State Insolvency
and
Foreign Bondholders

General Principles

Volume I

State Insolvency
and
Foreign Bondholders

General Principles

By

Edwin Borchard

Justus S. Hotchkiss
Professor of Law,
Emeritus
Yale University

Volume I

BeardBooks
Washington, D.C.

YALE LAW SCHOOL STUDIES

Volume I

PUBLISHED ON THE FUND ESTABLISHED
IN MEMORY OF
GANSON GOODYEAR DEPEW

PREFACE

THE present work developed from an earlier effort to discover to what extent rights of priority among different classes of creditors appear to have been established in the course of reorganizations of the debts of insolvent states. In 1930, with the collaboration of Mr. George Nebolsine, I prepared a report on this question at the request of Mr. Dwight W. Morrow, then Ambassador to Mexico, whose interest was prompted by certain priority issues which had been raised in connection with the Mexican foreign debt situation. From this brief inquiry, based on readily available sources of information, it became apparent that the subject of state insolvency as a whole called for more intensive and realistic examination than it had so far received. The Carnegie Corporation thereupon made a grant to Yale University to finance such an investigation. Completion of the undertaking was delayed several years by long, unavoidable interruptions, but, with the support and coöperation of the Yale University Press, the results are here finally published.

Detailed historical studies were first made of some of the world's major insolvencies. These are presented in Volume II. They deal with the insolvencies of Mexico, Peru, Santo Domingo, Greece, Portugal, Turkey, Bulgaria, and Egypt—countries selected from three continents. Corresponding but less complete studies, not intended for publication, were also prepared for Serbia, Venezuela, Nicaragua, Salvador, Honduras, Haiti, Tunis, and Morocco. In each instance the studies trace the development of the foreign bonded debt, indicate the causes and extent of defaults, outline the course of negotiations for a settlement, describe and analyze the terms of readjustment, and examine the outcome of reorganizations.

With these case histories as the chief factual source, Volume I discusses topically the main problems and practices which have arisen out of defaults by national governments on their foreign bond issues and examines how far past experience in the regulation of state insolvencies appears to have resulted in the establishment of principles and rules governing the matter.

The problems involved in the protection of foreign bondholders and the regulation of state insolvency have long been given attention and study. They will not lose importance because the number of outstanding foreign bond defaults has, in recent years, been substantially reduced and because most countries will, for some time to come, have to look to the International Bank for Reconstruction and Development and to United States Government agencies, rather than to private investors, for new external loans. Many governments are still in default on their foreign bonds. In due course, moreover, a moderate revival of public issues of governmental external bonds may again be witnessed. It is hoped, therefore, that this record and analysis of the legal, diplomatic, and economic developments which have characterized the relations of governments with their foreign bond creditors in the past will be found to have, in addition to intrinsic historical interest, some practical value. It may shed light on problems encountered in the arrangement of new debt readjustments; it may also prove useful to those who may be concerned in any way, whether as legislators, government officials, bankers, investors, or simply as students of international finance or international law, with external loans which foreign governments may seek to contract in the future.

It was my task to initiate and plan the work. Together with Dr. Joachim von Elbe, I also prepared Volume I. Extensive revisions were made throughout the manuscript of this volume to incorporate a considerable number of changes suggested by Mr. Wynne, whose contribution included the writing of the Introduction and Section XI. While I assume full responsibility for Volume I, Volume II is entirely the work of Mr. Wynne who, in addition to the eight case studies there included, wrote the unpublished studies on Serbia, Venezuela, Nicaragua, Salvador, Honduras, and Haiti. The unpublished studies on Tunis and Morocco were prepared by Dr. Eugene Gaulis.

My best thanks are due to the Carnegie Corporation for financing preparation of the work, to the Yale University Press for undertaking its publication, to Mrs. S. E. Seibert for skillful and patient secretarial assistance, to Mrs. Frank McMullan for careful styling of the volumes, and to the many individuals and organizations, mentioned in the separate preface to Volume II, from whom assistance was received in connection with the research for the case studies.

EDWIN BORCHARD

New Haven, Conn.

CONTENTS

Volume I: General Principles

Volume II: Selected Case Histories of Governmental Foreign Bond Defaults and Debt Readjustments

DETAILED CONTENTS VOLUME I

PART II. TYPES OF LOANS

PART III. THE DEFAULT ON GOVERNMENT LOANS

PART IV. BONDHOLDERS' REMEDIES

PART V. FINANCIAL CONTROL

PART VI. READJUSTMENT OF GOVERNMENTAL DEFAULTS

ABBREVIATIONS

Volume I

A.C.—English Law Reports, Appeal Cases

All E. R.—All England Law Reports, Annotated

Am. Bar. Assn. Jour.—American Bar Association Journal

Am. Econ. Rev.—American Economic Review

Am. Jour. Int. Law—American Journal of International Law

Am. Jour. Int. Law, Supp.—American Journal of International Law, Supplement

Am. Pol. Sci. Rev.—American Political Science Review

Ann. Am. Acad.—Annals of the American Academy of Political and Social Science

Archiv. civil. Prax.—Archiv für die civilistische Praxis

Association Nationale—Association Nationale des Porteurs Français de Valeurs Étrangères

Bing.—Bingham, English Common Pleas Reports

B.I.S.—Bank for International Settlements

Bost. Univ. Law Rev.—Boston University Law Review

Brit. and For. St. Pap.—British and Foreign State Papers

Brit. Year Book—British Year Book of International Law

Bull. de l'Inst. Jur. Intern.—Bulletin de l'Institut juridique international (The Hague)

CCH—Commerce Clearing House

Clunet—*Journal du droit international privé*

Ch. D.—Chancery Division (British)

Col. Law Rev.—Columbia Law Review

Com. and Fin. Chron.—Commercial and Financial Chronicle

Conf. Int. Law Assn.—Conference of the International Law Association

Cong. Rec.—Congressional Record

Corp. For. Bondh. Rep.—Annual Report of the Council of the Corporation of Foreign Bondholders

C. P. D.—Law Reports, Common Pleas Division, British, 1875–80

Coun. For. Bondh.—Council of the Corporation of Foreign Bondholders

Dalloz—*Jurisprudence générale; Recueil périodique et critique de jurisprudence, de legislation et de doctrine*

Dept. of St. Bull.—Bulletin of the Department of State, Washington, D.C.

Dipl. and Cons. Rep. on Trade and Fin.—Great Britain, Foreign Office, Annual Series, *Diplomatic and Consular Reports on Trade and Finance*

D.L.R.—Dominion Law Reports (Canada)

Entsch. Reichsg. Zivil.—*Entscheidungen des Reichsgerichts in Zivilsachen*

Exec. Agree. Ser.—*Executive Agreement Series,* United States Department of State

F.O.—Foreign Office Papers in the Public Record Office, London

For. Aff.—*Foreign Affairs*

For. Bondh. Prot. Coun. Rep.—*Foreign Bondholders Protective Council Report*

For. Pol. Assn. Bull.—*Bulletin of the Foreign Policy Association*

For. Pol. Rep.—*Foreign Policy Reports*

For. Rel.—*Papers Relating to the Foreign Relations of the United States* (Department of State)

40th Conf. Int. Law Assn. Rep.—*40th Conference of the International Law Association Report*

Gaz. des Trib. Mix.—*Gazette des Tribunaux Mixtes d'Egypte*

Gaz. du Pal.—*Gazette du Palais*

Geo. Wash. Law Rev.—*George Washington Law Review*

Grot. Soc.—*Grotius Society* (Transactions of the)

Hansard—*Hansard's Parliamentary Debates*

Harv. Law Rev.—*Harvard Law Review*

Institut de Rome—Société des Nations, Institut International de Rome pour l'Unification du Droit Privé

Inter-Am. Monthly—*Inter-American Monthly*

Inter-Am. Quar.—*Inter-American Quarterly*

Jour. Comp. Leg.—*Journal of Comparative Legislation*

Jour. des Trib. Mix.—*Journal des Tribunaux Mixtes*

Jour. du Droit Int.—*Journal du Droit International* (Clunet)

Jour. Int. Law and Dipl.—*Journal of International Law and Diplomacy*

Jur. Rev.—*The Juridical Review*

Jur. Woch.—*Juristische Wochenschrift*

Law Quar. Rev.—*Law Quarterly Review*

League Study Committee—League of Nations, Committee for the Study of International Loan Contracts

L.J.—Documents Diplomatiques (Livres Jaunes, France)

L.J.Q.B.—Law Journal Reports, New Series, Queen's Bench

L. of N.—League of Nations

L. of N. Doc.—League of Nations Document

L.R.—Law Reports (British)

L.T. Rep.—Law Times Reports (British)

L.T. Rep. (n.s.)—Law Times Reports (New Series)

Mich. Law Rev.—*Michigan Law Review*

Moo. C. P.—J. B. Moore's Common Pleas Reports (British)

Moore's *Digest*—J. B. Moore, *A Digest of International Law* (Washington, Government Printing Office, 1906)

Niemeyer's *Zeitschrift*—Niemeyer, *Zeitschrift für internationales Recht*

No. Car. Law Rev.—*North Carolina Law Review*

N.R.G.—De Martens, *Nouveau Receuil Générale*

N.Y. Univ. Law Quar. Rev.—*New York University Law Quarterly Review*

Ops. Atty. Gen.—*Opinions of the Attorney General*

Parl. Pap.—*Parliamentary Papers* (British)

Perm. Ct. Int. Just.—Permanent Court of International Justice

Pol. Sci. Quar.—*Political Science Quarterly*

Proc. Am. Soc. Int. Law—*Proceedings of the American Society of International Law*

Q.B.—Queen's Bench Division (British)

Rec. des Arb. Int.—*Recueil des Arbitrages Internationaux*

Rec. des Cours—*Recueil des Cours de l'Academie de Droit International*

Rec. des déc.—*Recueil des décisions*

Rec. Sirey—*Recueil général des lois et des arrêts* (founded by Sirey)

RFC—Reconstruction Finance Corporation

Rep. on For. Loans—"Report from the Select Committee on Loans to Foreign States," *Parl. Pap.* (1875), XI

Rev. de Droit Int.—*Revue de Droit International et de Législation Comparée*

Rev. Générale—*Revue Générale de Droit International Public*

Schweiz. Jur.-Zeit.—*Schweizerische Juristen-Zeitung*

SEC, *Rep.*—Securities and Exchange Commission, *Report on the Study and Investigation of the Work, Activities and Functions of Protective and Reorganization Committees, Pursuant to Section 211 of the Securities Exchange Act of 1934* (Washington, D.C., 1936–38).

Part I: *Strategy and Techniques of Protective and Reorganization Committees*

Part II: *Committees and Conflicts of Interests*

Part III: *Committees for the Holders of Real Estate Bonds*

Part IV: *Committees for the Holders of Municipal and Quasi-municipal Obligations*

Part V: *Protective Committees and Agencies for Holders of Defaulted Foreign Governmental Bonds*

Part VI: *Trustees under Indentures*

Part VII: *Management Plans without Aid of Committees*

Senate Hearings—Hearings on the Sale of Foreign Bonds or Securities in the United States before the Senate Committee on Finance, 42d Cong., 1st Sess., 1931–32.

S.W. Pol. and Soc. Sci. Quar.—Southwestern Political and Social Science Quarterly

T. L. Rep.—Times Law Reports (British)

Trade Inf. Bull.—United States Bureau of Foreign and Domestic Commerce (Department of Commerce), *Trade Information Bulletin*

Univ. Pa. Law Rev.—University of Pennsylvania Law Review

U.S. Sen. Doc.—United States Senate Document

Yale Law Jour.—Yale Law Journal

Yale Rev.—Yale Review

ZaöRVR—Zeitschrift für ausländisches öffentliches Recht und Völkerrecht (Berlin)

INTRODUCTION *

THE growth of foreign investment and its effects upon the economic development of the lending and borrowing countries have often been traced and analyzed.[1] The present work makes no attempt to re-survey this broad field but deals only with one segment of it—namely, private investment in foreign governmental loans. Focussing on the pathological aspect of this investment—the defaulted loan—the work aims to be a systematic treatise on what has come to be generally known as state insolvency. Although there is a considerable literature on the subject in foreign languages, particularly in German, French, and Spanish, a comprehensive study in English was lacking. These volumes will, it is hoped, fill the gap.

Volume II is devoted to detailed histories of some of the leading cases of state insolvency. Together with a number of similar studies not included in the published work, they cover virtually every type of default and illustrate the variety of economic, diplomatic, and legal questions that have arisen out of state insolvency and the subsequent debt reorganizations. These case histories were compiled as far as possible from first-hand documentary sources of information, including much material not previously utilized by writers on the foreign debt history of the countries concerned.[2] As a result, it was possible to base the topical analysis of the juridical and other problems of state insolvency, presented in Volume I, on a much larger and more precise body of facts than was available to earlier writers on the subject.

There have been numerous sporadic defaults by governments on their

* Introduction written by W. H. Wynne.

1. Important works in the field include: C. K. Hobson, *The Export of Capital* (London, Constable & Co., 1914); L. H. Jenks, *The Migration of British Capital to 1875* (New York, Knopf, 1927); H. Feis, *Europe, the World's Banker: 1870–1914* (New Haven, Yale Univ. Press, 1930); *The Problem of International Investment*. A Report by a Study Group of Members of the Royal Institute of International Affairs (London, 1937); Hal B. Lary and Associates, *The United States in the World Economy*, U.S. Dept. of Commerce, Economic Series, No. 23 (Washington, D.C., Govt. Printing Office, 1943).

2. Particular mention must be made of such material relating to the negotiations for and details of debt readjustments to which access was obtained in London through courtesies extended by the Secretary of the Council of the Corporation of Foreign Bondholders and the Librarian of the Foreign Office. (See Preface to Volume II.)

foreign bond issues which can be fitted into no neat chronological pattern but three periods stand out conspicuously as eras when these defaults were most general and widespread.

The first two periods, which occurred in the nineteenth century, 50 years apart, were described in 1935 by the present writer in the following terms:

During the years 1822 to 1825 the revolted Spanish American colonies besieged London for loans. The young republics had not yet succeeded in establishing internal order or settled government, while they were so feeble and impoverished that even their ability to maintain their independence was still in doubt; nevertheless, they all succeeded in their quest. In rapid succession issues were floated on behalf of Colombia, Chile, Peru, Buenos Aires, Brazil, Mexico, and Guatemala. The houses—mercantile firms rather than banks—which undertook the bulk of this business issued prospectuses, circulated news and disseminated pamphlets, all representing the political situation, economic resources and potentialities of the borrowing states *couleur de rose*. The English investor, like his American counterpart of our own times, was inexperienced, eager for high yields and in a feverishly speculative temper. Throwing discretion to the winds, he readily swallowed these puffed and highly colored descriptions. The bonds were offered at considerably below par, the prices ranging from 58 for a 5 per cent Mexican issue to 88½ per cent for a 6 per cent Colombian loan. A 6 per cent loan floated by Greece in 1825, while it was still engaged in a fight for freedom against the Turks, was offered, it may be noted, at as low as 55¼. The bankers' contract price was, of course, several points below the subscription price. From the proceeds the contractors retained, in each instance, the sum required to meet the interest and amortization charges for at least two years; further deductions were made for commissions and sundry expenses, thus reducing still further the balance available for the borrowing state. This residue—a slender proportion of the face value of the debt incurred—the borrower quickly expended on armaments, or otherwise wastefully dissipated, with little regard to the quite different purposes for which, in many instances, the loan had been ostensibly raised. The service charges were met as long as the sums reserved by the banker lasted, but, when these were exhausted, the debtor country, with only one or two exceptions, found itself utterly unable to make any payments out of its own resources, and default inevitably and promptly ensued. Eventually some part of the principal—at least the equivalent of the sum the borrower had actually received—was redeemed, while, in some instances, part of the interest in arrears was also liquidated, although, generally, thirty or forty years elapsed before the debtor republic was in a position, economically and politically, to effect a workable and acceptable settlement with its creditors. Meanwhile, however, the bonds had largely passed out of the hands of the original purchasers into the possession of speculators who bought them up at next to nothing and, in due time, reaped a handsome profit.

The second period of widespread default fell in the seventies and brought to an abrupt end a foreign loan mania of unprecedented intensity. The collapse in foreign loans had many ugly features which were brought into the limelight by the well-known report drawn up in 1875 by the Select Committee of the House of Commons on Loans to Foreign States. Again the worst abuses occurred in the negotiation and marketing of loans for weak Latin-American Republics. But although the Committee confined its investigations to the loans which had been floated on behalf of Honduras, Paraguay, Santo Domingo and Costa Rica, these were only the most notorious specimens of a numerous class of disreputable loan transactions.[3] . . . Close upon the failure of these loans came the far more serious defaults—having regard to the enormous sums which had been borrowed—on the Peruvian, Turkish and Egyptian external debts."[4]

During World War I belligerent countries necessarily suspended the transfer of bond service to enemy nationals but, apart from these suspensions and the repudiation by Russia of the huge Czarist foreign debt, the conflict engendered relatively few defaults on external public debts owed to private investors. The third general collapse of foreign debt structures did not occur until more than a decade after Versailles, when the world-wide economic slump precipitated an avalanche of defaults.

Many of the defaults stemming from the Great Depression took the

3. A few passages from the concluding part of the report may profitably be cited: "In respect of all these loans, those who introduced them to the public seem to have been regardless of the financial resources of the borrowing State; such resources, if inquired into, would have been found to have been totally inadequate to meet the liabilities incurred. . . .

"In order to induce the public to lend money upon a totally insufficient security, means have been resorted to which, in their nature and object, were flagrantly deceptive. . . .

"When the money of the public had been received, its application to the alleged purposes of the loans depended upon the good faith of those issuing them. In some instances these funds have been flagrantly misapplied. . . .

"It is true that the credulity and cupidity of certain classes of the community have blinded them to the danger of embarking in speculations such as your Committee have described. They appear to have measured the value of the promises held out to them, not by any rule of experience, but by their own sanguine expectations; and thus they have fallen a prey to those who, by trading on their credulity, have obtained their money, and then betrayed their interests. . . ." Parl. Pap. (1875), XI.

4. William H. Wynne, "Foreign Bonds and the American Investor," Journal of the Canadian Bankers' Association, XLII (1935), 472.

form of the suspension of sinking fund payments or of the transfer into the bondholders' currencies of part of the coupon liabilities, rather than of definitive reductions of interest or capital. Some of the defaults were terminated prior to World War II, while a few others (of Latin American countries) were adjusted during the war years by arrangements accepted by the bondholders. But the war brought new defaults, on the part of the enemy countries themselves, the lands they occupied, and the areas absorbed by Russia.[5] Since the war several debt settlements have been effected, though these have been characterized in the main by a considerable scaling down of the bondholders' contractual claims. Of seventeen Latin American countries which, during the course of the 1930's, defaulted in some degree on their external bond issues,[6] only three—Bolivia, Costa Rica, and Ecuador—were still in default in April, 1950.[7] Elsewhere, political and economic conditions continued to militate against the efforts of bondholders' organizations to obtain settlements. Countries remaining in default on their external bond issues included those under occupation (Austria, Germany, and Japan), those within the communist orbit (Russia—including Latvia, Estonia, and Lithuania—Romania, Hungary, Poland—including Danzig—Bulgaria,[8]

5. The table below shows the extent to which the outstanding foreign dollar bonds of national governments were in default at the end of 1938, 1945, and 1949, respectively. Similar data are added for the bonds of political subdivisions of these governments and for government guaranteed corporate bonds.

Issues	Amount Outstanding			Percentage of This Amount in Default		
	End of 1938	End of 1945	End of 1949	End of 1938	End of 1945	End of 1949
	$ billions			Per cent		
All issues	5.5	4.5	3.7	36.7	45.8	37.5
National	3.0	2.4	2.0	40.6	58.5	46.3
State, etc.	1.1	0.9	0.6	33.6	19.1	12.2
Municipal	0.5	0.4	0.4	37.9	42.7	31.0
Corporate *	0.9	0.7	0.7	27.0	38.8	38.4

* (Government guaranteed)

Data from *For. Bondh. Prot. Coun. Reps.*, 1938, p. 1138; 1945, p. 117; and 1946–49, pp. 376–377.

No comparable figures can be offered for sterling bonds. But notwithstanding the serious and extensive defaults of the thirties, the League Study Committee Report, II. Econ. and Finan., 1939, II.A. 10, p. 7, estimated that, of the total amount outstanding of external issues made on the London market, the amount in default (i.e., just before the war) did not exceed 30%.

The foreign bond defaults of national governments shown as aggregates in the table above are subdivided below, by geographical area.

Yugoslavia, and China), Greece, and Denmark (dollar sinking fund only).

The bondholders affected by the state insolvencies of the nineteenth century were mainly British but during its closing quarter bondholders of other nationalities, particularly French and German, steadily increased their share in the financing of foreign governments. American investors, with abundant openings for profitable use of their capital at home, did not enter the field on any appreciable scale until after World War I, when they became the chief participants in the business.

It has not been open to holders of the defaulted bonds of foreign governments to obtain a settlement of their claims through court procedures. In the main they have had to rely upon their own negotiations with the

Foreign Dollar Bond Issues of National Governments, Outstanding and in Default on Interest and/or Sinking Fund Payments, as of December 31, 1938, December 31, 1945, and December 31, 1949, respectively.

	Amount Outstanding			Outstanding Bonds in Default					
	1938	1945	1949	1938	1945	1949	1938	1945	1949
	$millions			$millions			Per cent		
Latin America	1129	1054	781	824	614	281	73.0	58.2	36.0
Europe	1073	720	634	388	618	493	36.1	85.8	77.8
Far East and Africa	339	317	358	2	163	162	0.6	51.4	45.2
Canada	449	293	248	Nil	Nil	Nil	Nil	Nil	Nil
All Areas	2990	2384	2021	1214	1395	936	40.6	58.5	46.3

Compiled from the tables in *For. Bondh. Prot. Coun. Reps.*, 1938, pp. 1132–1135, 1945, pp. 108–111, and 1946–49, pp. 374–375.

As the tables show, the percentage of the outstanding bonds of Latin American governments in default declined between 1938 and 1945 and fell considerably more during the ensuing four years. For European and Far Eastern issues, by contrast, the corresponding percentage rose sharply during the war, since when it has dropped, but only to a relatively small extent.

Between the end of the war and April, 1950, settlements were concluded with Mexico (in respect of her huge National Railways obligations), Chile, El Salvador, Italy, and Czechoslovakia. While a debt agreement was effected with Bulgaria in December, 1948, this had not been implemented. A unilateral offer by Peru, though not favored by the bondholders' organizations, was accepted by a large proportion of the bondholders. (The settlement with the Mexican National Railways did not become operative until March, 1950, and is consequently not reflected in the above tabulations.)

6. One of the three remaining republics was Venezuela, which redeemed the outstanding balance of its foreign debt in September, 1930. Argentina and Honduras, the other two, maintained the contractual debt service punctually and in

debtor and in England, France, Germany, Belgium, Holland, and, most recently, the United States, special institutions were established to represent the interests of holders of foreign bonds. British and Continental bondholders were early furnished with a powerful and persuasive weapon to help bring a delinquent debtor to terms in the form of rules under which the leading European stock exchanges refuse a listing to any new issue proposed by a defaulting state. The keener the desire of the latter for fresh loans, the more eager has it been to reach an agreement with its creditors, and a large proportion of the settlements which terminated the numerous defaults of the past and present centuries were in fact followed by a reëntry of the outcast into foreign money markets almost as soon as the ban of exclusion was withdrawn. Although the New York Stock Exchange has no such specific rule,[9] it seems unlikely that it would approve an application for listing a new bond issue of a foreign government still in default on its old privately held external loans.[10]

Bondholders have frequently appealed to their governments to support their efforts to effect a settlement with a defaulting foreign state. The British Government has, of course, had the longest experience in dealing with such requests. Generally its response has been none too sympathetic. It has freely reminded the bondholders that they purchased their bonds voluntarily and at their own risk. Nevertheless, it has seldom remained completely indifferent to the treatment of its nationals by a defaulting foreign government. At the least it has encouraged the bondholders' representatives to keep it informed of the progress of negotiations with the debtor. Occasionally, it has permitted its representatives abroad to perform unofficially certain services for bondholders. From time to time, however, it has seen fit to give the bondholders official aid. These occasions have as a rule arisen only when specific revenues assigned as security for the payment of bondholders have been willfully diverted to other uses; such conduct the government has regarded as deliberate bad faith and in a different category, therefore, from nonpayment of debt charges through simple inability to pay. The Government of the

---

full. Honduras, however, it should be noted, had settled a long-standing default in 1926, on terms which canceled huge arrears of interest and also greatly reduced the principal of the debt.

7. But see, as to Peru, the paragraph above, n. 5.

8. But see n. 5, last paragraph.

9. Letter, dated December 6, 1946, received from the New York Stock Exchange, in answer to an inquiry on the point.

10. The Exchange requires an application for listing foreign government bonds to include, along with other data, information as to the "past debt record with respect to: (a) defaults; (b) scaling down interest payments; (c) suspending

United States has adopted practically the same policy. Generally speaking, the French and German governments showed greater readiness than the British and American to support the bond claims of their nationals against an insolvent state.

Governmental intervention has sometimes gone far beyond mere diplomatic exhortation and resulted in the establishment of alien control over the part or whole of the finances of a defaulting state, or even over its entire administration. Turkey, Greece, Egypt, Tunis, Morocco, Haiti, and Santo Domingo have all been subjected, in greater or lesser degree, to foreign financial control as a means of ensuring that their external debts would be paid. But in most or all of these cases the intervening powers were motivated more by political considerations than by solicitude for the bondholders.

In rare instances—as in the historic cases of Mexico (1861) and Venezuela (1902)—bondholders' governments have even resorted to armed force for the collection of debts; they based their action, however, not on the mere neglect of bondholders' claims but on the contention that the defaulting state had broken international agreements respecting payment which it had made with the intervening powers, or that the lives and property of their nationals were being menaced by disorder and revolution.

The state insolvencies discussed in these volumes reflect a considerable waste of economic resources. A large proportion of the loans which fell into default failed to promote the best economic interests of either the borrowing or lending countries and tended to foster international suspicion and distrust rather than to advance peaceful coöperation among nations. But, notwithstanding their abundance, defaults were by no means endemic to foreign bond investments. Countries which remained politically stable and put the funds they borrowed abroad to productive use were, as a rule, able to meet their obligations without interruption, with beneficial results to themselves and to the countries from which the loans came. Moreover, although foreign governmental bond issues accounted for the bulk of the long-term investments made abroad by the United States during the twenties,[11] they absorbed a substantially smaller proportion of the total stream of capital which in the nineteenth and twen-

---

sinking fund payments." The letter cited in the preceding note states: "If an application were filed for the listing of a new bond issue of a foreign government then having outstanding external debt to private investors remaining in default, such fact would be considered along with all other facts when action was taken on the application."

11. During the years 1913–30 (inclusive) American new long-term investments abroad (i.e., disregarding amortizations and retirements) amounted to $11,600,-

tieth centuries flowed from Europe to relatively undeveloped lands.[12] After due allowance is made for the speculative excesses, financial abuses, exploitation of native peoples, and international friction which may be attributed to this capital migration, there can be little question that on balance it had highly desirable results. By and large, it contributed materially to the economic progress of the borrowing countries, provided the capital-lending countries with growing sources of supply for cheap raw materials and expanding markets for their manufactured products and commercial services, and, by promoting world-wide trade relations, helped to raise standards of living generally.

Foreign bond investment was usually induced by the prospect of higher returns than those offered by comparable domestic investments. Despite the extensive defaults on foreign governmental loans, it is probable that, prior to World War I, if not since, this expectation was on the whole realized.[13] The considerable discount at which the bonds were often issued raised the effective rate of interest well above the nominal rate. Complete repudiation of foreign bonded debts was comparatively

---

000,000. Of this amount $8,300,000,000 represented subscriptions to foreign bond issues (nearly all governmental offerings); the remaining $3,300,000,000 went into direct investments.

Lary, *op. cit.*, pp. 89–100, and Table III.

12. Over one half of the pre-World War I French foreign investment consisted of loans to foreign governments; a somewhat similar situation obtained in Germany, where substantially more than half of the foreign investment was in fixed interest-bearing securities, especially the bonds of foreign governments. But of the total foreign investment of the British Isles, as it stood in 1914, only a quarter was in the form of loans contracted by governmental bodies—national, state, and municipal. Moreover, over two thirds of these loans were made to dominion and colonial governments, so that less than one twelfth of the total investment was represented by loans to governmental bodies outside the British Empire. The aggregate British foreign investment was, of course, much greater than the French or German. Feis, *op. cit.*, pp. 26, 57, and 78.

13. French foreign investment was particularly hard hit after 1914 as a consequence of the Russian repudiation. This wiped out practically the entire French holdings in Russia, which in 1914 represented about a quarter (11,300,000,000 frs. out of 45 billion) of all French foreign long-term investment. Feis, *op. cit.*, p. 51.

With reference to British foreign investment, A. K. Cairncross, "Did Foreign Investment Pay?" *Review of Economic Studies*, October, 1935, states: "There is at least a prima facie case for believing that British investment in other countries has been economically advantageous to the investors . . . ." He offers some statistical estimates in support of this thesis. These cover, however, only the decade 1870–80.

On the same question, C. K. Hobson, *op. cit.*, p. 143, writes: "The losses caused through defaults were, in the long run, almost insignificant compared with the large gains derived by British investors over the whole field of foreign and colonial securities. By 1881, it was found that, not only had foreign Government stocks

rare. Many defaults were partial, rather than entire; payments for debt service were reduced but they did not cease, and, though the subsequent settlements sometimes involved a permanent and drastic reduction in interest, capital, or both, not infrequently they were of such a nature that, notwithstanding the default, the loan, besides being eventually redeemed at its issue price or better, produced over its entire life at least a small average annual net yield upon the original investment.

Prior to the world economic crisis of 1929 to 1933, the failure of certain classes of foreign loans gave only a temporary setback to the process of capital exports. For a time European money markets remained unreceptive to requests for new loans by foreign governments but other forms of lending abroad continued and before long investors proved willing to venture again into the financing of foreign states. The depression of the early 1930's was aggravated by the abrupt cessation of virtually all private foreign lending. A majority of the defaults dating from that period have now been terminated. The political and economic dislocation resulting from the war has, however, precluded a repetition of the historical pattern by resumption of at least a moderate degree of external bond investment.[14]

Not all capital exports ceased during the thirties; American and even British corporations continued, though at a declining rate, to expand their direct investments abroad, especially in Latin America. In addition, the loans made by the United States through the Export-Import Bank, also mainly to the republics to the south, filled part of the void created by the drying up of private loans.

Since World War II the United States has been the only country capable of supplying any appreciable portion of the financial aid urgently needed in Europe and elsewhere for the relief of economic distress resulting from the war and for the promotion of economic recovery and de-

---

been a profitable holding to British investors taken as a whole, after deducting the losses incurred upon defaulting securities, but that they had been more profitable than colonial government bonds, in spite of the fact that no colonial securities were, or have been, in default."

Hobson cites, as authority for the above statement, R. L. Nash, *A Short Inquiry into the Profitable Nature of Our Investments* (3d ed. London, E. Wilson, 1881), p. 9. Nash adds, *idem*, p. 23: "It is a fact that Foreign stocks as a whole now command a higher market than they did ten years back, and that a great many loans issued, even in the years of mania, now stand at a good premium upon their issue price."

14. It need hardly be pointed out that, during these depression years, considerable default occurred also on domestic securities in the United States—the largest exporter of capital in the post-World War I world. No one would condemn domestic investments as a class because some of them turned out badly.

velopment. From July 1, 1945, through December 31, 1949, the United States Government made available for these purposes (including contributions to the United Nations Relief and Rehabilitation Administration but not subscriptions to the International Bank for Reconstruction and Development and the International Monetary Fund) a total of $33,600,000,000. Of this sum, $25,900,000,000 had been utilized by the end of 1949, $15,700,000,000 to provide outright grants, and $10,200,-000,000 to extend loans and property credits. Aid to Europe accounted for $20,100,000,000 out of the $25,900,000,000, most of the rest going to Asia. Latin America's share amounted to only $400,000,000, furnished mainly in the form of Export-Import Bank Loans.[15]

A substantial volume of American private capital has also flowed abroad since the war, but almost entirely in the form of direct investments. In each year from 1947 to 1949 these in fact exceeded the previous peak established in 1929, while for the three year period as a whole, they totaled approximately $2,200,000,000. Practically all of this, however, constituted additional advances by parent companies to subsidiaries and branches. The bulk of the investment was made in Latin America, chiefly by the petroleum industry, which was also responsible for the major part of the direct investment channeled to other areas, mainly the Middle East.[16] The revival of direct investment in new enterprises, in Latin America particularly, continues to be deterred by a nationalist viewpoint which has resulted in the imposition of vexatious and discriminatory restrictions against foreign-owned or -managed operations and in some instances in their virtual expropriation.[17] Exchange restrictions which sharply limit the convertibility of foreign currency into dollars also discourage investment in new ventures abroad.

During the decade 1920–29, 60 per cent of new American private foreign investment flowed into the purchase of dollar bonds offered publicly,[18] predominantly by foreign governments. While political and economic conditions in most countries which might desire dollar loans

15. National Advisory Council on International Monetary and Financial Problems, Report to the President and to the Congress for the period, October 1, 1949—March 31, 1950, Appendix C, Tables 1, 2 and 3.

16. Source: Department of Commerce. See Milton Abelson, "Private Direct Investments Abroad," *Survey of Current Business*, November, 1949, pp. 3–4, and *idem*, June, 1950, p. 18, Table 5. The $2.2 billion figure is exclusive of the reinvested earnings of the foreign subsidiaries of American companies.

17. For examples of such expropriation, see Cleona Lewis, *The United States and Foreign Investment Problems* (Washington, D.C., Brookings Institution, 1948), pp. 150–156.

18. Department of Commerce, "The Balance of International Payments of the United States 1946–1948," p. 134. The direct investment figures for the twenties included the reinvested earnings of foreign subsidiaries.

are still too unfavorable to make flotations in the open capital market possible, sufficient improvement may in time be achieved to make it possible for a number of them to float new bond issues in the United States at a fairly moderate rate of interest.

Meanwhile, foreign governments seeking long-term dollar loans will, as a rule, have to look to the United States Government, operating through the Export-Import Bank or otherwise, or to the International Bank for Reconstruction and Development. Loan commitments by the International Bank down to the end of June, 1950, after four years of operations, totaled only about $816,000,000.[19] The Bank, it is true, was established to provide machinery through which areas unable for the time being to attract private investment at all, or to secure it only on very onerous conditions, might be able to obtain long-term loans at fairly low rates. The Bank has, however, set itself against being hurried into ill-considered loans and has made them only where domestic conditions in the borrowing country were deemed to afford a firm basis for development and reasonable prospects for repayment.[20]

The Bank may make loans out of its own or borrowed funds. It may also guarantee loans made by private investors through the usual investment channels. The Bank is not designed to replace ordinary private investment but to supplement it. Before the Bank makes or guarantees a loan, it must be satisfied that the borrower would otherwise be unable to obtain one at a reasonable rate of interest.

The lending practices the Bank is required to pursue are designed to minimize the risk of default. No loan may be made or guaranteed by the Bank until the project has been carefully studied and recommended by a competent committee of its own selection. It must make arrangements to ensure that the proceeds of the loan are used in an economical and effective way, without regard to political considerations, and solely for the purposes for which the loan was approved. The interest rate must be reasonable and the amortization schedule appropriate to the project. The Bank must feel satisfied that the borrower has good prospects of being able to meet his obligations. To safeguard the borrower against the stigma of default through inability to meet the service charges in the contractual foreign currencies during a period of acute exchange stringency, the Bank may accept payment in the borrower's own currency for as long as three years and may also modify the terms of amortization or extend the life of the loan.

19. Fifth Annual Report of the International Bank (1949–50), p. 51.
20. See, e.g., "The International Bank and World Trade," an address by Mr. John J. McCloy, then President of the Bank, Bank Press Release No. 119, November 8, 1948.

It is to be hoped that financial houses which may in the future undertake public issues of foreign bonds will be guided by similar standards to those set for the Bank. Prudence in lending is, after all, the primary safeguard against default.

PART I

The International Government Loan

Section I

LEGAL NATURE OF THE LOAN CONTRACT AND ITS BREACH

THE usual public loan contract is concluded directly or through intermediary bankers between a state as the borrower and an unknown number of private lenders, the terms of the legal relationship being embodied in the loan agreement between state and underwriting banker, by the fiscal agreement between state and paying agent, by a trust indenture expressing the bondholder's remedies, by the bearer bond in the hands of the bondholder. In one or more of these contracts the state, having received the money its offer or prospectus solicited, promises—except for "perpetual" *rentes* or consols, redeemable at the pleasure of the debtor—to repay to the bearer of the bond or a registered owner the principal amount at a fixed time and interest at a specified rate at given periods.

Where the loan is issued directly to individuals and is not underwritten, it has been doubted whether separate contracts are concluded with the individual bondholders, because the transaction may remain uncompleted. A preference has thus been expressed for the view that the invitation to subscribe is merely an offer to the public generally to participate in a final contract which, when concluded, will be embodied in certain instruments carrying out the terms of the prospectus or offer, the participation certificates or individual bonds being issued against the payment of the money loaned.

There is no legal relationship between individual bondholders, who have, however, a common interest in the fulfillment of the contract and who, in case of need or default, may unite in common defense of their interests. Trustees and bondholders' protective associations or committees have this function of representing the bondholders. They have been called a *de facto* association and the state loan a collective contract, by which a certain number of bondholders is united into an association for the purpose of lending collectively a certain sum to a foreign state at whose initiative the contract is concluded.[1]

1. H. M. Imbert, *Les Emprunts d'états étrangers* (Paris, 1905), p. 186. Alberto D. Schoo, *Régimen jurídico de las obligaciones monetarias internacionales* (Buenos Aires, 1940), pp. 160 ff., 193 ff.

The fact that one of the contracting parties is a sovereign state and that the lenders are private individuals whose remedies are limited has naturally given rise to a variety of theories as to the nature of the obligations contracted and assumed by the state and of the rights acquired by the bondholders. The theories adopted are themselves the reflection of the major premises or points of view of their proponents.

DEBTORS' THEORIES

Where the interest of the debtor state is the primary consideration, emphasis will be placed on the sovereign character of the borrower, on the impossibility of suing the state judicially, and the conclusion is reached that the debt is essentially one of honor only. This was the view of Foreign Minister Luis Drago of the Argentine and is shared by a number of others who, looking primarily to the lack of remedy on default, are less concerned with the legal theory than with the facts. They regard the sovereign as above the law—a view having a long historical background [2]—and conclude that the sovereign cannot be subject to legal rules; that he who contracts with the sovereign or the state has nothing but the state's honor and credit as a sanction, because the state cannot be sued effectively either in its own courts or in those of the bondholder; that the contract is, therefore, aleatory or a gambling contract, depending for its performance entirely on the good faith and capacity of the debtor to pay. This school of thought concludes that, if a state becomes insolvent or repudiates, such eventuality is a contingency which the creditor had or should have had in mind in concluding the contract or buying the bond, and that the state is as privileged to alter the terms of the contract or to violate it as it was originally to enter upon it. Stressing the law of the debtor state under which the bonds were issued, it is concluded that another law can extinguish or modify the debt. For this school, a decided minority, the relations between the parties escape not only judicial control but, in effect, legal character.[3] Thus they readily

2. See Borchard, "The Relation between State and Law," *Yale Law Jour.*, XXXVI (1927), 780.

3. "There can be not the slightest doubt but that State loans are legal acts, but of a very special nature as cannot be confused with any other kind. The common civil law does not apply to them. Emitted by an act of sovereignty such as no private individual can exercise, they represent in no case an engagement between definite persons. For they stipulate in general terms that certain payments shall be made, at a certain date, to the bearer who is always an indeterminate person. The lender, on his part, does not advance his money as he does in loan contracts; he confines himself to buying a bond in the open market; there is no certified individual act nor any relation with the debtor Government. In ordinary contracts the

Government proceeds in virtue of rights which are inherent in the juridical person or administrative corporation, by exercising that which is called the *jus gestionis* or the right with which the representative or administrator of any joint-stock company whatever is invested.

"In the second case it proceeds *jure imperii*, in its quality as sovereign, by effecting acts which only the public person of the State as such could accomplish. In the first case we understand that the Government may be summoned before the tribunals or courts of claims, as happens day by day, so that it may make answer with regard to its engagements in private law; we could not conceive in the second case that the exercise of sovereignty might be questioned before an ordinary tribunal. It would at least be necessary to establish this distinction of a practical nature, to which I permitted myself to refer in the plenary Commission; for ordinary contracts, courts are available; there are no courts available to sit in judgment upon public loans.

"If, on the other hand, it were said that national loans really imply a contract as is entered into with regard to ordinary loans, in the sense that they create exact obligations on the part of the borrowing State, it might be answered generally that it is not contracts alone that give rise to obligations; but that, even if it were so, it would be necessary to admit that they are a very special class of contracts with well-marked differential signs which, by that very fact, deserve to be put in a class by themselves." L. M. Drago, in James Brown Scott, ed., *The Proceedings of the Hague Peace Conferences, The Conference of 1907* (New York, Oxford University Press, 1921), II, 557 f.

The jurist Hugo, often called the father of the historical school of jurists (*Lehrbuch des Naturrechts* [2d ed. Berlin, 1819]), says: "A national bankruptcy is by no means illegal, and whether it is immoral or unwise depends altogether upon circumstances. One can hardly ask of the present generation that it alone shall suffer for the folly and waste of its predecessors, for otherwise in the end a country could hardly be inhabited because of the mass of its public debts."

Zachariae, "Über das Schuldenwesen der Staaten," *Jahrbüchern der Geschichte* (Leipzig, 1830), p. 291, says: "The State is entitled to reduce its debts, indeed to repudiate them entirely, in so far as it is no longer in a condition to raise the funds, aside from current expenses, to pay the interest and principal of the public debt." Zachariae admits that, if the rights of the creditor rested upon a contract, rather than on the duty of the state to compensate those who have borne a burden in place of the state, the rights of the creditors would then be unconditional and the nation would have to pay, so far as humanly possible, down to the last cent. He takes, however, the other view. He admits that no nation may arbitrarily break its word and simply decline to pay, when it can. But he maintains that a government has a higher duty than the payment of its debts, which is to keep its citizens alive, and that creditors must be disregarded when there is no alternative. He does make a distinction between those who have voluntarily lent their money and who have concluded an aleatory contract and those who were the victims of a forced loan. Only under *force majeure* would he consider the state entitled to disregard these involuntary creditors. (The analogy to involuntary tort creditors is significant.) Zachariae attributes no importance to the form of the contract, which, indeed, is sometimes but not always not unlike the usual corporate loan contract. Occasionally it reads like a decree or law.

F. K. von Savigny, *Obligationenrecht*, II (Berlin, 1852), 110, doubtless influenced by a Prussian law of 1823 which provided that the state could not be sued on its public debts, concluded that public debts are "not under the private-law protection of a judge."

G. Rolin-Jaequemyns, a Belgian jurist, in the *Rev. de Droit Int.*, 1869, p. 146, took the position that the making of a loan was an act of sovereignty, as was the payment. He added that any interference of another state was out of the question.

Numerous French jurists take the same view. We may cite Louis Berr, *Étude sur les obligations* (Paris, 1880), p. 236, who says: "The Frenchman who concludes a contract with a foreign government subjects himself in advance to the laws of that government concerning the jurisdiction and the law of its courts; he renounces voluntarily the protection of his own national laws. In consequence, questions concerning the performance and liquidation of obligations directed against a foreign state can only be brought before its own courts in accordance with the rules of public law there in force."

Sir Robert Phillimore, in *Commentaries upon International Law* (3d ed. London, Butterworth's, 1882), II, 18, says: "The English courts have decided that bonds payable to bearer issued by the government of a state only create a debt in the nature of a debt of honor, which cannot be enforced by any foreign tribunal nor by the tribunal of the borrowing state itself, unless with the consent of its government," citing *Crouch* v. *Credit Foncier of England,* L.R. 8 Q.B. 374 (1873); *Twycross* v. *Dreyfus,* 5 Ch. D. 605 (1877).

K. von Bar, a well-known authority, *Theorie und Praxis des internationalen privatrechts* (Hannover, Hahn, 1889), II, 663, says: "If all the creditors could actually levy execution upon the state property, they could bring the state machinery to a standstill. Public debts, therefore, issued under a special law, contracted with an uncertain number of creditors, rest upon the condition that the State is in a position—of which the State by legislation is the judge—to perform its obligations. The State has, so to speak, a *beneficium competentiae* in the widest sense; it must first preserve itself, and the payment of its debts is a secondary consideration."

N. Politis, *Les Emprunts d'état en droit international* (Paris, 1894), p. 16, states that the public loan is neither controlled by civil law nor is it a natural debt, but that a state which does not perform its contracted obligations merely loses credit and its honor. To some extent, Politis differs from von Bar, because he does regard the loan as creating rights and duties, notwithstanding the fact that the state cannot be sued or levied against. Politis declines to admit the distinction between internal and external creditors. He adds: "The assumption of a debt by a state cannot be regarded as a purely private act of a government, as would be the act of a private debtor, but constitutes a political act which the state concludes, in its sovereign capacity as a public power, in the interest and in the name of the whole people."

Another Greek writer, Kebedgy, in an article in *Jour. du Droit Int.*, XXI (1894), 59, 504, maintains that the loan of money to a foreign state is a speculative transaction or a more-or-less aleatory operation.

H. Appleton, a French writer, *Des effets des annexions de territoire sur les dettes de l'état* (Paris, 1895), pp. 17, 18, remarks: "Creditors who are affected by a state bankruptcy entered into a speculative contract which did not give them the hoped for result; that is for them a misfortune. But their government cannot intervene in so far as the debtor acts in good faith and gives its creditors everything which it is in a position to give."

Wuarin, *Essai sur les emprunts d'états* (Paris, 1907), p. 24, also regards the

arrive at the conclusion that they are "debts of honor," as the English Court of Chancery remarked in *Twycross* v. *Dreyfus*.[4]

This theory, while vulnerable, is not without practical importance.[5] Based on the analytical view that there is no right without a remedy and noting the absence of judicial remedy against the state, it is readily concluded that there is no legal right involved. But that confuses the nature of the contract with the means for its enforcement. No foreigner would lend his money on such precarious terms, though in many cases his protection may be no greater in fact than these views prescribe.

Indeed, the argument that the absence of an effective judicial remedy demonstrates the absence of legal right proves too much. If true, it would be wrong to speak of a "contract" between a private individual and the United States Government prior to 1855, when for the first time the United States permitted itself to be sued in contract. The fact is that the Austinian view, given modern currency by Holmes and somewhat loosely applied to public relations, was confined by its authors to private relations under a system of municipal law and was not intended to characterize relations in which one of the parties was the state. Even if the

---

contracts as of an aleatory character, giving the creditor no legally enforceable right.

Zorn, *Bankarchiv* (Berlin), VI, 106, points out that "the payment of interest on . a public debt is not a matter of private law, but is the result of the exercise of sovereign powers, and on this point there is no fluctuation in theory." He adds that "for extreme cases legal rules are unavailing." In this connection, he is thinking of losses occasioned by war or revolution, and he considers these in the field of *force majeure*.

C. Cavanagh, *The Law of Money Securities* (2d ed. London, W. Clowes and Sons, Ltd., 1885), p. 120, maintains that the relationship between a sovereign state and the individual borrower "does not amount to a legal contract and does not create a legal right against the Foreign Government, to whose *bona fides* and honesty alone, therefore, the lender must look for satisfaction of his claim." For a catalogue of the views of many authors, see Schoo, *op. cit.*, pp. 206 ff.

4. 5 Ch. D. at 616 (1877) Jessel, M. R.

5. The jurisdiction of civil courts in disputes between lenders and the borrowing government may depend on the determination of the loan contract as either an act of sovereignty or a private law transaction. See *Negrotto* v. *Egyptian Government, Gaz. des Trib. Mix.*, XXVI, 121, and comment by Gamil Chalom, *idem*, p. 119 (March, 1936). It was pointed out that in the matter of the public debt, the mixed courts have no jurisdiction if (1) the act of issuing a loan is to be considered an act of sovereignty or (2) the decision of the Egyptian authorities violating the loan contract can be characterized as an act of sovereignty. In the instant case, the court held that a governmental loan contract is in the nature of a binding engagement by the government toward the creditors. A French court, however, held that national loans floated in France by a foreign government are "political acts of sovereignty," involving immunity of the borrowing government from suit in the country of the lender. See *infra*, p. 165, n. 21.

state cannot be sued on its bonds in municipal courts, arbitral tribunals and foreign offices, in the cases in which they assume jurisdiction, and private creditors dealing with defaulting states have acted on the theory that the bond established a legal relationship.

Nor is the bondholder as remediless as the "debtor's sovereignty" school professes to assume. The diplomatic protection of his own state is a remedy which he may invoke when there is a bad-faith repudiation, discrimination, or diversion of security. And there are economic sanctions which lending groups may invoke, not to speak of foreclosure of "pledges." But, when there is an inability or total incapacity to pay, it is true that the bondholder's legal rights will be hard to vindicate in any forum and that he is then thrown back on such forms of pressure and such economic or political sanctions as may persuade the debtor state to make the best terms possible with its creditors.

If the theory were sound, it would be a privileged act for a country to repudiate its debt or violate clauses in the bond or divert security or diminish its obligation as to principal or interest; and it is very important to settle the fact that a unilateral change of the obligation by the debtor state is not legally privileged, to whatever extent the injured creditor may for lack of effective remedy have to submit. The United States Supreme Court under trying circumstances held that the repudiation of the gold clauses by the joint resolution of June 5, 1933, was not a privileged act but a breach of contract, although in fact the court could not find that the plaintiff had suffered any actual damage by the substitution of paper for gold dollars, and hence denied relief.[6]

CREDITORS' THEORIES

A second school of jurists approaches the subject from the point of view of the creditor. It observes that the relations between the state and the bondholders are recorded in contracts, just as in the case of any private corporation debtor. It therefore concludes that the obligation is controlled by the private law of contracts. It is not concerned with the question what the remedy for breach may be, regarding remedy as independent of substantive right. This school maintains that when the state contracts a loan it tacitly waives its sovereign character and subjects itself voluntarily to the rules of private law.

Whatever truth there may be in the views of this school, the assumption that the state waives its character as a sovereign by contracting a loan is gratuitous and is not susceptible of proof. It is important perhaps to be able to assert that, when the state fails to pay its bonded debt, there

6. *Infra*, p. 29 n. 12, and p. 158.

has been an unprivileged breach of a legal obligation and not a mere privileged act of sovereignty. While this does not immediately afford the disappointed bondholder an effective remedy, it is well to know that he is legally and not merely morally injured and that under certain circumstances public international law will protect him against bad faith or discrimination on account of nationality and that the default, even when irremediable, is not privileged. His claim is not wiped out but in the absence of readjustment may be vindicated if the fortunes of his debtor should improve.[7]

7. Not all the writers in this group are as clear or categorical as might be desired for purposes of classification, but it may be worth while to quote a few whose views differ materially from those of the first group. This second group regards the relationship as governed, in whole or in part, by private law concepts, and considers the creditor as having a legal claim upon his debtor, the state. This group considers him, in the event of bankruptcy, not the helpless victim of a sovereign act but a creditor entitled to such rights as practice and arbitration may be deemed to have given him as a matter of law.

Von Gönner, *Von Staatsschulden* (Munich, 1826), pp. 173, 174, 196, 197, says, though not altogether unequivocally, that "public bonds fall in the category of a contract to pay money, both in the relation between debtor and creditor as in the matter of the circulation of the bonds among private holders, notwithstanding the fact that the character of the debtor, who regards the debt as a matter of State, may introduce modifications which cannot always be measured by the rules of private law."

Thol, *Handelsrecht* (6th ed. Leipzig, 1879), Vol. I, sec. 215, p. 644, explains that the circumstance that the debtor is a state involves no particular legal peculiarity apart from exceptions raised by positive law. He defends the position, as do many others, that we are dealing here with duties or obligations of a private law character, regardless of whether the state uses the money loaned for fiscal or administrative or other purposes.

Cosack, *Lehrbuch des Handelsrechts* (5th ed. 1900), sec. 66, says: "The emission of a loan constitutes the sale by the borrower of his loan obligation and the attached promise to pay, to the holder of the bond. The bond is the subject of purchase and sale. The creditors are the purchasers. The purchase price is the sum which they pay to the debtor. Practically speaking, the partial creditor is in the legal position of the possessor of a bearer bond: the defenses which the debtor has are limited."

Meili, *Der Staatsbankerott und die moderne Rechtswissenschaft* (Berlin, 1895), p. 18, says that the contract of loan is a legal obligation, legally binding upon the debtor. He thinks the contract is governed by the objective law of the debtor at the time of the making of the loan, and admits that the obligation has been characterized differently by various jurists.

Freund, *Die Rechtsverhältnisse der öffentlichen Anleihen* (Berlin, 1907), pp. 55 ff., 249, says: "The legal relations arising out of a loan contract between a state and private individuals are of private-law character. The floating of a loan is not an act of sovereignty, but a legal transaction of private law. The state acts in its business capacity, not in the exercise of its public authority as it is the case in levying taxes."

Ruff, *Die Rechtsnatur der Aufnahme öffentlicher Anleihen* (Naumburg, 1912), pp. 52, 54, says: "Contracting a loan is not a unilateral act of the state in the exercise of its imperium; on the contrary, the state faces the money lenders as a partner to the transaction on the footing of perfect legal equality. It steps onto the bottom of the civil law and acts as fiscus. The legal relationship between the state and its money lenders arising out of this transaction is of private-law character."

Guggenheim, *Beiträge zur völkerrechtlichen Lehre vom Staatenwechsel* (Berlin, 1925), p. 120, says: "With respect to its creditors, the public debts of a state are purely of private-law character."

Sack, *Les effets des transformations des états sur leurs dettes publiques* (Paris, 1927), pp. 30 f., says: "Whether the loan of a state, like any other public loan, is based upon a contract for a loan for consumption, or on a contract for the sale of bonds—the debts of a state, so far as their substance is concerned, are always governed by the rules of private law. Elements of public law are lacking in those contracts and the sovereign power of the state does not appear.—A government issuing a loan or selling bonds obtains money from its creditors or the buyers of bonds by means of a free agreement with the latter, like any other private or juristic person.

"The substance of the rules of private law applying to the loan contract of a state is the same as in the case of loan contracts concluded by any private or juristic person."

Michaelis, "Anleihe [öffentliche]," *Handwörterbuch der Rechtswissenschaft*, I, 205: "It is no longer disputed that a state which issues a loan performs a private law transaction. The borrowing state does not act in its sovereign capacity, but as fiscus, viz., as a juristic person whose transactions are to be judged according to civil (private) law. Both parties to the contract, the state as well as the private creditors, are in a position of perfect legal equality. That is—with certain qualifications—even true with regard to compulsory loans."

Laband. *Das Staatsrecht des Deutschen Reiches* (Freiburg, 1891), IV, 371: "A loan whether issued by the Reich, a state, a municipal corporation, a joint stock company or a private individual, is a private law transaction consisting in the sale of bonds which embody the debt."

M. Devèze, agent of the Yugoslav Government, in a speech on May 22, 1929, Publications of the Perm. Ct. Int. Just., Ser. C, No. 16, III, pp. 177 f., said:

"On the contrary, a contract whereby a state for the purpose of increasing its financial resources obtains from a private individual or a private institution of whatever nationality certain funds in return for a promise to pay interest and to redeem the principal is unquestionably in the nature of a private law contract."

Von Daehne van Varick, *Le Droit financier international* (The Hague, 1907), p. 14, says: "In contracting a loan, a state, though always sovereign, does not perform an act of sovereignty which requires obedience, but an act of common law whereby it renounces its sovereign privileges towards its creditors. If entering into a loan contract with a state would mean that the creditor is at the mercy of the state, it is obvious that nobody ever would consent to such a bargain. It is therefore necessary that the two parties stand on the footing of perfect legal equality, and that the sovereign state be subject to the law of the place where the contract is made."

Pflug, *Der Staatsbankrott und internationales Recht* (Munich, 1898), pp. 15 f.: "According to the weight of authority, the legal relationship created by the loan contract between a state and its creditors is strictly in the nature of a private law relationship. It is true, the credit of which a state makes use is public in character, and whenever a state decides to issue a loan, it performs an act of sovereignty. While contracting the loan, however, the state does not exercise its sovereign power, for the individuals who lend their money to the state are under no obligation to do so. The legal transaction which is accomplished between the private money lenders and the state is essentially a private law contract."

The Swiss Federal Court on May 26, 1936 (*Obligations-interessenter* v. *The Bank for International Settlements, Die Praxis des Bundesgerichts*, XXV, 335) decided: "According to the unequivocal wording of the loan conditions 'the payment of the Principal, Interest and Sinking Fund is the direct and unconditional obligation of the German Government to the Bondholders.' It follows that the claims of the individual bondholders, although they rest on a common obligation, namely, the loan contract entered into by them jointly, nevertheless are mutually independent claims against the Reich which the latter may discharge by payment to the Bank for International Settlements with direct effect vis-à-vis the bondholders."

Chile and France. Award of the Franco-Chilean Arbitral Tribunal, July 5, 1901. Descamps and Renault, *Recueil international des traités du xxᵉ siècle* (Paris, 1901), p. 370: "In point of fact, the relations existing between the borrowing state and the individual bondholders fall exclusively within the purview of private law and can never be governed by principles of international public law which applies to the legal relations between the states as subjects of rights and duties, but not to the contractual relations between states and private individuals.

"It is true, states sometimes intervene in disputes arising between a state and its creditors, in order to safeguard the interests of their nationals. This is particularly true if the execution of a promise is at stake whereby a state undertook to assign certain values or revenues for the payment of the debt. Such intervention, however, although exercised by virtue of international law, never purports to achieve anything more than the fulfilment of an obligation the nature and extent of which is determined by such rules of private law as are applicable to it."

Decision of June 15, 1925, of the Mixed Tribunal of Cairo, *Jour. des Trib. Mix.*, Vol. IV, Pt. II, No. 350, p. 4: "A Government which enters into an agreement with a private individual to pay a certain sum of money thereby contracts a civil obligation; with regard to disputes arising out of this purely civil obligation it is subject to the jurisdiction of the common law. From its character as public authority a Government derives no right to liberate itself from its obligation by deciding on its own will that it is released for reasons that render it the only judge of the civil obligation entered into by it.

"In point of fact, the refusal to pay by alleging extinction of the contractual obligation which gave rise to the duty to pay, has never been an act of sovereignty, or an act of public authority, because any private individual may do the same. The mere fact that the debtor is a state, can make no difference."

French literature is also represented by this school. Lewandowski, *De la protection des capitaux empruntés en France* (Paris, 1896), pp. 27, 32, 33, regards a public loan as a purely private contract. He believes that, when a state takes up a loan, it renounces all its sovereign rights and steps into the arena of private interests, subjecting itself thereby to the common law of contracts. He nevertheless concedes, in the light of the present positions of international legislation and of the facts involved in state bankruptcy, that, if the state debtor is in bad faith, the

Closely affiliated with this school of thought are those jurists who, observing the fact that the foreign creditor occasionally receives through foreign pressure better treatment than the national, make a distinction even in legal theory between the contracts of the domestic and the foreign creditor. Professor Kaufmann, for example, argues that the domestic creditor in his relation with the state deals only with a single sovereign. He acquires certain contractual rights against the debtor but at the same time is subject to the legislative power of the debtor to alter the terms of the contract and deprive him of his contractual rights. As to foreign creditors, however, the state is a subject of international law. Though a contractual relation is involved, Kaufmann considers it a fiction to regard the alien as subject to the law and the courts of the contracting state and an even greater fiction to assume that this subjection relates not only to the time when the contract was concluded but to all future time and subsequent changes which the legislation of

creditor can legally do but very little, so that he concludes that perhaps after all it is only a moral obligation of the debtor.

Jozon, "Des Conséquences de l'inexécution des engagements pris par les gouvernments relativement au paiement de leur dette publique," *Rev. de Droit Int.*, I (1869), p. 279, believes that every time a bond is transferred, a new contract between state and creditor is entered into.

Gerlach, in the 5th edition of Roscher's *Finanzwissenschaft* (Stuttgart, 1901), p. 277, regards the loan contract as subject to the general principles of the civil law. Every invasion by the debtor state of the rights of the creditors is regarded as an arbitrary and wrongful act. He makes no such distinction as do Kaufmann and Freund between native and foreign creditors.

Among the writers who hold that the loan contract of a state creates legally binding obligations may be listed Bosch, *De Staatsschulden in het internationaal Recht* (The Hague, 1929), pp. 3 ff. His line of reasoning may be illustrated by the following excerpt: "In our opinion, the theory which attributes sovereign character to the state act of borrowing money lacks moral foundation. The state applies to the public with a request to lend it money in exchange for some definite and expressly stipulated obligations. We cannot assume that a state, at the conclusion of a loan contract, makes a mental reservation to the effect that it will refuse to perform the contract whenever it becomes difficult to do so, and that, in this case, it will alter the terms of the contract to its own advantage since it cannot be forced to perform its obligations.

"It is true, a state may render any breach of contract formally valid. In most cases, the subjects of the state will have to acquiesce, at least in countries where judicial review of acts of government does not exist, while foreign creditors may have a possibility of bringing suit. In both cases, however, the state infringes the rights of its creditors. The state, like any individual, may, in case of financial emergency, act like an unwilling debtor and may refuse to perform its obligations. But this is a fact, and not the consequence of a legal agreement; it rests upon a factual state of power and is not the result of a legal relationship. We therefore believe that a public loan, whether external or internal, is a contract of private law, subject, as far as possible, to the private law of the debtor state."

the state might effect. Such legislative changes in the contractual relations are deemed a breach of legal rights, whereas the native creditor is
in a different position and cannot successfully avail himself of these con-
tentions.[8]

But this supposed distinction in legal theory is exceedingly questionable. In the first place, it is based on the nationality of the holder, not
on the place where the debt was contracted or is to be performed or on
the internal or external character of the loan. As we shall observe, the
question of the law to be applied and the distinction between an external
and an internal loan is complicated.[9] But in fact the nature of the contractual relation is in no way affected by the consideration that the bond
is in the hands of a national or an alien, resident or nonresident, or
passes from hand to hand, national or alien. The alien may occasionally
under favorable circumstances be able to avail himself of diplomatic
protection and economic reprisals not open to the national but this does
not affect the character of the loan or contract. It affords to the alien,
in certain cases, an exceptional remedy,[10] but the contractual rights of
both national and alien are the same.[11] The diplomatic remedy is not

8. Kaufmann, *Das Internationale Recht der egyptischen Staatsschuld* (Berlin,
1891), pp. 14, 15.

Freund, *op. cit.*, p. 257, takes somewhat the same position. He thinks the internal creditor is subject to the legislation of the state, whereas the external
creditor has the protection of international law. He has equal rights with his
debtor, the state, and the state cannot change its obligations unilaterally.

Pflug, *op. cit.*, pp. 12, 13, follows somewhat the same view.

9. *Infra*, pp. 64 ff., 75 ff.

10. In the case of weak states, like Egypt, it was a great advantage to be a
foreign bondholder, because special courts, the mixed courts, were set up to
pass upon the claims of foreigners.

In 1894, on the protest of the British Council of Foreign Bondholders to the
Greek Government against any reduction in the interest of the external debt or
against any alteration in the system of collecting the hypothecated revenues without full accord with the bondholders, the Greek Government, through the chargé
d'affaires at London, replied, January 22, 1894 (*Corp. For. Bondh. Rep.*, No. 21
[1893], p. 86): "I am instructed to acknowledge the receipt of your letter to my
Government, and to assure your Committee and the Bondholders, that while the
Government thoroughly recognize the obligations undertaken by Greece, they
have acted under imperious and immediate necessity, and are convinced they
can satisfy the Bondholders that it is impossible for them to carry on the Government of the country and meet their engagements in full; but whatever may be the
provisional measures imposed on the Government by the imperious necessities of
the situation, the Government consider that no Obligations or *Securities* can
undergo any modification of a permanent character *except by agreement with the
Bondholders*." (Italics supplied.)

11. Laband, one of Germany's foremost jurists of the past generation, in an
article in the *Archiv für öffentliches Recht*, XXIII (1908), 200, opposes the

available as a matter of right in any event but depends upon the relations between the two states and upon a variety of political factors often beyond the bondholder's control.[12]

Nor is it accurate to say that the foreign bondholder is protected by international law against unilateral changes in the contract by the debtor state, or that he is not subject to the law of the debtor state, or that the subscription to a foreign loan is an "international" contract. International law creates obligations between states alone; there is an element of ambiguity and fiction in considering the individual as a subject of international law, although an increasing number of conventions confer rights upon him.[13] He is often the object and beneficiary of international agreements but, except for treaty or municipal law, may not vindicate these rights himself. The international obligation runs from state to state. His own state may in its discretion claim redress from the defaulting state because, as the theory has it, his state has been injured by an unredressed injury to its national. Yet the state vindicates its own right, not the national's, to have him treated without discrimination and without bad faith.

In the matter of defaulted bonds, there are many limitations upon a state's willingness to espouse the cause of its citizen, limitations which the defendant state may invoke and which are therefore part of international law. The bondholder has for many purposes been obliged to submit to the law of the issuing country, such as the interpretation of the terms of local law under which the loan was issued, and to domestic changes, such as the introduction of transfer prohibitions, and possibly,

alleged distinction between the legal position of national and foreign creditors. He maintains that the state as a corporation cannot be under the law and then, as a legislator, above the law. He admits that it may become incapable of paying its debts, like any private debtor. It may be unable to perform its legal obligations, in whole or in part, but these are facts and not consequences of legal principles. This legal position is not altered by the fact that the creditors, internal and external, may be unable to enforce their rights against a state acting even in bad faith.

Rotteck, in the 2d edition of his *Staatslexikon,* had already taken this position. It is also adopted by Escher and by Manes, *Staatsbankrotte* (3d ed. Berlin, 1922), at p. 166–167. Lippert, *Handbuch des internationalen Finanzrechts* (2d ed. Wien, 1928), p. 927, also refuses to distinguish between the domestic and foreign bondholder.

12. *Infra,* pp. 230 ff.

13. Cf. Borchard, *Diplomatic Protection of Citizens Abroad* (New York, Banks Law Publishing Co., 1915), pp. 16–18. Dr. Politis is a strong proponent of the theory that the individual is a subject of international law and has reiterated this theory in his introduction to Professor Sack's work: *op. cit.,* p. iv. For further refutation of the theory, see Ernst Feilchenfeld, *Public Debts and State Succession* (New York, Macmillan, 1931), pp. 582 ff.

in certain circumstances, changes in clauses, like the gold clause. These matters will be considered in separate sections.[14]

The relation between the state as debtor and the foreign bondholder as creditor, if not entirely controlled by the law of the debtor, is nevertheless not a contract of international law, which, as observed, can be concluded only between states. It is in fact a unique relation,[15] depending in its various aspects on the laws of several countries—the country of the borrower, of issue, of payment—and, when diplomatic protection is invoked and extended, on certain rules of international law. But, in spite of earlier theories to the contrary,[16] a mere failure to pay a public loan is not a breach of international law, although it may be a breach of contract. To constitute a breach of international law, it must be so flagrant in character as to evidence bad faith or arbitrary discrimination justifying the bondholder's state, according to approved practice, in advancing a diplomatic claim for redress on behalf of its injured national. The conditions of such interposition will be discussed presently.

THEORY OF CONTRACT SUI GENERIS

Perhaps we should classify in a third school those who cannot subscribe wholly either to the view that the flotation of a public loan is an act of sovereignty or that it is subject to the rules of private contract. As we have seen, the views themselves are the reflection of certain premises: on the one hand, a defense of the state's privilege to repudiate or change the terms of the loan; on the other hand, a defense of the view that the state is strictly bound to perform its contracted obligations.

14. *Infra*, pp. 64 ff., 123 ff.

15. Cf. Sack, *op. cit.*, p. 30; Schmitthoff, "The International Government Loan," *Jour. Comp. Leg.*, XIX (1937), 180, 188, 196 ("the international government loan of the ordinary type is a contractus sui generis"); De Lapradelle and Politis, *Rec. des Arb. Int.*, II (1923), 546 (*note doctrinale*).

16. Especially Vattel, *Law of Nations*, Bk. II, chap. xiv (Fenwick, tr. [Classics of International Law, ed. 1916], III, 186). Vattel considered a public loan, lawfully contracted, like a treaty, binding on the state and on all successors of the contracting authority. He argued that the obligations of treaties and of public loans are identical, and denied the legality of unilateral alteration of the contract. He sustained the view that financial contracts can be deemed invalid only on the same grounds that render treaties invalid. As Dr. Feilchenfeld says with great relevance (in Quindry, *Bonds and Bondholders, Rights and Remedies* [Chicago, Burdette Smith, and Kansas City, Vernon Law Book Co., 1934], II, 161), Vattel should not be cited as the inventor of an extreme theory considering public loans as a matter of international law, but as the first commentator on the complicated legal relations arising out of a public loan.

This third school regards the transaction as a contract of public law,[17] thus admitting the sovereign character of many of the motives and laws which authorize and support the loan, while yet insisting that the obligation is legally binding, whatever remedy the bondholder may or may not have.[18]

The contract of public loan is indeed *sui generis*, both in the form of its creation and in the results attending nonpayment. It is created by laws of the debtor state and in order to bind the state must conform to all requirements of those laws. Yet the purchaser of the bond and the issuing state both contemplate that they are entering not a gambling contract, a contract subject to repudiation by one party, but a definite and clearly stated obligation to make certain payments. Dr. Drago did not intend to contradict this view but only to emphasize the fact that the remedy of armed force should not be used for the collection of a public debt from a sovereign nation. In the event of default, the very fact that the debtor is a state is a clear indication that the ordinary procedure of bankruptcy and sale of the debtor's assets for the benefit of creditors cannot prevail. Hence members of this third school, if we may so classify the dissenters from the first and second groups, refuse to consider the nonpayment as either privileged or unprivileged but as an operative fact which creates a number of consequences, legal and factual. Practice, if not law, has determined the nature of some of these consequences, portrayed in the studies of national insolvencies printed in Volume II. Inasmuch as these differ considerably from the consequences attaching to insolvency and bankruptcy in private law, it is perhaps convenient to consider the whole transaction as one of public law, if that is any help.

17. Dr. Feilchenfeld rightly considers that "the attempts to make general statements as to whether debts of public debtors are debts of public or private law are necessarily futile," because some of the rules of municipal law will govern the rights of creditors and others the administration of the public debt, i.e., domestic fiscal law. *Public Debts and State Succession*, p. 653.

18. Jèze, *Cours de science des finances* (6th ed. Paris, 1925), p. 202; Jèze, "Les Principes juridiques dominants en matière de garantie des emprunts publics d'état," *Rec. des Cours*, VII (1925), 174, 176; Jèze, "Public Debt," *Encyclopaedia of the Social Sciences*, XII, 601: "Juridically, a public loan is a contract in the proper sense of the term; that is to say, a meeting of the minds setting up a juridical obligation on the part of the state to pay the interest and to restore the capital at the rate, the time and in the money agreed upon." De Lapradelle-Politis, *loc. cit.*; Lippert, *Code of International Financial Law* (Graz, 1935), p. 304; Lippert, *Handbuch des internationalen Finanzrechts*, p. 927; speech of M. Devèze, agent of Yugoslav Government, before Permanent Court of International Justice in Serbian loan case, May 22, 1929, Publications of the Perm. Ct. Int. Just., Ser. C, No. 16, III, pp. 178 ff., a good analysis of the sovereign functions and characteristics of a public loan and of its private law contractual aspects; speech of M. Basdevant, Agent of France, *op. cit.*, pp. 106 ff.

But, while a legal obligation is created under a definite system of municipal law, the peculiar nature of the remedies available, if any, warrant a refusal to subscribe to any categorical school of thought or submit to any particular classification.

Section II

THE TECHNICAL CONTRACT

THE view expressed in the preceding section that the legal relations created by the international government loan are of such unique character as to warrant its qualification as a contract *sui generis* is fortified by the procedure for floating these loans. As already noted, the public loan contract is concluded either directly between the borrowing government and the individual lender by the purchase of bonds from the issuer or through intermediary bankers who underwrite the loan issue and assume responsibility for the sale of the bonds to individual investors. In the field of governmental borrowing, the former method is distinctly the exception; it is available only to governments of high credit standing whose bonds are everywhere assured of a ready market. The great majority of governments in need of funds from private lenders abroad are forced to resort to the procedure of selling the entire bond issue to one or several banking houses for placement on foreign money markets.

This makes for a rather complex transaction. Even when only one single market is approached, the terms of the contract are ordinarily embodied in at least three documents: the loan prospectus, the contract between the debtor and the issuing bankers, and finally the actual bonds, with coupons attached, which are either sold to the bearer or registered in the name of the individual owner. In more complicated cases, for example, where the loan is issued in several *tranches* on different markets, or where a trustee is appointed, or where the loan is guaranteed by third parties, additional documents, like trust indentures or so-called "general bonds," are required. The documents used in each case show a great diversity both in form and expression; they reflect "the differences in legislation, still more in habits and tradition, in outlook and experience" [1] prevailing in the various debtor and creditor countries.

---

1. League Study Committee Report, II. Econ. and Finan., 1939. II.A. 10, p. 9. Loan contracts of the period of reconstruction after the war of 1914–18 were mostly drafted in the manner common to Anglo-American corporation practice. See Feilchenfeld, in Quindry, *Bonds and Bondholders, Rights and Remedies*, Vol. II, sec. 634, p. 175. See also Felix Weiser, *Trusts on the Continent of Europe* (London, Sweet & Maxwell, Ltd., 1936), p. 72.

Their legal significance, frequently a subject of considerable doubt, merits a somewhat closer examination.

THE LOAN PROSPECTUS

The "prospectus" or "bond circular" is a document setting forth in detail the elements of the proposed bond issue and soliciting subscriptions from the general public.[2] It is either published in the form of an advertisement or sent directly to prospective investors. Its function within the framework of the loan contract differs according to the method adopted in issuing the loan. In the event of a direct flotation, the borrowing government also is responsible for the prospectus, which usually bears the signature of a government official.

As to the binding nature of statements made in the circular in such a case, conflicting theories have been advanced.[3] A minority view maintains that the prospectus contains a genuine offer for the conclusion of a loan contract submitted by the government to an indefinite number of persons. Acceptance by the individual lender automatically consummates the bargain on the terms stated in the prospectus.[4] The prevailing school of thought, however, denies the binding character of the bond circular. It attributes to it the preparatory function of advertising the loan, to be followed by a bilateral agreement between borrower and

2. See Glenn G. Munn, *Encyclopedia of Banking and Finance* (New York, Bankers Publishing Co., 1937), pp. 94 f. It usually contains the following: title of the bond and brief description of its security; dates of issue, maturity, and interest payments; denomination and form; amount authorized and amount issued; redemption price; name of the trustee; guaranties; economic and financial condition of the borrowing government; authorizing laws. Stock exchange regulations at the place of issue may specify further the requirements for the prospectus before registration is granted. See, in general, F. E. Farrer, *The Law Relating to Prospectuses* (London, E. Wilson, 1913). As to the information required in prospectuses of foreign government bonds to be issued in the United States, see Federal Securities Act, sec. 10, a, 2, sec. 7, Schedule B. CCH *Federal Securities Law Service*, para. 2515, 2401, 641 ff.

3. See, for a general discussion of the question, Société des Nations, Institut de Rome, Preliminary Study (Rome, May, 1938), Études XX, Emprunts internationaux, Dec. 4, pp. 24 f. See also the conclusions of Procureur Général Matter in the case of *Port of Rosario* v. *Thirion et al., idem,* pp. 81 ff.

4. This was the position taken by the French Tribunal Civil de la Seine in the case of *Mouren et Comité de la Bourse d'Amsterdam* v. *Société des Services Contractuels des Messageries Maritimes, Bull. de l'Inst. Jur. Intern.,* XL, (1939), 98. It held that "the contract was concluded by the acceptance, on the part of the subscribers, of the offer contained in the prospectus and therefore cannot be modified by the silence in the bonds or even by terms in the bonds contrary to the statements of the prospectus, because the bonds were delivered after the conclusion of the contract."

lender embodied in the definitive bond.[5] Up to the moment of the final contract, the government remains free to alter the statements in the prospectus; those not repeated in the final document are not binding on the borrower. This, however, does not mean that the prospectus is without legal significance within the scheme of the loan. In interpreting the contract as a whole, courts may refer to it as a subsidiary means for the purpose of clarifying and supplementing ambiguous terms. Or, as stated by the Permanent Court of International Justice in the case of the Brazilian loans:

Where the Government itself becomes responsible for the prospectus and invites subscriptions for the bonds, it is reasonable to treat the prospectus as a part of the transaction with the bondholders, at least so far as may be necessary to clarify the meaning of the bonds.[6]

Where a loan is issued not directly by the government but through intermediary bankers, the prospectus forms part of the latter's advertising campaign for the placement of the bonds on the market and the government is not a party thereto.[7] Its function in such a case is usually

5. Institut de Rome, Preliminary Study, p. 25. See also the dictum in *Twycross* v. *Dreyfus*, 5 Ch. D. at 617 (1877): "First of all, a prospectus is set out which contains certain statements of what is about to be hypothecated, but the prospectus stated also that bonds would be issued. Bonds were issued and accepted by the subscribers to the prospectus, and those bonds stated in a definite way, under seal of the financial agent of the Republic of Peru, the terms on which the loan was issued. It appears to me that after that there was an end of the prospectus. *A fortiori,* that observation applies with respect to all bonds purchased in the market by persons who had nothing whatever to do with the prospectus."

6. Publications of the Perm. Ct. Int. Just., Ser. A, No. 20/21, p. 113. Similarly, judgment of the French Cour de Cassation (Ch. Civ.) of July 9, 1930, in the case of *Port of Rosario* v. *Thirion et al., Jour. du Droit Int.,* LVIII (1931), 124 f. Reference to the prospectus, therefore, is justified only where the terms of the bonds need clarification. See A. Nussbaum, *Money in the Law,* Chicago, Foundation Press, 1939), p. 463, criticizing the decision of the French Cour de Cassation in the case of the prewar loans of the city of Tokyo, where it was held that the French *tranche* of the loan, although exclusively running in terms of francs, was also payable in pounds sterling rather than francs because in the prospectus of the loan the total of interest and amortization to be supplied annually for the service of the various *tranches* was phrased in terms of pounds sterling. "No more was obviously intended by the prospectus than to give a survey of the cost of the service, probably contrasted with the receipts of the city, and this could properly be done only on the basis of a unified currency, the English currency being the most appropriate under the circumstances. No change in the unambiguous terms of the bonds and coupons could fairly be inferred therefrom."

7. See Sauser-Hall, "La Clause-or dans les contrats publics et privés," *Rec. des Cours,* LX (1937), 691. Its function as a means of attracting subscribers in the past led to the insertion of "puffing" statements that were often false or misleading. See SEC, *Rep.,* Pt. V, pp. 9, 18. Strict registration laws at the place of issue,

to acquaint the subscribing public with the terms of the fiscal agreement between the government and the issuing house. It thereby becomes a subsidiary means of interpreting the loan contract in much the same manner as in the case of direct flotation.[8]

THE LOAN AGREEMENT

Where the government engages the services of a banking house for the issuance of foreign bonds, its relations with the bankers are embodied in the so-called "loan agreement" or "loan contract." This usually is a lengthy document and, if American banks are involved, appears in printed form.[9] It invariably stipulates the duty of the borrowing government to create a bond issue in accordance with its laws. The bankers promise to purchase these bonds at a certain price for the purpose of placing them for sale on the market; or they simply undertake to make the necessary arrangements for the flotation of the loan without assuming the risk of the operation.

Other provisions customarily included in the loan agreement concern the purpose of the loan; the legal qualifications of the representatives of the government and the authority of the government to negotiate the loan, thereby assuring the bankers of the validity of the issue from the point of view of the debtor's municipal law; [10] a detailed description of the terms of the bonds, their denomination, form of payment, maturity, sinking fund provisions; security clauses engaging the full faith and credit of the borrower or establishing special liens. In the great majority of cases, the loan agreement is coupled with a fiscal agreement, appointing the bank of issue the fiscal or paying agent of the government and determining its rights and duties in that capacity.[11] An unusual feature in

prescribing in detail the information required in prospectuses before bonds may be sold have considerably lessened the danger of misrepresentation or fraudulent statements. See *supra*, p. 19, n. 2. See also the statement by Lord Coleridge, C.J., in *Twycross* v. *Grant*, 2 C.P.D. 469 (1877); 46 L.J.Q.B. 636, as to the reasons for the enactment of the English statute providing for the presentation of certain material in the prospectuses.

8. Institut de Rome, Preliminary Study, p. 33.

9. Instances of loan agreements may be found in *Hearings before the Subcommittee of the Senate Committee on Foreign Relations, Relative to Engaging the Responsibility of the Government in Financial Arrangements between Its Citizens and Sovereign Foreign Governments* (S. Con. Res. 22), 68th Cong., 2d Sess. (February 25 and 26, 1925), pp. 109 ff.

10. See C. C. Hyde, "The Negotiation of External Loans with Foreign Governments," *Am. Jour. Int. Law*, XVI (1922), 525.

11. SEC, *Rep.*, Pt. V, p. 11, and *infra*, p. 42. A special "authenticating agent" sometimes is a third party to the agreement. See *For. Bondh. Prot. Coun. Rep.*, 1937, p. 620.

two recent American loan agreements has been the involvement of the United States Government by providing for its assistance in the selection of a collector of customs pledged as security for the loan and by arbitration clauses providing for the submission of disputed points to a member of the federal judiciary.[12] The loan agreement, being primarily a private contract between the bankers and the government, is not always released for publication, although it is usually open for inspection by the bondholders.[13] If by reference incorporated in the bond certificates, its terms become binding on the bondholders also.[14] However, no direct legal relationship between the bondholders and the issuing house is thereby created.[15]

12. See, for example, the Salvador loan of 1923. *Com. and Fin. Chron.*, 1923, p. 1616.

13. Feilchenfeld, *op. cit.*, Vol II, sec. 633a, p. 171.

14. See the Finnish loan case, *Bull. de l'Inst. Jur. Intern.*, XXXVIII (1938), 280. A clause in the loan agreement between the Finnish State and an association of banks making American law applicable to the agreement was held to be binding on the bondholders because the bonds were stated as being issued "on the basis of the aforesaid agreement." The Dutch Supreme Court, however, in the Rotterdam loan case, affirming the Court of Appeals at The Hague, held that mere reference in the bonds to the loan agreement between the city and American bankers stipulating the applicability of American law did not subject the bonds to American law. *Idem*, p. 282. See also M. Domke, "International Loans and the Conflict of Laws," *Grot. Soc.*, XXIII (1937), 57. See also SEC, *Rep.*, Pt. V, p. 512. As to the desirability of including certain provisions of the loan contract in the prospectus or the individual bonds see the Note submitted by M. Golay to the League Study Committee (Basle, September 1, 1937), Doc. I.L. 46: "I have noticed in practice that loan contracts very often contain provisions regarding the law applicable, the court which is competent and the procedure of arbitration to be followed in case of dispute. These provisions have in certain cases given rise to difficulties, because the debtor has attempted to declare them applicable only to relations between himself and the banks of issue, and not to direct relations between himself and the holders of the securities. In future it should therefore be stipulated in contracts of issue that legal provisions of this nature should apply also to relations between the holders of the securities and the debtor, and these provisions should accordingly be reproduced in the prospectus or in the text of the securities themselves." See also J. Weigert, "The Abrogation of Gold-Clauses in International Loans and the Conflict of Laws," *Contemporary Law Pamphlets*, Ser. 4, No. 4 (New York, 1940), p. 18.

15. See the case of the holders of *rentes*, *Republic of Haiti* v. *White and Hartmann*, decided by the French Tribunal of Commerce, June 13, 1877 (Imbert, *Les emprunts d'états étrangers*, pp. 37 f.). Creditors of the Haitian Government alleged that by subscribing a loan or by buying bonds they entered into contractual relations with the issuing firm which acted as the agent of the Haitian Government. The court held that the defendants were merely intermediaries promoting the issue of the loan, but that they did not assume any personal obligation toward the bondholders. It was only the Government of Haiti to whom trust was

THE BOND

The principal document containing the terms of the contractual relations between the debtor government and the individual lender is the bond issued by the bank in accordance with the loan agreement or directly by the government pursuant to the loan prospectus. It evidences the promise by the borrower to pay the agreed interest on the loan, the principal at maturity, and to amortize the issue in a specified manner.[16] It defines the currency and the place of payment and, in the case of secured loans, indicates the revenues pledged as security for the fulfillment of the obligation. It may be either a negotiable instrument, payable to the bearer, or may be registered in the name of the owner.[17] In case of dispute between the parties as to the performance of the contract, recourse must first be had to the stipulations in the bonds; they should therefore be drafted in such manner as clearly to express the intentions of the parties. The prospectus and the loan agreement, as mentioned above, may under certain conditions be resorted to as subsidiary means of interpretation.

The coupons ordinarily attached to negotiable bearer bonds are interest warrants for each installment of interest; they contain, as a rule, only the most elementary statements, such as the name of the loan, the amount of interest represented by the coupon, and the date of payment.[18] Although they are separately negotiable and payable to the bearer, silence with respect to essential stipulation of the loan contract, such as currency and gold clauses, does not alter or invalidate the original obligation. The fact that the coupons of the Brazilian loan of 1909 did not contain a provision for payment in gold identical with the payment clause in the bonds was deemed by the Permanent Court of International Justice "not to detract from the express promise of the bond." The court proceeded to define the relations between bond and coupon in the following terms:

given. See also the case of Dreyfus Bros. Vol. II, pp. 127–134, of this work. (Hereafter, references to Volume II will be made in the following manner: II, oo.)

16. "The distinguishing feature of a bond is that it is an obligation to pay a fixed sum of money, at a definite time, with a stated interest." Quindry, *Bonds and Bondholders, Rights and Remedies*, Vol. I, sec. 2, pp. 3 f.; a bond is "a formal promise by the borrower to pay to the lender a certain sum of money at a fixed future date with or without security, and signed and sealed by the maker (borrower)." Munn, *op. cit.*, pp. 93 f.—"Temporary bonds" or interim receipts are sometimes given by the banking houses prior to the issuance of, and exchangeable for, the "definitive bonds" which usually require time for engraving after the loan has been floated.

17. See Cavanagh, *The Law of Money Securities*, pp. 120 ff.

18. Quindry, *op. cit.*, sec. 6, p. 6.

As regards bearer bonds, sometimes the coupons contain all that is necessary to make a complete engagement of independent negotiability; sometimes they are mere tokens which do not purport to set forth the entire obligation for the payment of interest. Thus, in the present instance, nothing is said in the coupons as to the place of payment, which is an integral part of the promise as contained in the bond.[19]

THE GENERAL BOND

International financing in the period of reconstruction after the war of 1914–18, in particular the loan practice of the League of Nations, produced a document hitherto unknown in the technique of governmental borrowing. The complicated mechanism of a modern external government loan issued in several *tranches* on various money markets with different currencies and coupled with pledges and guaranties which require independent machinery for control and enforcement creates the need for one single general document containing the terms of the issue. Anglo-American practice of corporate finance provided for this purpose the form of the so-called "general bond." [20] It has been used in particular where trustees were appointed or where the loan was guaranteed by third parties, such as the Austrian League loan of 1923.

The documents which one finds under the name of "general bonds" in various loan issues are by no means of uniform type. The only characteristic common to all is the fact that they embody in detail the obligations of the debtor government with respect to the loan. Sometimes the general bond is a unilateral promise issued and signed by the debtor whereby it binds itself to create a loan in conformity with the clauses of the general bond.[21] In other instances, the general bond takes the form of a contract among the government, the trustees, the issuing bankers, and possibly the guaranteeing governments.[22] Doubts have arisen with regard to its legal character. While admitting that the general bond, in the case of the Austrian League loan of 1923, is an "international legal

19. Publications of the Perm. Ct. Int. Just., Ser. A, No. 20/21, p. 110. If, on the other hand, the gold clause is mentioned only in the coupons and not in the bonds, the whole debt, principal as well as interest, is owed in terms of gold since it seems inconceivable that a debt, while losing its value, may still produce interest in gold. See Sauser-Hall, *op. cit.*, p. 688.

20. See Sir John Fischer Williams, *Chapters on Current International Law and the League of Nations* (London, Longmans, Green & Co., 1929), p. 398.

21. See Kingdom of Yugoslavia, 5% funding bonds, general bond, July 1, 1936, *For. Bondh. Prot. Coun. Rep.*, 1936, p. 760; see also the bonds mentioned in Institut de Rome, Preliminary Study, p. 30.

22. General bond of the Austrian Government guaranteed loan, 1923. Fischer Williams, *op. cit.*, p. 412; German Government (Dawes) loan, 1924.

act formed by the common will of representatives of different international persons" and therefore alterable only by their concurrence, Jèze [23] denies the contractual nature of its terms. He sees in them nothing but "regulations" similar to the rules governing the organization of a public service.[24] The general bond, he maintains, deals with matters "of a general and impersonal legal character, statutory and non-contractual in nature." This view seems to be supported by the fact that the Austrian bond, although signed by both the Austrian Government and the guaranteeing states and consequently embodying an "international engagement," was not registered with the League of Nations under Article 18 of the Covenant.[25] On the other hand, it appears from the wording of most of the general bonds that the debtor intends to establish thereby a direct liability toward the subscribers to the loan.[26] This is often emphasized by incorporating the general bond, either literally or by reference, in the individual (definitive) bond. Being the most complete and authoritative statement of the loan contract, the general bond is likely to prevail in case of disagreement among the various documents embodying the terms of the legal relationship among the parties to the transaction.

23. In *Rec. des Cours*, VII (1925), 227.

24. See also Institut de Rome, Preliminary Study, p. 31: "One may assimilate the 'general bond' to the regulations of enterprises or agencies of the State performing public services."

25. Fischer Williams, *op. cit.*, p. 399.

26. See Institut de Rome, Preliminary Study, p. 30. The general bond of the Belgian conversion loan of 1936 states: "Whereby the Government of the Kingdom of Belgium covenants and binds itself in the manner hereinafter appearing . . ."; the preamble of the general bond of the Czechoslovakian loan of 1922 stipulates: "The Minister of Finance empowered to represent the Czechoslovak Government do by these Presents duly countersigned by the President of the Supreme Accounting Control Office bind the Czechoslovak State and the Government thereof to observe and carry out the following conditions . . ."

Section III

CURRENCY, GOLD, AND ARBITRATION CLAUSES

WHEN it has been decided to make a foreign investment, draftsmen devote their attention to making the loan as secure as possible by inserting appropriate clauses in the loan contract. The security clauses designed to insure the prompt service of the loan and its repayment we shall leave for later discussion. Here we shall examine the currency clauses in which a loan is expressed, to avoid the risk that the creditor may receive lower value than he parted with when the loan was made. The dangers to be safeguarded against are two—that the currency in which the loan is repayable may depreciate in the terms of the lender's currency and that the lender's currency may itself depreciate in terms of gold or goods or other currencies.[1]

As a means of protecting the creditor against loss from these contingencies various devices are possible. Repayment of the loan might, for example, be required in an amount of money equivalent in purchasing power to the money lent. But purchasing power is difficult to define in terms of particular goods and services to which it is to be related, nor can it be measured with precision. For these and other reasons this device has never been used in foreign lending. Extensive use has, however, been made of the expression of the obligation in terms of some third currency, or in terms of several currencies, any one of which the lender may select at prescribed rates of exchange. The possibility, though, that even the best of these optional currencies may suffer depreciation leaves the creditor still facing some risk of loss. Better protection is afforded by stating the obligation in terms of gold, especially by specifying gold of a definite weight and fineness.[2] But, as we shall see, courts have given varying interpretations to clauses alleged to constitute "gold clauses" and to the effect of their breach when the promised currency no longer exists or is unobtainable.[3]

1. *The Problem of International Investment*, p. 347.
2. *Idem*, pp. 348–349.
3. *Idem*, p. 350.

CURRENCY CLAUSES

The most desirable method, from the point of view of both the creditor and the debtor, of fixing the substance of a money obligation in terms of a monetary unit undoubtedly consists in expressing it in a single currency. But even in the simplest case of an external government issue, when only the market of one country is approached, at least two different currencies are available for this purpose: the national currency of the debtor and that of the creditor country. The interest of the debtor suggests the choice of the former, primarily because it guards against the difficulties arising from the conversion of internal revenues, collected to discharge the foreign debt, into foreign currency and their transfer abroad. However, only countries of high credit standing and with stable monetary systems may expect to place such a loan on international money markets. The great majority of borrowing governments, in order to assure the marketability of their loans, will be compelled to submit to the wishes of their prospective lenders with respect to the currency of the issue. The individual creditor, conscious of the fact that the issuing state has control over its own currency [4] and may easily interfere with it to the detriment of its creditors,[5] will prefer to receive interest and principal either in the currency of his own country, thus being assured of the integral return of his loan, or in some other currency known to be both stable and internationally acceptable. If a loan is issued in several *tranches* in different countries, the currencies in which the debt may be expressed multiply accordingly.

During the periods of widespread currency depreciation between the two world wars,[6] bondholders tended to interpret clauses in loan contracts providing for the payment of the debt in more than one currency as conferring on the creditor the right to demand payment in the most appreciated currency mentioned in the bond, as a means of minimizing his losses due to currency depreciation. No doubt, a "multiple-currency

4. Case of the Brazilian Loans, Publications of the Perm. Ct. Int. Just., Ser. A, No. 20/21, p. 44.

5. Fischer Williams, *Chapters on Current International Law and the League of Nations*, p. 291, maintains that the sovereign power of a government over its own currency extends to the point where it may diminish and even destroy the value of the rights of its creditors, unless restrained from so doing by the terms of the loan contract. See, however, Nolde, "La Monnaie en droit international public," *Rec. des Cours*, XXVII (1929), pp. 253 f., 261 f., 263 ff., with respect to international restrictions on the monetary autonomy of states. See also *infra*, section on Currency Devaluation.

6. See, e.g., James W. Gantenbein, *Financial Questions in United States Foreign Policy* (New York, Columbia University Press, 1939), pp. 10 ff.

clause" may have the function of preserving the substance of a debt in terms of the currency having the highest rate of exchange at the moment of payment, if such intention is clearly expressed by the parties.[7] A great number of multiple-currency clauses in international government loans, however, date back to a time when the monetary systems of most countries were linked to a common gold standard and the parties could hardly have anticipated such serious disruptions of the equilibrium existing among various currencies as occurred after the first World War. The question, therefore, arises under what circumstances a multiple-currency clause may be interpreted as a genuine "currency option," namely, a device for affording bondholders some protection against loss from exchange depreciation by allowing them to elect payment, at each due date, in what they deem the most favorable of the optional currencies.

Multiple-currency clauses occur in various forms.[8] Principal among them is the clause which expresses the face value of a bond in terms of various currencies related to each other according to their respective rates of exchange, frequently adding the place at which payment of each of the alternative currencies may be required.[9] Or the debt is expressed in one currency only, which is considered basic, coupled with a promise to pay at holder's option at other places mentioned in the bond in local currency at the current rate of the basic money.[10] Finally, the bond may

7. II, 515. See also *Corp. For. Bondh. Rep.*, No. 61 (1934), with respect to the currency option granted the holders of the Greek public works loan of 1931. The Council "insisted upon the Bondholders' rights in respect of this currency option."

8. See, in general, Nussbaum, *Money in the Law,* pp. 447 ff.; F. A. Mann, *The Legal Aspect of Money* (London, H. Milford, 1938), pp. 147 ff.; Weigert, "The Abrogation of Gold-Clauses in International Loans and the Conflict of Laws," *Contemporary Law Pamphlets,* Ser. 4, No. 4 (1940), pp. 30 ff.; Seignol, *L'Option de change et l'option de place* (Thèse, Lyon, 1935); M. Domke, "International Loans and the Conflict of Laws," *Grot. Soc.,* XXIII (1938), 47.

9. A good example of such a clause is afforded by the provisions of the bonds involved in the case of *Guaranty Trust Co., Trustee* v. *Henwood, Trustee, et al.,* 307 U.S. 247 (1939): "St. Louis Southwestern Railway Company . . . for value received, hereby promises to pay . . . at its office or agency in the Borough of Manhattan, City and State of New York, One Thousand Dollars in gold coin of the United States of America, of or equal to the standard of weight and fineness as it existed Jan. 1, 1912, or in London, England, £205 15s 2d, or in Amsterdam, Holland, 2490 guilders, or in Berlin, Germany, marks 4200, D.R.W., or in Paris, France, 5180 francs . . . ." For other instances see Institut de Rome, Preliminary Study, p. 52; Note submitted by M. Golay to the League Study Committee. Doc. I.L. 46 (September 13, 1937).

10. The coupons of the Serbian loan of 1909 involved in the case before the Permanent Court of International Justice were made payable "at Belgrade, Paris, Brussels and Geneva, at the rate of frs. 11.25; at Berlin, Frankfort-on-Main, Hamburg, St. Petersburg, Vienna and Amsterdam at the rate of exchange at sight

indicate that principal and interest, couched in one currency, are, in addition, payable at alternative places without fixing the number of monetary units or the rate of conversion for the payments to be made at those places.[11] Only clauses of the first-named type may be said to contain a genuine "option of payment" (*option de change*), entitling the holder to demand payment in the best currency at the due date, regardless of whether or not the effect of safeguarding the creditor against currency depreciation was originally intended by the parties. In the bonds, as they appear to the bearer, a definite amount is promised in terms of each currency and these alternative promises "are entirely independent; each provides for the payment of a particular sum in a particular place in a particular way." [12] In the other instances of multiple-currency clauses mentioned above, merely a so-called "option of place" (*option de place*) is involved. It means that the debt is owed in one currency only, but "collectible" at the option of the creditor in various other places mentioned in the bond for the convenience of the holder. If collected at one of the alternative places in local currency, the amount payable to the holder is determined by the value of the basic currency at the rate of exchange current at the time of payment. A mere option of place, in other words, does not afford protection against currency fluctuations and devaluations.

The creation of an effective currency option, therefore, requires a clear stipulation as to the independence of the alternative promises by fixing in the bond itself and on every coupon the number of monetary units of each foreign currency which the bearer may select for payment

---

on Paris." Publications of Perm. Ct. Int. Just., Ser. A, No. 20/21, p. 27. The bonds of the Finnish loan of 1928 were couched in currency of the United States but it was "indicated that the principal of and the interest on the bonds may be collected, at the option of the bondholders, among others at the . . . Twentsche Bank, in the City of Amsterdam, Netherlands, in Dutch Gulden, at a rate of exchange applied by the Bank at the time when buying sight bills of exchange, payable in New York." *Bull. de l'Inst. Jur. Intern.*, XXXVIII (1938), 281.

11. Mann, *op. cit.*, p. 150.

12. *International Trustee for the Protection of Bondholders . . .* v. *The King* [1936], 3 All E. R. 407, 431; Mann, *op. cit.*, p. 148; Nussbaum, *op. cit.*, pp. 448, 461 f. In *Guaranty Trust Co., Trustee* v. *Henwood, Trustee*, 307 U.S., 247 (1939), the Supreme Court of the United States took the position that a multiple-currency clause which results in protecting the lender against monetary devaluations is equivalent to a gold clause and therefore invalid because of the abrogation of gold clauses by the joint resolution. The latter, however, never envisaged currency options which, as pointed out by Justice Stone in his dissenting opinion, contain "alternative and mutually exclusive undertakings." For a general discussion of the Supreme Court decision, see Nussbaum, *op. cit.*, pp. 452 f.; Weigert, *op. cit.*, pp. 33 ff.

at the places mentioned in the respective documents.[13] As pointed out by the League Committee for the Study of International Loan Contracts in its final report, a country not participating in the flotation of a loan may not allow its currency to be mentioned in the contract, and a place of payment to be specified in its territory, because this might lead to movements of capital which would upset its international financial relations.[14] Where such a country has a strong currency, exclusion of this currency from the options may appreciably weaken the protection accorded bondholders by a multiple-currency clause. Moreover, it is possible that all the currencies included in the option may depreciate. As a safeguard against these contingencies some other device must be adopted. The one that has been most frequently employed is the so-called gold clause.

GOLD CLAUSES

The term "gold" in connection with payment clauses in international government loans appears in various forms. Sometimes the discharge of the debt is promised in "gold coins" of a specified country "of or equal to the standard of weight and fineness existing" at a specified time; [15] or the debt is stated in terms of the gold standard of a certain national monetary system by adding the word "gold" to the description of the currency in which the contract was concluded, such as "gold francs," "United States gold dollars," "gold pesos," etc.; or the term "gold" is mentioned in the caption of the loan, impressing itself on the issue in its entirety.[16] These and other forms of connecting the term "gold" with a monetary obligation have been interpreted by creditors as affording

13. It must, however, be stated that the loan, though couched in different currencies, is a single issue and constitutes an indivisible whole. With regard to attempts of governments to "break up" the loan contract bearing a multiple-currency clause by legislative measures discriminating between different bondholders and allowing payment in the "sound" currency only to those who originally subscribed in the country of that currency, see Nussbaum, *op. cit.*, p. 452, n. 23. If the loan is divided into several *tranches*, floated in various countries in their local currencies, each *tranche* is payable in its proper currency without regard to the other *tranches*. See Basdevant, in Institut de Rome, Preliminary Study, p. 50.

14. League Study Committee Report, II. Econ. and Finan., 1939, II.A. 10, p. 29.

15. This clause is customarily inserted in American-sponsored loans. See Munn, *Encyclopedia of Banking and Finance,* p. 339; Nussbaum, *op. cit.,* p. 307; Mann, *op. cit.,* p. 102. It appears in the general bond of the German Government loan of 1930 (Young). See also "Draft of a Financial Plan to Be Proposed by the Republic of Liberia," *For. Rel.,* 1920, Vol. III, Art. VI, p. 66. For an English equivalent of the clause, see Mann, *op. cit.,* p. 102, n. 8.

16. Loans of Latin American states are usually called "gold loans" like "4% External Gold Loan of Mexico, 1904," "Argentine 6% Sinking Fund Gold Bonds, 1924," etc.

protection against currency fluctuations by tying the substance of the debt to the relatively stable value of gold, namely, obliging the borrower to pay in legal tender a sum approximately equal to the amount of wealth, measured in terms of its gold value, which he received from his creditors.

Such interpretation seems justified where a clause of the first-named type is involved. It clearly indicates the intention of the parties to dissociate the obligation from variations in the gold equivalent of a national currency and to stabilize the amount owed by reference to gold itself.[17] In all other cases, however, such intention appears less clear. Certainly, the mere mentioning of the term "gold" in the caption of the loan does not prove that the debtor is obliged to pay principal and interest in gold or its equivalent.[18] A loan has occasionally been styled a "gold loan" because the revenues by which it was secured are made collectible in gold, as distinguished from the domestic currency of the debtor which be highly unstable.[19] The mode of collecting revenues pledged as security for the loan does not permit a definite inference as to the gold character of the debt.[20] Nor does the description of the currency, in which payment is promised, as "gold francs," "gold dollars," etc., necessarily imply an in-

17. *Norman* v. *Baltimore & Ohio Railway Co.*, 294 U.S. 240 (1935); *Perry* v. *United States*, 294 U.S. 330 (1935); *Feist* v. *Société Intercommunale Belge d'Électricité* [1934], A.C. 161; *British and French Trust Corporation* v. *The New Brunswick Railway Co.* [1937], 4 All E. R. 516.

18. See *Derwa* v. *Rio de Janeiro Tramway Light and Power Co.* [1928], 4 D.L.R. 542, 553, 554, where the Ontario Supreme Court held that the fact that a bond providing for payment of francs in Paris, Brussels, or Toronto was headed by the words "5% Gold Bond" did not involve the stipulation of a gold clause. Mann, *op. cit.*, p. 95.

19. See the controversy between the United States Government and France with respect to the latter's claim that principal and interest of the Haitian Government loan of 1910 were to be paid according to their gold value, not in depreciated French francs, because of the description of the loan as "gold loan." In his note to the French Ambassador of May 12, 1923 (*For. Rel.*, 1923, II, 415 ff.), the Secretary of State pointed out that the expression "gold" in the caption of the loan "emphasized the fact that the bondholders would not be dependent for their security on revenues collected in the then fluctuating Haitian currency—a feature of the loan to which the prospective investors at that time would probably have attributed more importance than to the promise to repay in gold coins as distinguished from ordinary francs . . . the use of the word 'gold' in the caption of the loan is satisfactorily explained by the nature of the security upon which the loan was issued."

20. Nussbaum, *op. cit.*, pp. 317, 388 ff.; Sauser-Hall, "La Clause-or dans les contrats publics et privés," *Rec. des Cours*, LX (1937), 692. Cf. Alberto Schoo, *La clausula oro* (Buenos Aires, 1937), 520 pp. See also the remark of the Civil Tribunal of Cairo in *Negrotto Cambioso et al.* v. *The Egyptian Government*, *Gaz. des Trib. Mix.*, XXIII, 263, 266, with respect to the independence of the character of a loan from the type of money collected for its service.

tention of the parties to place the debt on the basis of the gold value of the currency as fixed at the time of the contract. True, the Permanent Court of International Justice, in the case of the Serbian and Brazilian loans, held a clause providing for the payment in "gold francs" (*francs-or*) to be sufficient evidence of such intention,[21] and various national jurisdictions have followed The Hague court, interpreting the term "gold" in connec-

21. Judgments Nos. 14 and 15 (case of the Serbian and Brazilian loans), Publications of Perm. Ct. Int. Just., Ser. A, No. 20/21, pp. 32, 116: "As it is fundamental that the terms of a contract qualifying the promise are not to be rejected as superfluous, and as the definitive use of the word 'gold' cannot be ignored, the question is: What must be deemed to be the significance of that expression? It is conceded that it was the intention of the parties to guard against the fluctuations of the Serbian dinar, and that, in order to procure the loans, it was necessary to contract for repayment in foreign money. But, in so contracting, the Parties were not content to use simply the word 'franc,' or to contract for payment in French francs, but stipulated for 'gold francs.' It is quite unreasonable to suppose that they were intent on providing for the giving in payment of mere gold specie, or gold coins, without reference to a standard of value. . . . One argument against the efficacy of the provision for gold payments is that it is simply a clause of 'style,' or a routine form of expression. This, in substance, would eliminate the word 'gold' from the bonds. The contract of the Parties cannot be treated in such a manner. When the Brazilian Government promised to pay 'gold francs,' the reference to a well-known standard of value cannot be considered as inserted merely for literary effect, or as a routine expression without significance . . . it cannot be admitted that when a Government places a foreign loan with a promise of payment having reference to a well-known standard of value, that reference is to be disregarded. The Government did not issue bonds simply for 'French francs' but for 'gold francs,' and if the expression 'gold francs' did in fact appropriately denote a standard of value, that standard must be deemed to be the subject of reference." See also the French Countermemorandum in the same case of September, 1928, *idem*, Ser. C, No. 16–III, p. 510.

This conclusion was directly contrary to that reached by French courts in similar cases. Hackworth, *Digest of International Law* (Washington, Govt. Printing Office, 1943), V, 633.

In the *Norman* and *Perry* cases, *supra*, p. 31, n. 17, the Supreme Court of the United States held that the gold clause had been breached by the United States on its bonds payable in gold of the present standard of weight and fineness. Since the plaintiff could prove no damage resulting from the 1933 cancellation of the gold clause, the purchasing power of the paper dollar remaining unaffected, the plaintiff obtained only a Pyrrhic victory. Damage could be proved, however, by Swiss and Dutch holders of United States bonds. Their countries had not departed from gold and they were entitled to payment in a 100-cent dollar rather than a 59-cent dollar. To foreclose actions on their part in the Court of Claims or the United States District Court, Congress passed an Act (49 Stat. 938–9, Sec. 2, 31 U.S.C.A. § 773b, August 27, 1935), prohibiting actions against the United States on these bonds after January 1, 1936. The Government could by statute nullify gold clauses in private loan contracts, but not in its own government bonds. Some countries have by statute prohibited further gold clauses in the bonds issued by national debtors.

tion with a national currency as implying a genuine gold value clause designed to protect the substance of the debt against depreciation.[22] There are, however, instances when the term "gold" was associated with the name of a monetary unit merely to indicate that the latter had been reorganized without tying it to a fixed amount of gold. Thus, the "gold peso" created by Argentina in 1899 for the convenience of foreign trade was made equivalent to a certain amount of paper pesos (44 gold pesos being equal to 100 paper pesos); the gold peso debtor did not intend to obligate himself in terms of gold.[23] The mere addition, therefore, of the word "gold" to the description of the currency in which payment is promised is of itself no proof that the parties intend to express the debt on a gold basis.

Nor does the fact that an external government loan is in the nature of an "international contract"[24] render the debt a gold obligation. In the famous "gold controversy" between the Egyptian Government and the commissioners of the Egyptian public debt, the Mixed Court of Cairo had advanced the theory that, even in the absence of a specific gold clause in the loan contract, the Egyptian Government was obliged to discharge its debt in gold because of the international character of the bonds, which implied reference to an international standard of stable value, such as gold.[25] This view, however, has not in practice prevailed. When a loan is denominated in a national currency without other indications, the obligation follows the fluctuations of the currency in question.[26] This is also true with regard to a certain type of the so-called

22. Especially France and Switzerland. See the cases quoted by Mann, *op. cit.*, p. 102, nn. 2, 3. See also the decision of the Alexandria Mixed Court of Appeal, March 9, 1939, U.S. Dept. of Commerce, *Comparative Law Series*, III (1940), 390.

23. Nussbaum, *op. cit.*, pp. 320 ff. (terms like "gold leva," "gold crowns" were not intended to refer to any specific gold value). See also Mann, *op. cit.*, p. 94, with respect to the Chilean gold peso.

24. In the sense of French monetary law. See Capitant, "Les Emprunts internationaux et le cours forcé," *Jour. du Droit Int.*, LV (1928), 561; Van Nierop, "International Loans Secured by Guaranty," *40th Conf. Int. Law Assn. Rep.* (Amsterdam, 1938), pp. 192 ff., 197. The criterion for the international character of a loan is the international supplying of capital. "By placing the loan abroad, the borrower enters into the sphere of international trade."

25. *Negrotto Cambioso et al.* v. *The Egyptian Government, Gaz. des Trib. Mix.*, XXIII, 263. See also *G. Atallah et al.* v. *Crédit Foncier Egyptien, idem,* p. 282; *Ottoman Bank of Nicosia* v. *Angelos Dascalopoulos,* 151 L.T. Rep. 151 (1934); Sauser-Hall, *op. cit.*, p. 691, n. 3.

26. Basdevant, Memorandum of April, 1937, submitted to the League Committee for the Study of International Loan Contracts. See also Reichert, *Die zwischenstaatliche Wirkung der Aufhebung der Goldklauseln* (Munich, 1938), pp. 14 ff.: "Loans which are international in character, *viz.*, those which are issued

multiple-currency clause whereby one currency is made "equivalent" to another.[27] French courts have taken the position that such clauses necessarily imply a gold clause since equivalence of currencies can exist only on a gold basis.[28] Although it is quite conceivable that the parties intended to insure the stability of the debt by referring to a currency of known immunity from depreciation,[29] it seems altogether inadmissible to disregard the monetary stipulations in the bonds, which, if adequately phrased, may offer the holder a choice of the best currency available at the moment of payment but are not expressive of an intention to create a gold obligation.[30]

In view of the reluctance of courts to spell gold clauses out of the extrinsic circumstances of the transaction, the intention to guard the debt against currency fluctuations by fixing its substance in terms of the stable value of gold should be given clear expression in the documents constituting the loan contract (prospectus, bonds, and coupons).[31] As already observed, the most effective method yet devised for achieving this end has been the American form of the gold clause which states the debt in terms of a certain number of "gold coins of the United States of America of or equal to the standard of weight and fineness" existing at the date of the issue of the loan.[32] The League Committee for the Study

in the whole of Europe or in non-European countries, are not for this reason alone protected against depreciation. True, the idea seems obvious that international bonds should be based upon an international standard of value. But the designation of a loan as 'international contract' cannot be decisive as to the obligation of the debtor to pay in terms of the gold value of his debt."

27. Loan of the city of Tokyo ("£4,000,000 equivalent to Frs. 100,880,000").

28. Appellate Court of Besançon, December 12, 1928 (*Jour. du Droit Int.*, LVI [1928], 1062); Nussbaum, *op. cit.*, p. 463, n. 70. See also the conclusions of the Attorney General Hugh Holmes in the case of the *Commissioners of the Egyptian Public Debt* v. *The Egyptian Government* before the Civil Tribunal of Cairo, *Gaz. des Trib. Mix.*, XXIII, 267, 272.

29. As to the position taken by the United States Supreme Court to the effect that in a case where one of the alternatively stipulated currencies calls for the payment of gold dollars, a "gold promise permeates the whole multiple currency," see *supra*, n. 12, and Nussbaum, *op. cit.*, p. 463, n. 70. The term "pound sterling" does not connote a gold clause. Nussbaum, *op. cit.*, p. 315, n. 6.

30. Nussbaum, *op. cit.*, p. 463.

31. If a loan is issued directly by the government without intermediary bankers, mention of the gold clause in the prospectus is sufficient, since this document may be used as a subsidiary means of interpretation to clarify the meaning of the bonds. See *supra*, section on the Technical Contract; also, Nussbaum, *op. cit.*, pp. 313 ff.; Mann, *op. cit.*, p. 94; Sauser-Hall, *op. cit.*, p. 688.

32. *Supra*, nn. 15, 17. According to Mann, *op. cit.*, p. 102, n. 8, the clearest method of expressing a gold value clause is embraced in the Order made by the House of Lords in the *Feist* case; it would read as follows: "to pay £100 in gold coin of the United Kingdom or in so much current legal tender of the United King-

of International Loan Contracts, which devoted a good deal of its work to the study of the gold clause, suggested in its final report that the liability of the debtor should be fixed "as the equivalent of a given weight of gold in money current at the time of payment, independently of the nominal amount expressed in monetary units in circulation at the time of the issue."[33] Since payment in bullion is difficult to conceive, a sentence should be added indicating that the debtor shall always be entitled to discharge his liability by paying in the required currency an amount sufficient to purchase the stipulated weight of gold.[34]

Debtor governments in the past have successfully defied attempts to enforce gold clauses in international loans.[35] Even if an international

dom that every pound comprised in the nominal amount of such payment represents the price in London in sterling (calculated at the due date of payment) of 123.27447 grains of gold of the standard of fineness specified in the First Schedule to the Coinage Act, 1870."

33. League Study Committee Report, II. Econ. and Finan. 1939. II.A. 10, p. 12; see also p. 30: "The very substance of the contract should be clearly shown to be based on a given weight in gold, so that the changes in the definition of any monetary unit will not affect the determination of this gold weight."

34. Other refinements suggested by the League Committee in the drafting of gold clauses concern the procedure to be employed in converting the weight of gold into the number of monetary units constituting legal tender at the time of payment. If conversion takes place at the moment when the bearer presents the mature coupon or bond, the debtor state will always be in doubt as to the actual amounts it will have to pay until every coupon has been paid or bond redeemed. For this reason, it is suggested that the conversion of the stipulated weight of gold into legal tender be calculated at the rate prevailing on a fixed date somewhat previous to the actual date on which payment becomes due to the bondholder. *Idem*, p. 13.

35. See the famous "gold controversy" between the Commissioners of the Public Debt of Egypt and the Egyptian Government, 1931–36. II, 629–631. The Greek Government, in a dispute with the International Financial Commission over the service of the so-called "Old Gold Loans," maintained that payment in gold francs "in this instance would recognize the validity of the 'gold clause' in general, which it refused to do." *Corp. For. Bondh. Rep.*, No. 61 (1934), p. 41. The International Financial Commission for a while retained enough drachmae to cover the difference between the sterling and gold values of the payments on these loans. See League Loans Committee, *First Annual Report*, May, 1933, p. 40, n. When asked by the Ottoman Debt Council to pay coupons in United States currency and not in devalued French francs, the Turkish Government in 1937 declared that the world crisis had destroyed for all countries the possibility of payment of debts on a gold basis and insisted on payment involving a devaluation of about 40%. *Corp. For. Bondh. Rep.*, No. 64 (1937), p. 70. See also H. M. Groves, *Financing Government* (New York, Holt & Co., 1939), p. 670. The annual reports of the Foreign Bondholders Protective Council for the years 1936–38 contained this note: "Insofar as the Council has information, no gold dollar bonds issued by any country, are now being served (either partially or in full) in gold, as to interest or sinking fund, even where the contractual obligation requires gold service, nor are

gold standard should be restored,[36] the disappointing experience with the gold clause as a means of protection against currency fluctuations should indicate the adoption in its place of the currency option which, as pointed out by the League Committee in its above-mentioned report, has been more often respected than gold clauses, because the latter have proved to be too rigid, while the currency option is less onerous and more adaptable to the needs of both creditors and debtor.[37]

ARBITRATION CLAUSES

The effort to introduce arbitration clauses into loan contracts between private lenders and government borrowers has a background of many years. Its justification lies in the fact that disputes as to the interpretation of the contract are very possible, that it is not only often difficult to determine the law to be applied but it is even more difficult to determine the court which might be invoked. While a government may espouse the claim of its national against another government after the event and thus make the proceeding international,[38] it is not usual to present

such gold dollar bonds being served in United States currency in amounts equivalent to gold service; on the contrary, all such gold dollar bonds (so far as the Council is informed) are being served in United States currency, dollar for dollar. In this respect, every gold dollar bond of every country is to this extent in default."

36. A development which many writers on monetary questions still regard as practicable and desirable.

37. Op. cit., pp. 15, 28 ff.: "With a gold clause . . . no future reduction in the obligations of the contract can be foreseen, even if the currency of the country in which the loan was contracted is devalued and even if all the principal currencies suffer the same fate; borrowers are apt to consider that this rigidity of gold clauses makes them intolerable, especially when their own currency has been devalued. . . . In a general monetary upheaval, therefore, respect for a currency option does appear to be less onerous than strict adherence to the gold clause." See also Sauser-Hall, op. cit., p. 667.

The Chinese attempt to regard the Boxer Indemnity, payable in gold, as merely a "gold standard debt" was resisted by the powers. Hackworth, op. cit., V, 629; Panama succeeded in enforcing her construction of the treaty obligation of the United States to pay Panama annually $250,000, "in gold coin of the United States," by payment of 450,000 balboas with back interest. Idem, p. 630. Reference has already been made to the Serbian and Brazilian cases before the Permanent Court of International Justice in which the clause "francs d'or" was construed as reflecting the intent of the parties to pay in France in "gold francs." Most commentators regard this as a misconstruction of the obligation.

38. E.g., as did France in the claims against Brazil and Yugoslavia as to the meaning of the clause "franc d'or" in the bonds of the debtor countries (Brazilian Loans Case, Publications of Perm. Ct. Int. Just., Ser. A, No. 20/21, July 12, 1929 [Judgments Nos. 14 and 15]). See also Dreyfus Brothers and Company v. Peru, decided by the Permanent Court of Arbitration, October 11, 1921, discussed in

bond cases diplomatically, and in the cases that have been submitted to claims commissions, like the Florida bonds before the British-American Tribunal of 1853, the commission generally maintains that it has no jurisdiction over bond claims unless it is expressly provided for in the protocol of submission.[39] Such matters do not fall within the obligatory jurisdiction of the Permanent Court of International Justice because they are not intergovernmental but involve a private claimant against a government. Courts other than those of the debtor state are likely to consider themselves incompetent; and suits in the courts of the debtor are not likely to be fruitful.

Practical efforts to afford an international solution of the problem by setting up a disinterested body to adjudicate disputes arising among the parties may be said to date from about 1920.[40] In these activities, the League of Nations and its Financial Committee played an important part not only in initiating arbitration proceedings and clauses providing for arbitration in the future but in furnishing impartial studies of the risks and supervision of the loans extended. The so-called "League loans" issued to meet pressing needs in Austria, Bulgaria, Danzig, Estonia, Greece, and Hungary [41] were all made with some supervision of

Scott, *The Hague Court Reports* (2d Ser. New York, Oxford University Press, 1932), pp. 31–38. A. Dutch report submitted to the 40th Conference of the International Law Association, at Amsterdam, listed the "standard clauses" for the settlement of disputes between individuals and governments in business contracts and loan contracts because national courts are not always impartial. M. Domke, "Arbitration Clauses and International Loans," *Arbitration Journal*, III (1939), 161.

39. See the discussion of the cases in Borchard, *Diplomatic Protection of Citizens Abroad*, p. 302; Schoo, *op. cit.*, p. 410. This also was the position of the Paris Court of Appeal, July 20, 1938, as to the gold clause in the French $7\frac{1}{2}\%$ dollar loan of 1924 (*Revue de Science et de Legislation financières*, XXXVI [1938], 424) and of Article XI of the Harvard *Research in International Law: Competence of Courts in Regard to Foreign States* (Cambridge, Harvard Law School, 1932), pp. 632–640.

40. Note, however, that at The Hague in 1907 the Porter Proposition was adopted by some thirty states, many with reservations. It prohibited the use of armed force to recover "pecuniary" claims arising out of contract unless the debtor state refused to submit to or abide by arbitration. It was misconceived, since debtors usually refuse to pay because they are unable to pay. See also Borchard, *op. cit.*, pp. 327–329. It has never come into force and some states have withdrawn from the convention. By "pecuniary" the Spanish-speaking states mean bonds only; others conceive it as covering all claims arising out of contract.

41. The Austrian loan, for example, provided that differences of interpretation should be submitted to the Council, while the Bulgarian $7\frac{1}{2}\%$ stabilization loan of 1928 provided for the submission of disputes to an arbitrator nominated by the Council of the League.

The clause read:

the debtor or control of the expenditure by League officials.[42] While the intergovernmental debt settlements of 1923 made by the United States with various European countries made no mention of disputes or their arbitration, the Dawes loan of 1924 and the Young loan of 1930 provided expressly for arbitration.[43] Germany, the debtor, brought several suits, notably one by which she sought a judgment that her payments to German nationals imposed as an obligation by Article 297 (e) of the Treaty of Versailles were within and not outside the Dawes commitments, which included all Germany's financial obligations.[44] The Czech loans of 1932 and 1937, guaranteed by France, and other recent loans contain an arbitration clause.[45] In a number of other cases, where the loan contract

"General Bond, Clause 19.

"Whenever any question arises as to the interpretation of the present text, such question shall be submitted to the Council of the League of Nations, and the decision taken by it, or by such person or persons as the Council may appoint to settle the question, shall be binding on all the parties concerned. When it is necessary to apply the present clause, the decision shall be taken by a majority vote." Quoted in League Study Committee Report, II. Econ. and Finan. 1939. II.A. 10, pp. 38–39.

42. Cf. *infra*, pp. 287 ff., for the international control commissions installed, during the nineteenth century, in Egypt, Turkey, and Greece.

43. *Die Entscheidungen des internationalen Schiedsgerichts zur Auslegung des Dawes-plans*, Schoch, tr., "Politische Wissenschaft," Vols. II, III, IV.

44. Germany lost this contention. See *ibid*.

45. The contract concluded with the French bankers read:
"Article 22.

"Any disputes which may arise as to the interpretation or execution of the present provisions shall be subject to the jurisdiction of the Permanent Court of International Justice at The Hague, acting in execution of Article 14 of the Covenant of the League of Nations. The Czecho-Slovak State undertakes to lay such disputes before the Permanent Court of International Justice, whose jurisdiction it accepts." Quoted in *idem*, p. 39.

See also the loan by British bankers to Czechoslovakia, 1922; the Lisman loan of 1922 to Salvador, in which the United States consented to a clause by which the Chief Justice or a federal judge might be selected as arbitrator; the Argentine 6% loan made by American bankers in 1925.

Article IX of the loan contract between Salvador and Minor C. Keith, dated June 24, 1922, read as follows:

"In case there shall at any time arise between the Republic, the Fiscal Agent, and the Fiscal Representative, or any of them, any disagreement, question or difference of any nature whatever regarding the interpretation or performance of this contract *such disagreement, question, or difference shall be referred to the Chief Justice of the Supreme Court of the United States of America, through the Secretary of State of the said United States of America, for determination, decision and settlement* by such Chief Justice and the parties hereto severally agree that any determination, decision or settlement made by such Chief Justice shall be accepted by them as final and conclusive and that each of them will abide by such determination, decision, or settlement, and will fully perform and conform to the

made no provision for the adjudication of disputes, an agreement was made to submit them to the Financial Committee of the League of Nations.[46] In 1932 the Council of the League, petitioned by a private committee organized to deal with League loans, made a declaration providing that "any country which is in default on a loan issued under the auspices of the League should avail itself fully of the technical help of League advisers, and keep the Council fully informed of the position through its Financial Committee."

Because of the alleged "uncertainty as to the competence of the courts to which they [the lenders] had access" and the resulting "demoralization" of lenders if not of the "international capital market," the Dutch Government proposed in 1935 at Geneva that the League of Nations study the means of improving loan contracts issued by public authorities

---

terms thereof. In case the said Chief Justice shall decline or be unable to act, then the Secretary of State of the United States of America shall be empowered to designate some other member of the federal judiciary of the United States of America to act in his place." Quoted in Robert W. Dunn, *American Foreign Investments* (New York, Viking, 1926), p. 227.

The Argentine arbitration clause reads as follows:

"Article V, Paragraph 5.

"Should the banker and/or the paying agents have any doubts in some particular case as to their rights or obligations under the present Agreement, any question or difficulty of this kind shall be settled by reference to an arbitrator appointed jointly by the Ambassador of the Argentine Republic in the United States of America and the bankers; the decisions of this arbitrator shall be final and without appeal." Quoted in League Study Committee Report, II. Econ. and Finan. 1939. II.A. 10, p. 38.

See also Article XXII of the loan contract of October 6, 1922, between the bankers and the Republic of Haiti (Dunn, *op. cit.*, p. 308), and Article XVIII of the loan contract with Nicaragua, September 1, 1911 (Dunn, *op. cit.*, p. 371).

See also the tobacco monopoly loan of the Free City of Danzig, 1927, clause 34, *idem*, p. 38. A similar provision is to be found in the Treasury bonds issued in 1934 by Dutch bankers to the French Government. Since these clauses stipulate for the jurisdiction of the Permanent Court of International Justice and are made between private lenders and the borrowing government, their efficacy, without the intervention of the lender's government, is not clear. But see the arbitration between the Greek Government and the Société Commerciale de Belgique, 1925. After two arbitral awards were made on the defaulted Greek bonds in 1936, the Belgian Government espoused their claim before the Permanent Court of International Justice under Article 36 of the statute providing for obligatory jurisdiction; in 1939, the court held that the arbitral awards were "definitive and obligatory."

See also the so-called Bruins Award on the gold clause, embodied in the Romanian monopolies loan, M. Domke, *op. cit.*, p. 165, and Article XIII of the Austrian loan contract of June 30, 1930, *idem*, p. 164.

46. See, for example, the case of the Disconto Gesellschaft loan to Bulgaria. II, 559.

and prepare model arbitration clauses which might be included in such contracts. Out of that initiative a committee was appointed for the study of international loan contracts. After holding numerous meetings and hearings, they issued in 1939 a valuable report.[47] They recommended the insertion in all contracts of a clause providing for the arbitration of all disputes arising under the contract.[48] Each arbitral tribunal was to be appointed by the President of the Permanent Court of International Justice from a panel of nine persons chosen by the court for five-year periods, with eligibility for reappointment. The tribunal was to be invocable unilaterally in the absence of agreement by the debtor government by any bondholder or bondholders possessing not less than ten per cent of the bonds outstanding, by any official representative of the bondholders or officially recognized protective committee, and by the trustee or supervisor of the loan. The arbitral tribunal was to act not as a committee of compromisers or adjusters but judicially, was to determine its own jurisdiction, and was to be paid a compensation to be fixed by the Permanent Court of International Justice, payable, except in frivolous cases, by the borrower. Like most arbitral tribunals it was to fix its own procedure in the absence of party agreement. The arbitrators in various cases, who might sit where they pleased, were, if possible, to be the same men, in order to establish a uniform jurisprudence.[49]

The committee stated that it was sensible of the fact that a complete solution of the legal difficulties could only be achieved if the question of currency, gold clause, the law applicable, and similar problems were taken out of the field of national law by international conventions. Under such a convention, it added, states would undertake to set up an international loans tribunal, which would be a single tribunal with competence extending to all international loans. The committee had before it a draft convention for such a tribunal which, without necessarily recommending, it printed in an annex to the report [50] as a matter of information. The permanent tribunal thus projected [51] would have been much

47. League Study Committee Report, II. Econ. and Finan. 1939. II.A. 10.
48. *Idem,* p. 24. See also the suggestion for such arbitration clauses in bond contracts by Weiser, *Trusts on the Continent of Europe,* p. 99.
49. League Study Committee Report, II. Econ. and Finan. 1939. II.A. 10, p. 26.
50. *Idem,* p. 40.
51. Its principal differences from the recommended arbitral tribunal are that it would be obligatory for states invoking the tribunal in the interests of their nationals. The judges would still be three, with three deputy judges, appointed for ten-year terms. The Permanent Court of International Justice would draw up its rules of procedure and its financial regulations. Its decisions would have the force of decision of the highest national courts. *Idem,* pp. 40–41.

like the arbitral tribunal, a court of specialists distinct, in contrast to Judge Manton's proposal to the American Society of International Law in 1934,[52] from the Permanent Court of International Justice. The committee did not anticipate early adhesion to such a convention.[53]

52. *Proc. Am. Soc. Int. Law,* 1934, pp. 146–155. This was to make of the Permanent Court of International Justice a sort of bankruptcy court under sec. 77-b of the Securities Act or Part X of the Chandler Act.

53. The position of public bonds before arbitral tribunals will be discussed in sec. 17, *infra,* on Diplomatic Protection.

Section IV

AGENCIES CONCERNED WITH THE EXECUTION OF THE CONTRACT

THE international government loan contract requires for its execution the setting up of special machinery. Since, as a rule, governments do not possess banking facilities of their own outside their territories, they are compelled to enlist the services of independent bankers or banking houses operating within the countries of issue to act as intermediaries between themselves and their creditors in the performance of the duties resulting from the loan contract, such as the payment of interest and sinking fund in the stipulated currency, the stamping and cancellation of coupons, and other functions in connection with the issue and service of the loan. While primarily assisting the debtor in the discharge of his obligations toward the bondholders, such banks incidentally serve the need of the latter for centralized agencies in their dealings with the debtor government during the life of the loan.

THE FISCAL OR PAYING AGENT

The organ appointed by the borrowing government to represent it at the place of payment is called "fiscal agent" or "paying agent." No conclusion as to the functions of the agent may be drawn from the use of one or the other term. In particular, the word "fiscal" instead of "paying" agent in no way implies a special authority to represent the debtor government before the fiscal authorities of the country in which the loan was issued.[1] If the loan is floated not directly by the government but through intermediary bankers, the latter are ordinarily appointed the paying agents of the borrower [2] and their powers and duties are defined

1. See League Study Committee Report, II. Econ. and Finan. 1939. II.A. 10, p. 15, where it was proposed to discard entirely the term "fiscal agent" and to replace it throughout by "paying agent," in order to avoid this misunderstanding.
2. SEC, *Rep.*, Pt. V, p. 513.

in the loan agreement between the government and the issuing house.[3] Otherwise, the rules governing the office of the paying agent are embodied in a special "paying agency agreement" concluded between the debtor state and the bank serving in that capacity.[4]

The principal duty of the paying agent consists in servicing the loan with the sums placed at his disposal by the debtor for this purpose.[5] The debtor will have discharged his obligation only by the complete satisfaction of the creditor's claims in accordance with the terms of the contract, namely, by actual payment through the agent. Currency fluctuations occurring between the date of transmission of funds abroad and the actual payment of the creditor or financial difficulties on the part of the agent are risks which the debtor government is obliged to bear.[6] While in the hands of the paying agent, the monies received by him for distribution among the bondholders remain the property of the foreign government and therefore are immune from attachment.[7] Except in cases where a special "authenticating agent" has been named,[8] the paying agent performs additional functions in connection with the issue of the loan, such as the authentication and registration of the bonds and the exchange of temporary for definitive certificates. The agent must perform his duties in good faith and with reasonable care.[9] His liability

3. See, for example, Republic of Poland 3% dollar funding bonds loan agreement, *For. Bondh. Prot. Coun. Rep.*, 1937, pp. 620 ff.

4. See, for example, the paying agency agreement of September 1, 1937, between the Republic of Uruguay and the National City Bank of New York, *idem*, p. 741; paying agency agreement between the Province of Mendoza (Argentina) and Manufacturers Trust Co., of June 1, 1938, *idem*, 1938, p. 60.

5. Where one bank has been designated by the debtor government to receive the whole of the service monies for distribution among other paying agents appointed for various countries, the duty to remit the necessary funds is discharged by the transmission of the service monies to the principal agent. See the case of the *Banque de Paris et des Pays-Bas* v. *The German Clearing Office*, decided by the Franco-German Mixed Arbitral Tribunal, May 16, 1925, *Rec. des déc.*, V, 397 (402 ff.).

6. League Study Committee Report, II. Econ. and Finan. 1939. II.A. 10, p. 16.

7. Feilchenfeld, in Quindry, *Bonds and Bondholders, Rights and Remedies*, II, 173, n. 70. See also the various dicta on this point in *Thomas W. Lamont et al.* v. *The Travelers Insurance Co.*, 281 N.Y. 362, 24 N.E. (2d) 81 (1939); *Am. Jour. Int. Law*, XXXIV (1940), pp. 349 ff.

8. See, for example, the authenticating agency agreement of June 30, 1937, between the Government of the Republic of Poland and the National City Bank of New York, *For. Bondh. Prot. Coun. Rep.*, 1937, p. 669.

9. See, for example, the paying agency agreement between Uruguay and the National City Bank of New York, Art. 8 (c), *idem*, p. 743; paying agency agreement between the Province of Mendoza and the Manufacturers Trust Co., June 1, 1938, Art. 9 (c), *idem*, 1938, p. 63.

toward his principal is, as a rule, limited to gross negligence and willful misconduct.[10] He may be dismissed or may tender his resignation of his own accord.[11]

No difficulties in the practical exercise of the agency functions are likely to arise if the paying agent remains the exclusive representative of the debtor and acts only on the latter's behalf. This, however, is almost never the case. In the great majority of cases, draftsmen of paying agency agreements, disregarding the legal notion of agency and insensible to the logic of the situation, have conferred upon the paying agent the duty to represent the interests of the bondholders as well, especially to take judicial action against the debtor government in default.[12] This dual position naturally divides the loyalties of the agent and is injurious to the interests of both creditors and debtor. Bankers, acting as fiscal agents of foreign governments in financial distress whose bonds they had sold, when questioned before the Securities and Exchange Commission as to whether they ceased to be the agents of the debtor government after default and became the sole representatives of the bondholders in enforcing the contract, denied any such shift from one allegiance to another but were unable to define precisely the anomalous status of an agent attempting to serve at one time two principals whose interests sharply conflict.[13] In a suit brought by a bondholder against the Province of

10. See, for example, State Mortgage Bank of Yugoslavia 5% funding bonds indenture and general bond, July 1, 1936, No. 16, *idem,* 1936, p. 834; authenticating agency agreement between Poland and the National City Bank, *idem,* 1937, p. 675.

11. See, for example, State Mortgage Bank of Yugoslavia 5% funding bonds indenture and general bond, Art. 16, *For. Bondh. Prot. Coun. Rep.,* 1936, p. 833; authenticating agency agreement between Poland and the National City Bank of New York, Art. 17, *idem,* 1937, p. 675.

12. SEC, *Rep.,* Pt. V, pp. 514 f. See, for example, State Mortgage Bank of Yugoslavia 5% funding bonds indenture and general bond, *supra,* n. 11, p. 832: "The Fiscal Agent or its successors are hereby irrevocably appointed the special agent and representative of the holders of the Funding Bonds, and vested with full power and authority on their behalf to enforce this Indenture for the benefit of said holders with full power and authority to bring and defend . . . any action or proceeding . . . in the Kingdom of Jugoslavia or elsewhere, for the enforcement of the Funding Bonds or for the interpretation and enforcement of this Indenture . . . ."

13. SEC, *Rep.,* Pt. V, pp. 517 ff. An "ingenious rationalization" of the fiscal agent's position in defending the bondholders' rights against the defaulting government was advanced by Mr. Schoepperle who maintained that the fiscal agent, when pleading for the bondholders, is "remonstrating" to his principal, the debtor, "that he was not treating decently the bondholders who were third parties in our relationship with the government." *Idem,* p. 427. The Securities and Exchange Commission concluded that "the ties of royalty and obligation of the fiscal agent to the

Santa Fé (Argentina) before the Argentine Supreme Court, the authority vested in the paying agent under the terms of the loan agreement to enforce the rights of the bondholders by instituting legal proceedings against the debtor in default was interpreted by the court in a manner directly detrimental to the interests of the private creditors. By purchasing a bond providing for the enforcement of his rights by the fiscal agent, a bondholder, it was held, had issued a power of attorney to the latter who thereby became the sole legal agent of the creditors and exclusively entitled to take judicial action against the debtor.[14] The suit was dismissed on the ground that the plaintiff had failed to show a refusal on the part of the fiscal agent to sue the defaulting province. As a result of this ruling, the bondholder is deprived of his legal remedies so long as the fiscal agent, even in the most perfunctory manner, requests payment from the defaulting government or negotiates for a settlement of the default. In order to avoid confusion and misapprehension, it seems advisable to draft the paying agency agreements so as to make it plain that the agent owes legal duties exclusively to the debtor.[15] The protection of the bondholders' rights should be entrusted to separate agencies, a matter which will be discussed presently.

TRUSTEES IN INTERNATIONAL LOANS

The inequality of the parties to a bonded governmental loan—a single debtor on the one hand and a multitude of individual creditors, anonymous and widely scattered, on the other—raises the question of a joint representation of the bondholders in order to safeguard their interests in their dealings with the debtor government. Whenever in the past the need for collective organization of bondholders became particularly acute, as in case of default, protective committees were formed for the purpose of negotiating the terms of a settlement with the debtor on behalf of the holders of the defaulted loan. The necessity of concerted action on the part of bondholders, however, exists not only for the readjustment of a default situation but in many instances during the life of

foreign debtor disqualify the agent from representing the bondholders" in default situations. *Idem*, p. 531.

14. *The New York Times*, September 5, 1935. See also SEC, *Rep.*, Pt. V, p. 517.

15. See League Study Committee Report, II. Econ. and Finan. 1939. II.A. 10, p. 16. The paying agency agreement of June 1, 1938, between the Province of Mendoza (Argentina) and the Manufacturers Trust Co. (*For. Bondh. Prot. Coun. Rep.*, 1938, pp. 60 ff.), provides in Article 9(b) that "in acting under this Agreement, the Agent is acting solely as agent of the Province and does not assume any obligation or relationship of agency or trust for or with any of the owners or holders of the Readjustment Bonds . . . ."

the loan, in particular, when certain decisions must be taken in connection with the loan or where accompanying security invites or requires supervision or administration by a body independent of the pledgor government. The task of representing the bondholders' interests in such cases has sometimes been assigned to international agencies like the International Financial Commission in Greece, the Ottoman Debt Council, and the Egyptian Caisse de la Dette Publique, which were set up by the great powers of Europe as the result of their intervention in the financial affairs of the respective debtor countries. In recent years, under the influence of the growing participation of American capital in foreign investments, a special device hitherto unknown among the institutions for the collective representation of holders of foreign government bonds has made its appearance in the field of international finance: the trustee for international government loans.

A well-known and tested institution in American corporate finance since the middle of the last century,[16] the trustee representing the interests of security holders was first used in international financial transactions in connection with loans made by American bankers to Continental industrial corporations during the period of reconstruction after the war.[17] The first example of the trust device in international state loans is afforded by the Austrian guaranteed loan issued in 1923 under the auspices of the League of Nations. It also appears in the German loans of 1924 (Dawes) and 1930 (Young) and in later League loans to certain central European countries.[18]

The introduction of the trust device in the pattern of international government loans was as sudden as it was ill-advised. Prior to its adoption for purposes of international government loans, no thought had apparently been given to the question as to how the legal concept of trusteeship could be fitted into the law of the debtor countries on the Continent of Europe, where it had to be chiefly applied. The Anglo-American trust is inextricably bound up with the trichotomy, peculiar to

16. See James Stetson, *Some Legal Phases of Corporate Financing, Reorganization and Regulation* (New York, Macmillan, 1930), pp. 6 ff., 11, 40 ff.; Herman M. Roth, *Der Trust in seinem Entwicklungsgang vom Feoffee to Uses zur amerikanischen Trust Company* (Marburg, 1928), pp. 226 ff.; Quindry, *Bonds and Bondholders, Rights and Remedies* (Chicago, 1934), I, 264 ff.; SEC, *Rep.*, 1936, Pt. VI; League Study Committee Report, II. Econ. and Finan. 1939. II.A. 10, p. 17. See also the Note on the literature of the subject submitted to the Committee, Doc. I.L. 50 (Geneva, November 18, 1937), pp. 2 f.

17. J. Zahn, "The Trustee in German-American Industrial Loans," *Bost. Univ. Law Rev.*, XII (1932), 189 f.

18. See League Study Committee, Doc. I.L. 45 (Geneva, September 2, 1937), for a list of international loans where the institution of the trustee has been used.

the English law, of legal rights, equitable interests, and contracts. While the legal title to property may be vested in one person, equitable interests with respect to it may be retained and asserted by others, and the confidence placed in the legal owner of the property by the person entitled to its beneficial use may become the source of rights and duties of the parties to the trust agreement. In addition, the parties may apply to an equity court for guidance and supervision in the execution of their agreement. Both the judicial machinery provided by the Anglo-American law of trusts for the implementation of an incomplete indenture and the division of claims to property into legal rights and equitable interests are unknown to the Continental system which is based on the rigid Roman law concept of *jura in rem* and *jura in personam*. There is no room for that restricted or "dual" ownership, "which, when all is said and done, remains the crux of the notion of trust." [19] To the Continental mind, ownership is necessarily all-embracing and exclusive. There cannot be more than one owner of a thing and all attempts made by Continental lawyers to construe the Anglo-American trust in terms of transactions familiar to them and authorized by the civil law failed.[20] For a better understanding of the difficulties that have arisen in connection with the use of the trust device in loan contracts with Continental debtor countries, it is well to remember that they have their origin in this fundamental cleavage between irreconcilable concepts of different legal systems.

19. F. Weiser, *Trusts on the Continent of Europe*, p. 3.

20. This has been conclusively shown by Weiser in his book, *supra*, n. 19. See also J. Escarra, *Traité de l'organisation des obligataires* (Paris, 1922), pp. 85 ff.; Schmitthoff, "The International Government Loan," *Jour. Comp. Leg.*, XIX (1937), p. 180, n. 3, Plesch and Domke, *Die Österreichische Völkerbundanleihe* (Zürich, 1936), pp. 73 ff.; and in particular the decisions of three Swiss Courts *in re Aktiebolaget Obligationsinteressenter* v. *The Bank for International Settlements* (English translations in League Study Committee, Doc. I.L. 18) which will be discussed *infra*. As to the reasons for introducing the trust device into international government loans without previous examination of its compatibility with Continental legal concepts, see Weiser, *op. cit.*, p. 79, n. 2: "The explanation is probably that the professional men at work . . . acted under duress. Here were countries clamouring for and deserving credit and there were Anglo-Saxon capitalists prepared to lend but feeling—to be sure with very little reason—that they simply must have a Trust. The great thing was to get the loan floated and it was probably the acme of practical wisdom to give the lenders their hearts' desire without so much as admitting that there was anything to be defined or explained." See also Fischer Williams, *Chapters on Current International Law and the League of Nations*, p. 411: ". . . . financiers with a sound and practical realism instinctively assimilate the business which they do with States to the business which they do with individuals."

APPOINTMENT OF THE TRUSTEE

In the practice of international government loans, various forms for the appointment of trustees have been developed. As a rule, the example set by the law of trusts for the establishment of a private law corporate trust has been followed in the international sphere; that is, a trust deed or contractual document to be executed by the debtor and the trustee and usually called the general bond constitutes the legal basis for the trusteeship.[21] In the case of the League loans (with the exception of Greece where their duties were assigned to the International Financial Commission), trustees were appointed by the Council of the League acting either in pursuance of a clause in the protocol concluded between the debtor and some of the League members principally concerned with the loan, or, in the Austrian scheme, under the general bond negotiated between the government and the issuing banks.[22] In other instances, the document setting up the trust is simply an agreement between the debtor government and a banking institution providing for the distribution of funds received by the latter for payment to the bondholders.[23] No general principles can be said to have been adopted with regard to the number or qualification of persons to be named loan trustees. It may be one or several individuals, or corporations, like banks.[24] Thus, the Bank for

21. See *supra*, section on The Technical Contract. The general bond as an agreement between debtor government and trustee was first introduced by the German 1924 (Dawes) loan; similar constructions were followed for the German 1930 (Young) loan and the Austrian loans of 1933 and 1934. See League Study Committee, Doc. I.L. 45, p. 9. In the case of the Austrian guaranteed loan of 1923, the governments which guaranteed the loan and the commissioner-general whose functions were later on transferred to the trustee were parties to the general bond. See Fischer Williams, *op. cit.*, pp. 397 f., and, with respect to its legal nature, Plesch and Domke, *op. cit.*, p. 75; Weiser, *op. cit.*, pp. 79 f.

22. See Report of the Financial Committee, League of Nations, *Principles and Methods of Financial Reconstruction Work Undertaken under the Auspices of the League of Nations*, L. of N. Publications, II. Econ. and Finan., 1930. II, 16, pp. 52 ff.; League Study Committee, Doc. I.L. 45, p. 13, for details of the appointment and replacement procedure; Weiser, *op. cit.*, pp. 79 f.

23. An agreement of this sort was involved in the case of *Thomas W. Lamont et al.* v. *The Travelers Insurance Co. and the Government of the United States of Mexico*, 281 N.Y. 362, 24 N.E. (2d) 81 (1939); *Am. Jour. Int. Law*, XXXIV (1940), 349. The plaintiffs alleged that by the terms of an agreement between the Government of Mexico and themselves they were constituted trustees of the funds coming into the hands of the International Committee of Bankers on Mexico and were obligated to distribute such funds to holders of obligations issued by the Republic of Mexico. For the outcome of this matter, see II, 103–104, n. 60.

24. As to the relative merits of appointing corporations or private individuals as trustees, see the remark of the League Study Committee, Doc. I.L. 50, p. 2: Corporate trustees have the advantage of being permanent and of being able to

International Settlements at Basle was appointed trustee for the German 5½% international (Young) loan of 1930 and the Austrian government international loan of 1930.[25] The trustees for the League loans were several private persons for each issue, domiciled in various countries of Europe.[26]

LEGAL POSITION OF THE TRUSTEE

As the introduction of the trust device into the scheme of international government loans was primarily designed to afford protection to the bondholders, the most general statement that can be made with regard to the legal position of the trustee is that he is the representative of the bondholders.[27] This excludes, on the one hand, his becoming the agent or

specialize in functioning as trustees. "Ordinary trustees cannot always be found when they are wanted: they take holidays, get ill, go abroad, and die; whereas a trust company is always ready to attend to business." See also Zahn, op. cit., pp. 1, 192. Difficult questions are likely to arise in connection with nationality and domicile of the trustee. Banks and trust companies are subject to the laws of the state of incorporation. If several trustees of different nationality, domicile, and residence are appointed for the same loan, the question arises as to what law is applicable in case action is brought against all of them by the bondholders. Should one law be applicable to all the trustees? Should it preferably be the Anglo-American law of trust? See, with respect to this question, the suggestion made by Messrs. Freshfield, Leese, and Munns in their Memorandum submitted to the League Study Committee, Doc. I.L. 14 (Geneva, December 7, 1936): "If it is decided that the English courts shall have jurisdiction, this can be done by a provision in the general bond that the trustees, whatever their nationality, shall for the purposes of the trust be deemed to be located in England, and the general bond should name an agent for the trustees in London capable of accepting service and· instituting proceedings in their behalf. Alternatively, some arbitration tribunal having authority analogous to that exercised by the English High Court over trustees might be set up."

25. Apart from its being trustee for the governments entitled to receive reparation payments under the plan. With respect to this function, see Fischer Williams, "The Legal Character of the Bank for International Settlements," Am. Jour. Int. Law, XXIV (1930), 668; John W. Wheeler-Bennet and Hugh Latimer, Information on the Reparation Settlement (London, G. Allen & Unwin, Ltd., 1930), p. 208.

26. See League Study Committee, Doc. I.L. 45, pp. 9, 13.

27. Plesch and Domke, op. cit., p. 76; Cosoiu, Le Rôle de la Société des Nations en matière d'emprunts d'état (Paris, 1934), p. 197. The trust contract between Bolivia and the Equitable Trust Company, New York, of May 31, 1922 (text in Hearings before the Subcommittee of the Senate Committee on Foreign Affairs Relative to Foreign Loans [S. Con. Res. 22], 68th Cong., 2d Sess. [Washington, 1926], pp. 130 ff.) provides in Article 9, sec. 3: "The Equitable Trust Company of New York is hereby appointed general representative of the bondholders, that is to say, trustee . . . ." This, however, is by no means a complete description of the legal position of the trustee. For example, in the case of the Austrian loan of 1923, the trustees held the reserve fund against the possible gold clause liability

representative of the debtor government.[28] On the other hand, the trustee is the legal owner of the funds paid to him by the debtor in satisfaction of the debt owed to the bondholders.[29] This is in some cases explicitly stated by a stipulation in the general bond to the effect that the borrowing government, besides being the debtor of the individual bondholders, is also indebted to the trustee in the amounts borrowed.[30] The latter,

---

upon the bonds of the American *tranche* for a threefold purpose. First, in order to be able to make payment to the bondholders on a gold basis if it should ultimately be decided that that was the proper basis. Secondly, as a safeguard to the guarantor governments so that, in the event of its being held that payment was due on a gold basis and of the debtor government's refusing to make payment on that basis, the guarantor governments would not be called upon to implement their promise to pay. Finally, they held the fund in the interest of the debtor government in order to be able to pay it to that government in the event of its being finally held that payment was not due on a gold basis. See Freshfield, Leese, and Munns, *op. cit.*, p. 3.

28. See Plesch and Domke, *op. cit.*, p. 75. The trustee may not plead immunity from suits if action is brought against him by the bondholders. The trustees of the League loans do not enjoy the extraterritoriality accorded to League commissions and officials.

29. *Thomas W. Lamont et al.* v. *The Travelers Insurance Company and the Government of the United States of Mexico*, 281 N.Y. 362, 24 N.E. (2d) 81 (1939). See also *Carl Boyoir and Associates* v. *Tsune-Chi Yu*, 112 F. (2d) 885 (C.C.A. 2d, 1940).

30. The clause providing for the indebtedness of the government to the trustee in the Austrian loan of 1923 runs as follows:

"Prior to or simultaneously with the issue of any portion of the said loan the Austrian Government shall give to the Trustees an acknowledgment in writing that the Austrian Government is indebted to the Trustees to an amount equivalent to and in the same currency as the portion of the said loan about to be issued carrying interest at the rate to be specified in the bonds of each issue payable by half-yearly instalments on the said first day of June and first day of December in every year." General bond, Clause 4.

With respect to the legal significance of the clause, see Weiser, *op. cit.*, pp. 79 ff. The clause usually contained in general bonds of international state loans reciting that the borrowing government is indebted to the trustee in the amounts borrowed "clearly smacks of legal title and Anglo-Saxon Trust." However, in order to avoid any semblance of a double indebtedness on the part of the debtor government, i.e., to the trustees as well as to the bondholders, the general bond of the German loans of 1924 and 1930 contains the following clause:

"No increased obligation on the part of the German Government shall be deemed to have been created by reason only of the fact that besides the acknowledgments of indebtedness of the German Government herein contained or provided for acknowledgments of indebtedness shall also be contained in the Temporary and Definitive Bonds issued in accordance with these presents."

The general bonds of the Austrian conversion loans of 1933 and 1934 provide:

"All payments made to the Trustees pursuant to the acknowledgment provided for by the first part of this Article shall be by them applied in discharging the

therefore, receives the payments due from the debtor to the bondholders in his own right and with the understanding, implied in his trust, that he distribute the sums among the bondholders as beneficiaries entitled to receive them. Nothing more concerning the general legal position of the trustee of international government loans can be said. For the Anglo-American lawyer, the very notion of trust "is pregnant with meaning";[31] possible gaps in the trust instrument can be filled by the elaborate law of trusts, and no further explanation of its general character is needed. To the Continental legal mind, as pointed out above, the trust relationship cannot be explained in terms of any of the accepted institutions of the civil law, and the construction of the rights and duties arising from a trust instrument in connection with an international government loan must in each particular case be left to the court that is called upon to interpret the agreement in accordance with its own law.

FUNCTIONS OF THE TRUSTEE

While the powers and duties of the loan trustee can reliably be determined only by reference to the detailed provisions of the trust deed, some general considerations with respect to his functions can, nevertheless, be deduced from various instruments. Where a loan has been divided into several separate *tranches,* each issued in a different country, expressed in different currencies, and contracted with different banks or issuing houses, as, for example, the Austrian Government loan of 1923 and the German Government international loan of 1930, a trustee is instituted primarily to act as a central agency for the collection and distribution of the service monies received from the debtor.[32] In the matter of this function, the institution of a loan trusteeship seems chiefly to benefit the debtor, to whom it affords valuable technical assistance in discharging his obligation. The question, however, remains whether the services rendered to the debtor by the trustee in his capacity as receiver of the loan payments are of such nature as to give him the status of a mere paying agent of the debtor, or whether the trustee, even when receiving the funds due from the debtor, still acts principally as the representative of the bondholders, to whom he owes the duty "to enforce their rights,"[33] namely, to see to it that the debt is discharged in accordance with the terms of the loan contract. It was this question which lay at the bottom of the famous case, *Aktiebolaget Obligationsinteressenter* v.

obligation of the Government to the Bondholders under the second part thereof."
See League Study Committee, Doc. I.L. 45.
31. Weiser, *op. cit.*, p. 79, n. 2.
32. League Study Committee, Doc. I.L. 45.
33. Fischer Williams, *Chapters On Current International Law,* p. 397.

The Bank for International Settlements,[34] the only one as yet in point on the subject of the trustee for international government loans. Three successive Swiss courts labored with the proper solution of the question, only to give evidence of the profound confusion created by the attempt to transplant the institution of the loan trust in the unfavorable soil of Continental law.

The case, briefly, involved an action brought by a Swedish bondholder against the Bank for International Settlements, as trustee for the German Government international loan of 1930 (Young), for the payment of the full gold value of his share in the service monies received by the defendant from the German Government. The latter, transmitting the loan service to the trustee, had given express instructions that the interest on certain *tranches* of the loan should be paid only at the nominal value. This measure, violative of the *pari passu* as well as of the gold value clauses of the loan contract, resulted in a discriminatory treatment of the holders of the various *tranches;* it was intended as a reprisal against those states which had gone off the gold standard and had prejudiced the interests of nationals of the German Reich. The Swiss Federal Court, affirming the rulings of the lower courts, dismissed the action on the ground that the defendant bank was merely the paying agent of the debtor government whose instructions with regard to the distribution of the service monies it was bound to follow.[35] In the teeth of the express and clear stipulation in the general bond that the German Government was indebted to the trustee for the whole amount of the loan, the court bluntly stated that the loan did not represent a global obligation of the German Government to the defendant but merely the

34. *Die Praxis des Bundesgerichts,* XXV, 331. English translations in League Study Committee, Doc. I.L. 18 (Geneva, February 11, 1937).

35. Weiser, *op. cit.,* p. 86, n. 11, calls it a "derogatory conclusion," at which the Swiss Court arrived, that the trustee was "no more than a paying agent—one of the dozen or so appointed in respect of the same loan." The dangers resulting for the trustee from his being made the agent of payment are pointed out by Basdevant in his Note submitted to the League Study Committee, Doc. I.L. 52 (Geneva, December 1, 1937): "Were he to become an agent of payment, that would undoubtedly tend to create the impression of an additional guarantee that payment would be made in accordance with the terms of the loan; but the actual nature of the debtor's undertakings might be disputed—for example, a mode of payment enjoined by the debtor on his agent of payment may be held by certain bondholders to be contrary to those undertakings; by taking sides, the trustee would place himself in a difficult position, and if, having done so and paid out more than the debtor claims to owe, the courts were to decide that he had in fact paid more than was due, he would himself be liable to the debtor . . . . It would be wrong to allow the trustees to be placed in such a position, and they must not therefore be made the debtor's agents of payment."

total of a number of mutually independent claims of the bondholders against the German Reich. If the court had followed the notion of the trust, it would have come to the conclusion that the German Government, after having paid the service monies to the trustee in fulfillment of its debt to the latter, had lost control over the funds which were held by the bank in trust for distribution among the bondholders in accordance with the terms of the loan contract. An agreement between the trustee and the debtor concerning the distribution of the service in violation of certain clauses in the contract would not have been binding on the trustee; on the contrary, compliance with it would have amounted to a breach of trust. The Swiss courts, however, unanimously refused to give effect to the Anglo-American notion of trust in the relationships created by the general bond, holding that, since the defendant bank was domiciled and had to fulfill its duties in Switzerland, Swiss law as the law of the place of performance was applicable. Even so, the courts experienced great difficulty in trying to fit the specific rights and duties arising under the scheme of the Young loan into the system of contractual relations admitted by the Swiss Code of Obligations.[36]

Besides receiving the service installments and performing other functions in connection with the payment of the debt,[37] the trustees are

36. In construing the terms of the loan contract, the court stated: "The legal relationship existing, under the terms of the loan contract, between the Bank for International Settlements and the German Reich on the one hand and the bondholders on the other, cannot simply be characterised as mandate (secs. 294 ff. of the Swiss Federal Code of Obligations) even though the position of the Bank as trustee (Treuhänderin) has been paraphrased in the German text as Agent of the Bondholders (*Beauftragter der Inhaber der Schuldverschreibungem*). In point of fact, the element of revocability at all times, which is the essential element of a mandatory relationship, is lacking. Furthermore, the Bank occupies a position of considerably greater freedom than an agent since instructions, whether from the Reich or the bondholders, are not under all circumstances binding upon it. The legal relationship here in question should rather be construed as a tri-partite contract *sui generis* similar to a mandate the purport of which, however, is to be determined exclusively upon the basis of the terms of the loan . . . ." For general criticism of the decision, see Weiser, *op. cit., passim,* and Fachiri, Memorandum submitted to the League Study Committee, Doc. I.L. 17, p. 6: "It is hardly necessary to point out that the decision is completely at variance with the whole conception of trusteeship as understood in England. Under English law a trustee is not the agent or representative of anyone. He is trustee of the trust fund and his duty is to administer it in the interests of the beneficiaries in accordance with the provisions of the trust deed."

37. The varied nature of the transactions in connection with the service of the loan through the trustee is described by Basdevant, *loc cit.:* "In considering the trustee's duties in regard to the service of the loan (coupons and redemption), it must be borne in mind that complicated operations are involved. The debtor State

or establishment does not merely have the necessary sums paid out as they fall due by its own cashiers. As a rule, it has such payments made through agents, to which it transfers the necessary funds. In some cases such funds are handed over in monthly instalments even though the payments are made quarterly or half-yearly. In other cases, the method adopted is the periodical transfer to the agent (weekly, fortnightly or monthly) of the income from the revenues or taxes assigned to the service of the debt. It is also conceivable that reserves might be constituted. Such being the case, the trustee might receive the funds from the debtor, be responsible for their custody and administration until the various due dates, and, lastly, pay out to the bondholders the sums due in respect of coupons or redeemed bonds. This is the method which would give the trustee the strictest control over the service of the debt, as the funds would pass through his hands or be paid into his account. It presupposes, however, that the trustee is a bank of some importance. Under this system the trustee would be the necessary intermediary between the debtor and the bondholders and it would therefore give rise to somewhat serious difficulties in the event of the trustee's becoming insolvent between receiving the funds from the debtor and paying them out to the bondholders, or in the event of a change in the rate of exchange between those two dates, resulting in the depreciation of the funds made over by the debtor. In such cases, should the debtor State be regarded as having discharged its obligations through the fact of having duly paid what it owed and should the bondholders solely be entitled to recover from the trustee, or, on the contrary, should the debtor State's liability to the bondholders subsist, in which case it is the State which bears the risk of the trustee's insolvency or of a currency depreciation against which it has been unable to cover itself? On the other hand this system of making over the funds or the reserves to the trustees implies an obligation on the latter to take proper care of them and use them in the best interests of the bondholders and of the debtor; that is a serious responsibility which raises the following question: How far should the bondholders and the debtor be entitled to require the trustee to account for the use of the sums confided to him, more particularly in the event of their claiming to have suffered through a change in the rate of exchange? But another system is possible, under which the funds would not pass through the trustee's hands or be placed at his disposal; they would be held by the debtor State or establishment, or be placed to its account in a bank to be selected by itself or designated in the loan contract: that bank would remain the debtor's bank, and the debtor would not be regarded as having discharged its obligations until the payments were made to the bondholders." See also the Report of the Financial Committee of the League of Nations, mentioned *supra*, n. 22, at p. 52. The procedure adopted by the trustees for the Austrian loan of 1923 for receiving the loan service and paying it out to the bondholders is described in League Study Committee, Doc. I.L. 45, p. 4. The general bond provided that the loan service shall be paid to the trustees "or as they may direct." The trustees thus had to set up the machinery for the various accounts to be kept by each paying agent for interest, amortization, reserve fund, etc. Since the trustees had no central organization themselves, to handle such accounting, they requested the Swiss National Bank, which acted as depository for the collateral bonds of the guaranteeing governments, to assume this burdensome task. The Swiss National Bank accepted and has carried out this considerable work throughout the life of the loan. Detailed instructions were sent by the trustees to the various paying agents as to the administration of the above-mentioned accounts.

usually assigned an important role with respect to the control and administration of the security and guaranties attached to international government loans. Thus, under a proviso in the general bond of the Austrian loan of 1923, the gross receipts from the revenues pledged as collateral to the loan had to pass through an account established in the name of the trustees. Out of this account there had to be paid every month one twelfth of the loan service and all further charges, commissions, etc. (general bond, clause 8). The balance remaining in the special account after the monthly service payments had been made was immediately placed by the trustees at the disposal of the Austrian Government. Under the scheme of the Hungarian League loan and the German (Young) loan, 1930, the trustees were authorized to block the amounts accumulated from the pledged revenues in special accounts in case the debtor governments failed to perform the debt service in accordance with the terms of the loan contract.[38] Under the terms of the arrangement made in September, 1937, with respect to the two Danzig League loans, the trustees were authorized to inspect at all times the special account at the Treasury to which the gross receipts of the assigned revenues were to be credited.[39]

In addition, the power of the trustees to control the security assigned to certain loans includes the right to demand from the debtor government its approval of any measure likely to affect the yield of the pledged revenues. Thus, under the terms of the general bond of the Austrian guaranteed loan of 1923, the Austrian Government was bound not to create any mortgage or charge on the assigned revenues without consent of the trustees or to do anything which would affect the charge created by the general bond. In the case of the League loans to Hungary (1924), Bulgaria (1926), and Estonia (1927), the respective debtor governments promised not to take any measures which, in the opinion of the trustees, would be likely to diminish the aggregate value of the pledged revenues

38. In Annex XI to the Hague agreement of January, 1930, it was provided that the whole of the proceeds of the pledged revenues should be remitted by the tax-collecting offices of the German Reich directly to the account of the trustees for the loan, or to the account of their fiscal agent, at the Reichsbank. When opening the account in May, 1930, the trustees gave a revocable standing order to the Reichsbank to the effect that as soon as a sufficient number of Reichsmarks had been received in the trustee's account to cover the amount of foreign currency required for the monthly service installment, the Reichsbank was authorized to release to the German Government the whole of the remainder of the revenues so entering the trustee's account. Bank for International Settlement, *Fifth Annual Report* (Basle, 1935), p. 57.

39. League Loans Committee, *Sixth Annual Report,* pp. 34, 35 ([5] of the respective Memoranda).

to such an extent as to threaten the security of the bondholders.[40] The trustees were furthermore authorized, in case the total yield of the revenues should fall below 150 per cent of the annual sum required to meet the service of the loan, to request the Council of the League of Nations to call upon the Reparations Commission to release from the general charge in favor of reparation payments such additional revenues as might be sufficient to assure the immediate restoration of the yield to the stipulated percentage; the additional revenues so released were to be assigned to the service of the loan.

In the case of the Austrian guaranteed loans of 1923 and 1934, special duties were assigned to the trustees to enforce the guaranties given by several European governments to insure the fulfillment by Austria of her obligations. As pointed out in note 37 above, the guaranteeing governments, in order to give their promise a commercial form capable of being utilized at short notice, had deposited with the Swiss National Bank collateral bonds in the names of the trustees. The duties of the trustees with respect to these bonds consisted, *inter alia*, in receiving them, in returning to the guaranteeing governments the coupons of their bonds in respect of any payment duly made by the Austrian Government, and, in case of the latter's default, in presenting the coupons to the guaranteeing governments for payment.

Since the function of the loan trustee is, in essence, "to ensure that the loan contract is properly carried out by the party responsible, that is, the borrower, in the interests of the real beneficiaries, that is, the bondholders," [41] it follows that the chief duties of the trustee arise in case of default. The general bond instituting a loan trusteeship usually contains

40. See League Study Committee, Doc. I.L. 45, p. 11. Instances where approval of the loan trustees to changes in the existing laws concerning pledged revenues was requested by the debtor may be found in the reports of the League Loans Committee. See *Third Annual Report*, p. 39: The Bulgarian Government asked the trustee's consent to the abolition of statistical and export duties to facilitate Bulgaria's external trade. The trustee did not object. *Fourth Annual Report*, pp. 33, 38; *Fifth Annual Report*, pp. 33, 34, 39 (change in the rate of certain assigned customs approved); *Sixth Annual Report*, p. 27; *Seventh Annual Report*, p. 26; *Eighth Annual Report*, pp. 11, 14 (approval of reduction of certain minor import duties, the revenue of which was assigned to the service of the Bulgarian Stabilization Loan). See also *Sixth Annual Report*, p. 29: The trustees for the Bulgarian refugee settlement loan, 1926, consented to a decree law for the relief of refugees reducing the rate of interest payable by the refugees.

41. See Basdevant, *op. cit.*, p. 1; see also League Study Committee, Doc. I. L. 32, p. 5: The trustee is the only agency avowedly designed for the protection of security holders during the entire life of the security . . . . The common understanding of the lay investor is that the trustee is his alter ego in safeguarding his rights." SEC, *Rep.*, Pt. VI, Introduction.

a clause in which such default is defined as a "breach of any of the terms of these presents" by the debtor.[42] Thus, in the absence of an express stipulation in the bond to the contrary, the trustee is in no position to agree to any departure, on the part of the debtor, from the strict fulfillment of the obligations assumed under the loan contract; he is in duty bound to take the steps indicated to him for the enforcement of the creditors' rights whenever the debtor fails to live up to the terms of his contract. This has resulted in the anomalous situation that debt settlements proposed by the debtor and offering, in the circumstances, a favorable adjustment of the default, have generally met with a stern refusal by the trustees to coöperate, because such procedure involved changes in the general bond; it had to be left to bondholders' committees to negotiate and carry out new terms designed to safeguard the interests of the bondholders.[43]

42. See, for example, the general bonds of the Danzig League loans of 1925 and 1927. League Study Committee, Doc. I.L. 45, p. 12. The trust deeds of international industrial loans usually contain a more elaborate definition of default, describing in detail the various possibilities of the failure of the debtor to perform his obligations. See Zahn, *op. cit.*, p. 217.

43. In its *Ninth Annual Report* (Basle, 1939), pp. 130 f., the B.I.S., as trustee of the German Government international loan of 1930 (Young), stated: "The German Government and certain other governments have concluded agreements as a result of which bondholders, as specified therein, are able to obtain payment of a part of the nominal value of their coupons in the currency of their country of domicile. The trustee is not a party to any of these agreements, has nothing to do with their terms or execution and has protested against them to the German Government as being incompatible with the terms of the General Bond." An instance where trustees declined coöperation in the negotiation of new terms is reported in League Loans Committee, *First Annual Report*, May, 1933, p. 35: "The Bulgarian Government have requested the Trustees to invite the bondholders of the loans to form a Committee authorised to enter into negotiations with the Bulgarian Government for the conclusion of an agreement regarding the terms for future service of the loans. It is the duty of the Trustees under the General Bonds to endeavor to obtain the complete fulfilment of the terms under which the loans were issued, and they are not empowered to consent to any variation in these terms. The Trustees, therefore, do not consider it desirable that they should be parties to any negotiations which involve a departure from the provisions of the General Bonds and Protocols." See also *Seventh Annual Report*, p. 12 (refusal by the trustee to release Treasury bills representing untransferred interest and sinking fund upon request of the Hungarian Government pursuant to an agreement with the League Loans Committee regarding the future service of the loan). In fact, among the reasons mentioned by the League Loans Committee in its *First Annual Report* for its constitution was the legal inability of the loan trustees "to enter into negotiations for anything less than complete fulfilment of the terms of their Bonds . . . . For all these reasons it appeared necessary to constitute some new body which could definitely undertake the particular task of protecting the rights of holders of

The measures to be taken by the trustees for the protection of the bondholders in case of default range from mere conservatory steps to coercive action against the recalcitrant debtor. Where the debtor pays the debt service in monthly installments to be distributed by the trustee among the bondholders at the due dates,[44] or where provision for a reserve fund has been made, failure to remit these payments may not immediately affect the bondholders if the trustee has accumulated a sufficient reserve fund or has already received a certain number of installments with which to maintain payment of the coupons. Such failure, nevertheless, constitutes default. In his capacity as representative of the bondholders, the trustee may take whatever action the bondholders are entitled to in attempting to remedy the situation; for example, he may institute suit against the defaulting debtor for the payment of principal and interest.[45] Sometimes special powers are con-

---

League Loans and safeguarding the special status of those loans." *Idem*, p. 7. How the work of the League Loans Committee superseded the functions of the trustees is illustrated, *inter alia*, by the readjustment of the Danzig and Hungarian League loans negotiated and carried out by the League Loans Committee. See *Sixth Annual Report*, June, 1938, pp. 8, 11, 37. Certain technical difficulties arose with regard to the legal position of the trustees of the loans. The Committee had hoped that in spite of the known legal difficulties some way might be found whereby the trustees could coöperate in the application of the new terms of service and thus continue to watch the interests of the bondholders. In the case of Danzig, there was a provision in the general bond which eventually enabled the trustee—with the assent of the Council of the League of Nations—to waive the default. The trustee, while in no way responsible for the terms agreed between the debtor government and the representatives of the bondholders, was therefore able legally to recognize and work the new arrangements. In the case of Hungary, however, there was no such provision. The trustees did not feel able "to depart from a strictly legal construction of their duties and in consequence, to the Committee's regret, the new settlement will have to function without their assistance." See also *Seventh Annual Report*, p. 21. The act of defiance of the Hungarian Government against the trustee's refusal to release Treasury bills was announced by the Committee as being "in accordance with the recommended terms of the settlement."

44. The general bonds of the Austrian, Hungarian, and Bulgarian League loans provide that the debtor governments shall transfer the service in monthly installments to the account of the trustees in foreign currency.

45. At the request of the Council of Foreign Bondholders, the Banco Frances de la Plata, Buenos Aires, instituted suit in its capacity as trustee for the bondholders of the Province of Corrientes 6% external gold loan of 1910. Judgment was given in favor of the trustees. *Corp. For. Bondh. Rep.*, No. 65 (1938), p. 14; No. 67 (1940), p. 11. The Central Hanover Bank, trustee for Bogotá's consolidation power and light dollar loan, formally demanded that the President of the Municipal Council of the City of Bogotá place in escrow to the account of the trustee all monies received from the revenues pledged for the service of the bonds. *The New York Times*, September 27, 1936.

ferred upon trustees to enforce pledges and mortgages established as security for the loan.[46] Under the terms of the general bond of the Austrian guaranteed loan of 1923, the trustees were given the right to present for payment, after default, the collateral bonds of the guaranteeing governments without awaiting action on the part of the bondholders. In the case of the 1925 and 1927 Danzig League loans, the trustees were authorized, after compliance with certain formalities establishing the default of the debtor, "to proceed to execution for the payment of the principal and interest" of the outstanding bonds falling due immediately after the failure of the Free City to pay.[47] Where the trustees exercise supervision over pledged revenues by the provision that the proceeds from these sources have to pass through an account in their names before they can be utilized by the debtor government, their power to block such account in case the government fails to fulfill the contract has been made use of to force the defaulting debtor to resume payment of his debt.[48] In addition, the trustees may themselves employ these

46. See the trust contract of May 31, 1922, between the Republic of Bolivia and the Equitable Trust Co. of New York (text in *Hearings before the Subcommittee of the Senate Committee on Foreign Affairs Relative to Foreign Loans* [S. Con. Res. 22], 68th Cong., 2d Sess. [Washington, 1926], pp. 130 ff.). The trustee was empowered in case of default to sell the shares of stock of the Banco de la Nacion Boliviana pledged as security and to foreclose mortgages constituted upon the properties and earnings of certain Bolivian railroads. As to the practicability of such action by the trustee, see the statement of the Chase National Bank, New York, as trustee for the Danzig Port and Waterways Board external gold bonds, 1927. *For. Bondh. Prot. Coun. Rep.*, 1937, pp. 288 f. The bank refrained from taking legal action against the property of the board because it believed that any attempt "to realize upon such mortgage or purported pledge through legal process . . . on the part of the trustee . . . would undoubtedly immediately be met by the passage of legislation by the Free City to deprive the trustee of such legal remedies as it might otherwise have had in the premises."

47. Clause 32 of the 1925 general bond (30 of the 1927 general bond). See League Study Committee, Doc. I.L. 45.

48. See League Loans Committee, *First Annual Report*, p. 42 (blocking of the account of the trustee for the Hungarian loan to force the government to resume transfer in foreign exchange of the service monies); B.I.S., *Fifth Annual Report*, p. 57 (blocking of the trustee's account with the Reichsbank when the German Government failed to furnish the foreign currencies required for the service installments on the Young loan). When Greece, in 1932, failed to transfer service on its League loan, the International Financial Commission, acting in its capacity as trustee for this loan, retained from the assigned revenues the amounts necessary to cover the service at the current rate of exchange. League Loans Committee, *First Annual Report*, p. 38; *Second Annual Report*, p. 13. However, the governments concerned often find ways and means of evading the coercive powers of the trustee. Thus, the retention of the assigned revenues by the International Financial Commission "caused little inconvenience" to the Greek Government

funds or reserve funds under their administration to make good the default or demand that other or additional revenues be assigned.[49]

Apart from powers vested in the trustee for the purpose of enforcing bondholders' rights, his duties in case of default are mainly to inform the bondholders, their representatives, or other agencies charged with the supervision of the loan, for example, the Council of the League of Nations with respect to the League loans, of the nature and size of the default and to take appropriate action for the preservation of the rights of the creditors, such as the lodging of formal protests against the non-fulfillment of the contract or the refusal to consent to readjustment schemes.[50]

RELATIONS BETWEEN BONDHOLDERS AND TRUSTEES

The Anglo-American law of trusts offers the beneficiary a number of ways in which the proper discharge of the trustee's duties with regard to the trust property may be enforced. Thus, the trustee is under a general obligation to the beneficiary to take reasonable steps to realize on claims which are part of the trust property.[51] If the trustee fails to take all due measures in defense of the trust estate, a beneficiary may intervene and compel the trustee to lend his name for the purpose of bringing any actions that may be necessary.[52] The question arises whether similar

---

which successfully prevented the conversion of the retained revenues into foreign currency and borrowed the amounts it needed from the Bank of Greece. See League Loans Committee, *Second Annual Report*, pp. 13 f. After the union of Austria and Germany, the revenues pledged for the service of the Austrian Government international loan no longer passed through the trustee's account. See B.I.S., *Ninth Annual Report*, March, 1939, p. 131. The trustee protested to the German Government against the infraction of the general bond by the failure to pass the pledged revenues through the trustee's account after April, 1938.

49. League Loans Committee, *First Annual Report*, pp. 42, 44.

50. See, with respect to these duties, Basdevant, *op. cit.*, p. 3: "The Trustee's essential functions will be to follow the various operations in the service of the loan and thus help to ensure the strict application of the terms of the loan contract. Should he perceive any departure from those terms, he would endeavor to put an end to it by bringing it to the debtor's attention . . . . Should the disagreement relate to the borrower's obligations to the bondholders (currency in which payments are to be made), the dispute is in reality one between the two parties to the loan: they must therefore settle it between themselves, or have it decided by a court of law. It would not be for the trustee to decide between the two parties, or to give either of them his support in judicial proceedings; his sole duty would be to bring the matter to the attention of those concerned."

51. American Law Institute, *Restatement of the Law of Trusts* (St. Paul, American Law Institute, 1935), Vol. I, sec. 177.

52. George W. Keeton, *The Law of Trusts* (London, Sir I. Pitman & Sons. 1934), p. 311.

rights accrue to the bondholder under a trust deed of an international government loan. That it is by no means idle to raise this point and to examine it somewhat more closely has been shown by the action, mentioned above, of Swedish bondholders against the Bank for International Settlements, as trustee for the Young loan of 1930, where a decision was sought against the trustee for distribution of the service monies according to the gold value of the various *tranches,* in disregard of the instructions given by the debtor to the trustee and directing the latter to discriminate among the various groups of bondholders. Another instance where this question became practical is offered by the refusal of the Austrian Government in 1934 to pay to certain holders of the American *tranche* of the guaranteed loan of 1923 interest in the equivalent of a certain weight of gold; it held that its legal liability extended only to payment in paper dollars. The question then arose whether the bondholders, after an unsuccessful attempt to bring suit directly against the Austrian Government, could compel the trustees to make use of their various powers under the general bond either to exact from the defaulting government compliance with the gold clause or to bring into operation the guaranty attached to the loan.[53]

If the legal relations between bondholders and trustees are construed in terms of the Anglo-American law of trusts, no reason exists why the principles governing the liability of the trustee for the proper administration of the trust estate should not be applicable to trusteeships in connection with international government loans.[54] However, since the majority of trustees for these loans are domiciled in places on the Continent of Europe which are also the places of performance and therefore, according to the view taken by the Swiss Federal Court in the case of *Obligationinteressenter* v. *Bank for International Settlements,* determine the law to be applied, the chances that effect will be given to the Anglo-American notion of the trust relationship are obviously slim. Apart from the so-called "immunity clause" usually inserted in the loan contract, exempting the trustee from any liability except for a "breach of trust knowingly and intentionally committed," [55] a simple stipulation

53. See the opinion of the Austrian Supreme Court of November 26, 1935, *Jour. du Droit Int.,* 1936, pp. 442, 717. The chapter on "Trustees" in Plesch and Domke, *op. cit.,* is mainly devoted to this question. See also Fachiri, *op. cit.,* p. 5.

54. See Freshfield, Leese, and Munns, *op. cit.,* p. 4, although it is admitted that English law cannot be applicable *in toto* to trusteeship of this kind because the supervision of the courts is lacking.

55. See League Study Committee Report, II. Econ. and Finan. 1939. II.A. 10, secs. 58, 60, p. 18. The Committee suggests maintaining this provision in future contracts "for it is unlikely that anybody would accept such a task if liability were involved outside the case of manifest breach of trust." The general bonds of the

to the effect that the trustee is "the representative of the interests of the bondholders" [56] cannot be construed as constituting the contractual basis essential under Continental law to support an action by the bondholders against the trustee for the fulfillment of his duties with respect to the loan contract.[57] While, in the oft-quoted Swiss case, the court of appeal and the federal court recognized in principle the existence of a *vinculum juris* between bondholders and trustee in the shape of a "mandate-like, three-sided contract *sui generis*," yet in the same breath both courts deprived the contract of its positive meaning in favor of the bondholders by stating that the defendant trustee, being merely an "intermediary between creditor and debtor" or "paying agent," had no authority to inquire whether or not the instructions given by the debtor for the distribution of the service monies among the bondholders were permissible under the contract; as they were not "manifestly untenable," the trustee was bound to follow them. Having in addition reserved the rights of the injured bondholders by proper protests and representations lodged with the debtor government, no claim for damages against the trustee appeared to be justified.[58]

TRUSTEESHIP IN FUTURE LOAN CONTRACTS

The small success encountered up to the present by the trust device in international state loans by no means affords an argument against its usefulness in the general scheme of such transactions. In fact, everyone interested in the increasing perfection of this type of contract, such as Dr. Weiser, a severe critic of the loan trust in its present form, and the League Committee for the Study of International Loan Contracts, which devoted much time to the study of the trustee, agrees that an office such as the loan trustee is a desirable and salutary institution in connection with state loans and that it is merely a matter of draftsmanship to insure

---

two Danzig League loans contain in addition clauses excluding the responsibility of the trustee for acts of others. See League Study Committee, Doc. I.L. 45, p. 15. Furthermore, under the Danzig general bonds, the debtor government guarantees the trustees against actions on the part of the bondholders. *Idem*, p. 17. Professor Basdevant, in his often-quoted Note, *op. cit.*, p. 4, suggests that the normal penalty for negligence should be relief from his duties. His civil liability should be restricted to cases of serious culpability.

56. See, for example, the protocol for the Hungarian loan signed by the Hungarian Government, March 14, 1924, and the protocols and general bonds of the Bulgarian loans of 1926 and 1928. League Study Committee, Doc. I.L. 45, p. 8.

57. Weiser, *op. cit.*, pp. 83, 85. *Contra:* Plesch and Domke, *op. cit.*, pp. 74, 76.

58. The practical result of the decision must be approved since the question whether payment was due on a gold basis "really concerns the debtor and the bondholders" and should not be left to a decision by the trustee. Basdevant, *op. cit.*, p. 4.

its successful operation in the future. Both Dr. Weiser [59] and the League Committee, the latter in its final report,[60] have submitted a number of suggestions for draft clauses designed to clarify the legal position of the trustee and to define the exact functions attached to his office. What matters first is to ascertain from the mechanism of the loan contract and its execution those tasks which require the establishment of a special agency in the interests of efficient and impartial performance. These are, briefly, the centralization of the loan service, supervision of pledged revenues, and enforcement of guaranties.[61] In view of the misapprehensions and confusion created by the term "trustee," the League Committee suggests the adoption of some other name "not encumbered with past legal associations," such as *contrôleur de l'emprunt* in French or "supervisor" in English, to describe the agent entrusted with these functions, while Dr. Weiser retains the name of "trustee," thus making it plain that the office is chiefly created to serve the interests of the bondholders and not, as the League Committee understands it, "to personify the common intention of the parties." Both the committee and Dr. Weiser agree that the "supervisor" or "trustee" shall not be made the general creditor of the debtor government, which would simply duplicate the functions of the body of the individual creditors and would expose him to the danger of becoming the debtor of the bondholders for the whole amount of the loan.[62] Other suggestions concern clauses with respect to the law to be applied and the court to invoke in case of disputes between the parties, the choice of the holder of the office, whether a natural person or a corporation. The answer to these questions will, of course, depend in each instance on the particular circumstances of the case.

59. Annex to his book on *Trusts on the Continent of Europe*, pp. 94 ff.

60. League Study Committee Report, II. Econ. and Finan. 1939. II.A. 10.

61. Thus, during the drafting of the loan documents for the Austrian guaranteed loan of 1923, it became clear "that machinery was required for the convenient supervision of the Reserve Fund, for the enforcement of the Guarantees and for the administration of the Pledged Revenues not only during the appointment but also after the termination of the functions of the League Commissioner General. Following the practice adopted in England in most cases where security was provided by the terms of a loan it was decided that there should be Trustees . . . ." Freshfield, Leese, and Munns, *op. cit.*, p. 1.

62. League Study Committee Report, II. Econ. and Finan. 1939. II.A. 10, sec. 56, p. 18; Basdevant, *op. cit.*, p. 1; Weiser, *op. cit.*, pp. 80, 82.

Section V

THE LAW TO BE APPLIED

EXCEPT in the rare case of direct flotation, which creates legal ties only between the borrowing government and its creditors, the international government loan involves a number of separate acts and functions establishing a variety of jural relationships among different parties, such as the issuance of the loan abroad through intermediary bankers acting as agents of the government, the purchase of the bonds by foreign lenders who thereby enter into contractual relations with the debtor government, trustee and agency functions to be performed on behalf of the debtor or the creditors outside the debtor country, and sometimes the accession of other states as guarantors of the contract. In the absence of clauses specifying the law to be applied to these various relations, the complicated nature of the international government loan is likely to raise difficult questions regarding the legal system applicable to the transaction as a whole or its constituent parts. For a number of years the League of Nations, through its Committee for the Study of International Loan Contracts and in coöperation with the International Institute for the Unification of Private Law at Rome, made a thorough examination of the subject with a view to elaborating a uniform code of rules applicable to international loans and to be adopted by the states in the form of an international convention, similar to the "Hague Rules" in respect of maritime transport.[1] This project had not passed the preparatory stage when the work of the League of Nations in these matters was discontinued. Since there is no body of international financial law to substitute for the lack of conventional rules,[2] the answer

1. See League Study Committee Report, II. Econ. and Finan. 1939. II.A. 10, p. 24. The Rome Institute submitted a Preliminary Study (May, 1938), Études XX, Emprunts internationaux, Doc. 4, and a Draft Convention, Études XX, Emprunts internationaux, Doc. 5, for discussion in the Committee. See Institut de Rome, Rapport, 1937–38 and 1938–39, pp. 25 f.; Schoo, *Régimen jurídico*, pp. 182 ff., 675 ff.

2. The attempt by Gfroerer, "Die auswärtige Staatsanleihe als Vertrag übernationalen Privatrechts" (Dissertation, Greifswald, 1914), to construe the international government loan as a contract belonging to some sort of supranational private law has no basis in the actualities of either the international or the domestic legal situation. The term "international financial law," as sometimes used

to the question as to what is the proper law in a dispute involving an international government loan must be sought in general legal principles.

INTERNATIONAL LEGAL RELATIONS

Where a direct relationship between several states is concerned, such as a guaranty promise given by one state or a group of states for the loan contracted by another, or where a state addresses itself diplomatically to the debtor government to protect its nationals against injuries arising from the nonfulfillment of the loan contract, the matter is clearly one of international law.[3] These situations, however, are exceptional. The international government loan primarily creates contractual relations between the government and private individuals and, therefore, is subject to the general rule that "any contract which is not a contract between States in their capacity as subjects of international law is based on the municipal law of some country."[4]

THE LOAN AGREEMENT

The loan agreement between the government and the issuing bank, as a rule, expressly states that it is concluded under the laws of the country where the bank is located and that it shall be interpreted in accordance with that law.[5] Even in the absence of such a clause, however, the nature

by writers, is meant to refer merely to international law cases "in which there is, on the one hand, a predominantly economic or financial element, and on the other a foreign or international element." See George Schwarzenberger, "The Development of International Economic and Financial Law by the Permanent Court of International Justice," *Jur. Rev.*, LIV (April, 1942), 21.

3. Fischer Williams, *Chapters on Current International Law and the League of Nations*, pp. 267, 347; *idem*, "La Convention pour l'assistance financière aux états victimes d'agression," *Rec. des Cours*, XXXIV (1930), 137. See also the sections on Diplomatic Protection and Guaranteed Loans, *infra*.

4. Perm. Ct. Int. Just., case of the Serbian loans, Judgment No. 14 (Publications of the Perm. Ct. Int. Just., Ser. A, No. 20/21, p. 41). See also Schmitthoff, "The International Government Loan," *Jour. Comp. Leg.*, XIX (1937), 181; Nussbaum, *Money in the Law*, p. 387; Feilchenfeld, in Quindry, *Bonds and Bondholders, Rights and Remedies*, Vol. II, sec. 632 [b].

5. See loan agreements in the case of the Finnish Government loan and the City of Rotterdam loan, quoted *supra*, sec. 2, n. 14, concluded between the European debtors and American bankers, both of which declared American law applicable. Similarly, Republic of Peru 6% external sinking fund gold bonds, agreement with American bankers, Art. IX, sec. 6: "This Agreement shall be interpreted and construed in accordance with the laws of the State of New York in the United States of America as though it had been made and were to be performed wholly within the territorial limits of the said State." Agreement between

of the transaction suggests the submission of the agreement to the law of the country where the loan is to be issued. The bonds may not validly be sold unless the bankers comply with the rules governing the flotation of foreign loans in their country. It is reasonable to assume that the foreign government consented to subject the agreement to the law of the place of performance in its other aspects also, for example, with respect to the classification of the agreement as an agency, mandate, guaranty, or other type of contract.[6]

AGENCY AGREEMENTS AND TRUST INDENTURES

Similar considerations weigh in favor of the place of performance in determining the law to be applied to paying agency agreements and trust indentures. As regards the latter, three successive Swiss courts, invoked in the famous case of *Aktiebolaget Obligationsinteressenter* v. *The Bank for International Settlements,* to determine the law applicable to the trust relationship, declared that it was the law of Switzerland where the trustee had its establishment and where he had to perform his functions, although the institution of trustees is unknown to Swiss law.[7]

THE LOAN CONTRACT

The fact, however, that certain preparatory acts and administrative functions in connection with the loan are governed by the law of the place of performance is not of itself decisive in subjecting the entire transaction to that law. Although, from an economic point of view, the loan constitutes a whole, the law applicable to the various relationships it creates must be determined in accordance with the specific legal nature

the Republic of Costa Rica and the Ceneral Union Trust Co. of New York, of October 20, 1926, Art. 22. Mere reference to the loan agreement in the bonds does not necessarily subject the loan contract between the government and the individual holder to the law mentioned in the clause. See *supra,* sec. 2, n. 14.

6. Sauser-Hall, "La Clause-or dans les contrats publics et privés." *Rec. des Cours,* LX (1937), p. 754.

7. See *supra,* pp. 51–53. See also Weiser, *Trusts on the Continent of Europe* pp. 86 ff. The trust agreement of July 1, 1927, between the Danzig Waterways Board and the Chase National Bank, provides in Art. XV, sec. 10: "This indenture is made pursuant to the laws of the State of New York, and this indenture and all rights and remedies of the parties thereto and of the Fiscal Agents and holders of bonds and coupons shall be governed by the laws of the State of New York, except as to matters in connection with the security given by this indenture and with the mortgage given pursuant hereto and the enforcement thereof upon the property in the Free City of Danzig as to which the laws of the Free City of Danzig shall govern."

of the several acts comprising the loan transaction.[8] Whether entering into an agreement with foreign bankers for the flotation of a loan or contracting with individual moneylenders—the rights and duties assumed by the borrowing government in each case vary greatly. As already observed, the law of the country of issue is the logical choice in the former case. With respect to the contractual relations between the government and its foreign creditors, a "traditional" doctrine, supported by the authority of the Permanent Court of International Justice, judicial precedents from various national jurisdictions, and a sizable body of opinion, maintains that the law of the debtor state applies.[9] A state, it is asserted, in the absence of a clear indication to the contrary, cannot be presumed to submit in its dealings with foreign private individuals to any law other than its own. Furthermore, since action against a state defaulting on its bonds must be brought in the courts of the defaulter, unless otherwise stipulated in the contract, it is reasonable to assume that the parties intend to submit the transaction to the law of the prospective forum. Finally, the fact that the funds with which to pay the debt are collected and located in the territory of the debtor state provides a strong argument in favor of the application of the debtor's law.

In the Serbian loans case it was contended on behalf of the Yugo-

---

8. Sauser-Hall, *op. cit.*, p. 754.

9. Perm. Ct. Int. Just., case of the Serbian and Brazilian loans, Judgments Nos. 14 and 15 (Publications of Perm. Ct. Int. Just., Ser. A, No. 20/21, p. 42). In English law, the doctrine that, where a government contracts a foreign loan, its law governs the transaction, was first established by a dictum in *Smith* v. *Weguelin*, L.R. 8 Eq. 198 (1869) and affirmed in *Twycross* v. *Dreyfus*, 5 Ch.D. (1877), 36 L.T. Rep. 752, 755. The maxim making the law of the debtor state authoritative was established in France by the decision of the Civil Tribunal of the Seine of March 3, 1875, in the case of *The Ottoman Government* v. *Comptoir d'Escompte et al.*, *Jour. du Droit Int.*, III, 271. For the German law, see the decision of the Supreme Court in the case of *B.H.* v. *The Municipality of Vienna*, decided November 14, 1929. *Decisions in Civil Matters*, CXXVI, 196. The position that the law of the debtor state applies was also taken by the Swedish Court of Appeal in the case of *Skandia Insurance Co., Ltd.* v. *The Swedish National Debt Office.* Text in A. Plesch, *The Gold Clause* (2d ed. London, Stevens & Sons, 1936) I, p. 66. See, furthermore, Sauser-Hall, *op. cit.*, pp. 751 ff.; G. C. Cheshire, *Private International Law* (2d ed. Oxford, Clarendon Press, 1938), p. 271; Joseph H. Beale, *A Treatise on the Conflict of Laws* (New York, Baker, Voorhis & Co., 1935), II, 1102; Wortley, in *Brit. Year Book*, XVII (1936), 117, 127 f.; M. Schmitthoff, "The Gold Clause in International Loans," *Jour. Comp. Leg.*, XVIII, 275 f.; *idem*, "The International Government Loan," *Jour. Comp. Leg.*, XIX (1937), 192 f.; Nussbaum, *op. cit.*, pp. 387 ff.; Meili, *International Civil and Commercial Law* (New York, 1905), p. 341; Bosch, *De Staatsschulden in het internationaal Recht*, pp. 9 f.

slavian Government that payment in gold francs had been rendered impossible by French law devaluing the franc. The court said:

In the first place, the law governing the obligations at the time at which they were entered into must be determined. In the Court's opinion, this law is Serbian law and not French law, at all events in so far as concerns the substance of the debt and the validity of the clause defining it. . . .

But the establishment of the fact that the obligations entered into do not provide for voluntary subjection to French law as regards the substance of the debt, does not prevent the currency in which payment must or may be made in France from being governed by French law. It is indeed a generally accepted principle that a State is entitled to regulate its own currency. The application of the laws of such State involves no difficulty so long as it does not affect the substance of the debt to be paid and does not conflict with the law governing such debt. In the present case this situation need not be envisaged, for the contention of the Serbian Government to the effect that French law prevents the carrying out of the gold stipulation, as construed above, does not appear to be made out.[10]

In the case of the Brazilian loan payable in France, the Permanent Court of International Justice considered the effect of the following clause in the special agreement under which the case was submitted to the court.

In estimating the weight to be attached to any municipal law of either country which may be applicable to the dispute, the Permanent Court of International Justice shall not be bound by the decisions of the respective courts.

The court, considering that this could be interpreted either as meaning that it was not bound to accept the interpretation placed upon local law by the national courts or that it was barred from considering such interpretations, decided:

Though bound to apply municipal law when circumstances so require, the Court, which is a tribunal of international law, and which, in this capacity, is deemed itself to know what this law is, is not obliged also to know the municipal law of the various countries. All that can be said in this respect is that the Court may possibly be obliged to obtain knowledge regarding the municipal law which has to be applied. And this it must do, either by means of evidence furnished it by the Parties or by means of any researches which the Court may think fit to undertake or to cause to be undertaken.

Once the Court has arrived at the conclusion that it is necessary to apply the municipal law of a particular country, there seems no doubt that it must seek to apply it as it would be applied in that country. It would not

10. Hackworth, *Digest of International Law,* V (1943), 632–633.

be applying the municipal law of a country if it were to apply it in a manner different from that in which that law would be applied in the country in which it is in force.

It follows that the Court must pay the utmost regard to the decisions of the municipal courts of a country, for it is with the aid of their jurisprudence that it will be enabled to decide what are the rules which, in actual fact, are applied in the country the law of which is recognized as applicable in a given case. If the Court were obliged to disregard the decisions of municipal courts, the result would be that it might in certain circumstances apply rules other than those actually applied; this would seem to be contrary to the whole theory on which the application of municipal law is based.[11]

However, since the advent of legislation in certain states abrogating gold clauses in private contracts, a tendency has become apparent to break with the traditional rule so as to enable debtor states to profit by such legislation. In the famous case of *The King* v. *International Trustee*,[12] the House of Lords, reversing the Court of Appeal, held that gold bonds issued by the Government of the United Kingdom and payable, at the option of the holder, either in New York in gold dollars or in London in pounds sterling, were subject to American law, thus permitting the British Government to discharge its debt at the nominal amount provided for in the bonds by invoking the joint resolution of 1933 which invalidated gold clauses in contractual obligations. In reaching this conclusion, the court followed the fundamental principle of private international law that the law of the contract is what the parties intended it to be and that therefore the judge's main duty consists in ascertaining such intention from all the circumstances of the transaction. From the fact that the principal associations of the bonds were American, since the place of issue and payment, the latter at least alternatively, were located in the United States, the court inferred the intention of the parties to submit the contract to American law. The practical consequence of the doctrine propounded by the House of Lords is that, in the absence of an express stipulation in the contract, the proper law applicable to the obligation must be determined according to the intentions of the parties as indicated by the circumstances of the transaction, among

11. Perm. Ct. Int. Just., Judgment 15, July 12, 1929 (Publications of the Perm. Ct. Int. Just., Ser. A, No. 20–21, pp. 93, 123, 124); Manley Hudson, *World Court Reports* (Washington, Carnegie Endowment, 1935), II, 404, 427, 428; Hackworth, *op. cit.*, VI, 121.

12. (1937) A.C. 500. See also *Brit. Year Book*, XVIII (1937), pp. 214 f.; Lorenzen, *Cases and Materials on the Conflict of Laws* (4th ed. St. Paul, West Publishing Co., 1937), p. 500 (with further references); Cheshire, *op. cit.*, pp. 271 f.

which the sovereign character of the borrowing government is only one, though an important, factor.[13]

If, then, the international government loan does not constitute an exceptional case warranting the application of a particular or "traditional" rule for the determination of its proper law, the question as to the law to be applied must be decided in accordance with the general principles of private international law. A variety of legal systems presents itself, especially where a loan is couched in different currencies or issued in several *tranches* in more than one country. The place of issue,[14] the currency chosen,[15] even the legal terminology used in drafting

13. In the same sense, Helsingfors City Court in the Finnish loan case (*Bull. de l'Inst. Jur. Intern.*, XXXVIII [1938], 280), holding that "notwithstanding the fact that the bond debtor is a sovereign State, when appreciating and interpreting the legal relationship between the bondholder and the Finnish State, based on the bonds in question, the law of the United States is to be taken into consideration." And Mixed Tribunal of Tangiers in the matter of *Tilley Dme Colgate* v. *Bengelloun-Maspero* (*idem*, XXXV [1936], 95). The Court held that a loan concluded between a state and private individuals is subject to the rules of private law contracts. A clause promising payment in Paris was considered indicative of the intention of the parties to submit the contract to French law. See also Weigert, "The Abrogation of Gold-Clauses in International Loans and the Conflict of Laws," *Contemporary Law Pamphlets*, Ser. 4, No. 4 (1940), pp. 4 f.

14. Moreau-Néret, in a Memorandum submitted to the League Study Committee (Doc. I.L. 61, May 31, 1938), sets forth the following considerations in favor of the law of the country of issue: "From the point of view of the bondholder, it is only logical that, in this matter as in any other, he should be subject to the legislation of his own country, which reflects the ideas and tendencies of the environment in which he lives and changes as they change. Besides, it is not too much to ask the borrowing Government to comply with the rules governing the bond issues in the country to which it applies for the loan . . . if [the law of the debtor] is accepted as the law of the contract—the debtor State obviously retaining the right to modify its own legislation—the party which has applied to the other for assistance might change the legal position established between them by unilateral act." See also League Study Committee Report, II. Econ. and Finan. 1939. II.A. 10, p. 23.

15. See Weigert, *op. cit.*, p. 4: ". . . the currency chosen is not only the strongest indication of the intention of the parties to have the contract governed by the law of this currency but the country of this currency is also the system with which the transaction has the closest and most real connection since money is the only object of such a contract." See, however, the dictum in the *Canevaro* case between Italy and Peru. Permanent Court of Arbitration, May 3, 1912 (Scott, *The Hague Court Reports*, p. 290): ". . . the fact that the evidences of indebtedness were to order and payable in pounds sterling . . . did not prevent the Peruvian law from being applicable to the debt created and payable in the territory in which the said law prevailed." If the bondholder is given an option to demand payment in several currencies, the law of the currency in which payment is claimed under the option should govern the debtor's obligation. See the Note submitted by Fachiri to the League Study Committee, Doc. I.L. 47. See also M. Wolff,

the loan documents [16] may serve as indications of the intentions of the parties as to the applicable law, quite apart from the considerations mentioned above, which tend to favor the law of the debtor state. Theoretically, the law of a third country, having no connection with any of the parties or transactions of the loan, may be specified as the proper law of the contract, although the practicability of this solution is subject to doubt.[17] There is a consensus with respect to the law applicable to certain questions, such as the formal validity of the contract, which depends upon the law of the place of making, or the authority of the debtor government to issue the loan, which is governed by the debtor's own constitutional law.[18] Furthermore, the foreclosure of the security assigned to the loan is subject to the law of its situs.[19]

PUBLIC POLICY CONSIDERATIONS

The public policy of the forum may be opposed to certain parts of the law intended by the parties to apply to their contract. This is of special significance in connection with gold clauses written into foreign government bonds. Although the traditional rule favoring the law of the debtor state was abandoned with the world-wide trend toward the abrogation of gold clauses in order to enable debtor states to participate in the benefits of such legislation, it seems more than doubtful whether a foreign law invalidating gold clauses in contractual obligations may be given effect in a suit in the forum of the debtor state. Like exchange restrictions, such laws are political measures designed to afford relief during an emergency and to enforce the economic policy of the government.[20] It is a settled principle of international private law that foreign political laws have no extraterritorial effect and may not be considered

Internationales Privatrecht (Berlin, 1933), p. 88, with respect to the law applicable in the case of several places of performance: "It is customary to apply the law of the place where the performance is demanded."

16. See Bosch, *op. cit.*, pp. 13 ff. He mentions the case of the Netherland-Indian dollar loan which provided for the loss of negotiable instruments in a manner unknown to the Dutch but analogous to Anglo-Saxon law, and concludes that the parties clearly had Anglo-Saxon law in mind when drafting the contract.

17. See League Study Committee Report, II. Econ. and Finan. 1939. II.A. 10, p. 23.

18. *Idem*, p. 21.

19. Jèze, *Rec. des Cours*, VII (1925), 177 f., and *infra*, section on Secured Loans.

20. The joint resolution of 1933 expressly declares that the gold clause is contrary to public policy and affects the public interest. 48 Stat. 112. See also Nussbaum, *op. cit.*, pp. 391 ff.; Van Nierop, "International Loans Secured by Guaranty," *40th Conf. Int. Law Assn. Rep.*, p. 195.

by the courts.[21] A state which relies on a foreign law abrogating the gold clause runs the risk of subjecting itself to a measure which may be directed against its own interests. Such a law, moreover, would be contrary to the public policy of a country which recognizes the validity of gold clauses.[22] French law expressly exempted "international payments" from the applicability of a statute invalidating gold clauses in contracts between Frenchmen.[23] Under the rule that a court applying a foreign law is bound to adopt the interpretation given it by the country where it was enacted, the joint resolution of 1933 could be relied upon by a debtor state, as it was by the House of Lords, claiming the applicability of American law to its contract. The Supreme Court, in *Perry* v. *United States* [24] and other cases, expressly held that, although the joint resolution does not serve to abrogate or impair gold clauses in bonds of the United States—since damages are unprovable by an American citizen paid in paper dollars—the resolution does enable public debtors to disregard the clause because of impossibility of performance.[25]

21. See, on the question, the valuable study by Weigert on "The Abrogation of Gold-Clauses in International Loans and the Conflict of Laws," *supra*, n. 13, pp. 45 ff. See also M. Domke, "International Loans and the Conflict of Laws," *Grot. Soc.*, XXIII (1937), 47 ff.

22. See the case of the Royal Dutch loan (text in Plesch, *op. cit.*, II, pp. 8 ff.), where it was held by the Dutch Supreme Court that the application of a foreign law impairing the rights of the creditors to receive the gold value of the debt as fixed by the contract was contrary to Dutch public policy. See also Alfred Wieland, *Schweiz. Jur.-Zeit.*, XXXII (1935–36), 274.

23. Weigert, *op. cit.*, p. 51; see also *supra*, section on Gold Clauses, n. 24.

24. 294 U.S. 330.

25. Sauser-Hall, *op. cit.*, p. 761, appears to be in error in concluding that the *Perry* case did not consider the gold clause breached in government contracts.

PART II

Types of Loans

Section VI

EXTERNAL AND INTERNAL LOANS

AMONG the various classifications of loans introduced by writers into the field of public debts, the division of governmental loans into external and internal, or foreign and domestic loans, occurs in almost every book on the subject.[1] As indicated by the terms themselves, the distinction refers to the origin of the borrowed money. According to the view most generally held, external loans are those marketed chiefly in a country or group of countries other than the debtor state, whereas internal loans are floated mainly within the borrowing country.[2]

1. See, for example, K. Th. von Eheberg, *Finanzwissenschaft* (Leipzig, 1915), pp. 486 ff.; M. von Heckel, *Lehrbuch der Finanzwissenschaft* (Leipzig, 1911), II, 381 ff.; Jèze, *Cours élémentaire de science des finances* (Paris, 1912), pp. 534 ff.; G. F. Shirras, *Science of Public Finance* (3d ed. London, Macmillan, 1936), II, 771, 775.

2."When a Government borrows money by floating a bond issue in a foreign country it is said to float an external loan and its bonds are external bonds . . . . Such loans are to be distinguished from Internal Bonds which the Government sells to investors within the country." Munn, *Encyclopedia of Banking and Finance*, p. 268; see also pp. 319, 401: ". . . a loan is called internal if it is issued in the domestic money market; an external loan exists if the State has applied to foreign money lenders. It makes no difference in either case whether the loan was floated directly or through intermediaries; the only thing that matters is the place where the loan has been issued." Zitelmann, "Der Canevaro Streitfall zwischen Italien und Peru," *Das Werk vom Haag*, Ser. 2, Vol. I, Pt. III, pp. 236 f.: ". . . the only factors which determine the character of a loan are the place of the original issue and the domicile of the original purchaser of the loan." John T. Madden and Marcus Nadler, *Foreign Securities* (New York, The Ronald Press, 1929), pp. 143 f. See also the dissenting opinion of Mr. Andrade in the Venezuelan bond case, J. B. Moore, *A Digest of International Arbitrations* (Washington, Government Printing Office, 1898), IV, 3652: "Respecting *the origin* of the capital realized, public loans are divided into *foreign* (exterior) loans, the evidences of which are issued *in favor of foreign capitalists*, and *domestic* or *internal*, the evidences of which are issued *in favor of national capitalists*." However, the name given to a loan by the issuing government may not always be an indication of its character. Thus, the Argentine loans of 1907, 1909, 1910, 1911, although floated abroad (London, Paris, and Berlin), were all included by the government under the head of "Internal Debt." *Corp. For. Bondh. Rep.*, No. 56 (1929). See also Manes, *Staatsbankrotte*, p. 68; Goertz, "Auswärtige Anleihen," *Arbeiten zum Handels-, Gewerbe-, und Landwirtschaftsrecht*, No. 45 (1926), p. 9 (foreign loans

Since the principal distinguishing feature is the place of issue, neither the nationality of the bondholders nor the currency in which the bonds are couched determines the character of the loan. The fact that the majority of bonds of a foreign loan are subsequently acquired by nationals of the debtor state or that foreign investors participate in a domestic issue leaves the original nature of the loan unaffected.[3] Likewise, if a debtor state whose currency is subject to frequent fluctuations

are those which have not been floated in the debtor country); Lippert, *Handbuch des internationalen Finanzrechts*, p. 927 (legal concepts or provisions have nothing to do with the distinction often made between external and internal loans: it refers merely to the place of issue which is either the debtor country or a foreign money market); Meyer Balding, "Die völkerrechtliche Anleihegarantien," *Niemeyer's Zeitschrift für internationales Recht*, XXVI (1916), 389 (a public debt is called internal loan if it is floated within the debtor country itself, irrespective of whether it is subscribed by nationals only or whether foreigners participate in it; external debts are those which have been contracted abroad, in one or more foreign money markets).

3. Madden and Nadler, *op. cit.*, p. 142: "An external bond may be considered as an obligation contracted with a foreign lender to be paid either in foreign or in local currency, and originally issued in a foreign country. Even if part or all of these securities should later be repurchased by natives of the borrowing country, they still remain external obligations." Sauvaire, "Procédures employées en droit international public contre les états qui ne remplissent pas leurs engagements financiers" (Thèse, Bordeaux, 1932), p. 12 (a loan is an external loan if it is floated in a foreign market; the nationality of the subscriber or eventual holder does not influence the character of the loan). See also League Study Committee Report, II. Econ, and Finan. 1939. II.A. 10, pp. 6 f.

A local debt held by resident foreigners is considered an internal debt. II, 232. Likewise, the 4% *rentes* floated by Greece in 1889 to redeem certain railroad loans were termed internal issues even though some bonds were held by nonresidents. *Corp. For. Bondh. Rep.*, XXXIV (1907), 221. Some authors, however, have used the nationality of the bondholders to establish a further distinction between external and internal loans in the formal and the substantive sense. See Von Heckel, "Staatsschulden," *Handwörterbuch der Staatswissenschaften* (3d ed. Jena, 1911), VII, 764: "A distinction may be made between external loans in the formal and the substantive sense. The former exists if an external loan is floated abroad, with fiscal agencies at foreign places; the latter, if the bonds of an external loan in the formal sense are in the actual possession of foreigners so as to constitute an indebtedness towards foreign countries. An internal loan may become an external loan in the substantive sense of the term if the bonds are sold to foreign creditors." See also Von Heckel, *Lehrbuch der Finanzwissenschaft*, II, 381 f.; Freund, *Die Rechtsverhältnisse der öffentlichen Anleihen*, p. 28; Zitelmann, *op. cit.*, p. 236: "A loan that is external in the formal sense of the term may essentially be an internal loan because the bonds may actually be acquired, either originally or later on, by nationals and vice versa. At any rate, this second distinction is useless for any legal treatment, because the criterion may change from day to day and cannot be ascertained with sufficient certainty."

bases its internal loans on foreign currencies of known stability, the character of such loans as domestic issues is not thereby altered.[4]

It has been maintained that the distinction between external and internal loans is a fundamental one "since it contains the question whether a creditor does or may enjoy the protection of international law." [5] The foreign holder of an internal bond, it is asserted, is in exactly the same legal position as the national of the debtor state. By accepting a bid for subscription to a loan which is primarily designed to serve as a means of investment for domestic capital, a foreigner subjects himself to the local law, viz., he is liable to taxation with respect to his share in the same manner as domestic creditors and must submit to any reductions or other modifications of the loan contract which the debtor state may decree under the authority of its legislation. The foreign bond, on the other hand, is said to lie outside the domain of the debtor's unrestricted jurisdiction. By soliciting capital from abroad, the borrowing state puts itself on the same legal level as the foreign creditor with whom it contracts; it acknowledges the loan contract as the unalterable law of the transaction, having binding force upon both parties alike.[6]

4. Madden and Nadler, *op. cit.*, p. 143: "The opinion is commonly held that a loan stated in terms of a foreign currency is an external obligation. This is not the case, because during the period of inflation certain countries, finding it impossible to issue loans in local currency, were forced to float bonds in dollars or other stable currencies. Thus, in 1923, the German Government issued short-term notes in dollars and the Polish Government still has outstanding an internal loan stated in dollars . . . That the currency in which the bond is stated is not the decisive factor in determining whether the loan is an external or an internal obligation may also be seen from the fact that the practice in pre-war days of issuing loans abroad in local currency, such as gold crowns or gold lei did not in any way affect the classification of these bonds as external obligations." Zitelmann, *op. cit.*, p. 236: "It is immaterial whether the loan is expressed in domestic or foreign currency; not seldom it happens that an external loan is expressed in domestic currency. On the other hand, special circumstances may require an internal loan to be issued in a foreign currency." See also Fischer Williams, *Chapters on Current International Law and the League of Nations*, p. 291: ". . . it may be observed that a foreign loan is very rarely issued in the currency of the borrowing country, and indeed if a general criterion were sought for distinguishing a foreign from an internal loan it might well be found in the distinction between a loan in a foreign currency or in gold on the one hand and a loan in a native currency on the other. It happens, however, occasionally, that countries in good credit will make issues on foreign markets—usually simultaneous with issues on their own markets—of loans in their own currencies, which thus may be largely held by foreigners."

5. Feilchenfeld, in Quindry, *Bonds and Bondholders, Rights and Remedies*, Vol. II, sec. 623.

6. See Jozon, "Des Conséquences de l'inexécution des engagements pris par les gouvernements relativement au paiement de leur dette publique," *Rev. de Droit*

The character of a loan as either internal or external has, no doubt, legal and practical significance in various ways. As was pointed out in a previous section, the place of issue may afford a clue as to the intention of the parties with respect to the law to be applied in interpreting the loan contract. Furthermore, the distinction between foreign and domestic loans may have a bearing upon the question of preferential treatment of bondholders' claims in readjustment procedures. For reasons ex-

---

Int., I (1869), 278: "In case bonds that were originally reserved to nationals pass, after their issuance, into the hands of foreigners, the latter, as mere assignees of the original holders, can have no more rights than the assignors; they are subject to all legal restrictions that the debtor State may place upon the execution of the bonds. By appealing exclusively to nationals for the subscription of the bonds, the State preserved the right to reduce them in case of public necessity. To such risks foreigners who acquired the bonds have submitted themselves in advance . . . . It frequently happens that certain loans are specially and exclusively issued for the benefit of foreigners . . . . As long as those bonds remain in the hands of foreigners, they cannot be legally subjected to any diminution or reduction, either of the principal or the interest, under whatever name or for whatever reason it may be, or whatever the formalities of the regulation. The foreign bondholders who would be affected by those measures are subject only to the law of their own country, but not to the law of the State to whom they lent their money. They may refuse to recognize or submit to that law. The agreement concluded at the time of the issuance of the bonds between the lenders and the debtor government is the only law that governs the execution of the loan contract. If nothing in that agreement provides for a reduction of the debt, no such measure may legally be imposed upon foreign bondholders." Phillimore, *Commentaries on International Law*, II, 16 f.: "Where the loan is internal, there seems to be no hardship in placing a foreign purchaser of any portion of it on the same footing as a domestic creditor, and when an income tax is imposed, it is, of course, a convenience to all parties that the Government, which is to receive the tax, should deduct it from the interest, which in this instance the Government owes to the payer of the tax, and thus avoid a double process. But the case is different where the loan is external, and it seems unjust for a State that has avowedly raised its loan amongst foreigners, to apply to a foreign creditor, if resident abroad and therefore not otherwise subject to taxation by that State, that machinery which, on the ground of convenience, is applied in the case of domestic creditors, in order to subject him to a tax to which he is not on principle liable." Cf. Gfroërer, "Die auswärtige Staatsanleihe als Vertrag übernationalen Privatrechts," pp. 19 f.: "A foreigner who subscribes to an internal loan or later on acquires bonds of such a loan subjects himself to the jurisdiction of the debtor State in the same way as the national does. The State, by issuing an internal loan within its own territory, shows its intention to deal primarily with persons living within its jurisdiction as partners to the loan contract. A foreigner who acquires bonds of such a loan agrees with the State that his rights in connection with the loan contract are to be determined according to the law of the debtor State. If, however, the loan is not exclusively an internal loan, i.e., if it has been floated either abroad, or in the home markets and abroad, no such intention on the part of the State to deal only with persons subject to its jurisdiction can be assumed. In this case, the foreigner does not submit himself

plained in a later section, debtor states in default have sometimes treated their internal creditors more favorably than their external creditors.[7]

However, to make the application of rules of international law concerning the protection of nationals dependent upon the character of the loan as an internal or external issue is not in accord with the accepted principles of international law. That law affords protection against certain acts or omissions committed by a government against the person and the rights of aliens because of the political tie existing between the injured alien and his home state. Arbitrary or discriminatory treatment of aliens is considered an international delinquency because it violates the respect due to the foreign state represented by its citizens abroad.[8] It makes no difference whether the rights encroached upon by the foreign government have their origin within or without the jurisdiction of the wrongdoer. If the debtor refuses to pay a bond owned by a foreigner in a manner compatible with its duties under international law—for example, if it discriminates against foreign bondholders—the fact that the bond is internal is no excuse. True, proof of treatment contrary to international law is more difficult in the case of an internal loan, since the debtor state can usually point out that the foreign holder of its internal bonds is treated on a footing of perfect equality with its own nationals.[9]

---

through the act of subscription or the subsequent acquisition of the bonds to the jurisdiction of the debtor State. Even if a purely internal loan is involved, the State may express its intention not to subject the loan entirely to its jurisdiction, for instance if it establishes fiscal agents abroad for the service of the loan. Madden and Nadler, op. cit., p. 141: "Internal bonds are subject to the jurisdiction of the individual sovereign debtor, who may alter the terms affecting the payment of principal and interest . . . The holder of an internal security, whether a citizen or a foreigner, is subject to the same laws and judicial decisions." See also letter of the Secretary of the Council of Foreign Bondholders to Musurus Pasha. II, 408, n. 46: "There is this cardinal objection in the opinion of the Council to the propositions of the Ottoman Government, that whereas the 1862 Loan is an external Loan, and as such held to be a contract, it would by being subject to the 'Law of 1866' become subject to Turkish Jurisdiction and thereby become an internal loan."

7. II, 436. The suspension of the service on the sinking fund of Argentine loans under the arrangement of January 30, 1933, did not include service on the new internal 6½% consolidation loan. Corp. For. Bondh. Rep., No. 34 (1907), p. 91. Preference of internal to external debt is likely when there is no pressing need for new foreign money.

8. Boeck, Rev. Générale, XX (1913), 370 f.

9. See the Note of the Austrian Foreign Minister to the Austrian Ambassador in Paris, May 26, 1868, Staatsarchiv, XV, pp. 159 f.: "The measures to be taken in this respect (the taxing of the coupons of the Austrian rentes) belong exclusively to the domain of domestic legislation, and, as a matter of principle, we cannot concede to a foreign government the right to interfere with general pro-

But the same argument applies if the act complained about relates to an external loan: as a rule, no international delinquency exists if the foreign and domestic holders of external bonds share the burden of a certain measure, e.g., taxation of coupons, alike. In both cases, the home government of the foreign bondholder may step in only if the injury to the rights of its nationals is due to denial of justice, arbitrary or discriminatory treatment, bad faith, or other violations of the international standard of treatment, and these acts, if committed against a foreign bondholder, constitute a wrong entailing international liability regardless of whether the rights of the injured alien originated in an internal or external loan.[10]

visions adopted with regard to the holders of *rentes* of the State. By subscribing to loans issued by the State, or by subsequently acquiring bonds of those issues, foreigners know in advance that they assimilate themselves thereby to nationals, that they are exposed to the same risks, that they receive the same benefits, and that they are not entitled to claim preferential treatment." See also decision of the German Supreme Court, January 27, 1927. Bruns, *Fontes Juris Gentium,* Ser. A, sec. 2, p. 82: "Foreign participants in the 3% German Imperial Loan of 1901 must accept the provisions of the Law concerning the Conversion of Loans (*Anleiheablösungsgesetz*) in so far as the law is to be considered as valid within the German Reich. Foreigners must let themselves be treated as nationals. They have subjected themselves to the law in effect at the time and its possible modifications by the acquisition of the securities. The question is not one of an external, but of an internal loan, viz. a domestic loan underwritten by a German banking group, whose securities are expressed to be payable solely in German marks." Does repudiation constitute an international wrong toward foreign holders of the debt? Not, says Belgium—like the Soviets—if it affects nationals and foreigners alike, as in the case of an internal loan. See League of Nations, *Conference for the Codification of International Law. Bases of Discussion: Reply of Belgian Government,* L. of N. Publications, V. Questions Juridiques. 1929. V. 3, p. 38: "Is the State responsible to foreigners for repudiation of debts? A distinction should surely be drawn according to whether the debt was contracted towards foreigners as such, e.g., by the floating of a loan in a foreign market, or whether, the debt having been contracted in the country itself, certain bonds were acquired by foreigners. In the latter case, foreign holders ought not perhaps benefit by treatment different from that imposed upon nationals by laws necessitated by circumstances."

10. See Zitelmann, *op. cit.,* p. 236: ". . . the answer that in determining the international law question as to the right of a State to reduce its obligations, the nature of the debt as external or internal is decisive seems in itself unconvincing; it is hard to conceive why this distinction should justify any difference in the legal treatment of the question." Practically speaking, intervention on behalf of private lenders by their home governments to protect their interest against harmful action on the part of the debtor is more likely in the case of foreign debts than in the case of a domestic loan. See Shirras, *op. cit.,* II, 864.

Section VII

SECURED LOANS

A STATE is, like a private debtor, liable for the fulfillment of its debts with all its assets and revenues, present and future.[1] It also enjoys the so-called *beneficium competentiae* which assures the debtor's continued existence by exempting the necessaries of life from seizure by its creditors.[2] The question, however, what in a given case constitute the legitimate needs of a government to be satisfied prior to the payment of foreign debts is largely left to the discretion of the individual government and, therefore, subject to arbitrary determination by states with a less developed sense of financial responsibility. To guard against abuses in the appropriation of funds to the various functions of the government, creditors of states of weak credit standing will be well advised to insist that certain assets and revenues—even if the assignment is unenforceable—be placed outside the reach of the govern-

1. See H. Lauterpacht, *Private Law Sources and Analogies of International Law* (London, Longmans, Green, 1927), pp. 256 ff. The Hague Arbitral Tribunal, in the Russian indemnity case, did not recognize the Turkish contention that the position of a state is not that of an ordinary debtor under private law and that its responsibility is limited by the assets at its disposal. In former times, even the nationals of the debtor state were held liable with their property for public debts. Madden and Nadler, *Foreign Securities*, pp. 165 f. See also, as a modern authority for this view, Phillimore, *Commentaries on International Law*, II, 17: "It is a clear maxim of International Law that the property of the subject is liable for the debts contracted by the State of which he is a member." Fischer Williams, *Chapters on Current International Law and the League of Nations*, p. 328, maintains that "the foreign debtor is justified in expecting that private citizens will not be allowed to retain wealth which can fairly be regarded as going beyond the proper needs of their several lives and occupations while the State debts remain unpaid." As pointed out by Feilchenfeld, in Quindry, *Bonds and Bondholders, Rights and Remedies*, II, 190 ff., the principle of general liability does not mean that every government loan is automatically a "secured" loan. See also Feilchenfeld, *Public Debts and State Succession*, pp. 736 ff., 742; Sack, *Les Effets des transformations des états sur leurs dettes publiques*, p. 54; Alexander Sack, "The Juridical Nature of the Public Debts of States," *N.Y. Univ. Law Quar. Rev.*, X (1932–33), 127. Cf. Schoo, *Régimen jurídico*, pp. 240 ff.

2. Von Bar, *The Theory and Practice of Private International Law* (2d ed. Edinburgh, W. Green & Sons, 1892), p. 1104; *infra*, sections on Readjustment, Priorities.

ment's unlimited spending power during the life of the loan and be devoted exclusively to the service of the debt.

GENERAL PLEDGES

Clauses frequently inserted in loan contracts to the effect that the "full faith and credit" of the debtor state are pledged to the fulfillment of the contract or that the promise is based "upon the entire revenue, assets and domains" of the borrower [3] cannot afford the desired protection. They merely confirm in emphatic terms a fact resulting by implication from the obligation, namely, that the debtor promises to pay out of its entire revenues; no additional security is thereby created.[4] A

3. A few examples of loan contracts over a period of more than a hundred years may illustrate this type of clause. The 1833 guaranteed loan of Greece stipulated "as guaranty and as a general mortgage of the present loan, all the property and revenues of the State . . . ." II, 285. By the terms of the Peruvian loan of 1823 "all the revenues of Peru are . . . declared to be generally mortgaged and pledged for the payment of the principal and interest of the loan." *Brit. and For. St. Pap.*, XXVIII, 1002. A security clause for other Peruvian bonds reads: "As a guaranty for the fulfillment of the obligations contracted in this bond, the Government of Peru, under the national faith, pledges the general revenues of the republic . . . ." *Twycross* v. *Dreyfus*, 5 Ch. D. 605 (1877). The 6% loan of 1871 of Costa Rica was secured upon "the entire revenues, assets and domains of the Republic." *Corp. For. Bondh. Rep.*, No. 56 (1929), p. 124. The Argentine 1887 conversion bonds were secured on "the general revenues of the Republic." *Idem*, p. 52. The security for the 6% 1888 loan of Santo Domingo was a "first charge on the entire Revenues of the Republic . . . ." *Idem*, p. 323. The 4% issue of 1895 by the same country was secured by "a first charge on the Budget." *Idem*, p. 324. Russian State Credit Notes of 1908 were secured "by all the property of the State."*Marshall* v. *Grinbaum and Others*, July 13, 1921, 37 T. L. Rep. 913. The security for the 6% Bulgarian loan of 1888 was "all revenues and resources of Bulgaria." *Corp. For. Bondh. Rep.*, No. 56 (1929), p. 90. The issue of 1916 for the Colombian Central Railway was secured "on the general revenues of the Republic." *Idem*, p. 111.

4. Fischer Williams, *op. cit.*, pp. 355 f.; Manes, *Staatsbankrotte*, p. 177; Lippert, *Handbuch des internationalen Finanzrechts*, p. 985; Feilchenfeld, *Public Debts and State Succession*, pp. 190, 195, 742; Feilchenfeld, in *Col. Law Rev.*, XXX (1930), 1126; Borchard, in *Proc. Am. Soc. Int. Law*, 1932, p. 151. See also Jèze, *La Garantie des emprunts publics d'état* (Paris, 1924), p. 54. Unless specifically stipulated in the loan contract, no priority of any kind is established by such clauses. Thus, the holders of the Greek loans of 1824 and 1825 which had been secured on all the revenues of the state, protested vainly against the pledge of all the revenues as a first charge upon the service of the guaranteed loan. II, 286. See also the Russian reply to an English note of November 14–26, 1881, *Parl. Pap.* (1882), LXXXI, C. 3197, No. 118, Inclosure 1: ". . . Every creditor who lends his money is undoubtedly supposed to count upon the solvency of his debtor according to the gross amount of his fortune. In case of insolvency, all debts of

"pledge" or "lien" is not really a pledge or lien or assignment unless it is handed over and committed to the administration of the creditors.

SPECIAL SECURITY

The effective establishment of such special security, however, presents one of the most difficult problems in the scheme of the international government loan. In earlier periods of history, when loans for the state were considered the personal transactions of the monarch, the pattern of the private law security was adopted, as exemplified by the pledging of crown jewels or the mortgaging of territory.[5] But the modern concept of state property as a sum of rights and privileges to be exercised in the public interest is opposed to the idea of surrendering it wholly or in part to the control of private lenders in the shape of pledges and mortgages, quite apart from the loss of political prestige which such submission inevitably entails.[6] If the claim of the creditors to a genuine security is to be satisfied without sacrificing essential public interests of the state, a compromise must be sought. The methods and devices of placing state property effectively under the control of foreign creditors as security for a loan will depend upon the type of assets available in each case.

this nature are on a footing of complete equality in the competition for the liquidation of the bankruptcy, and no priority of date or of other kind is admitted. Each creditor is indemnified in the proportion existing between the assets and liabilities of the bankrupt. But if the loan is made upon special security, the creditor can take legal proceedings for the seizure of the special pledge upon which his debts are secured." Fischer Williams, *op. cit.*, p. 356, is of the opinion that "possibly in some cases," general charges may contain a "covenant that the service of the particular loan in question shall have priority over other similar claims against the State, over other loans, that is, foreign or domestic, but not priority over the payment of the necessary current expenses of the State." Doubts as to the value of special pledges are expressed by J. Jensen, *Government Finance* (New York, Thomas Y. Crowell, 1937), p. 486. A specially pledged source of revenue may cease to yield the required amount; the yield from the exercise of the power to tax is much less likely to be so restricted. Cf. Schoo, *op. cit.*, pp. 423 ff.

5. Nys, "Le Credit et les emprunts publics au moyen age," *Rev. de Droit Int.*, XXIX (1897), 433 ff. Fischer Williams, *op. cit.*, pp. 263, 335; Jèze, *Cours de science des finance*, pp. 413 ff.; Manes, *op. cit.*, pp. 27, 69 f.; Lippert, *op. cit.*, p. 985. A reference to the older doctrine may be found in the opinion of the law officers of the British Crown, Dodson and Philimore, in the case of the Mexican loan of 1846. They maintained that Mexico had hypothecated her territory and entire revenues to the payment of the bondholders under the loan contract and that she owed the British creditors part of the proceeds she received when she alienated part of her territory to the United States in 1848. II, 11, n. 20.

6. Jèze, *Rec. des Cours*, VII (1925), 156 f., 172, 176; Jèze, *Cours de science des finances*, pp. 409 ff.; Fischer Williams, *op. cit.*, p. 353. See also SEC, *Rep.*, Pt. V, p. 16.

REAL ESTATE

If the borrower owns real estate not used for governmental purposes and therefore available as security for the loan, an ordinary private law mortgage may be constituted in accordance with the law applicable to the res.[7] This rather unusual type of security is best illustrated by the hypothecation of real estate owned by the Khedive of Egypt for loans issued in the interest of the Egyptian State. Thus, a deed of hypothecation on the Khedivial estates was deposited with the Bank of England as security for the Daira loan of 1870; another mortgage was created by the Daira debt of 1877.[8] Under the terms of the so-called Convention of Paris of October, 1861, between Colombia and her creditors, 30 hectares of land were assigned to each £100 active and 16 to each £100 deferred bond of 1845,[9] and loans of the Province of Buenos Aires in 1926 and 1928 were secured, *inter alia*, by a lien on the real estate owned by the borrowing municipality.[10] A French bank, advancing money to pay off claims by German concerns against the Government of Morocco took a mortgage on land reclaimed by harbor works.[11] The 1925 Danzig (League) loan was secured by first mortgages on the land, buildings, etc., of the electric, gas, and water works of the municipality and on a number of freehold lands and buildings. The mortgages were registered in the name of the trustee who could authorize the debtor to withdraw land from the mortgages on the condition that other land of adequate value be substituted and mortgaged in its place.[12]

TANGIBLE PROPERTY

Tangible property offered by governments as collateral for loans mainly includes bullion, cash, and securities. Thus, a Russian loan to Bulgaria was secured by four million francs in silver held by the Bulgarian National Bank against its note issue. The silver remained in the vaults of the bank under Russian seals.[13] A short term loan by the Na-

---

7. This type of security, however, is ill suited for government loans where guaranties for the regularity of the service are of primary concern, while a mortgage on real estate is mostly used to secure the repayment of the principal of the debt. See Jèze, *Cours de science des finances*, pp. 409 f.

8. See II, 593; Goertz, "Auswärtige Anleihen," *Arbeiten zum Handels-, Gewerbe-, und Landwirtschaftsrecht*, No. 45 (1926), p. 120.

9. *Corp. For. Bondh. Rep.*, No. 56 (1929), pp. 106 f.

10. *Idem*, pp. 76, 77. See also, with respect to the mortgaging of forests by Honduras, Bosch, *De Staatschulden in het internationaal Recht*, p. 63.

11. *Documents diplomatiques, Affaires du Maroc*, V, 1908–1910, No. 242.

12. League Loans Committee, *First Annual Report*, p. 32.

13. II, 539, n. 29.

tional City Bank of New York to Mexico in 1930 was guaranteed by gold.[14]

The device of depositing securities with the issuing bankers or trustees was used in the case of the English loan to Argentina in 1900, where Argentine Treasury bills and railway bonds were deposited with the banking house of Baring Brothers and Company,[15] and by Tunis in 1867 when oil warrants were handed over to the trustees as security for the first and fourth conversion issues.[16]

In many instances, unissued portions of previous loans have been considered of sufficient value to serve as collateral for new loans; [17] the bankers with whom they were pledged could sell them to the public. It is obvious that a default by the debtor government would cause a considerable drop in the value of these pledges and probably would make them unacceptable as collateral except where the previous loan carries more substantial security than the new issue.

In a few cases, commodities in the hands of the borrowing government have been utilized in the same fashion as private law pledges. Thus, in 1922 the Brazilian Government obtained a loan from London banking

14. *Corp. For. Bondh. Rep.*, No. 57 (1930), p. 265. In October, 1914, Russia deposited with the Bank of England 75 million gold roubles as security for a £12,000,000 loan. Lippert, *op. cit.*, p. 986. See also *ibid.*, for further instances of depositing gold and other valuables as security for state loans.

15. *Corp. For. Bondh. Rep.*, No. 56 (1929), p. 56. The 1916 6% gold bond issue by Buenos Aires was secured by the deposit with the London County and Westminster Bank, as trustee, of the Province's 5% consolidated gold bonds, such bonds not to be sold below 85%. *Idem*, p. 75.

16. These were two of four operations in 1867 by which the claims of foreign merchants resident at Tunis against the Tunisian Government were converted into secured bonds. F.O. 102/83, No. 11. See also Venezuelan settlement agreement of 1876. According to the agreement, on or before January 1, 1879, the Government was to place in the hands of the bondholders' committee the sum of £200,000 in 8% preference shares of the projected La Guayra railroad as security for the promised payment of £100,000 per annum. Text given in leaflet at p. 230 of Venezuelan Extract Book, No. 1 (Archives, Coun. For. Bondh.). The 1931 Republic of Bolivia external 8% sinking fund gold bonds were secured on the shares of the Banco Central de Bolivia and payments were made from dividends paid on the bank's shares. *Com. and Fin. Chron.*, CLIV (December 4, 1941), 1352.

17. Turkish temporary short-term loans in 1874 and 1875 were secured by unissued bonds of the issues of the 1873 and 1874 loans. II, 412. 5½% gold notes of Santo Domingo of 1924 were secured on $3,300,000 unissued 5½% twenty-year customs administration bonds of 1922. *Corp. For. Bondh. Rep.*, No. 56 (1929), p. 331. Advances to Greece in 1930 were guaranteed by bonds of the unissued portion of the 1914 loan. *Idem*, No. 57 (1930), p. 210. Parts of the Huerta loan of Mexico of 1913 were deposited with Peat & Co. in London as security for £700,000 of 6% trust certificates sold in 1914 by the Reuter's Bank. II, 63.

houses by pledging as security 4,500,000 bags of coffee.[18] The hypothecation of art treasures was suggested by a Dutch author because of the
high prices they yield. Their loss was deemed preferable to the injury
caused to the national honor of a debtor in default.[19] However, when
Austria, after World War I, offered her art collections as collateral
security for loans, prospective lenders refused to accept the proposal.[20]

ASSIGNMENT OF REVENUES

The method of direct pledges of state-owned property is the exception. In the great majority of cases, the security for government loans
consists in the assignment of revenues to the service of the debt. Governmental revenues are derived from a great number of sources: commercial enterprises (mines, factories, warehouses, etc., run by the state);
public services (monopolies, transportation, public utilities); and the
exercise of the taxing power. Their suitability as security for the service
of an external government loan depends on various considerations. Those
revenues may be said to be most useful for this purpose which promise
a fairly steady yield, even under adverse economic conditions; are easy
to administer; and are either payable in or produce foreign exchange.[21]
Such favorable combination, however, will seldom occur in practice.

The outstanding example of the significance of the publicly owned
natural wealth of a country as a credit basis for external borrowing is
provided by the public debt of Peru, which rested almost entirely on the
security offered by the rich guano deposits owned or controlled by the
state.[22] In other instances, the comparatively steady and readily acces-

18. Lippert, *op. cit.*, p. 986. See also State of São Paulo . . . coffee realization
loan of 1930 ("Governments and Municipalities," *Moody's Manual of Investments* [1937], p. 2147). The loan is "a direct obligation of the State of São Paulo
and originally secured by pledge to the extent of 50 shillings per bag of 3,000,000
bags of coffee and to the extent of £1 per bag of about 13,500,000 other bags of
coffee. Documents of title for pledged coffee are deposited with Banco do Estado
de São Paulo; documents of title for newer coffee of at least equal quality may
be substituted for documents on deposit."

19. Von Daehne van Varick, *Le Droit financier international*, pp. 14 f.

20. See Bosch, *op. cit.*, p. 64.

21. Chile, when submitting her readjustment plan of 1935 to the bondholders
for acceptance, pointed out that the revenues from the copper and nitrate industry
produced most of Chile's foreign exchange and, therefore, were preferable to
other revenues as security for the debt. See *infra*, section on Readjustment. See
also Golay, Note submitted to the League Committee for the Study of International Loans, May 8, 1936. A security should preferably "relate to revenue which
can be cashed outside the debtor country." Furthermore, Hyde, "The Negotiation
of External Loans with Foreign Governments," *Am. Jour. Int. Law*, XVI (1922),
534 ff.

22. For details with regard to the guano security for Peruvian loans, see
study on Peru, *passim*. See also *Twycross* v. *Dreyfus*, 5 Ch. D. 617 (1877).

sible revenues from certain industries operated under state monopoly, like the manufacture of matches, tobacco, alcohol, playing cards, or the production of salt and petroleum, have been assigned as security for governmental loans.[23] In fact, the popularity among foreign lenders of this source of income as security for loans has apparently been so great that monopolies have been specifically created for the purpose of serving as "pledges" in securing public loans.[24]

Similar to proceeds from state monopolies are revenues derived from public business enterprises. Out of a great variety of possible activities,[25] only those types of government enterprises have recurrently been used as security for foreign lending as are assured of relatively stable income. Of foremost importance in this respect are publicly owned or state-operated railways; the form of security is either a mortgage on the entire enterprise,[26] or the pledging of the railroad proceeds,[27] or the deposit of

23. Instances are: the Bulgarian so-called "refugee loan" of 1926 (net receipts of the match monopoly), II, 554; Colombian loans of 1854 (net revenues from the tobacco monopoly); Costa Rican loan of 1872 (revenues from the liquor and tobacco monopolies), *Corp. For. Bondh. Rep.*, No. 56 (1929), p. 124; salt bonds of Ecuador of 1908 (Government salt monopoly), *idem*, p. 148; Nicaraguan loan of 1909 (sums received by the Government from English firms holding the liquor and tobacco monopolies); *idem*, p. 263; Peruvian 5% loan of 1920 (revenues from the opium monopoly), II, 186, n. 11; Greek loan of 1887 (proceeds from the government monopolies on salt, petroleum, matches, playing cards, cigarette paper, and Naxos emery), II, 300; Serbian issues of 1902, 1906, 1909, and 1913 (state monopolies); Turkish loan of 1881 (salt and tobacco monopolies), II, 436, 439.

24. Instances are: the match monopolies created by Danzig, Poland, Germany, and certain Baltic states as security for loans by Ivar Kreuger; the tobacco monopoly given by the Portuguese Government to a Franco-German and a Portuguese bank syndicate in return for the issuance of a loan. II, 363. See, however, Gross, in *Encyclopaedia of the Social Sciences*, X, 621, who maintains that "there is nothing in the public monopoly as such which makes it particularly suitable to serve as security for public loans; ordinary taxes or customs duties serve the purpose equally well."

25. See Stacy May, "Government Ownership," *Encyclopaedia of the Social Sciences*, VII, 111.

26. Instances are the following: The Bulgarian 6% state mortgage loan of 1892 (secured by a first mortgage on the Kaspitshan-Sofia-Kustendil and Rustchúk-Varna state railroads—in case of default for two years, the bondholders were entitled to sell the railroads). *Corp. For. Bondh. Rep.*, No. 56 (1929), p. 90. See also Bulgaria, II, 534. The Greek loan of 1890 for the Piraeus-Larissa Railway (net receipts of the railway as well as a registered first mortgage on the railway itself). II, 302. By Egyptian decree of November 18, 1876, a special mortgage on the railways was created as security for the public debt. II, 590. The Argentine 1887–88–89 mortgage bonds (secured on the railway extensions for the construction of which the loan was raised). *Corp. For. Bondh. Rep.*, No. 56 (1929), p. 52. The outstanding amount of the second issue of the Northern Central Railway bonds of Argentina of 1903 was charged on the extensions of the Northern Central Railway as defined in the general bond, *idem*, p. 57. See also, for similar security on issues

railroad shares for the benefit of the bondholders.[28] Also frequently used for securing external loans are earnings of the government from the operation of or participation in banking institutions.[29] The same is true for revenues from national forests,[30] state domains,[31] salt and nitrate

---

of Buenos Aires, *idem*, pp. 73, 75. Colombian Government bonds of 1906 (mortgage on the Bogotà-Sabana Railway), *idem*, p. 109. Bonds of Santo Domingo of 1890 (mortgage on the first section of a railroad line), *idem*, p. 323. See also *idem*, p. 324, for the 1893 loan which was secured by a first mortgage on the Central Dominican Railway. The 1886 Nicaraguan bonds (first mortgage on the railways of the country), *idem*, p. 262; Honduran loans of 1867, 1869, 1870, 1872 (first mortgage on the incomplete Interoceanic Railway), *idem*, p. 227; Salvadorean loan of 1889 (first mortgage on the railroad from Sonsonata to San Salvador), *idem*, p. 311. Bonds issued by the San Domingo Improvement Co. (first mortgage on the railroad and its accessories). II, 214.

27. The "Baghdad railway loan" of 1904 (first series) was secured on the tithes of certain *vilayets*, the Government's share in the gross receipts of a certain section of the line, and on the railroad itself. II, 477. The 1910 Turkish railroad loan was secured by the general receipts of the line. II, 478, n. 84. Railway revenues secured the 7% Egyptian loan of 1873. *Corp. For. Bondh. Rep.*, No. 56 (1929). The Costa Rican loan of 1871 was secured "upon the entire revenue, assets, and domain of the railways." *Idem*, No. 34 (1907), p. 168. The Pacific railway loan of Costa Rica of 1926 was made a direct obligation of Costa Rica and secured by a first lien on the gross revenues of the railway and on the electric plant to be erected. *Idem*, No. 56 (1929), p. 127.

28. For interest arrears on the 1871 and 1872 loans, fully paid shares in the Costa Rican railways were deposited. *Corp. For. Bondh. Rep.*, No. 34 (1907), p. 168.

29. The 1884 loan of Argentina was specially secured on the dividends of the shares of the Government in the National Bank. *Idem*, 1929, p. 52. The 1910 loan of Buenos Aires was secured, among others, on the yield from the bank's share capital held by the Government. *Idem*, p. 73. The 1931 loan of Guatemala was secured on the share of the Government in the profits of the Central Bank. *Idem*, p. 264. The Bulgarian loans of 1896 and 1897 were secured by a first charge on assets and earnings of the agricultural banks. II, 534, and *Corp. For. Bondh. Rep.*, No. 56 (1929), p. 90. See also Minister Reinsch to the Secretary of State, January 10, 1917 (*For. Rel.*, 1917, p. 114): "Any loan made to the Chinese Government for the purposes above stated would have as its security the general guaranty of the Chinese Government fortified more especially by the assignment of some special tax, such as the tobacco and wine tax, which is assigned for the Chicago loan; the security would further embrace the assets of the industrial bank and would therefore rest back upon every enterprise, the development of which would be facilitated through this organisation."

30. The 1867 Honduran loan was secured on the railway, its revenues, and the produce of the mahogany forests. *Corp. For. Bondh. Rep.*, No. 56 (1929), p. 227. The 1869 bonds of Santo Domingo were secured by a first charge on customs duties and revenues from forests and mines. *Idem*, p. 333.

31. The security assigned for the 5% loan of Greece of 1881 included the revenues from national lands and plantations. *Idem*, No. 61 (1934), p. 220. The Honduran railway loan of 1870 was secured on the produce of state domains. *Idem*, p. 227.

mines,[32] the manufacture of tobacco,[33] water works,[34] port facilities,[35] telegraphs,[36] and other minor enterprises.[37]

Under the fiscal systems of most of the debtor states, proceeds from state-owned industrial property or public utilities operated by the government constitute but a minor fraction of the public income. Revenues derived from taxes occupy by far the first rank among the assets ordinarily utilized as security for government loans. Their prospective yield can, as a rule, be fairly well estimated, and a state which is determined to honor its obligations can increase taxation if the yield should fall below expectations.[38] The taxes actually used for securing the service of loans are in the vast majority of cases indirect taxes, with customs duties leading as the favorite,[39] while the pledging of direct taxes

32. In Chile and Colombia. See *idem,* No. 56 (1929), p. 106, and No. 34 (1907), p. 28. Annuities from the proceeds of quicksilver mines secured a Spanish loan of 1870. *Ibid.*

33. Peruvian loan of 1927 (secured by "a direct first lien and charge on the revenue from the manufacture and sale of tobacco . . ."). II, 185, n. 10.

34. The 1892 work bonds of Argentina were secured upon the work done by the water company and its revenues. *Corp. For. Bondh. Rep.,* No. 56 (1929), p. 54. The security for the City of Mexico loan of 1903, assumed by the government in 1903, included the water rates of the City of Mexico. *Idem,* p. 248.

35. Argentine debentures of 1892, 1899, and 1903 were secured by a first charge on the port works, on their revenues, and on the reclaimed lands and their products when sold. *Idem,* p. 53. The 1897 Province of Buenos Aires bonds were secured specially by the works, lands, and appurtenances of the La Plata Port. *Idem,* p. 55.

36. The Egyptian preference debt as part of the consolidated debt had as security the revenues of railways and telegraphs and the revenues from the port of Alexandria. II, 607, n. 117.

37. The 1911 loan of the Province of Buenos Aires was secured on the revenues of the Parade which was to be constructed with the loan proceeds. *Corp. For. Bondh. Rep.,* No. 56 (1929), p. 73.

38. This is sometimes expressly stated in the loan agreement. In loan contracts with Mexico from 1888–1913, a stipulation was inserted to the effect that customs duties assigned as security were to be increased should their proceeds fail to exceed a certain annual sum. II, 48, n. 4. See also II, 302. On the other hand, a reduction of the assigned percentage of certain revenues may be provided for if their yield should rise beyond a certain point. See the 1922 loan contract, United States and Salvador, Art XII (f). A country may not plead inability to pay until it has fully exhausted its taxing powers. See J. Reuben Clark, *Am. Jour. Int. Law,* XXXIV (1940), 125.

39. B. H. Williams, *Economic Foreign Policy of the United States* (New York, McGraw-Hill, 1929), p. 197; Jèze, *Rec. des Cours,* VII (1925), 215; income and inheritance taxes are of comparatively recent origin, and economically immature countries are not in a position to employ them effectively. Such countries necessarily have to depend largely on customs duties, which are easier to collect and to control.

distinctly constitutes the exception.[40] Customs duties, generally the principal source of income,[41] have in most instances constituted the main special security assigned for loans issued by Central and South American Republics [42] and by the small and predominantly agricultural countries of Europe and North Africa.[43] The kind of tax pledged has often varied with the nature of the debtor's economy; in some instances a tax on the production and consumption of tobacco has been assigned; [44] in others, a salt tax,[45] a tax on sheep [46] or on olive trees.[47] The Hungarian League loan of 1924 was made a first charge not only on the customs and the sugar tax, but also on the tobacco and salt monopolies.[48]

Other revenues which have occasionally been used to secure foreign loans are annuities received by the debtor from a third state under an international agreement. The Turkish loans of 1854, 1871, and 1877 were secured by the tribute due by the Khedive of Egypt to his Turkish overlord.[49] Under the terms of the decree of Mouharrem of 1881, the tribute of Bulgaria and the eastern Roumelian annuity were pledged as security for the Ottoman debt.[50] The Panamanian Readjustment Plan of 1941 provided for a first lien on the canal annuity which Panama receives from the United States.[51] The suitability of those annuities as security for long-term loans depends largely on the political stability of the debtor country. Because of changes in the position of Turkey following the Congress of Berlin, the annuities due to her from subject nations

40. The 1930 gold loan of the Province of Buenos Aires was based on the inheritance tax. *Corp. For. Bondh. Rep.*, No. 56 (1929), p. 83; the 1888 Mexican loan was, among others, secured on the proceeds from direct taxes on land, houses, industries, etc., within the Federal District of Mexico. *Idem*, p. 246.

41. B. H. Williams, *op. cit.*, p. 183; Jèze, *Rec. des Cours*, VII (1925), 215.

42. Numerous instances may be found in the debt history of Argentina, Colombia, Costa Rica, Ecuador, Mexico, Nicaragua, Honduras, Paraguay, Peru, Santo Domingo.

43. Such as Greece, Bulgaria, Turkey, Morocco, and Egypt.

44. Bulgarian loan of 1900. II, 535, 538, 540, 543. Greek and Turkish loans. II, 320, 443.

45. Peruvian salt loan of 1909.

46. Sheep taxes secured the Turkish loans of 1863, 1864, 1865, 1872, 1908. II, 402, 405, 456.

47. The Tunisian loan of 1864.

48. If the yield of the assigned revenues should fall below 150% of the sum required for service, additional security could be demanded. *The Problem of International Investment*, pp. 241, 243.

49. See II, 394, 404, 424. Furthermore, Braun, "Emprunts Ottomans et tribut d'Égypte," *Jour. du Droit Int.*, LII (1925), 518 ff.

50. II, 460 f.

51. See *Com. & Fin. Chron.*, CLII (March 29, 1941), 1993. The 1836 3½% loan of Portugal was secured on a debt due from Brazil; it merged for the most part with Brazilian stock. *Corp. For. Bondh. Rep.*, No. 56 (1929), p. 287.

were successively reduced during the life of the loans which they were designed to secure.[52] Bulgaria, after the proclamation of her independence in 1908, and Egypt, at the outbreak of the war in 1914, stopped paying tribute to Turkey, thus demonstrating the unreliable character of political payments as debt guaranties.

ADMINISTRATION AND COLLECTION OF ASSIGNED REVENUES

As already mentioned, a revenue pledge can become a real security in the hands of the creditors only if the assignment of the revenues to the service of the debt is coupled with some device removing them from the debtor's unhampered control and committing them directly to the administration of the creditors.[53] Such implementation of a pledge, however, is feasible only in exceptional cases. Public opinion in debtor countries will oppose the surrender of essential administrative rights to foreign creditors.[54] On the other hand, undue regard for local susceptibilities may be harmful to the effectiveness of the pledge. As instances of direct administration of pledged revenues through foreign creditors or their agents mention may be made of the management of Nicaragua's steamship and railroad lines by the bankers under the loan contract of March, 1912;[55] the sale by the bondholders of guano under agreements with Chile in 1880.[56] More common are methods of direct collection of pledged revenues by bondholders or their agents, especially in the case of customs and excise duties.[57] Less onerous for the debtor but also a weaker safeguard for the bondholders is the establishment by the former of a special organization for the purpose of administering or collecting pledged revenues on behalf of the creditors.[58] This is sometimes done by

52. II, 458 ff.

53. Cf. Part V, *infra*.

54. See Hyde, *op. cit.*, p. 536. Cf. Schoo, *op. cit.*, p. 277. See *infra*, section on Financial Control.

55. *The United States and Nicaragua: A Survey of the Relations from 1909 to 1932* (Dept. of State, Lat. Amer. Ser., No. 61, 1932), pp. 17–18.

56. II, 139.

57. II, 13 (bondholders' agents in the ports receive the sums necessary for the service of the debt); II, 232–233 (direct collection of the pledged import duties from the importers by creditors of the Republic); Uruguay, 1891, 1896, 1905 (customs receipts transmitted daily to agents of the bondholders); Honduras, *For. Rel.*, 1912, pp. 560–562; *Corp. For. Bondh. Rep.*, No. 53 (1926), pp. 246–249 (pledged Consular Service Charges automatically collected on behalf of the bankers through the sale of special stamps to exporters by the National City Bank).

58. See, in general, Jèze, *Rec. des Cours*, VII (1925), 160.

creating a semi-independent agency, like the Portuguese "Junta de Credito Publico" [59] or the Chilean "Autonomous Institute for the Amortization of the Public Debt." [60] In other instances, private companies are formed which assume the duty to service a public loan in return for a monopoly on some of the resources of the debtor nation.[61] Again, the national banks of the debtor states may be appointed the recipients of the pledged revenues for direct disbursement to the creditors.[62]

59. Established by the law of May, 1893, after diplomatic pressure had been exerted on behalf of German Bondholders. The "Junta" was composed of five members, all Portuguese; one was named by the Chamber of Peers, one by the Chamber of Deputies, one by the Government and two by the holders of the consolidated bonds. The "Junta" was to receive and disburse the assigned revenues, II, 373, 376.

60. *For. Bondh. Prot. Coun. Rep.*, 1935, p. 103. The proceeds of the assigned revenues were to be paid into the "Caisse Commune des Revenues Concédés" under a "Board of Administration of the Conceded Revenues."

61. Dreyfus & Co. received a monopoly of the sale of guano in Europe by the Peruvian Government. The sales agents of the company were to service the Peruvian loan of 1865. II, 115 ff. The Portuguese 4½% Tobacco monopoly bonds of 1891 were guaranteed by the Société des Tabacs de Portugal, which was to deduct from the monthly rent payable to the Government the amount of the service. *Corp. For. Bondh. Rep.*, No. 56 (1929), pp. 289, 290. By agreement of July 14, 1925, the collection of revenues pledged for the payment of the Greek public debt was handed over by the Greek State to a company, the Société Régie des Revenus Affectés à la Dette Publique Hellénique, in pursuance of the Treaty of 1897 between Turkey and Greece establishing an international control of Greek finances. When the régie in 1932 sued the Greek Government for changes made in the agreement which, it was maintained, was of an international character by reason of its connection with the Treaty of 1897, the Greek Supreme Court dismissed the action on the ground that no municipal remedy was available against the violation of such undertakings; the remedy was to be an international one. See H. Lauterpacht, *Annual Digest of Public International Law Cases, 1931–1932* (London, Longmans, Green, 1938), p. 11.

62. The 1896 loan of Haiti was secured by a special tax on each 100 pounds of coffee exported; the tax was to be collected by the Banque Nationale d'Haiti which was also to handle the debt service. Prospectus of loan, Archives, Coun. For. Bondh. The National Bank of Mexico was charged to pay the coupons of the 1886 loan out of funds which it was to receive directly from the customs house at Vera Cruz. II, 39. The same bank was to sell to the public for cash the certificates by which all import and export duties were paid for the benefit of the holders of the 1899, 1910, and 1913 loans. II, 60, n. 5. The customs duties assigned as security for the diplomatic loan of Venezuela of 1905 were to be paid separately by the merchants and placed in a separate account with the Banco de Venezuela. *Corp. For. Bondh. Rep.*, No. 61 (1934), pp. 490 f. Under the contract of September 30, 1908, concerning the Guayaquil railway bonds, the banks of Ecuador in which the customs revenues are deposited were directed to place daily to the account of the Council of Foreign Bondholders as representing the

Where the debtor government has surrendered administration or collection of revenues to agencies acting on behalf of the bondholders, it
is a safe assumption that it has also renounced its property rights in the
monies once they have passed into the possession of the collecting agencies. They either become the property of the bondholders [63] or of the
collecting agency,[64] or are held in trust for them to be distributed in
accordance with the loan agreement.[65]

LEGAL SIGNIFICANCE OF SECURITY CLAUSES

If the "pledge" is not implemented by any such device, the question
arises as to the legal significance of security clauses. To be sure, the mere
use of the terms "pledge," "security," "mortgage" in connection with
the assignment of government revenues to the service of a debt does not
admit of any inference as to the nature of the bondholders' rights with
respect to them. As justly observed in the report of the League Study
Committee, "a moment's reflection makes it clear that the implementing
of such pledges cannot be achieved in the same conditions in an international loan as in a domestic loan, unless the pledged assets or revenues
are situated outside the national territory of the borrower." [66] However,

holders of the bonds a certain part of the total amount required to remit to London the gold value of the annual service. *Idem*, No. 66 (1939), pp. 32 f.

63. See II, 309 (tobacco and stamp revenues, when paid over to the Monopoly
Company, became the absolute property of the bondholders).

64. See the case of *De Neuflize* v. *Deutsche Bank et al.*, decided by the Franco-
German Mixed Arbitral Tribunal on October 24, 1924 (*Rec. des déc.*, IV, 798),
where it was held that the Ottoman Debt Council, possessing a legal personality
of its own, became the owner of the revenues collected by it; third parties to
whom these sums were lent became debtors of the Council and not of the bondholders.

65. This was the position taken by the Inspector-General of the Chinese customs with respect to customs revenues accumulated for the protection of the bondholders. See *For. Rel.*, 1921, I, 353 f.

66. League Study Committee Report, II. Econ. and Finan. 1939. II.A. 10, p. 10.
See also Mixed Court of Appeal of Egypt, *In re Sursock* (March 16, 1880), quoted
in *Gaz. des Trib. Mix.*, XXIII (March, 1936), 119: "The subscribers to a loan
with a [foreign government] cannot be unaware of the fact that the first duty of a
State, that which dominates all others and which it cannot evade, is to provide
first of all for the public expenditure required for the maintenance of the social
life . . . . The special pledges assigned by the State to the service of its debt,
quite apart from the impossibility of enforcing them by legal means, can in the
eyes of the creditors never be more than aleatory guaranties." See also Jèze, *Rec.
des Cours*, VII, 156 f. (". . . the public domain nowadays is assigned to a public
service which means that it is inalienable. A forced transfer, which mortgaging the
property would imply, would disrupt the functioning of the public service") and

to conclude from this inability of creditors of governments to assert their rights by the same means as private law creditors that security clauses in government loans are nothing but "boilerplate" and "not worth the paper they are written on" [67] would mean to ignore entirely the clear manifestation in these clauses of a will on the part of the debtor government to obligate itself over and above its promise to pay interest and principal to the lender.[68] The revenues are "earmarked" for a specified purpose, which is the subject of a legally binding obligation.[69] They thereby "cease to be at the free disposal of its debtor-owner." [70] That means that the debtor state is not at liberty to alter their contents or

---

p. 176 ("The legal obligation of the State with regard to security of its debt may not imperil the functioning of its vital public services.") Jèze, *Cours de science des finances*, pp. 409 ff.; SEC, *Rep.*, Pt. V, p. 16.

67. See the testimony of Allen W. Dulles before the SEC. SEC, *Rep.*, Pt. V, pp. 17, 22. See also C. Lewis, *America's Stake in International Investments* (Washington, The Brookings Institution, 1938), pp. 417 f.

68. See the award of the French-Chilean Arbitral Tribunal in the case of *Chile v. France*, July 5, 1901. Descamps and Renault, *Recueil international des traités du xxᵉ siècle*, p. 370: ". . . public debts of a State may be secured not only by real pledges constituted according to the rules of private law, but also by legal relations of a purely obligatory character by virtue of which certain goods or revenues are assigned by the State to the payment of its creditors."

69. See Feilchenfeld and others in *Col. Law Rev.*, XXX (1930), 1124. The pledging of specific revenues, however, does not free the debtor's general assets from liability for the debt. This is sometimes expressly stated in the contract by a clause stipulating that any deficiency of the assigned revenues is to be made up from the general revenues of the state. See e.g., II, 116 (payment from the general revenues if the guano deposits should be exhausted or the sales of guano be insufficient). In other instances, the specific pledge is coupled with a general charge on the revenues of the state. See II, 190, n. 1; II, 207. When Chile, under the terms of the Adjustment Law of 1935, assigned the proceeds from the copper and nitrate industry exclusively to the service of the readjusted debt, the Foreign Bondholders Protective Council pointed out that the loans were originally issued upon the full faith and credit of the Chilean Government and that Chile was not entitled to limit her liability for the debt to the proceeds from specified revenues. The bondholders were advised to reject the proposal. *For. Bondh. Prot. Coun. Rep.*, 1935, pp. 33, 49. See also SEC, *Rep.*, p. 465.

70. Fischer Williams, *op. cit.*, pp. 353 ff.; Fischer Williams, "International Law and International Financial Obligations Arising from Contracts," *Bibliotheca Visseriana*, II (1924), 61. See also the case of Italy in the Venezuelan arbitration before The Hague Tribunal, 1903 (text in S. Doc. 119, 58th Cong. 3d Sess., p. 861): "The condition prohibiting the alienation of customs revenues (assigned as security for the payment of the unascertained debts) deprived Venezuela of the property in it and transferred it to the Italian Government and their allies." Revenues that are assigned as security but have never been made use of, are free for assignment to another loan. II, 316, n. 33.

to abrogate them altogether; it has in this respect submitted to a partial control of its domestic fiscal policy by its foreign creditors.[71]

VALUE AND IMPORTANCE OF SECURITY CLAUSES

Attaching a security clause, moreover, enhances the economic value of the loan and gives it a standing of priority in the reorganization of the public debt of the borrower. Secured loans sometimes have stood the test of financial or political crises in the debtor country better than unsecured ones. Thus, apart from a brief period following the Revolution of 1911, China's customs-secured foreign obligations were regularly paid.[72] Even the profound dislocations caused in Chinese political and economic life by the invasion of Japan did not materially affect the security of China's foreign debt. In spite of the fact that the majority of the principal revenue-producing ports of China came under Japanese domination, the larger portion of the total Chinese foreign debt was for a while properly serviced,[73] and Japanese authorities expressly declared that the customs would still go to servicing the country's foreign obligations.[74] Another example of the ability of secured debts to survive the vicissitudes of the political and economic life of the debtor country is provided by Bulgarian Treasury bills discounted by the Banque de Paris et des Pays-Bas in 1913 upon the condition that, if they were not redeemed at maturity, they should be retired "out of the proceeds of the first financial operation undertaken by Bulgaria abroad." [75] The covenant securing the redemption of the bills was expressly maintained by

71. Fischer Williams, *Chapters on Current International Law*, pp. 353 ff.; Jèze, *Rec. des Cours*, VII, 161; Jèze, *Cours de science des finances*, p. 411; Feilchenfeld, *Public Debts and State Succession*, pp. 194–195; W. E. K. Fournée, *Wanbetaling van Staten* (Amsterdam, 1895), p. 29. See also II, 443–44 (Debt Commission refused to grant permission for a change of the assigned revenues which Turkey insisted was her right); Egypt (no modifications in the land tax without assent of the powers).

72. Young, "China's Financial Progress," *For. Pol. Rep.*, XIV (April 15, 1938), p. 33.

73. *Corp. For. Bondh. Rep.*, No. 65 (1938), p. 36.

74. *Far Eastern Survey*, Vol. VII, No. 19 (1938), p. 219. The picture changed, however, in 1939, when the Chinese Government ceased to make advances to the Inspector-General of customs in Shanghai for the payment of the service on customs-secured loans, since none of the customs duties collected at Chinese seaports under the control of the Japanese Army and Navy had been made available for the payment of service charges on Chinese bonds held by foreigners. See K. Bloch, *Far Eastern Survey*, Vol. VIII, No. 4 (1939), p. 43; also *idem*, pp. 81 ff.

75. II, 554, n. 21.

Article 139 of the treaty of Neuilly which recognized the right of the Banque to be reimbursed out of the "next financial operation," and the amount of the Bulgarian refugee loan issued under the auspices of the League of Nations in 1926 was actually increased so as to provide a sum sufficient for the redemption of the bills.[76]

Cases where holders of foreign government bonds have been able to satisfy their claims against the defaulting debtor state out of the pledged security in the same manner as private law pledgees are comparatively rare. Foreclosure actions by foreign creditors of necessity require that assets of the debtor government be found beyond the latter's jurisdiction and within reach of the creditors. As shown above, that type of security is the exception rather than the rule. However, when the Turkish Government in 1873 failed to repay an advance given by the Compte d'Escompte, the latter sold bonds given as security for this debt in accordance with the Turkish law governing the foreclosure of pledges.[77]

The majority of the cases where the pledging of revenues as security for government loans proves to be of material value to bondholders occur when the debtor government seeks new credit or seeks to adjust its debts after default on its external obligations. In both cases, the promise on the part of the debtor state to satisfy the holders of secured loans out of specified revenues creates a distinctly advantageous position for the latter; it may result either in strong diplomatic action on their behalf by their home government or in a preferential treatment of their claim in the reorganization of the debts of the borrowing state.

As to the relation of secured loans to later issues by the same debtor, mention may be made of the fact that the pledging of revenues substantially limits the future borrowing capacity of a country.[78] The investing public as well as issuing houses is reluctant to extend credit to a state whose principal resources have already been pledged for the service of previous loans, and this in itself enhances the value of existing secured issues. Furthermore, holders of secured loans have repeatedly succeeded in asserting their prior rights to pledged revenues either by having them expressly recognized before the flotation of a new loan or by preventing their double assignment for the later issue. Thus, Article 7 of the agreement of December 16, 1926, between the Bulgarian Government and certain bondholders' committees stipulated that "the new Loan to be issued under the auspices of the League of Nations shall not in any way

76. II, 554.
77. II, 410 ff.
78. Madden and Nadler, *op. cit.*, p. 181; John T. Madden, Marcus Nadler, and Harry C. Sauvain, *America's Experience as a Creditor Nation* (New York, Prentice-Hall, 1937), p. 217.

affect the rights and guarantees belonging to the Holders of Bonds of the existing Loans." [79] When Turkey, after her war with Russia in 1878, negotiated a loan with an Anglo-French group of financiers, one of the conditions of the new issue was that it should be secured by a prior charge on all revenues assigned for previous loans; i.e., that it was to have priority over the entire existing debt of Turkey. Protests of the holders of previous loans, supported by a strong criticism on the part of the British Foreign Secretary, defeated the scheme.[80] When an American loan to Liberia was contemplated in 1920, the United States Government expressly asked the British Government to consent to a surrender of security assigned to British investors under the loan agreement of 1912. The British Foreign Office replied that they felt bound to stipulate "that the *status quo* should not be altered to the detriment of British economic interests." [81] It is true, double assignment of pledged revenues occasionally occurs.[82] But apart from the fact that

a State, at a period of great emergency, and in order to obtain a fresh loan which might avert a national disaster, might be thought excusable for disposing temporarily of resources at its command without immediate reference to prior obligations,[83]

such double assignment in most cases is not the result of deliberate dishonesty on the part of the debtor; it is rather to be attributed to the failure of certain debtor countries with undeveloped fiscal systems to distinguish clearly, in law and in fact, between the various sources of income, thus causing the same revenues to be pledged twice under different names.[84] This assumes good faith.

79. II, 554.

80. II, 427–28.

81. *For. Rel.*, 1920, III, 97 f.

82. Thus, the once-assigned (for the loan of 1872) tithes of the Turkish *vilayets* of the Danube and the sheep tax of Anatolia were also hypothecated for the loan of 1873. II, 409; see also II, 412, 427. Nearly 90% of the Mexican customs revenues in 1884 were assigned for the repayment of short-term advances from the National Bank and other internal obligations, notwithstanding assignment of part of the same customs revenues to the 1851 bondholders. E. Turlington, *Mexico and Her Foreign Creditors*, p. 204.

83. The Marquis of Salisbury to Sir A. H. Layard, February 20, 1880. II, 430, n. 44.

84. See Minister Reinsch to the (Chinese) Foreign Office, May 1, 1917 (*For. Rel.*, 1917, p. 131): "The [Continental Commercial Bank of Chicago] was solemnly assured that the Tobacco and Wine Sales Revenue, which was pledged for the loan, had not theretofore been pledged as security for any other loan. Unfortunately it turns out that this revenue is not clear from other claims upon it.

.   .   .

"2d. Under the language of its contracts the Banque Industrielle de Chine claims, through the French Legation, that it has a right to all taxes and imposts on

It is, however, in cases of threatened or actual defaults and during readjustment proceedings that the real value of security becomes evident. In the first place, experience shows that lending houses and investors, when they appeal to their governments for diplomatic interposition, have usually a better chance of obtaining governmental coöperation if there exists a specific "pledge." [85] Diplomatic protection in such cases has been exercised for the purpose of safeguarding existing security either against acts of the debtor government directly or indirectly violating the rights of bondholders or against acts of third parties threatening to disturb the pledged revenues in their dealings with the debtor. Thus, when in 1879 the British Government was informed about certain plans of the Peruvian Government to dispose of guano pledged to the holders of Peruvian bonds, the British minister at Lima was instructed "to protest against any acts of the Peruvian Government which may tend to weaken the security hypothecated to the holders of Peruvian bonds." [86] Similarly, when the Government of Guatemala withdrew the coffee duties pledged as security for loans and after the failure of the bondholders to obtain relief from the debtor, the British Government addressed a request to Guatemala for restitution of the security and eventually invoked the good offices of the United States to move the Guatemalan Government to refer the matter to arbitration.[87] During the negotiations preceding the Congress of Berlin, 1878, Great Britain was able to impress Russia with the necessity of respecting the prior rights of secured creditors of Turkey, when the latter had consented, under the terms of the Treaty of San Stefano, to the payment of a war indemnity to Russia out of her entire revenues. While maintaining that, in principle, all creditors are entitled to an equal share in the assets of their debtor, Russia nevertheless recognized a "claim of priority" for the foreign obligations of the Porte which had been secured by special hypothecations prior to the Congress of Berlin, and both Russia and Turkey agreed at

tobacco and wine of whatever kind present and future. This claim, which on the face of it might seem unreasonable, is unfortunately to some extent borne out by the fact that in some cases, for instance in the province of Chihli, all tobacco and wine taxes have been consolidated under the form of the Public Sales Revenue. This would bear out the French claim, as their security could, of course, not be defeated by swallowing up the security in some other form of the same tax." See also *For. Rel.*, 1916, pp. 143 f.

85. Madden and Nadler, *op. cit.*, pp. 184 f. In Mexico, II, 23, where a security like customs revenues was assigned, the British Government took an active interest in the discharge of the debt.

86. The Marquis of Salisbury to the Peruvian minister, November 26, 1879. J. B. Moore, *A Digest of International Law* (Washington, Govt. Printing Office, 1906), VI, 724.

87. *For. Rel.*, 1913, p. 566.

the Congress that the payments designed to discharge the political obligation of the war indemnity should have no precedence over the secured claims of the foreign holders of Turkish bonds.[88]

In reorganization proceedings, various forms have been evolved which reveal the intrinsic value and the legal significance of security attached to government loan contracts. During the different stages of the liquidation and readjustment of the Turkish and Egyptian public debt, as well as in other settlements, holders of secured bonds have received preferential treatment either in the form of priorities in payment and amortization,[89] by being subjected to a smaller reduction of interest than the holders of unsecured bonds,[90] by being spared any reduction in interest,[91] or by being left entirely unaffected by the readjustment procedure.[92]

Another important advantage accruing to holders of loans with assigned revenues as security may be observed in a claim to adequate participation in the control or administration of those revenues, if the debtor state, on default, should be compelled to surrender those functions, wholly or in part, to its creditors.[93]

From these precedents, it may safely be concluded that creditors of

88. *Brit. and For. St. Pap.*, LXIX, pp. 1000 ff. II, 485, 496–98.

89. Borchard, *op. cit.*, p. 152, nn. 30, 31; II, 590. See also II, 545. In the readjustment made as a result of the currency depreciation, the Bulgarian loans of 1902, 1904, and 1907 were regarded as having superior security to those of 1892, 1896, and 1909.

90. The 1858 and 1862 Turkish loans received a higher rate of interest under the debt settlement than the less-secured and later loans. II, 506.

91. In the 1884 conference of the great powers on the readjustment of the Egyptian debt, the British Government proposed reduction of interest on certain loans, but not on the Domains loans because they had been issued "under special conditions which would not have been granted unless the security had been regarded as absolute." *Corp. For. Bondh. Rep.*, No. 12 (1886), p. 40.

92. In March, 1891, a committee formed by the Bank of England, concluded an arrangement with the financial agent of the Argentine Government in London, whereby the interest on the Argentine national external loans was to be funded for three years into 6% funding bonds. The 1886 customs loan was excepted from the arrangement; its service continued to be in cash. See H. E. Peters, *The Foreign Debt of the Argentine Republic* (Baltimore, Johns Hopkins Press, 1934), p. 46; *Corp. For. Bondh. Rep.*, No. 20 (1892), pp. 16 ff. By the Egyptian Law of Liquidation, the rights of those holding mortgages on the Daira properties, now transferred to the State, were maintained. II, 608, n. 123.

93. See the French Ambassador to the Secretary of State, December 22, 1919 (*For. Rel.*, 1919, I, 551). ". . . It cannot be denied that the taxes on alcohol and tobacco constitute . . . the first mortgage of the loan floated in 1913[1914?] by the Industrial Bank. It therefore seems to us that our countrymen have a right to ask when the internal revenue service is reorganized to have a part commensurate to their interests and, in particular, the administrative direction of the service, assigned to them."

secured loans are legally entitled to demand preference for their claims in a readjustment of the debtor's finances. They furthermore indicate that bondholders possessing a security in the form of a revenue assignment stand a good chance that their claim to preferential treatment in reorganization proceedings will be honored by the debtor and recognized by the nonsecured creditors.

OTHER FORMS OF SECURITY

Revenue pledges are frequently strengthened by a special undertaking of the debtor not to assign any of its assets to future loans.[94] On the other hand, the assignment of certain revenues as special security to a loan may, at the same time, benefit a prior issue with what may be called a "most-favored-loan" clause which automatically extends revenue pledges of later loans to the previous debt.[95] Other clauses designed to make the payment of the principal debt more certain and, therefore, belonging to the category of security clauses include the promise by the debtor government not to incur another debt during the life of the loan [96] or to pay the debt according to its gold value or in the currency selected by the creditor as the most favorable one at the time of payment.[97]

94. See, in general, with respect to this so-called "negative pledge clause," Feilchenfeld, in Quindry, *Bonds and Bondholders, Rights and Remedies,"* Vol. II, sec. 635 (a); Madden and Nadler, *op. cit.*, pp. 162 f. Instances of those clauses may be found in the Annual Reports of the Foreign Bondholders Protective Council under the various issues. The Argentine Republic 4% bonds of the external conversion loan *(For. Bondh. Prot. Coun. Rep.*, 1937, p. 34) provides: ". . . The Government covenants that, so long as any of the Bonds of this issue shall be outstanding, it will not create or permit the creation of any mortgage or pledge or other lien on any of its revenues or assets . . ."

95. See, for an instance of such clause, Madden and Nadler, *op. cit.*, pp. 162 f. "The loan constitutes a direct obligation of the borrower. None of the revenues or assets of the borrower . . . is specifically pledged for any loan, and the borrower . . . covenants that if, in the future it shall sell, offer for public subscription, or in any other manner dispose of any bonds or contract for any loan secured by any charge or pledge on or of any revenues or assets of the borrower, the service of this loan shall be secured equally and ratably with such bonds." Sometimes the prior claim of the first loan on the pledged revenues is expressly stated in the clause. See the 8% loan of Uruguay, 1946, quoted by Madden and Nadler, *op. cit.*, p. 163.

96. The Egyptian Government, when issuing the loan of 1868, promised the contractors not to float any further public loan for the next five years. II, 581. Under the terms of the Venezuelan loan of 1896, no new loan was to be contracted with equal or superior rights until its amortization. *Corp. For. Bondh. Rep.*, No. 61 (1934), p. 489.

97. See the sections on Gold and Currency Clauses, *supra;* J. Sulkowski, "Questions juridiques soulevées dans les rapports internationaux par les variations de valeur des signes monétaires," *Rec. des Cours*, XXIX (1929), 77 ff.

Section VIII

GUARANTEED LOANS

ASIDE from pledging parts of their own assets, movable or immovable, to the fulfillment of their obligations, debtors since early times have offered to their creditors the property of others as security by attaching to the principal contract the promise of third parties to fulfill payment of the debt in case they default (suretyship, guaranty). The practice of public lending and borrowing has developed a similar device by which a financially well-established community lends its name and credit to another of weak credit standing in order to enable the latter to obtain a loan or to improve the terms offered.[1]

DOMESTIC GUARANTIES

Political subdivisions or public corporations within a state may find it necessary to secure the express backing of the central government before they are able successfully to float a loan on foreign money markets. The assistance of the central government in these cases may assume the form of a direct guaranty by which the government obligates itself to make good any deficiency resulting from the default of the principal debtor [2] or it may consist in a promise to maintain the solvency of the

1. See Jèze, *Rec. des Cours*, VII (1925), 158; Jèze, *La Garantie des emprunts publics d'état*, p. 7; John H. Wigmore, "The Pledge Idea: A Study in Comparative Legal Ideas," *Harv. Law Rev.*, X (1897), 321, 389; Madden and Nadler, *Foreign Securities*, p. 186; Meyer Balding, "Die völkerrechtliche Anleihegarantien," in Niemeyer's *Zeitschrift*, XXVI (1916), 416. The French Government withheld its guaranty from the Moroccan loan of 1910 for reasons of internal French policy; sometimes, however, the soundness of extending a guaranty is challenged in principle. When England, in 1898, suggested to France and Russia that the three powers should guarantee a loan in order to enable the Greek Government to discharge its obligations under the terms of the peace treaty with Turkey, the French Foreign Minister replied that such guaranty "would constitute a bad precedent . . . a fatal encouragement to minor Powers to disturb the peace of Europe and escape the due penalty by transferring the chief responsibility to the shoulders" of others. II, 315, n. 31.

2. The Bulgarian railway conversion loan of 1907 was secured by the direct guaranty of the Government. *Corp. For. Bondh. Rep.*, No. 56 (1929), p. 91. The Peruvian (1869) railroad loan was guaranteed by the Government, unconditionally

borrowing community through certain administrative measures such as the grant of regular subsidies or exemption from transfer restrictions.[3] Only relationships of the former type are in the nature of direct pecuniary obligations of the government, to be performed and, if necessary, enforced in the same manner as the principal debt.[4] The promise in the

and absolutely. II, 116. The Cedulas of the Argentine National Mortgage Bank were guaranteed by the nation. *Corp. For. Bondh. Rep.*, No. 56 (1929), p. 60. Loans issued by the Mortgage Bank of Chile between 1922 and 1930 were guaranteed by the Government. *Idem*, No. 58 (1931), p. 22. The Haitian Government guaranteed 6% interest on the railroad bonds issued by the American concessionaire. A. C. Millspaugh, *Haiti under American Control, 1915–1930* (Boston, World Peace Foundation, 1931), pp. 22–23. In May, 1914, the Mexican Government guaranteed the Mexican National Packing Co.'s bonds, issued in 1911. *Corp. For. Bondh. Rep.*, No. 56 (1929), p. 249. A Mexican loan of 1889 for the completion of the Tehuantepec Railway was secured by a promise of the Government to make good any deficit. II, 49. The Portuguese 4½% State Railway loan of 1912 was guaranteed by the Government. *Corp. For. Bondh. Rep.*, No. 56 (1929), p. 291. A direct responsibility of the Argentine Federal Government for bonds of the Province of Mendoza resulted from the latter's instruction to the Federal Government to make all payments on the bonds of the Province in accordance with the Unification of Taxes Law. *For. Bondh. Prot. Coun. Rep.*, 1938, p. 77.

3. Instances of indirect guaranties in the form of subsidies by the central government to its political subdivisions may be found in the 1921 6% gold loan of the City of Soissons and the 1927 6½% loan of the City of Rome. In both cases, the central governments of the respective municipalities promised to pay annually to the latter certain grants in aid and, at the same time, guaranteed that these sums would not be diminished by possible depreciation of the exchange. See Madden and Nadler, *op. cit.*, pp. 189 f., where further instances of indirect guaranties are mentioned. Administrative measures amounting to an indirect guaranty for loans issued by municipalities are exemplified by certain promises on the part of the central government to facilitate the transfer of the debt service abroad. See, for example, the 1934 loan of the City of Marseilles which provided that "the Government has agreed to undertake, in order to permit the City to pay the interest or principal amount of the loan in gold in the City of New York, to furnish it, if necessary, . . . with gold in the amount needed and authorize its exportation for said purpose." See *idem*, pp. 195 f. When the states and cities of Brazil failed to meet their external obligations because of lack of foreign exchange, federal intervention in the transfer question led to extended responsibility in regard to these state and municipal debt services. In February, 1934, a Presidential decree was issued dividing all external loans of the Federal Government as well as those of the states and municipalities into eight grades according to the amount of foreign exchange assigned to the service of each. *Corp. For. Bondh. Rep.*, No. 60 (1933), pp. 23 ff. By agreement with the holders of defaulted bonds of the City of Riga, the Latvian Government undertook: (1) to provide adequate guaranties for the carrying out of the terms of this arrangement, either by withholding a proportion of taxes payable to the municipality or by other means; (2) that no restrictions would be imposed upon the remittance of service monies. *Idem*, No. 61 (1934), p. 17.

4. Fournée, *Wanbetaling van Staten*, p. 32, calls it a case of negligence if a state

latter case involves certain administrative decisions which, according to legal doctrines prevalent in many countries, are left to the discretion of the competent authorities and are not cognizable in a lawsuit before ordinary courts.

INTERNATIONAL GUARANTIES

PURPOSE

In the field of international finance, the guaranty given by one or more states to a loan issued by a fellow member of the community of nations is in practically all cases undertaken for political reasons in consideration of some actual or anticipated advantage to the guaranteeing governments.[5] The guaranty of the Turkish loan of 1855 by France and England and of the Sardinian loan of 1855 by England during the Crimean War constituted a form of financial aid to a weak ally for the pursuit of a common war. The concept of collective security recently brought forth the suggestion of financial assistance to the victim of aggression through an international guaranty of the service of a loan to be floated by the attacked state.[6] A loan guaranty may offer an effective means for the stabilization and preservation of a political situation created under the auspices of the guaranteeing states. Thus, the great powers of Europe, after their intervention in the struggle of Greece for her independence from Turkey, in 1833 assumed responsibility for a loan which was to insure the independent existence of the new nation.[7] Similarly, Austria was saved from internal collapse in 1923 by a loan which was guaranteed by the powers principally interested in her continued existence as a sovereign state.[8] The international guaranties of the Egyptian loan of 1885 and of the Greek loan of 1898 were designed permanently to stabilize the work of financial reconstruction undertaken by the guaranteeing governments for the purpose of protecting capital invested by their nationals in these countries.[9]

---

has guaranteed the loan of a public body or corporation and then refuses to fulfill the promise.

5. Jèze, *Rec. des Cours*, VII, 185 ff.; Schoo, *Régimen jurídico*, pp. 419 ff.; 430 ff.

6. Fischer Williams, "La Convention pour l'assistance financière aux états victimes d'agression," *Rec. des Cours*, XXXIV (1930), 105 ff.

7. II, 290–291; Jèze, *Rec. des Cours*, VII, pp. 187 ff.

8. Fischer Williams, *Chapters on Current International Law and the League of Nations*, pp. 378 f.; Jèze, *Rec. des Cours*, VII, pp. 196 ff.; Plesch and Domke, *Die österreichische Völkerbundanleihe*, pp. 92 ff.

9. Jèze, *Rec. des Cours*, VII, pp. 192 ff.; Meyer Balding, *op. cit.*, pp. 405 ff.

EFFECTIVENESS

A guaranty involving the financial responsibility of a state for the debt of another can become effective only if the nature and extent of the guarantor's liability are fixed in precise terms. It therefore presupposes the conclusion of an international agreement stipulating the exact legal relationship between the various participants in the transaction; it cannot be implied from extrinsic circumstances. Thus, the mere fact that the British Consul-General in Venezuela was authorized to forward the interest payments on the Venezuelan loan of 1862 in no way created a guaranty of the British Government for the continued performance of the loan contract by Venezuela.[10] Many people believed that the issuance of loans to certain of the smaller European countries after World War I "under the auspices of the League of Nations" implied a genuine guaranty by the League for these loans.[11] Such interpretation of the function of the League in the flotation of the loans was, however, unwarranted. The League merely provided the center where the loans were initiated; it would send a committee of investigation to the country applying for financial assistance and, through its Financial Committee and in agreement with the country concerned, would draw up the terms and conditions of the loan which then was floated in the international money markets.[12] The "special responsibility" which the Council of the League realized that it incurred by these loans [13] involved a promise to extend all technical aid in case the borrower needed assistance to overcome financial difficulties. If it meant more than that, the guaranty assumed by certain powers for the Austrian loan of 1923 would have been superfluous. Likewise, the special part taken by the United States in the preservation of the financial stability of certain Latin American countries through the institution of financial control has not engaged its pecuniary liability toward the foreign creditors of these countries.[14] Even the use of the term "guaranty" in connection with a promise made by a state with respect to the loan of another state does not always offer irrefutable evidence of an intention to create an obligation commonly implied in that

10. Statement in loan prospectus (Archives, Coun. For. Bondh.).

11. See *The Problem of International Investment*, p. 95.

12. See League of Nations, *The Financial Reconstruction of Austria*, General Survey and Principal Documents, Geneva, November, 1926. Also, Fischer Williams, *Chapters on Current International Law and the League of Nations*, pp. 378 ff.; Plesch and Domke, *op. cit.*, pp. 92 ff.; Jèze, *Rec. des Cours*, VII, 196 ff.; *Com. and Fin. Chron.*, CXXXV (October 1, 1932), 2249.

13. Resolution of the Council of the League of Nations, October 7, 1932. League of Nations, *Official Journal*, XIII (December, 1932), 1927.

14. Jèze, *Rec. des Cours*, VII, 166 ff.

term. When France and England, in 1846, intervened in the Uruguayan Civil War in favor of the liberal government by guaranteeing a loan issued by the latter, their intention was not

to assume any pecuniary liability towards the bondholders. Their only purpose was to give the loan a sort of authenticity which would distinguish it from ordinary contracts with the Uruguayan government which sometimes were concluded under such circumstances as to make it impossible for diplomatic agents to support the claims of foreign creditors in case of non-performance of the contract. The guaranty simply implied the promise to assert in case of need the claims of the subscribers; it went no further than that. The guaranteeing powers failed to reserve to themselves control over the service of the loan which they would have done if they had intended to become sureties for Uruguay.[15]

In other words, the two powers simply promised to grant their diplomatic protection against the defaulting debtor, which is a privilege to be exercised by the state at its discretion but under no circumstances a duty enforceable against it by those who may benefit from its exercise.

LEGAL SIGNIFICANCE

The promise to guarantee a loan means that the guarantor undertakes to be answerable for the payment of the debt in case the principal debtor should fail to perform his engagement.[16] This duty exists toward the debtor state which issues the loan on the strength of the guaranty, as well as toward the individual creditor who lends his money to an uncertain borrower in consideration of the security offered by the superior financial means of the guarantor. As the guaranty is designed to insure the continued performance of the loan contract, the obligation of the guarantor to pay becomes due the moment the principal debtor fails to fulfill the

---

15. De Lapradelle and Politis, *Rec. des Arb. Int.*, II (1932), 119 ff.

16. Meyer Balding, *op. cit.*, pp. 413 f.: "The guarantor obligates himself, like the surety in private law, to fulfill the principal obligation in case the debtor defaults." Pradier-Fodéré, *Traité de droit international public*, II, (Paris, 1885–1906), 641 ff.: "A State which guarantees a loan does not undertake simply to use its influence to assure the execution of the contract . . . it goes farther: it undertakes to perform accessorily the promise given by the borrower and, if necessary, to execute it himself." Bosch, *De Staatschulden in het internationaal Recht*, p. 62: A guaranty creates a legal, not merely a moral obligation to pay. Fauchille, *Traité de droit international public*, Vol. I, Pt. III, No. 891 (Paris, Rousseau & Cie., 1921), pp. 416 ff.; Vignéras, "Des Garanties offertes au porteurs française de fonds d'état étrangers" (Thèse, Paris, 1905); Jèze, *Rec. des Cours*, VII, 158 ff.; Plesch and Domke, *op. cit.*, p. 99: "The assumption of a guaranty is equivalent to the creation of an independent obligation, irrespective of the existence of the original debt." Feilchenfeld, in Quindry, *Bonds and Bondholders, Rights and Remedies*, Vol. II, sec. 646 (b); Madden and Nadler, *op. cit.*, pp. 188 ff.

contract, regardless of whether the default results from inability or un-willingness to pay; the cause of the debtor's failure is irrelevant, unless it furnishes a valid excuse such as *force majeure,* in which case the legal consequences of the default remain in abeyance.[17] Nor is the duty of the guarantor limited to special cases of default. If the debtor, in dis-regard of an express gold clause, refuses to pay the gold value of his debt, the guarantor may be obliged to make good the difference.[18]

RELATIONS BETWEEN GUARANTOR AND DEBTOR

The guarantor and the debtor both being states, the relations between them are determined by international law. In defining their legal nature, the theory has been advanced that the loan guaranty constitutes a form of financial intervention, entitling the guaranteeing state to interfere with the fiscal affairs of the debtor and, in particular, to take all measures necessary to protect the rights of the creditors.[19] The practice of states seems to bear out this theory. As already observed, the international guaranties of the Egyptian loan of 1885 and of the Greek loan of 1898 were part of the reconstruction scheme which gave the intervening powers considerable influence in the management of the finances of the two countries. In 1843 the powers that had guaranteed the loan of 1833 called upon Greece to reduce expenditures to such extent as to permit her to meet her obligations on the loan and to substitute a specific se-curity for the general assignment of revenues.[20] In 1864 the guaranteeing powers asserted the priority of their own claims and refused to allow the Greek Government to appropriate a fixed annuity for the service of the defaulted independence loans.[21]

The payment of the debt by the guarantor, in whole or in part, pur-suant to his promise, creates a corresponding duty of the principal debtor to reimburse the guarantor; the latter's payments are not in the nature of a gift but are advances to the defaulting government for the purpose of discharging the loan.[22] Various means have been employed by guaran-

17. See *infra,* section on Default.

18. In 1932, when the Greek Government defaulted on its external loans, the difference between the amount transferred in paper and the sum required to pay interest on the guaranteed loan of 1898 in gold. *Corp. For. Bondh. Rep.* No. 60 (1933), p. 261 was made up by France and Great Britain, guarantors of the loan. See also Plesch and Domke, *op. cit.,* p. 99, who maintain that a decision on the part of the principal debtor not to fulfill the contract in gold, as originally stipu-lated, has no influence whatever on the obligation of the guarantors to pay the debt in accordance with its terms.

19. Meyer Balding, *op. cit.,* p. 393; Bosch, *op. cit.,* p. 120; Fournée, *op. cit.,* p. 72, n. 1.

20. II, 287–288.

21. II, 290; see also Jèze, *Rec. des Cours,* VII, 164.

22. See the French law of April 24, 1838, concerning the guaranty of the Greek

tors to exact from the defaulting government the fulfillment of this obligation. Under the terms of the unratified convention of Athens of September 14, 1843, between Greece on the one hand and the three guaranteeing powers on the other, the Greek Government undertook to issue Treasury bonds to be deposited with the individual guarantors to the extent of the payments to be made in pursuance of their guaranty commitment. To secure the discharge of this debt, the proceeds from the salt mines were specifically assigned.[23] The general bond of the Austrian Government guaranteed loan of 1923 provided that the sums owed by Austria to the guaranteeing governments for advances made under their guaranty should carry interest "one half per centum higher than the rate of interest payable on the Bonds upon which default has been made" and that they should rank as a second charge, immediately after the bondholders, on the gross receipts of the customs and of the tobacco monopoly pledged as security for the principal obligation, that charge to be utilized by the trustees for the repayment of the guarantor governments.[24]

RELATIONS BETWEEN GUARANTOR AND CREDITOR

The legal relations between the guarantor and the creditors of the guaranteed loan are similar to those existing between the latter and the principal debtor. The duty assumed by the guarantor toward the indi-

loan of 1833 (Jèze, *La Garantie des emprunts publics d'état*, p. 55), Art. II: "Payments made by virtue of the authorization given in the preceding article are in the nature of advances to be recovered from the Government of Greece." French financial law of February 26, 1887, also speaks of "advances" made with regard to the portion of the Greek loan guaranteed by France. *Idem*, p. 62. See also Meyer Balding, *op. cit.*, p. 423.

23. Jèze, *op. cit.*, p. 57. See also the agreement between the Greek Government and the British Treasury of August, 1932, concerning the reimbursement of Britain and France by the former for sums paid by the two governments as guarantors for the 1898 loan (*Corp. For. Bondh. Rep.*, No. 60 [1932], p. 265) and the further agreements of 1934 and 1935 between the guarantor governments and Greece providing for compensation for sums disbursed by the guarantors on account of their guaranties for the 1833 and 1898 loans (*Corp. For. Bondh. Rep.*, No. 62 [1935], p. 269, and No. 63 [1936], p. 269).

24. Article XV of the general bond. Text in League of Nations, *The Financial Reconstruction of Austria. General Survey and Principal Documents*, pp. 154 ff. See also Fischer Williams, *Chapters on Current International Law*, p. 417. Under the terms of the Anglo-German transfer agreement of July 1, 1938, the German Government agreed to reimburse the British Government for any sums which might be expended by them under their guaranties for the Austrian loans. *Corp. For. Bondh. Rep.*, No. 65 (1938), p. 45. Since September, 1939, Great Britain, France and certain other countries have made payments on the Austrian loans in fulfillment of their guaranty. See *idem*, No. 75 (1948), pp. 13 f. The British claims

vidual bondholder is in the nature of a pecuniary obligation: he agrees to pay a certain sum of money upon default by the debtor. Nothing more is promised. The creditor, in particular, may not ask the guarantor to exercise political pressure upon the recalcitrant debtor nor to interfere with the latter's fiscal administration on his behalf.[25] The use of the political power of a state cannot be made the subject of a contract with private individuals. Intervention in the internal affairs of another state is a privilege granted in certain circumstances by international law but never becomes a duty to be exercised at the behest of private individuals.

The claim of the creditors against the guarantor for payment is based on the bond, not on the legislative act required by the constitution of some countries to authorize or sanction the assumption by the state of a new pecuniary obligation.[26] The intention of the guarantor to make the debt of the borrower his own obligation and to enter into direct legal relationships with the creditors is sometimes clearly expressed by certain acts of the guarantor. Thus, the bonds of the Turkish guaranteed loan of 1855 and of the Egyptian guaranteed loan of 1885 were quoted among British funds in the official list of the stock exchange.[27] In the case of the Austrian loan of 1923, the guaranteeing powers deposited their own bonds with the National Bank of Switzerland in the names of the trustees of the loan. It was furthermore provided that in the event of the Austrian Government's defaulting on its obligations, these bonds should, at the instance of the trustees and without any action on the part of the bondholders, become immediately payable by each of the guaranteeing governments to the extent provided by its guaranty.[28] In the absence of such

for reimbursement by Germany, resulting from the Anglo-German transfer agreement of July 1, 1938, and the supplementary agreement of August 12, 1938, remain, however, unadjusted. *Idem*, p. 35.

25. Meyer Balding, *op. cit.*, p. 413, and Fournée, *op. cit.*, p. 72, n. 1. Both hold the contrary view.

26. French law of April 24, 1838, concerning the guaranty of the Greek loan of 1833. Jèze, *La Garantie des emprunts publics d'état*, p. 55. Acts of the guaranteeing states concerning the Egyptian loan of 1885. II, 620. Acts of the guaranteeing states concerning the Austrian loans of 1923 and 1933, Plesch and Domke, *op. cit.*, p. 78, in particular, French act of December 31, 1922, to authorize the Government to guarantee a loan issued by the Austrian Government. *Journal Officiel*, January 1, 1923 (*Jour. du Droit Int.* [1923], 734). The Austrian Loan Guarantee Act, 1933. 23 & 24 Geo. 5, c. 5. (*The Law Reports, 1933, The Public General Acts*, p. 10).

27. *Corp. For. Bondh. Rep.*, No. 56 (1929), p. 355.

28. This was done in order to give the guaranty a commercial form, capable of being utilized at short notice. League Study Committee, Doc. I.L. 45 (September 2, 1937), p. 7. By thus commercializing the guaranty obligation, the guarantor governments, moreover, intended to make sure that the individual guarantor could not invoke its right of immunity from suit in case the promise became due

clauses providing for the automatic operation of the guaranty, the enforcement of the claim of the creditors against the guaranteeing government is governed by the latter's municipal law. While the government may not deny the existence of its direct liability toward the bondholders, an action against it is otherwise subject to all the limitations and restrictions imposed by the public law of the guaranteeing state on suits of this nature.[29]

RELATIONS AMONG SEVERAL GUARANTORS

As previously noted, the guaranty of the foreign loans of a state is invariably based on political motives. The participation of more than one state on the guarantor's side raises the question as to the respective shares of the various guaranteeing powers in the liability for the debt. The guarantors usually undertake to answer for the principal debt "jointly and severally."[30] This, however, does not always mean that every one of them promises to be liable for the entire debt, relying for reimbursement on the right to contribution from his coguarantors. Russia, although a joint and several guarantor for the Egyptian loan of 1885, expressly declared that in no case would she be bound beyond the amount of one sixth of the guaranteed interest.[31] Similarly, the procedure devised for the implementation of the guaranty in the case of the Turkish loan of 1855 shows that each of the two guaranteeing powers was liable for only half of the guaranteed debt.[32] The division of liability into shares

---

and thereby increase the liability of its coguarantors. Plesch and Domke, *op. cit.*, p. 80. See also *idem*, p. 84, the quotation of a letter by the Austrian Government to Morgan & Co., of May 26, 1923, wherein it is stated that the collateral bonds of the guarantors are payable like any other government obligation, e.g., Treasury bonds, and that no action by the bondholders is required to make the guaranty operative.

29. Jèze, *Rec. des Cours*, VII, 177 ff. He maintains that the legal duty of the guaranteeing government to pay results from a diplomatic convention or governmental act (*acte de gouvernement*) which is not cognizable either by the ordinary courts or by administrative tribunals under the present doctrine of the French law. This view, however, disregards the fact that the claim of the creditor against the guarantor, like that against the principal debtor, is based upon the loan contract, which is not in the nature of an *acte de gouvernement* in the technical sense of the term.

30. See the Turkish loan guaranty of 1855, *idem*, p. 206, and II, 395; Egyptian guaranty of 1885, *idem*, p. 193; Greek guaranty of 1898, *idem*, p. 195, and II, 317.

31. Russian declaration of March 18, 1885 (*Brit. & For. St. Pap.*, LXXVI [1885], 350). See also Meyer Balding, *op. cit.*, p. 421.

32. In the Declaration of London of July 27, 1855 (*Brit. & For. St. Pap.*, XLV [1855], 20), Great Britain and France agreed that: "in the event of the Turkish Government failing, in the whole or in part, so to remit the amount of the half-year's interest [on the loan], the British Government shall advance the amount

is sometimes regulated by the treaty of guaranty, as in the case of the Greek loan of 1833 [33] and the Austrian loans of 1923 and 1933.[34] While in respect of the Greek loan and the Austrian loan of 1933–53 each of the guaranteeing states assumed responsibility only to the extent of the *tranches* issued within their respective countries,[35] the percentage assigned to the guarantors under the scheme of the Austrian loan of 1923

which may be necessary to enable the Bank of England to pay the said interest at the appointed time; that the British Government shall then transmit to the French Government an account of the amount so advanced; and that the French Government, on its part, shall immediately remit to the British Government the half of such amount; it being understood that any sums so advanced by the British and French Governments shall be proportionally repaid to them out of any funds which may be remitted by the Turkish Government to the British Government."

33. II, 290, 292. Each of the guaranteeing governments was liable for one third of the guaranteed sums.

34. Interest, principal, and redemption payments of the Austrian Government guaranteed loan of 1923 were guaranteed by the following countries in the proportion stated:

					%
Great Britain	to	the	extent	of	24.5
France	"	"	"	"	24.5
Czechoslovakia	"	"	"	"	24.5
Italy	"	"	"	"	20.5
Belgium	"	"	"	"	2.0
Sweden	"	"	"	"	2.0
Denmark	"	"	"	"	1.0
Holland	"	"	"	"	1.0

This guaranty was maintained by these countries in the same manner for the Austrian guaranteed conversion loan of 1934, which was issued for the purpose of providing for the redemption of the loan of 1923. The Austrian Government international guaranteed loan 1933–53 was guaranteed by Great Britain, France, Italy, Belgium, Switzerland, and Holland. Each of the guarantors was liable only for the *tranches* issued in their respective countries. Article II of the so-called "Austrian Protocol" signed at Geneva on July 15, 1932, between Austria, Great Britain, France, Italy, and Belgium (text: *British Law Reports* [*1933*]. *The Public General Acts*, p. 11 ff.; *Austrian Federal Law Gazette*, 1933, No. 12) provided: "There will be no joint guarantee as between the Governments. Each Government shall be responsible solely for the share in the total operation which it is to guarantee or to provide. No guarantor government will be liable for the service or the repayment of a bond of the loan not included in the portion guaranteed by it. As regards the public issues, the Austrian Government will prepare separate bonds for the portions of the loan issued in each country, specifically stating which Government is the guarantor." The portion (630,000,000 crowns less 585,000,000 guaranteed) not guaranteed, was chiefly an advance from the Swiss Government of 20,000,000 and the Spanish *tranche*. *The Problem of International Investment*, p. 241.

35. Jèze, *La Garantie des emprunts publics d'état*, p. 53.

had no relation to the amounts floated by bankers of the various states which participated in the issue.[36]

VALUE OF GUARANTIES

Whenever in the past the guaranty obligation has arisen, the guarantors themselves have either paid the amounts due on the service of the loan [37] or forced the debtor, as in the case of the seizure of the revenues from Cyprus by Great Britain in 1881 for the payment of the Turkish loan of 1855, to apply certain funds to the fulfillment of his obligations.[38] In addition, guaranteed loans have shown a greater stability and resistance to reduction in readjustment procedures than other state debts.[39] The record presented by the few examples of guaranteed loans fully justifies the confidence placed by their subscribers in this type of security device for governmental borrowing.

36. Jèze, *Rec. des Cours*, VII, 198 f.; Jèze, *La Garantie des emprunts publics d'état*, p. 74.

37. As in the case of the Greek guaranteed loan of 1833. See II, 291, n. 24.

38. II, 441–42.

39. The Turkish guaranteed loan was not included in the debt reduction under the Turkish agreement of 1881. II, 444. By Egyptian decree of November 28, 1904, the guaranteed loan was to continue to be regularly amortized by sinking fund, while the preference and unified debt sinking funds were to be discontinued for several years. II, 627.

PART III

The Default on Government Loans

Section IX

CONCEPTION OF STATE INSOLVENCY

"INSOLVENCY"

STATE insolvency may be defined as the condition of affairs when the state or its government fails to perform its financial obligations to its creditors, by nonpayment in whole or in part of interest, principal, or sinking fund.[1] The reasons for the nonpayment, inability, or unwillingness do not change the fact, although they may affect the remedy and the consequences in international law. A government may default in good faith through sheer inability to perform or default in bad faith when ability is present. But it has not always been possible for the bondholders to feel assured into which of these two

1. Lehr, for example, in *Handwörterbuch der Staatswissenschaften* (1st ed. Jena, 1893), says: "When a government, with or without express declaration, openly or tacitly fails to fulfill its obligations toward its creditors, we speak of a state bankruptcy." Pflug, in his work *Der Staatsbankrott und internationales Recht*, p. 1, says: "State bankruptcy is the refusal of a state to pay its legally undoubted money obligations toward private persons, whether this be caused by inability or unwillingness, or both." Wuarin, *Essai sur les emprunts d'états*, p. 62, says: "The bankruptcy of a state, from a legal point of view, consists in the official declaration, by law or decree, of the non-performance by the state of its obligations on its public debt, whether the violation of the rights of its creditors proceed from the insolvency of the state or from its unwillingness to pay." Von Heckel, in his *Lehrbuch der Finanzwissenschaft*, p. 450, says: "State bankruptcy is present whenever a state violates the rights of its creditors, with or without express declaration, by failing in whole or in part to perform its obligations as a debtor." Von Heckel, "Staatsschulden," *Handwörterbuch der Staatswissenschaften* (3d ed. Jena, 1911), VII, 764; Lotz, *idem* (4th ed. Jena, 1926), VII, 811; Terhalle, "Staatsbankrott," *Staatslexikon* (Freiburg, 1931), IV, 1855: "State bankruptcy is the non-performance of an obligation, resulting from the credit transaction of a State, to pay interest or redeem the principal." Bosch, *De Staatsschulden in het internationaal Recht*, p. 88, says, too broadly: "A breach on the part of the State of the contract with its creditors is called state bankruptcy." According to Körner, *Staatsschuldentilgung und Staatsbankrott* (Wien, 1893), pp. 75 ff., "the non-performance, on the part of the State, of obligations arising out of debts is a violation of the rights of the creditors . . . . According to private-law analogy, such violation is called state bankruptcy." Cf. Schoo, *Régimen jurídico*, pp. 347 ff.

categories a particular default fell, for the unwillingness was usually accompanied by a plea of disability.[2] The investigations of the Financial Committee of the League of Nations into the financial situation of countries which, in recent years, defaulted on League loans [3] illustrated the value and importance of an authorized procedure for deciding the issue impartially.

"DEFAULT"

Nor is default easy to define precisely.[4] Any departure from the terms of the loan contract would be a breach of contract but some, such as a payment at a place different from that agreed on or a payment in different currency or a substitution of security, may not result in material damage to the bondholder. In other cases debtor and creditor may on request of the debtor modify the terms of the contract without stopping payment. In still other cases, now common, part payment may be offered and sometimes accepted voluntarily or reluctantly or under duress of circumstances. In other cases there may be a payment in domestic cur-

2. See Gantenbein, *Financial Questions in United States Foreign Policy*, pp. 168 ff., with respect to reasons for default advanced by Latin American governments. See also H. C. Wallich, "The Future of Latin American Dollar Bonds," *Am. Econ. Rev.*, XXXIII (June, 1943), 321.

3. See e.g., II, 352–353, and 564 ff.

4. See the opinion of the Attorney General of the United States upon the Act to Prohibit Financial Transactions with Any Foreign Government in Default on Its Obligations to the United States, *Am. Jour. Int. Law*, XXIX (1935), 160 f., at 164: ". . . in general it may be said, in the words of the statute, that a 'foreign government, political subdivision, organization or association is in default' if it has failed 'in the payment of its obligations, or any part thereof, to the Government of the United States,' according to its promise or undertaking to pay a fixed amount at a definite time, unless such default has been postponed or waived in some competent manner or by a transaction having that effect in law or good morals." According to Jèze, "Les Défaillances d'état," *Rec. des Cours*, LIII (1935), 382, default exists in all cases where a state violates its obligations. Depending upon the seriousness of the default, one distinguishes between insolvency and bankruptcy. *Halsbury's Laws of England* (2d ed. London, 1935), XVI: "The word 'default' . . . apart from its statutory signification, is a purely relative term, just like negligence, meaning nothing more, nothing less, than not doing what is reasonable under the circumstances, not doing something which one ought to do, having regard to the relations which he occupies towards other persons interested in a particular transaction." See also Madden and Nadler, *Foreign Securities*, pp. 239 ff., 263. As to the question whether a government which has made small token payments on its debt can be said to be in default, see the debate in the House of Representatives, April 4, 1934, on the occasion of the adoption of the Johnson Act, *Cong. Rec.*, LXXVIII, 73d Cong., 2d Sess., 6048–6057. It appears that the term "default" was held not to be applicable in those cases.

rency into the creditor's account, as in Germany, but a prohibition of transfer or refusal to supply the necessary foreign exchange to convert the local into a foreign currency, or a permission to use the currency for certain purposes only, as in the case of the Standstill Agreements with Germany after 1932 and the successive debt readjustments with Greece and Bulgaria. In still other cases there may be a complete cessation of payments, with or without express declaration or explanation.[5] In all these cases there is some degree of default in the purpose of the contract but there are manifestly great differences in the various types and in the loss or disadvantage suffered by the bondholder. The word "default" therefore is not very different from the word "breach" and fails to describe the character of the default or its consequences, factual or legal. And, obviously, not every default or breach in the terms of the contract is an admission of insolvency.

"BANKRUPTCY"

The term "insolvency" has no precise legal connotations and is descriptive only. Even less appropriate, therefore, is the favorite Continental descriptive term "bankruptcy," which in private law conveys to the mind an impression of a recognized legal institution, with a fairly precise code of municipal rules for the administration and disposition of the debtor's estate. Such conceptions or provisions are totally lacking in the case of states, so that the use of the term "bankruptcy" is decidedly loose if not metaphorical. It is in fact a term of opprobrium and was prohibited by the French National Assembly in 1789 when they issued a decree "placing the creditors of the state from now on under the protection of the honor and loyalty of the French nation"[6] and not long thereafter issued the famous or infamous assignats practically wiping out the public debt and the credit of France.

Before 1914, when public debts enjoyed a prestige and moral sanction not now prevalent, state insolvency was regarded as a weakness if not delinquency of feeble and impecunious states only, the victims of internal mismanagement or corruption. It was overlooked that even in the nineteenth century war and revolution had played havoc with the finances of many states. As late as 1907, perhaps still a relatively tranquil period, a Dutch writer felt justified in saying:

In point of fact, bankruptcy is more fatal than war. A war may be just; bankruptcy never. It adds moral injury to the material loss. The violation,

5. Cf. *The Problem of International Investment*, p. 298.
6. Denais, "Banqueroute des collectivités publiques," *Dictionnaire de Sociologie*, III (Paris, 1936), 258. Manes, *Staatsbankrotte*, pp. 16, 23, 37, 79.

committed from so high an authority, of other people's property rights strikes a blow at the conception of property among all classes of society; one of the fundamental bases of internal order is destroyed.[7]

It has been denied that a state can in theory become insolvent, because it has an unlimited taxing power, even to the point of levying a capital tax, and that it may even alienate a part of its public domain for the benefit of creditors. Practice belies the theory. Most states prefer not to take the hard road, and the frequency of the practice of default has taken away some of its moral opprobrium. At all events, the depth of the financial morass in which many weak states found themselves even before 1914 and the devastating consequences of two world wars and the economic collapse which intervened, have indicated that taxation has both economic and political limits of feasibility and that alienation of territory will never be voluntarily undertaken. The insolvency of weak states may give rise to various forms of political intervention by states whose nationals have suffered and the reasons may not be exclusively financial protection of the creditors, as in the case of Egypt. And creditors may have to or may prefer to consent to a readjustment of the debt to minimize their losses or may themselves through creditor organizations institute a form of receivership in which they may participate in the financial administration of the debtor country and collect for themselves a part of the revenues, as in the cases of Egypt, Turkey, Greece, Nicaragua, Haiti, and Santo Domingo. A later section will discuss the various methods of financial control which creditors have exercised for their protection in these countries.[8]

INTERNATIONAL RESPONSIBILITY

In considering the legal consequences of default in international law, some writers maintain that the failure by a state to fulfill its contractual obligations amounts to an international delinquency, entailing the legal responsibility of the defaulter. They either assimilate the loan contract

7. Von Daehne van Varick, *Le Droit financier international*, p. 4. He also thought that bankruptcy was a scourge analogous to martial law in war time and that the protection of private property against bankruptcy would be as beneficial as the protection against the devastation of war. In neither case did he indicate how this desirable aim was to be accomplished, except by reducing the principal of state loans. He also thought that bankruptcy breeds burdensome military expenses and in part accounted for Europe's state of armed peace in 1907 (*idem*, p. 5).

8. See *infra*, section on Bondholders' Control.

to an international treaty, the breach of which automatically involves an international wrong,[9] or they regard the nonperformance of public debt obligations as an illegal confiscation of the rights of foreigners, making the wrongdoer liable under international law.[10] Besides misconstruing the loan contract as an international agreement which presupposes the participation of states on both sides of the transaction,[11] the broad statement that any kind of default constitutes an international wrong is neither sound in law nor borne out by the diplomatic practice of states. A distinction has to be made as to the nature of the default. Only acts which purport to wipe out the obligation permanently and in its entirety, such as repudiation or cancellation, may be classified as confiscatory and contrary to international law, regardless of the reasons advanced by the guilty state in justification of the measure.[12] In view of

9. See Schmitthoff, "The International Government Loan," *Jour. Comp. Leg.*, (1937), 184 f., quoting with approval Sir John Fischer Williams.

10. See F. K. Nielsen, *International Law Applied to Reclamations* (Washington, J. Byrne & Co., 1933), pp. 35, 37: "These principles relating to confiscation seem clearly to be applicable to contractual arrangements when a government obtains loans from private alien sources and later defaults in payment . . . it would appear obviously proper to take account of the sanctity which the law of nations attaches to international covenants. A violation of a treaty is a violation of international law . . . . When the [Permanent] Court [of International Justice, in the case of the Serbian and Brazilian loans] found that adequate payment was not made in satisfaction of these loans, it would seem that it might properly have held that there was confiscation to the extent of the inadequacy."

11. See *supra,* section on the Legal Nature of the Loan Contract. See also Nussbaum, *Money in the Law,* pp. 402 f.; Lippert, "Internationales Finanzrecht," in Strupp, ed., *Wörterbuch des Völkerrechts* (Berlin, 1929), III, 918; Schmitthoff, *op. cit.,* p. 183.

12. This question was among the subjects of discussion submitted to the Conference for the Codification of International Law under the auspices of the League of Nations in 1930 at The Hague, but not considered by the Conference. The Bases of Discussion, No. 4, drawn from the replies made by various governments to the question whether a state becomes responsible by repudiating its debts, stated that a state "incurs responsibility if, by a legislative act, it repudiates or purports to cancel debts for which it is liable." League of Nations, *Conference for the Codification of International Law. Bases of Discussion.* Vol. III. L. of N. Publications, V. Questions Juridiques. 1929. V. 3, p. 40. The committee of experts, at whose request the replies were made, observed that "examination of the replies suggests that a distinction ought to be drawn between repudiation pure and simple and legislation suspending or modifying the service of a debt; as regards the first, a reservation for the case of financial distress appears superfluous, since that ground could not justify final repudiation of the debt." *Idem,* p. 40. See, in particular, the reply of the Swiss Government, *idem,* pp. 39 f.: "The repudiation of debts is a typical instance of the violation of acquired rights. It involves the responsibility of the States even if the latter, in contracting them, has not acted *jure imperii* but *jure gestionis,* i.e., in the capacity of a private person." See also Isidoro Ruiz

the character of the state as a permanent organization, financial distress, however serious, is no valid excuse for complete cancellation of foreign debts. Nor does a change of its regime free a state from previous engagements; [13] even where a state loses its personality by annexation or incorporation into another state, the successor is bound by the debts incurred by the former.

The situation, however, is different if the debtor state, without repudiating its debt, temporarily suspends the service payments or in some other way defaults on its obligations. The international liability of the state in such a case is involved only if the failure to pay is accompanied by some act violative of the international standard of treatment due to foreigners, such as arbitrary or discriminatory treatment or denial of justice.[14] But if the default results from a situation beyond the debtor's control, no cause for complaint on the part of the creditors exists and, consequently, no claim in international law may be advanced by the governments of the injured creditors on their behalf.[15]

Moreno, *Economia y finanzas contemporaneas* (Buenos Aires, 1938), p. 221; SEC, *Rep.*, Pt. V, p. 26. The claim frequently advanced by governments that the violation of domestic rules concerning the contracting of external loans affords a valid reason for denying the binding character of the contract has no foundation in law. See the Note of the Secretary of State to the Minister in Bolivia with respect to the contract of the Bolivian Government of 1922 for a loan from American bankers, of April 9, 1923, *For. Rel.*, 1923, I, 443 f.: "Setting aside the question of the legality of the loan, the Department would direct attention to the fact that the Bolivian Government, after having accepted and used the proceeds of the loan seem to be estopped from asserting now that the loan was illegal." The exposé prepared for the Council of Foreign Bondholders in the matter of Greek external loans (II, 306 n. 41) stated: "According to International Law principles all contracts made by a Government on the faith of laws promulgated by the Parliament and then published in the Law Gazette cannot be contested on the ground of a technical mistake in the form of publication." With respect to attempts by the Cuban Government to deny liability for loans contracted by former President Machado allegedly contrary to the Constitution, see *For. Bondh. Prot. Coun. Rep.*, 1934, p. 54. According to a report to *The New York Times* of January 20, 1931, from Bolivia, the general opinion of the country with respect to certain loans contracted by former governments without obtaining Congressional authorization required by the Constitution was that even obligations thus illegally contracted had to be met.

13. See *infra*, section on State Succession.

14. See Strupp, "L'Intervention en matière financière," *Rec. des Cours*, VIII (1925), 68.

15. Permanent Court of Arbitration, Award of November 11, 1912, the Russian indemnity case (*Russia* v. *Turkey*), in Scott, *The Hague Court Reports*, 1916, p. 317: "The exception of *force majeure* . . . may be pleaded in opposition in public as well as in private international law . . . . It is incontestable that the

PRIVATE AND PUBLIC INSOLVENCY

It is obvious that state insolvency or bankruptcy differs materially from the private law insolvency or bankruptcy from which it has taken its name. The private law insolvency is established by definitely determined facts and results either in a composition with creditors or in a judicial proceeding resulting in a decree which authorizes the creditors to liquidate the assets of the bankrupt and pay the debts so far as possible. In state insolvency or bankruptcy, there is no judicial proceeding resulting in a decree. There is no sale of the assets of the insolvent state. Indeed, the state must go on; [16] and, in the absence of political interven-

Sublime Porte proves by means of the exception of *force majeure* . . . that Turkey was, from 1881 to 1902, . . . placed in a position where it could meet its engagements only with delay and postponements, and even then at great sacrifice." See also draft convention submitted by Isidoro Ruiz Moreno to the American Institute of International Law, Session of Montevideo, March, 1927 (Moreno, *op. cit.*, p. 222). He remarks, however, that a state which pleads the exception of *force majeure* to justify suspension of the service of a loan should, within three months from the date of the suspension, offer to its creditors a plan for readjustment, or, failing such action, should ask for international financial assistance. Furthermore, Bases of Discussion, No. 4, submitted to The Hague Codification Conference (*supra*, n. 12): "A State incurs responsibility if, without repudiating a debt, it suspends or modifies the service, in whole or in part, by a legislative act, unless it is driven to this course by financial necessity." Jèze, *Rec. des Cours*, LIII (1935), 391: "A Government is entitled to suspend or reduce the service of its public debts whenever it appears that essential public services would be impaired or neglected by the fulfillment of those obligations. In other words, the public debt is not a service to be satisfied preferentially." The scarcity of foreign exchange, caused by inevitable economic conditions, is frequently advanced in excuse for the failure to transfer the debt service abroad. See *infra*, section on Transfer Default. A debtor in transfer default, however, should continue to show the full debt service in his budget in local currency. See article by Sir Austen Chamberlain on "The League Loans," January 19, 1934 (League Loans Committee, *Second Annual Report* [June, 1934], p. 25). Acts by third states may create valid reasons for default. Orders freezing accounts held by the German and other governments in the United States made it impossible for these governments to continue making payments on their bonds in the United States out of those funds. "Axis Debtors and American Creditors," *Com. and Fin. Chron.*, CLIV (1941), 818. The payment of only the nominal, not the gold value of the interest due on the Dawes and Young loans in disregard of the gold and *pari passu* clauses of the loans was justified by the German Government as a measure of reprisal against those states which had given up the gold standard and had failed to recognize gold clauses in private contracts, thereby violating interests of German nationals. See the decision of the Swiss Federal Court in the case of *Obligationsinteressenter* v. *The Bank for International Settlements*, May 26, 1936, *Die Praxis des Bundesgerichts*, XXV, 335 f.

16. "The property of a State is not subject to proceedings of the nature of sequestration or seizure. Any such process would be inconsistent with the con-

tion, the state usually effects a composition with its creditors. In private law, bankruptcy may constitute a penal offense subjecting the bankrupt to the jurisdiction of the criminal courts. In the case of a state, the inability or unwillingness to pay has no criminal connotations in spite of the fact that the insolvency may have been the result of the grossest mismanagement. In the case of a private concern, the reason for insolvency is almost exclusively inability to pay. In the case of a state, the nonpayment may result from either inability or unwillingness to pay. In the case of an insolvent individual who goes into bankruptcy, all his property, with trifling exceptions, becomes subject to attachment and sale for the benefit of creditors; in the case of a private corporation, all the property may be sold. The state is subject to no judicial forum, cannot be compelled to pay, except through the need for credit or through diplomatic political pressure, and its assets are not at the disposal of its unpaid creditors. For economic, political, or moral reasons, a defaulting state usually endeavors to effect a composition with its creditors in order that its credit and reputation may not too greatly suffer.[17]

tinued existence of the State as an independent community. It is obvious therefore that it is impossible to apply to States the procedure of bankruptcy as it is applied to individuals or societies." *The Venezuelan Arbitration before The Hague Tribunal, 1903*, S. Doc. No. 119, 58th Cong., 3d Sess., Case of Italy, p. 858. "International law knows no such procedure as bankruptcy of a nation, nor does it provide any machinery by which the assets of an insolvent State can be administered or distributed among creditors. Indeed, any such procedure must necessarily be incompatible with the continued existence of the insolvent State as an independent sovereign State." Counter Case of Great Britain, *idem*, p. 977. See also Schwarzenberger, *Die Kreuger-Anleihen* (Munich, 1931), pp. 30 f.: A state cannot, like a private corporation, discontinue its operations and assign its assets to the creditors for the purpose of liquidation. The only common feature that exists in the case of bankruptcy of a private individual and of a state lies in the fact that both fail to fulfill their obligations because of inability to pay.

17. Wuarin, *op. cit.*, p. 60; Meili, *Der Staatsbankerott und die moderne Rechtswissenschaft*, pp. 11 ff.; Manes, *op. cit.*, pp. 17–23; Lauterpacht, *Private Law Sources and Analogies of International Law*, pp. 253, 256.

Section X

TYPES OF STATE INSOLVENCY

CLASSIFICATIONS

STATE insolvency may take various forms, some mild, some drastic; it may be open and acknowledged or disguised, such as devaluation of the currency or unit of payment; it may relate only to interest, principal, or sinking fund, or to some or all of these in combination; it may be in good faith or bad, unavoidable or willful; it may be formally acknowledged by legislation or be undeclared and left to inference. It may involve discrimination among different creditors or among different groups of creditors, nationals or foreigners, or among foreigners of different nationality.[1] It may involve discrimination between large and small bondholders, between holders of the floating debt and long-term bondholders, between secured and unsecured creditors, according to or in violation of the terms of the loan.[2]

The types of state insolvency have been classified as follows:[3]

1. As in the case of Germany, which claimed in 1933 that its favorable trade balance with Holland and Switzerland enabled the Reich to treat bondholders of those countries more favorably than American bondholders. See Charles R. S. Harris, *Germany's Foreign Indebtedness* (London, Oxford University Press, 1935), p. 53.

2. Cf. Manes, *Staatsbankerotte*, pp. 25 ff.; Bosch, *De Staatsschulden in het internationaal Recht*, pp. 89 ff.; Denais, "Banqueroute des collectivités publiques," *Dictionnaire de Sociologies*, III, 258; Von Daehne van Varick, *Le Droit financier international*, p. 11; Von Heckel, "Staatsschulden," *Handwörterbuch der Staatswissenschaften*, VII, 765; Terhalle, "Staatsbankrott," *Staatslexikon*, IV, 1856; Jèze, "Les Défaillances d'état," *Rec. des Cours*, LIII (1935), 381 ff.; Schoo, *Régimen jurídico*, pp. 343 ff.

3. For other classifications of the types of state insolvency, see Madden and Nadler, *Foreign Securities*, pp. 264 ff., who distinguish between defaults as to interest (suspension of interest; reduction of interest without consent of the lender; cancellation of interest and agreement to pay principal only; imposing of new coupon taxes which reduce the interest on the loan) and defaults as to principal (forced conversion of loan without consent of the lender; suspension of amortization charges; alienation of pledged revenues; compulsory prolongation of a loan that has matured). Körner, *Staatsschuldentilgung und Staatsbankrott*, pp. 80, 87: state bankruptcy may be divided into (1) the total nonperformance of (a) the obligation to pay the principal, (b) the duty to pay interest, or (c) of both duties

1. Nonpayment of interest—by reducing the rate,[4] by postponing

simultaneously; (2) the partial nonperformance of the obligations mentioned under (a), (b), (c). Jèze, *loc. cit.*, says: "History affords many examples of States failing to fulfil their engagements. Thus, States may suspend the payment of interest or sinking fund; they may perform their obligations in a currency different from the one stipulated in the contract; or they divert revenues assigned for the service of the debt to other purposes." Feilchenfeld, in Quindry, *Bonds and Bond-holders, Rights and Remedies*, Vol. II, sec. 647, distinguishes between default, quasi confiscatory measures, confiscation and repudiation, voiding. Winkler, "Defaults and Repudiation of Foreign Loans," *Foreign Policy Association, Information Service*, August 3, 1928, IV, 235, enumerates the following forms of government default: (1) reduction of the rate of interest; (2) delay in the payment of interest; (3) suspension of payment of interest; (4) reduction in the rate of interest through the levy (subsequent to the flotation of the loan) of taxes upon the rate of interest agreed upon; (5) delay in payment of principal; (6) forced conversion of loans; (7) reduction in the principal amount of the loan; (8) payment of "gold" loans in depreciated currency; (9) reduction in the amount of sinking fund payments; (10) suspension of sinking fund; (11) reduction of both interest and sinking fund; (12) repudiation of both interest and principal.

4. This occurred in the case of Greece after 1893, which for many years paid only 30% of its coupon interest; and Portugal, which, after 1891, reduced its interest payments for a number of years by two thirds. See II, 307, and 371.

The South American countries are prolific in instances of this type. Under this heading might be included the payment of interest in promissory notes instead of in cash—a typical example of which is the Turkish default of 1875, after which Turkey for five years resolved to pay one half of its interest in cash and to give 5% notes for the other half. Even this undertaking was not carried out, for in 1876 a complete insolvency took place and coupons were no longer paid.

Argentina in 1891 paid part of the interest in cash, part in new bonds, funding the interest on certain external bonds for the years 1891–93. *Corp. For. Bondh. Rep.*, No. 20 (1892), pp. 16 ff. This also happened in Spain, 1872. In Nicaragua, in 1895 settlement, interest was reduced from 6% to 4% and coupons in arrears exchanged for certificates at 50% of face value. *Idem*, No. 23 (1895), pp. 234–237. In Haiti, interest in arrears on internal debt was scaled in 1922 from 5% to 25% and paid. *Report of the American High Commissioner*, January 1, 1923, p. 3. In Santo Domingo, interest on the Westendorp loans was reduced from 6% to 4%. II, 213.

The question whether the reduction of the rate of interest constitutes a form of bankruptcy was much discussed at the beginning of the nineteenth century. See Körner, *op. cit.*, pp. 87 ff., who answers the question in the affirmative, quoting from the debates in the Austrian Parliament of June 4, 1868, the remark of the Deputy von Mende: "The Majority expects the Government to reduce the rate of interest, in other words, to proclaim the bankruptcy of the State. As far as I am concerned, I consider the reduction of the interest as contrary to the law." The minutes of the proceedings in the French Chamber of Deputies at the beginning of the nineteenth century offer an interesting picture of the various opinions on the subject. On the one hand, it was asserted that the state has an unconditional right to reduce its debts at its discretion; on the other hand, the measure of reducing the interest was assailed in an equally uncompromising manner and was called a case of state bankruptcy. However, if the creditor is offered redemp-

the payment for a period,[5] by complete and indefinite suspension of interest payments,[6] by reduction of the coupon interest by a special tax on the coupons in breach of the contract. [7]

---

tion of the principal before the rate of interest has been reduced, the state merely exercises a right without hurting anybody. *Idem*, p. 87.

5. This has not been an uncommon practice, for war and revolution have placed many states in temporary default, requiring postponement in payments. Cf. Schoo, *op. cit.*, p. 365.

When Holland became independent the debt amounted to 1,253,500,000 florins. To avoid a complete breakdown, the Government decided in 1802 to pay interest on one third of the debt, deferring interest on the remaining two thirds. It was to begin with no interest but by the gradual drawing of lots convert the unpaid part into an interest-bearing debt. An equal amount of the first third was to be redeemed. Bosch, *op. cit.*, p. 90. This was carried out, and in 1814 payment on the full debt was resumed.

6. An example of this form of default will be found in the Spanish insolvencies of 1820, 1834, 1851, and 1867. These defaults were made good only in part, when refunding or reorganization or consolidation of loans, helped by a new loan, was undertaken. In 1834, for example, Spain declared that one third of its foreign debt would be considered as not subject to payment of interest, whereas the other two thirds were to be subjected to compulsory conversion into new 5% bonds. Even on these, interest was defaulted. Greece, after 1827, completely defaulted on interest for nearly 50 years. Argentina paid interest on its first loan from 1825 to 1829 but then remained in default of interest from 1829 to 1857. In 1890 an agreement with the Bank of England provided for a partial payment of the defaulted interest. Mexico, which effected its first loan in 1825 in Europe, suspended payment of interest in 1827, resumed in 1836, suspended in 1846, resumed in 1850, suspended from 1859 to 1863, and in 1886 entered into an agreement with its creditors to pay, after 1889, 3% interest. Mexico in 1942 agreed to pay about 1% on interest accrued from 1922. San Salvador suspended interest from 1828 to 1859; Guatemala from 1828 to 1855; Ecuador from 1834 to 1854 and from 1868 to 1899. Since 1931 many of the Latin American and some European countries have suspended the payment of interest, in whole or in part. The Foreign Bondholders Protective Council in its 1934 report lists 197 issues of foreign bonds payable in dollars which were in complete or partial default, either as to interest or sinking fund or both. 182 of these issues, it is said, were sold to the public since 1920. Most of them bore interest rates from 6% to 8%. SEC, *Rep.*, Pt. V, p. 7.

7. Obviously, not every tax on coupons can be regarded as the result of insolvency. Where the coupon, however, is tax exempt by contract, such tax constitutes a violation of the obligation to pay interest. An example of this type of unlawful reduction of coupon interest was the Austrian coupon tax of 1868, after the union with Hungary, when a coupon tax of 16% was levied on the "consolidated state *rente*," thus reducing the rate of interest from 5% to 4.2%. Although it affected foreigners and nationals alike, France protested the tax on behalf of French nationals. Aegidi and Klauhold, eds., *Das Staatsarchiv*, LV (Leipzig, Duncker and Humblot, 1893), 159 ff.; Freund, *Die Rechtsverhältnisse der öffentlichen Anleihen*, p. 242; Jèze, *Cours de science des finances*, pp. 140 ff.; Wuarin, *Essai sur les emprunts d'états*, pp. 75 ff.

2. A failure to fulfill obligations as to repayment of principal, either by postponing the duty to repay,[8] by transforming the obligation into a different type, including compulsory conversion,[9] by reducing the

---

Russia in 1885 levied a 5% tax on the coupons of her internal bonds. Freund, *op. cit.*, p. 242.

Italy, from 1894 to 1906, levied a coupon tax of 20% on all bondholders, regardless of nationality. But foreign bondholders were paid in gold if they proved their foreign nationality by affidavit. By the conversion law of 1906, the tax was abolished. *Idem*, p. 243.

Spain in 1898 taxed the coupons, exempting the 4% external loan of 1882 if held by foreigners. Proof was required that no Spaniard had any interest in the bond. *Idem*, p. 243.

France in 1937 deducted 10% from the coupons of French bonds but exempted United States holders, on presentation of the bonds for stamping. *The New York Times*, September 20, 1937.

Some writers regard this practice as a form of compulsory conversion. Cf. Schoo, *op. cit.*, p. 376.

These examples of coupon taxes inspired the clauses for tax exemption of foreign holders by the borrowing state. A general income tax on all residents, native and foreign, which income might include the interest on the bonds, would probably not be deemed a violation of the exemption.

8. Such a default may occur in the failure to redeem at the time promised, the failure to draw a lottery loan at the time promised, or the failure to pay annuities. In this category one often cites the case in 1770 of Louis XV, whose Finance Minister Terray diverted to other uses for eight years funds set aside for the payment of debts. South American countries and states in federal governments, like Argentina and Brazil, have frequently suspended the payment of capital sums or failed to carry out the amortization covenants of loan contracts.

Haiti obtained the consent of the United States, which had assumed certain responsibilities to the bondholders, for a temporary suspension of amortization payments. U.S. Executive Agreement Series 117; Dept. of State, *Press Releases*, No. 434 (January 22, 1938), pp. 123–130; *idem*, No. 458 (July 9, 1938), p. 28.

9. The compulsory character of the obligation is sometimes difficult to prove, though it may well be assumed that no creditor willingly submits to a diminution of his claim. Older forms of loan contracts frequently contained a clause that a conversion was not to take place for a given number of years. Nevertheless, the practice was so common that certain writers on finance seem to have regarded a conversion as something inevitable. If creditors are given an option to take the new converted debt or payment of their old debt, there is nothing objectionable in the transaction.

One form of conversion has been the compulsory exchange of a short-term or floating debt for a permanent consol uncallable. Philip II of Spain in 1557 converted a debt of 7,000,000 ducats into permanent consols, cancelling the security on the debt and reducing the interest at the same time. In 1852 Portugal forced a conversion of the whole external debt to 3% bonds. II, 364, n. 6.

A more modern example was the conversion in 1880 of the 7% and 9% Egyptian debt into a 4% to 5% debt, at the time of the institution of financial control. In Serbia a 5% consol was converted into one of 4%. Another form of conversion

capital amount of the debt,[10] by depreciation of the prescribed standard
of payment either through devaluation, through going off a metallic

is the so-called "nationalization of bonds," namely, the conversion of bonds payable in foreign currency into bonds payable exclusively in domestic currency. See
infra, section on Readjustment.

In France, by the law of September 17, 1932, converting French *rentes* from 5%
and 6% to 4.5%, it was asserted that the time for the privilege of conversion had
been shortened. Denais, *op. cit.,* III, 259. Bosch, *op. cit.,* pp. 25, 92. Germany reduced the rate of interest on the American *tranche* of the Dawes and Young loans
from 7% and 5½% to 5% and 4%, respectively (*For. Bondh. Prot. Coun. Rep.,*
1935, p. 119), while blocking payment through transfer difficulties on most of the
other loans of German cities and corporations. *Idem,* 1937, p. 345. *For. Pol. Assn.
Bull.,* Vol. XVII (June 24, 1938), No. 35. It has been argued that the subsequent
acquiescence of the creditors makes these conversions contractual and hence
unobjectionable. This seems an evasion, because the creditors, doubtless, in the
absence of any other remedy, must perforce accept their lot. As to the probable
consequences of a creditor's adding to the debtor's burden, see Floyd F. Burt-
chett, *Investments and Investment Policy* (New York, Longmans, Green, 1938),
p. 746.

Some authorities justify compulsory conversions, when not too seriously violative of the terms of the original contract, on the ground that new conditions, such
as political, financial, or social upheavals, make it necessary to effect some new
arrangement with creditors for the benefit of the taxpayers. Cf. Wallich, "The
Future of Latin American Dollar Bonds," *Am. Econ. Rev.,* XXXIII (June, 1943),
321 at 325. These equitable considerations, they maintain, require creditors to
forego a portion of their claims in the general interest. This, however, seems a
dangerous argument and would seek to introduce into the debtor-creditor relationship something like the clause *rebus sic stantibus* in international treaties, which
assumes that treaty promises are made on the assumption of the continuance of a
certain condition of affairs.

States whose credit is good are likely to reserve the privilege of paying off the
debt before the due date, and if market conditions are satisfactory are likely to
refund the loan at a lower interest rate. Inasmuch as there is everything to gain
and nothing to lose by the reservation of this privilege, it is becoming common in
corporation practice and will probably become more common in state practice.

10. A well-known illustration is the reduction of the French debt in 1797 by the
National Assembly. After the payment of interest had been reduced to three
fourths, for which the creditors received assignments on national assets, the
principal of the debt was in 1797 reduced by the Directorate to one third of its
amount. For the other two thirds, the creditors received coupons which would be
accepted for payment if they purchased state property. These coupons sank in
value to one sixth. Holland and the Kingdom of Westphalia followed the French
example. Foreign writers occasionally cite the case of Minnesota, which, in 1858,
reduced $100,000,000 of railroad bonds to $50,000,000.

In practice in the reorganization of a bonded indebtedness or voluntary composition with creditors, some reduction in the capital of the debt is usually effected.
The Foreign Bondholders Protective Council objects in principle to such reduction in capital.

standard on to an inconvertible paper basis,[11] or through a marked inflation.

3. A reduction or repudiation of interest payments and the simultaneous reduction or repudiation of the capital debt.[12]

4. The "blocking of foreign exchange" by transfer prohibitions or licenses, with a deposit in untransferable currency of funds representing the debt charges. This amounts to retardation or suspension of payment, possibly for an indefinite period, although the debt is not repudiated nor open insolvency admitted.

Some of these types of state insolvency are examined more closely below.

11. This type of insolvency was known even in ancient Rome. In ancient times the amount of metal in the coin was debased so as to make it less valuable. In modern times, the unit of currency is depreciated or "devalued" or a promise to redeem in gold is repudiated by redeeming in paper of an arbitrary or uncertain value. Thus, under the French law of June 28, 1928, the French franc lost four fifths of its value. The devaluation may confirm an existing depreciation, as in France, or it may deliberately and suddenly depreciate or "go off gold" as in England in 1931 and the United States in 1933. From 1864 to 1879 the United States currency was not redeemable in gold. The French assignats of the French Revolution, bonds issued as currency and "secured" on state lands, became worthless. Managed currency has left the paper without a reliable basis for redemption in any fixed value. Excessive issues of paper money constitute a method of depreciating the monetary unit in which a debt is "repaid." The unit retains its character as legal tender. Germany had this experience in 1922, and the German courts, down to the time in 1923 when the currency was completely destroyed, held that "a mark is a mark." Foreign holders of German mark bonds had to bear the loss as did nationals. *Ginlini* v. *The Reich*, R.G. IV, 359/26, January 27, 1927. Mortgages, insurance policies, and other obligations were by statute revived or revalued (Aufwertung) at $12\frac{1}{2}\%$ of their face amount.

After World War I the payment in an inflated paper currency of an obligation contracted in a metal currency became common throughout many of the exbelligerent countries. It is a form of confiscation and admission of insolvency. Russia entered on such a transaction in 1839, though in Russia it affected practically only Russian creditors. This Russian affair has been characterized by writers as an intentionally fraudulent transaction, for they took silver away from the people and gave them worthless paper in its place.

Jèze, *Cours de science des finances*, p. 293; Jèze, *Rec. des Cours*, LIII, 303 ff.; Denais, *op. cit.*, III, 259; Bosch, *op. cit.*, p. 92.

12. Both types of reduction have been known in connection with a single debt. This was done in Austria in 1811, where the interest was cut in half and the capital converted into a different currency. It was also done in Egypt, Turkey, Greece, and Santo Domingo. South America offers other illustrations. In Colombia, notwithstanding a considerable gold production, foreign exchange decrees after 1932 prohibited a payment of dollar bonds. Some financial journals considered this an act of bad faith, e.g., *Financial World*, July 18, 1938.

REPUDIATION

Repudiation constitutes a refusal to admit the binding character of an obligation. The repudiation may extend to the debt as a whole, or only to some part of it or its contractual terms. Simple default, on the other hand, admits the binding character of the debt but pleads inability to meet its terms. Borrowers have, by unilateral action, reduced the burden of a debt in various ways, such as by cutting interest payments, either directly or by the imposition of a special tax on the coupons, or by paying gold debts in depreciated paper money. But as long as this action is attributed only to current inability to pay, and does not involve an actual denial of liability, it is better regarded as a default rather than as a partial repudiation.[13]

Repudiations have often followed revolutions, when the new government repudiated obligations contracted by a previous *de jure* or *de facto* government, on the allegation that the prior government had no authority to bind the nation.[14] Repudiation has, however, sometimes occurred without any antecedent revolution.[15] As a justification in such circumstances, it has usually been alleged that the loan was not contracted according to law, the defect including lack of legal authority of the officials purporting to represent the state.[16] Where in fact the loan contract is defective in law, either because there was no constitutional or legislative authority to contract the debt or because in other respects the rules of law governing a binding obligation were not observed, the repudiation may have a legal justification, and the creditor may not be deprived of any legal right, for in such cases his obligation from the beginning was not legally binding.

13. Cf., however, Shirras, *Science of Public Finance*, II, 863.

14. The outstanding example is the repudiation by the Soviet Government of the Czarist debt of some $20,000,000,000. Portugal declined to be bound by the debts contracted by Dom Miguel, 1832. Mexico declined to be bound by the debts contracted by Maximilian. In 1922 Mexico also repudiated the B, C, and D bonds of the Huerta loan of 1913. II, 68.

15. As in the case of the states of Mississippi, Florida, Alabama, North Carolina, South Carolina, Georgia, Louisiana, Arkansas, and Tennessee, which repudiated various debts around the middle of the nineteenth century. See B. Randolph, "Foreign Bondholders and the Repudiated Debts of the Southern States," *Am. Jour. Int. Law*, XXV (1931), 63; R. C. McGrane, *Foreign Bondholders and American State Debts* (New York, Macmillan, 1935); W. A. Scott, *The Repudiation of State Debts* (New York, T. Y. Crowell, 1893); P. Studenski, *Public Borrowing*, National Municipal League Monograph Series (New York, 1930).

16. This allegation was made by a number of the repudiating American states.

The debts of the unsuccessful revolution would of course not be assumed by the constituent government [17] or anyone else.[18]

TRANSFER DEFAULT AND EXCHANGE CONTROL

External government bonds are, as a rule, couched in a foreign currency and payable outside the debtor country.[19] For the proper discharge of this obligation more is, therefore, required than the mere collection of sufficient funds from domestic sources. The debtor must procure foreign money for the holder in the manner and at the place stipulated in the contract. While in the possession of sufficient funds in their own currencies, debtor countries may be unable to convert these sums into the money required by the bond because of lack of foreign exchange normally accruing to them from favorable trade balances, new loans, gold production, or other sources,[20] and during the nineteen-thirties this type of default occurred even on issues such as the League loans which were placed on the market after a thorough examination by experts of the debtors' economic and financial conditions and were provided with safeguards inspiring the highest confidence among investors.

The fact that a government's capacity to meet its external obligations is not simply a matter of internal solvency but may depend in part on

17. See Amendment XIV, sec. 4 (1868): ". . . But neither the United States nor any State shall assume or pay any debt or obligation incurred in aid of insurrection or rebellion against the United States . . . ."

18. We cannot here enter into the power of *de facto* governments to bind the state, although, in principle, it may be said that general *de facto* governments having actual control of a country are in international law its legal representatives and have authority to bind the nation.

19. See *supra*, section on Currency Clauses.

20. See Willy Feuerlein and E. Hannan, *Dollars in Latin America* (New York, Council on Foreign Relations, 1941), pp. 9 ff., 19; Herbert Feis, *The Changing Pattern of International Economic Affairs* (New York, Harper & Bros., 1940), pp. 74 ff.; Madden, Nadler, and Sauvain, *America's Experience as a Creditor Nation*, pp. 166 ff.; SEC, *Rep.*, Pt. V, pp. 292 ff.; Lewis, *America's Stake in International Investments*, pp. 403 ff. For reasons advanced by various governments in explanation for transfer defaults, see Memorandum of the German Government, delivered to the United States Secretary of State on June 15, 1934, concerning the German transfer situation and the action taken in connection therewith in regard to Germany's foreign indebtedness. Dept. of State, *Press Releases*, No. 248 (June 30, 1934), p. 436; Memorandum of the Brazilian Ministry for Foreign Affairs, May 5, 1938, *For. Bondh. Prot. Coun. Rep.*, 1938, pp. 164 ff.; Advertisement of the Republic of Uruguay in *The New York Times*, July 29, 1933; Publication of the Hungarian Government, July 1, 1932, League Loans Committee, *First Annual Report*, May, 1933, p. 42; II, 564 ff. Cf. Schoo, *op. cit.*, pp. 825 ff.

economic factors largely beyond its control calls for special treatment of the default resulting from transfer difficulties.

The debtor government may, with the consent of the creditor, be freed for a time either wholly or in part from the responsibility for transferring the debt charges into foreign currency. Such suspensions of transfers, sometimes effected unilaterally by the debtor country but generally by direct agreement between debtor and creditor,[21] were the characteristic

21. See, for example, the protocol signed on December 22, 1932, between the Romanian Government and representatives of various European bondholders' committees by which the latter agreed to recommend to their principals the suspension of the transfer of the sums necessary for the amortization service of the Romanian external debt, *Corp. For. Bondh. Rep.*, No. 59 (1932), p. 353. For instances where the League Loans Committee and the Financial Committee of the League of Nations suggested suspension of the transfer of debt service on League Loans see League Loans Committee, *First Annual Report*, p. 13 (with respect to Bulgarian loans); p. 15 (Greek loans); p. 16 (jointly with the Council of Foreign Bondholders); p. 35 (with respect to Bulgarian loans); *Fifth Annual Report*, p. 50 (with respect to Danzig loans): "The Committee are of the opinion that the Danzig Government . . . have some justification in the circumstances in asking for a measure of relief in the burden of their foreign debt service. They can see nothing to be gained by insistence on the transfer of full service until the actual moment of default; such action, in the Committee's opinion, would create a situation which might seriously endanger the bondholders' interests." See also II, 556, 564 f., 567, 568, and *Corp. For. Bondh. Rep.*, No. 66 (1939), p. 20, with respect to Brazil. Although the reparation payments due by Germany under the Dawes plan were of a different order to those payable by a debtor government to foreign private holders of its bonds, the transfer system instituted as part of the plan merits notice here.

The report of the Dawes Committee of the Reparations Commission sharply distinguished between the internal collection of the debt and its transfer abroad. With the payment of the reparations in gold marks or their equivalent in German currency into the bank of issue to the credit of the agent for reparation payments, Germany was deemed to have discharged her obligations toward her creditors. Report of the Dawes Committee, *The Experts' Plan for Reparations Payments* (Paris, Reparations Commission, 1926), p. 31. The delicate task of converting these funds into foreign currency to be transmitted abroad was entrusted to an independent international authority, the so-called "transfer committee," which was allowed to perform this operation only to such extent as seemed compatible with the maintenance of the stability of the debtor's monetary system. Fischer Williams, *Chapters on Current International Law*, p. 342; Harris, *op. cit.*, p. 15. The commission wrote: "There has been a tendency in the past to confuse two distinct though related questions, i.e., first, the amount of revenue which Germany can raise available for reparation account, and, second, the amount which can be transferred to foreign countries . . . . We propose to distinguish sharply between the two problems, and first deal with the problem of the maximum budget surplus and afterwards with the problem of payment to the Allies." *The Experts' Plan for Reparations Payments* (Paris, Reparations Commission, 1926), p. 19. The realization that internal collection and transfer abroad are two separate acts occurs

type of default during the decade preceding World War II. These transfer defaults were part of a network of restrictions on the normal international flow of trade and capital. Strict exchange control and a growing bilateralism in economic relations left creditors in some instances largely dependent on clearing systems or similar arrangements as a means of obtaining payment of their debts in the stipulated currency.

Many examples of these arrangements may be cited. The so-called Roca-Runciman agreements of 1933–36 between Great Britain and Argentina reserved for British traders and bondholders the bulk of the sterling exchange arising from the export of Argentine goods to the United Kingdom.[22] Under the Anglo-German payments agreement of November 1, 1934, provision was made for resuming the service on the Dawes and Young sterling loans by limiting Germany's imports from Great Britain to somewhat over one half of her exports to that country.[23] A notable example of commercial collaboration between debtor and creditor countries for the purpose of insuring the payment of external debts in foreign currency may be found in the Franco-Turkish debt agreement of May, 1936.[24] By this accord the Turkish Government undertook to pay the debt service in Turkish pounds to the Ottoman Debt Council which was then to hand over these sums to a Franco-Turkish trading company for the purchase of minerals and other Turkish goods to be sold in France for the account of French bondholders. The French Government in its turn promised to facilitate the entry of these goods into France.[25]

---

first in the Report of the Financial Committee on the Financial Reconstruction of Hungary, submitted to the Council of the League of Nations December 20, 1923. *Official Journal*, February, 1924, pp. 413 ff.; C. 772 (I). M. 317. (I) 1923. II. (F. 120): "It is also necessary, in order to avoid a danger of the value of the crown being depreciated, that any Treaty charge payments made by Hungary should be paid in Hungarian crowns into an account in the name of the Reparations Commission at the Bank of Hungary; and that it should be the duty of the Chairman of the Bank to convert these sums into foreign currencies at the earliest moment, but at such times and in such a manner as to prevent them depreciating the value of the crown." See also Kastl and Liefmann, *Das Transfer-problem* (Leipzig, 1926), pp. 9 ff.

22. Gantenbein, *op. cit.*, p. 81, n. 32; Feuerlein and Hannan, *op. cit.*, pp. 63, 72–73.

23. League of Nations, *Enquiry into Clearing Agreements*, 1935, p. 25 n. Similar agreements were made by Germany with France, Switzerland, and Holland. See B.I.S., *Fifth Annual Report* (May, 1935), p. 58.

24. *Corp. For. Bondh. Rep.*, No. 63 (1936), pp. 367 ff.; II, pp. 513 ff.

25. For details on the operation of the scheme, see II, 514 ff.

In connection with Latin American transfer problems, it may be mentioned that some of the loans extended by the Export-Import Bank, notably those

The plea of *force majeure* as an excuse for transfer default is acceptable only if the failure to provide the debt service in foreign currency is actually due to circumstances beyond the debtor's control, such as a collapse in the prices of his major exports,[26] and is not the result of mismanagement or bad faith in allocating available foreign exchange. The debtor must give unmistakable evidence of his willingness to live up to his engagements. This he may do by providing and placing in a blocked fund the full debt service in local currency.[27] The use of available foreign

---

made to Brazil, looked specifically to the unfreezing of funds due to American citizens. See the press release of the Department of State of March 9, 1939 (*For. Bondh. Prot. Coun. Rep.*, 1938, pp. 165 ff.); Feuerlein and Hannan, *op. cit.*, pp. 37 ff.; "Export-Import Bank Loans to Latin America," *For. Pol. Rep.*, XVII (June 15, 1941), 85 ff.

As a solution of the Latin American debt transfer problem, it may be added, Boris Eliacheff, "A Scheme for Handling Latin American Debts," *Inter-Am. Quar.*, III (April, 1941), 21 ff., suggested that the entire dollar indebtedness of these countries should be converted into a domestic currency debt to be owed to the United States Government and that the latter should pay to the creditors the dollar equivalent of their bonds. This scheme could, however, hardly be called one for "a settlement" of the defaults. It would, in effect, merely amount to a proposal that the United States should lend these countries in dollars the full amount of their debts (i.e., by paying off creditors) and accept in return claims payable only in the debtor currencies. In other words, the general taxpayer of the United States would be asked to make good the losses of American investors in Latin American bonds. Insofar as the debtor countries are concerned, the effect would be virtually the same as if they were able to induce the bondholders to accept claims payable in the debtor currencies for their claims to payment in United States dollars. For proposals for a more equitable solution, see Wallich, *op. cit.*, p. 321.

26. *Supra*, nn. 20, 24.

27. This principle has often been stated by the Financial Committee of the League of Nations and the League Loans Committee. See the latter's *Second Annual Report*, pp. 8, 25. For a list of countries where full service was set aside in local currency which could not be transferred, see William O. Scroggs, "Foreign Treatment of American Creditors," *For. Aff.*, XIV (1936), 347. See also SEC, *Rep.*, Pt. V, p. 21. The payment of the service into blocked accounts in local currency does not discharge the debt. The sums thus set aside may be considered "a special collateral security for the ultimate payment of the corresponding instalments in the respective foreign currencies." See B.I.S., *Fourth Annual Report* (Basle, 1934), p. 42. The economic dangers of the accumulation of large amounts in domestic currency are pointed out by Paul Einzig in his book on *Exchange Control* (London, Macmillan, 1934), pp. 126 ff. He even calls the practice of paying the amounts due into blocked accounts in national currency and reborrowing these sums a method of "concealing" the transfer default and adds: "It is important to realize that the security provided by the system to the creditors is very slender indeed. The belief that, once the transfer difficulties have ceased to exist, the creditors can recover their blocked balances immediately, is sheer illusion. In

exchange for the "repatriation" of his bonds, i.e., their purchase at the low prices caused by the transfer default, is clearly an act of bad faith.[28] The question, however, what government expenses may claim a right to be satisfied prior to the fulfillment of external debts is dependent on the circumstances of each case. If the maintenance of essential government services requires the use of all the foreign exchange in the hands of the debtor, bondholders have no just cause for complaint.[29] While discrimination in allocating foreign exchange to bondholders according to their nationality would violate the international legal principle of equality of treatment,[30] the division of loans into grades for the purpose of preferential allocation of foreign exchange to the service of those which deserve special consideration may not appear objectionable, if such classification is based on reasonable grounds.[31]

order to be able to release the blocked balances, the debtor country has to be in a position to recover the funds lent directly or indirectly out of the blocked resources."

28. See *infra*, section on Repatriation.

29. The use of foreign exchange by Germany for the purchase of military equipment in preference to the service of her external loans was considered by the United States Government an infraction of the obligation under loan contracts. See Note of the United States Secretary of State to the German chargé d'affaires of June 27, 1934. Dept. of State, *Press Releases*, No. 248 (June 30, 1934), p. 444. When announcing her transfer default in July, 1933, Uruguay pointed out that "the continued full payment at this time of interest on its foreign obligations in the currencies in which they are expressed to be payable would have a disastrous effect on the gold reserves of the Bank of the Republic, which have already been substantially reduced. These reserves cannot be further depleted without endangering the industrial and commercial structure of the country." *The New York Times*, July 29, 1933. The Hungarian transfer moratorium of 1932 was stated to be due to a "position of constraint, which is quite independent from [*sic*.] the Government's desire." The Government promised to procure sufficient foreign currency for the payment of the loan service "as soon as the Government is in a position to do so consistently with safeguarding the vital interest of the country." See League Loans Committee, *First Annual Report*, May, 1933, pp. 42 ff.

30. This point was stressed during the negotiations between Germany and the United States Government on the question of discrimination against American holders of the Dawes and Young loans by Germany in 1934. See *aide-mémoire* of the American Ambassador to Germany of July 17, 1934, Dept. of State, *Press Releases*, No. 251 (July 21, 1934), p. 60; SEC, *Rep.*, Pt. V, pp. 419 ff.

31. By decree of the President of Brazil of February 5, 1934, the Brazilian external loans of the federal government, the states, and the municipalities were divided into eight grades which were to receive (with the exception of the eighth) varying amounts in foreign exchange, ranging from the full service (in the case of Grade I) to different percentages of the full nominal value of the coupons without sinking fund. See *Corp. For. Bondh. Rep.*, No. 60 (1933), pp. 23 ff., 109; *For. Bondh. Prot. Coun. Rep.*, 1936, pp. 105 ff. See also *infra*, sections on Readjustment and Priorities.

REPATRIATION OF BONDS

"Repatriation" of bonds literally means their return from foreign possession to the country of their origin. In international finance, the term applies both to the repurchase of securities from foreign holders by the debtor through the operation of sinking-fund provisions and to the purchases of foreign bonds by nationals of the debtor country.[32] Under normal conditions, i.e., while the bonds are fully serviced and sell at reasonable prices, the practice of repatriating foreign loans is a perfectly legitimate means of repaying debts and constitutes a sound technique of reducing the foreign indebtedness of a country. As such, it has been widely used by debtors of all descriptions, private as well as public, without injurious effects on the rights and interests of the creditors.[33] Repatriation, however, becomes tainted with bad faith and objectionable to the bondholders if it is carried out by a debtor in default on its bonds. By buying up its own bonds at the low prices caused by the default, a debtor "profits by its own wrong." [34] Governments, in particular, while pleading lack of foreign exchange as an excuse for their failure to transfer the debt service, have often found enough foreign currency to retire their depreciated bonds by profitable purchases in the open market.[35] They are thus cancelling their foreign debts at the expense of their creditors.[36]

32. SEC, *Rep.*, Pt. V, p. 5, n. 12; pp. 494 ff.

33. See B.I.S., *Eighth Annual Report* (Basle, 1938), pp. 69 ff.; *Eleventh Annual Report* (Basle, 1941), p. 108, with respect to Portugal; *For. Bondh. Prot. Coun. Rep.*, 1936, p. 6.

34. SEC, *Rep.*, Pt. V, p. 505.

35. Representatives of banking houses, testifying before the Securities and Exchange Commission, declared that they would carry out such purchases at the request of customers even if they knew that the transactions served to repatriate depreciated government bonds. SEC, *Rep.*, Pt. V, pp. 502 ff. Holders, they asserted, are not obliged to sell; but if there is an offer in the open market to buy and a customer is willing to sell at the price offered, no banker or broker would feel entitled to refuse to make the deal.

36. The Foreign Bondholders Protective Council, in recent years, has sharply condemned various practices of repatriation as "bootlegging operations," by which foreign governments in default have succeeded in cancelling their external indebtedness. See, in particular, *For. Bondh. Prot. Coun. Rep.*, 1938, pp. 7 ff. Among the practices of repatriation, the Council lists the following ones: (1) permission by a country, which has instituted exchange control and pleads lack of foreign exchange as the reason for not servicing its bonds, to its provincial or municipal debtors to use dollar exchange for the purpose of buying up their defaulted bonds on the American market; (2) speculation by a government which pleads poverty in dollar exchange in its own defaulted bonds on foreign markets; (3) permission given to its nationals to use controlled foreign exchange to buy

The retirement of defaulted bonds, whether it be done openly or in secret,[37] clearly violates the spirit, if not the very terms,[38] of the loan contract to the detriment of the creditors and, therefore, in itself constitutes default. For this reason, bondholders have objected to the insertion in readjustment plans of clauses providing for the redemption of bonds out of the limited assets of the debtor before the market value of the bonds has been restored to normal or near normal by adequate provisions for the interest service.[39]

CURRENCY DEVALUATION

Bondholders frequently sustain injury because the currency in which the debt is expressed depreciates during the life of the loan by changes in the monetary standard. In the absence of special devices in the loan contract designed to guard against this contingency, such as gold clauses or currency options,[40] the risk of currency depreciation must be borne by the creditor. The bondholder is entitled to claim, and the debtor is obliged to pay, only so much in a certain currency as is stated on the face of the bonds and coupons.[41] By choosing a foreign currency as the

the defaulted government bonds abroad; (4) resale of repatriated bonds at advanced prices at a favorable moment secured by market manipulations. See, for estimates of the amounts thus repatriated, J. Reuben Clark, "Foreign Bondholdings in the United States," *Am. Jour. Int. Law,* XXXII (1938), 445.

37. SEC, *Rep.,* Pt. V, p. 495.

38. The withdrawal of bonds at the low prices caused by the debtor's default would be contrary to the terms of the contract where the latter provides that redemption must take place at par, by drawings or purchases, or that the whole of the interest must be satisfied before any money is applied to the redemption of the principal.

39. See *infra,* section on Readjustment. The League Loans Committee, in its *Third Annual Report,* June, 1936, pp. 10 f., remarked that there are "obvious reasons on moral and other grounds against encouraging a debtor Government which is in default to use its resources in buying up its own bonds while these stand at low prices precisely because of the Government's default . . . . The Committee have not excluded the possibility of applying some part of the debtor's payments to a regular sinking fund service when the time comes to make a permanent settlement; but they have concluded that it does not seem practicable to recommend any such arrangement until the debtor countries are meeting a higher proportion of the service of their loans than any of the countries which are in partial default on their League Loans are at present providing."

40. See *supra,* section on Currency and Gold Clauses. See also J. Sulkowski, "Questions juridiques soulevées dans les rapports internationaux par les variations de valeur des signes monétaires," *Rec. des Cours,* XXIX (1929), 77 ff.

41. Wharton's opinion (*A Treatise on the Conflicts of Laws,* Vol. II [Rochester, N.Y., Lawyer's Coöperative, 1905], sec. 517, p. 1231) that, in case of depreciation of currency, a creditor may, even in the absence of specific protective clauses

standard of their respective rights and duties, both debtor and creditor submit to the vicissitudes of the international rate of exchange and are subject to the law of the state which creates that currency and determines its value.[42]

The situation, however, may be different in case the loan is issued in the national currency of the debtor government. If the failure to redeem the debt in money of the original standard is due to a "collapse," a "catastrophic depreciation" of the debtor's currency as a result of circumstances beyond the debtor's control,[43] the plea of *force majeure* would be a valid excuse for the default in accordance with the principle already stated.[44] But if the monetary devaluation and, consequently, the injury to the bondholders' rights arises from a deliberate act on the part of the debtor government, foreign creditors would be justified in further examining the situation with a view to determining whether or not the debtor has thereby incurred an international liability. It has been maintained that governments, in the exercise of their sovereign power, are absolutely free to regulate their own monetary systems, regardless of the effects of such action on the rights of their creditors.[45] But, just as international law may, and sometimes does, limit the monetary autonomy of states,[46] the loan contract creates an obligation, binding upon the government, not to alter its terms to the disadvantage of the creditors by unilateral action, such as reducing the principal or rate of interest, or in some other way modifying the substance of the engagement for

---

in the contract, "according to the principles of international law . . . recover that which would give him an equivalent in currency to that which he would have been entitled to had no such depreciation taken place" has remained isolated. See Wahl, "Der Einfluss der Geldwertveränderungen auf internationale Rechtsbeziehungen," in *Deutsche Länderreferate zum II. Internationalen Kongress für Rechtsvergleichung im Haag 1937*, "Zeitschrift für ausländisches und internationales Privatrecht," XI (1937), 342. Furthermore, Midas, "Die Goldklausel im Währungsverfall" (Dissertation, Erlangen, 1924), pp. 16 ff. Cf. Schoo, *op. cit.*, pp. 509 ff.

42. Nolde, "La Monnaie en droit international," *Rec. des Cours*, XXVII (1929), 275; Nussbaum, *Money in the Law*, pp. 414 ff.

43. See Mann, *The Legal Aspect of Money*, p. 40.

44. *Supra*, section on the Conception of State Insolvency.

45. See Fischer Williams, *op. cit.*, p. 291: "Where the loan is issued in the national currency, it is no doubt within the power of the issuing government, and it is difficult to say that it is not within its right, to regulate its own coinage in such a fashion as to diminish, and even to destroy the value of the rights of its creditors. . . . If for domestic reasons the borrowing government depreciates its currency and is not restrained from so doing by the terms of the contract of the loan, I see no foundation for any legal complaint by the bondholder, though as a matter of morality he may have a case." See also Nussbaum, *op. cit.*, p. 417.

46. Nolde, *op. cit.*, pp. 261, 263 ff., 275.

the purpose of alleviating the burden of the debt, unless driven thereto by financial necessity.[47] Losses sustained in consequence of currency depreciation through a change of the monetary standard may vary considerably, depending on whether the bonds are held by nationals of the debtor government or by foreign creditors. If domestic prices rise relatively little, the damage to the internal creditor may be small, whereas the external bondholder suffers at once a loss, measured in his own currency, proportional to the devaluation. The partial confiscation of his rights, together with the discrimination which may result from currency devaluation between internal and external holders of a debt couched in the national currency of the debtor government, may well form the basis of a claim against the defaulting government.[48]

ABROGATION OF GOLD CLAUSES

Similar considerations apply with regard to the abrogation of gold clauses. Where the intended effect of a legislative act invalidating gold clauses in contractual obligations is to free the government from a promise to pay the gold value of a debt,[49] such act would amount to a unilateral alteration of the substance of the debt, seriously infringing upon the rights of the creditors.[50] Again, while internal creditors may remain entirely unaffected by the act, foreign creditors would have a cause of action against the defaulting government if they are able to show damages sustained by the breach of the contract.[51]

47. *Perry* v. *United States*, 294 U.S. 330, 349 ff. (1935).

48. Feilchenfeld, *op. cit.*, Vol. II, secs. 650, 651, 652. See also Jèze, "Public Debt," *Encyclopaedia of the Social Sciences*, XII, 601.

49. Under the doctrine of *Perry* v. *United States*, 294 U.S. 330 (1935), bonds of the United States Government were also affected by the joint resolution of 1933, abrogating gold clauses. The obligation of the French Government arising from guaranties of franc loans of foreign governments was exempted from the French statutory invalidation of gold clauses by the concept of the "international contract," first developed by the courts and later adopted by the act of June 25, 1928, and the Monetary Law of October 1, 1936. See Nussbaum, *op. cit.*, pp. 336 ff.

50. "Should a State appeal to is own legislation invalidating the gold clause in order to render the clause inoperative in a loan issued by itself, it would be defaulting on its own obligations." Basdevant, Memorandum submitted to the League Study Committee, April 13, 1937. The Polish Government refused to carry out the gold clause of the Polish stabilization loan of 1927, relying on the Polish law of 1934. See Nussbaum, *op. cit.*, p. 390, n. 45. See also Jèze, *Encyclopaedia of the Social Sciences*, XII, 601.

51. *Perry* v. *United States*, 294 U.S. 330 (1935). See also Charles Fenwick, "The Gold Clause Decision in Relation to Foreign Bondholders," *Am. Jour. Int. Law*, XXIX (1935), 310; Nussbaum, *op. cit.*, pp. 365, 367, 402 ff. Groves, *op. cit.*, p. 670: "clauses in Government bonds requiring payment in gold have proved

In the matter of the abrogation of gold and currency clauses, a division between creditor and debtor countries is not possible. In fact, the creditor countries are largely responsible for the action taken against the gold clause. The United States gave the lead not only in the abrogation of the gold clause in private obligations but even abrogated it in its own bonds (Liberty bonds). Moreover, a multiple-currency clause was also regarded as being contrary to public policy.

The abrogation of the gold clause by creditor countries benefited foreign debtors who were no longer obliged to meet the service of their external bonds in gold.

GOVERNMENTAL INTERFERENCE WITH SECURITY

Governments in the past have interfered with security pledges in various ways. Most frequent has been the simple diversion of revenues assigned to the service of loans to other governmental purposes. There seems to have been little hesitation to encroach upon funds intended for foreign creditors when needed for budgetary purposes, like the payment of overdue salaries,[52] or the discharge of local debts,[53] or for unspecified general liabilities of the government.[54] In some cases administrative or financial reforms have been carried out with the aid of revenues pledged as security for foreign loans.[55]

unavailing as a defense by creditors against the power of the State to devalue the currency." In fact, the abrogation by statute was held illegal, but a domestic holder obtained no redress because he was unable to prove damage. Not so, the citizen of a country like Holland and Switzerland, still on the gold standard. For that reason Congress passed a statute, 49 Stat. 938, placing a short period on the statute of limitations (January 1, 1936) within which suit could be brought against the United States in the Court of Claims.

52. Serbia in 1894 raided a fund into which revenues pledged as security for various loans had been paid, in order to pay overdue salaries. *The Daily News* (London), April 13, 1894; *The Times* (London), April 28, 1894; *The Economist*, April 28, 1894. Similar inroads on the caisse appear to have been made on other occasions when the governments had no other way of meeting current expenses. Y. Zivkovitch, *La Garantie des emprunts publics du royaume de Yougoslavie* (Paris, 1931), p. 62.

53. Santo Domingo in 1893 diverted customs duties from the Regie to the merchants of Santo Domingo for the payment of local debts. II, 220.

54. The abortive decree of May 7, 1876, projected a unification of Egyptian debts which would have deprived the Daira loan of its special guarantees. II, 589. From 1875 to 1877 the Egyptian tribute assigned as security for Turkish loans was diverted by Turkey for general budgetary purposes. II, 479.

55. In 1885 Mexico attempted to put her financial house in order by the suspension of pledges of public revenues. II, 43–45. She also used pledged funds to provide capital for a new bank. II, 74–75. Revenues promised to bondholders were used by Turkey in 1907 for Macedonian reforms. II, 481.

In other instances revenues have been assigned to a later debt in disregard of a previous pledge, irrespective of whether their proceeds would suffice to satisfy the service of both issues, or a previous loan has been altogether deprived of its security by transferring it to a new loan by the same debtor.[56]

Administrative measures by which a number of governments have interfered with pledged revenues range from total abrogation [57] and temporary suspension [58] to reduction either of rates or yield [59] of the

56. Ecuador in 1909 assigned the whole of the customs duties to the service of the 6% loan, although these revenues had been preferentially pledged to the holders of the Guayaquil and Quito railway bonds. *Corp. For. Bondh. Rep.*, No. 56 (1929), p. 149. The Mexican bondholders' committee of 1871 protested against the assignment of customs revenues to the Mexican railway bonds because of a previous charge for their benefit. II, 34. When Serbia in 1899 assigned the receipts from the state railroads as security to the Austrian loan, the French and German ambassadors protested because the same revenues had been pledged as security to the 1895 loans. The matter was adjusted by substituting the receipts from the match and cigarette-paper monopolies. Zivkovitch, *op. cit.*, pp. 66–67. Turkey in 1879 gave the customs revenues of Constantinople to a group of bankers who were allowed to place agents in customhouses to collect their share, despite the fact that the entire customs were pledged to the loan of 1862. II, 436.

57. Juárez, Mexican President, cancelled the assignment of 25% of the customs revenues to the 1851 Convention loan because of alleged illegality of the pledge. II, 29. The duties which had been hypothecated to the service of the Venezuela loan of 1864 were reduced to two thirds in 1866 and entirely abolished in 1869. E. B. Eastwick, *Venezuela . . . with the History of the Loan of 1864* (London, 1868), p. 351.

58. By decree of May 29, 1861, Juárez suspended payment of the import duties assigned as security to foreign creditors of Mexico, claiming that these revenues were needed for the establishment of a stable government. II, 22. Ecuador in 1915 defaulted on the deposit of salt revenues pledged as security for the 4% salt bonds. *Corp. For. Bondh. Rep.*, No. 43 (1916), p. 134.

59. An interesting case of indirect reduction of the yield of pledged revenues, leading to diplomatic action, was reported by the Council of Foreign Bondholders in its *Annual Report*, No. 64 (1937), p. 32. When the increase of petroleum duties, decreed by the Chilean Government in 1937, threatened to affect adversely the profits from the nitrate industry and also the yield of a nitrate tax assigned as security to foreign loans, the British Government intervened on the ground that the Chilean Government, when assigning the security, had undertaken not to reduce its yield by taxation or other act. The 20% of the gross receipts of the Republic of Colombia assigned to the service of the external bonds of 1890 were reduced in 1929 to 7%. *Corp. For. Bondh. Rep.*, No. 56, 1929, p. 107. By decree of 1937, the Government of Paraguay reduced the export duties on *yerba-maté*, assigned as security to the external debt service under the 1924 agreement, by 50%. The Council of Foreign Bondholders took action to protect the bondholders against this breach of the agreement. *Idem*, No. 64 (1937), p. 32. By granting release from customs duties and changing goods from dutiable to

specific revenues and alterations in the mode of payment or collection.[60]

Doctrine and international practice agree that in case of a genuine emergency the debtor government may utilize revenues at hand for pressing needs in disregard of a pledge assigning them for the service of external loans. Thus, the utilization of assigned revenues for the relief of destructive natural catastrophies, such as floods and earthquakes, may be justified,[61] and the same may be said in the case of external wars or internal uprisings.[62] Where, however, such a crisis is lacking, the use of pledged funds simply to overcome financial difficulties which might have been solved without disturbing the rights of the creditors, for

free goods, the Dominican Government in 1892 connived at avoidance of paying the custom revenues which were the chief security of its external debt. II, 212.

60. By decree of April 20, 1932, the Bulgarian Government ordered revenues assigned as security for the League loans to be paid to the Bulgarian Public Debt Administration instead of to the special accounts of the League Commissioner. The trustees drew the attention of the Secretary General of the League to "the serious nature of the default." League Loans Committee, *First Annual Rep.*, May, 1933, pp. 34 f. In 1893 the Greek Government instructed officials to collect taxes hypothecated for foreign loans in paper currency instead of in gold and to pay the funds into the Treasury. II, 307. When the Government of Honduras leased the Interoceanic Railway to W. S. Valentine, British holders of bonds secured on the revenues of the road protested. J. E. Paredes, *La Contrata Morgan —Sus Antecedentes*, p. 8. In 1931 the Government of Peru ordered the Caja de Depositos, a domestic corporation charged with collecting the revenues for the national loan and transferring them to New York, to pay the revenues in to the Treasury. II, 188.

61. After the earthquake in Chile in 1939, a law provided that funds set aside for the service of Chile's external debt were to be placed at the disposal of the Reconstruction and Relief Corporation created for the purpose of reconstructing the devastated areas. *Com. and Fin. Chron.*, CXLIX (July 29, 1939), 653; CLII (January 18, 1941), 353: temporary assignment to the purposes of the earthquake decree of funds reserved for the amortization of external bonds. The *For. Bondh. Prot. Coun. Rep.*, 1938, p. 214, however, pointed out that the bondholders cannot be asked to assume the burden for the reconstruction of the earthquake damage "as it is a matter wholly disconnected with them and their investment in Chilean bonds." A disastrous hurricane in Santo Domingo in September, 1930, was partly responsible for the diversion to the Government's own use of revenues pledged to the service of the foreign debt. II, 275.

62. In 1932 the Government of Salvador took over pledged customs revenues to meet obligations under a large floating debt which had arisen from internal disturbances (communistic uprisings). The text of the decree is given in *Nuestro Diario* (Guatemala City), March 2, 1932. See also Charles A. Thompson, "The Caribbean Situation: Nicaragua and Salvador," *For. Pol. Rep.*, Vol. IX (August 30, 1933), No. 13, p. 148, n. 48. The Tampico and Vera Cruz customs pledged by Mexico for the service of the 1824–25 loan were diverted by the Government in 1831 for the discharge of expenses connected with the outbreak of a revolution. II, 8.

instance, by increasing the tax rate,[63] clearly constitutes a breach of contract.

It has already been observed [64] that holders of loans secured by revenue pledges are more likely to obtain governmental protection than less careful investors. By the same token, interference with the security on the part of the debtor has frequently given rise to prompt action by the governments of the bondholders.[65] Sometimes the bondholders themselves or representatives of their interests have succeeded in defeating the attempted diversion of security by appropriate remedial measures.[66] Moreover, where the promise to pay the loan service out of special revenues is part of the debtor's municipal law, a court action against the government or against the guilty official may lie.[67]

63. Charles C. Hyde, *International Law* (2d rev. ed. Boston, Little, Brown, 1945) II, 1005–1007. SEC, *Rep.*, Pt. V, pp. 415 ff.; Strupp, "L'Intervention en matière financière," *Rec. des Cours*, VIII (1925), 58; Jèze, *Rec. des Cours*, LIII (1935), 381. In the reply made by the Austrian Government to questions submitted by the Committee of Experts on the Responsibility of States, to be discussed by The Hague Codification Conference, the diversion of security from its proper destination is called an arbitrary act violative of the international obligations of the state. League of Nations, *Conference for the Codification of International Law. Bases of Discussion.* Vol. III. "Responsibility of States for Damages Caused in Their Territory to the Person or Property of Foreigners" (Geneva, 1929). Questions Juridiques. 1929. V. 3, p. 38.

64. *Supra*, section on Secured Loans, pp. 98 ff.

65. When Turkey diverted the Egyptian tribute pledged as security for various loans, Great Britain and France intervened on behalf of the bondholders. II, 42 ff. The diversion of revenues pledged for the Tunisian loan of 1868 drew a protest from the French agent in Tunis. L.J. 1869, *Affaires de Tunis*, pp. 179–191. See also *supra*, nn. 56, 59, 60.

66. French and Belgian bondholders protested in 1905 against the diversion of the customs receipts of Santo Domingo and Macoris. II, 241. The quotation of the Turkish loan of 1872 on the London Stock Exchange was refused in retaliation for the failure by Turkey to pay pledged revenues as covenanted. II, 405. The Imperial Ottoman Bank, as negotiators of the 1867 loan, protested to the Khedive of Egypt against the diversion of pledged revenues. II, 589. See also *supra*, nn. 56, 59, 60.

67. Counsel for the bondholders' committee with respect to certain Greek loans argued that any official who permits imposts known to be assigned to a debt to be paid elsewhere would be personally liable. In 1884 the commissioners of the Egyptian public debt (Caisse) sued the Egyptian Government for violation of the law of liquidation committed by diverting funds pledged for the sinking fund of the external debt. The lower court pronounced judgment in favor of the Caisse. II, 619.

Section XI

CAUSES OF INSOLVENCY*

GENERAL

THE majority of the governmental loans which fell into default, at least prior to 1914, were made to countries which were primarily agricultural and where the standard of living was far below that of the industrialized states in which the loans were raised. Sometimes the debtors proved unable to maintain internal political stability or to keep free from civil or foreign wars; often they borrowed excessively and used most of the proceeds for nonproductive expenditure; only too frequently they failed to develop prudence and efficiency in fiscal administration. Where such circumstances were present, default was the usual outcome.

Although financial mismanagement in various forms helped engender the wave of insolvencies which disrupted the contractual relations between borrowing states and their foreign creditors during the early 1930's, that cataclysm was largely attributable to circumstances beyond the debtors' control. The steep fall in prices and shrinkage of trade which characterized the world-wide economic slump was accompanied by an abrupt cessation of foreign loans. As a consequence debtor countries suffered a severe depletion of their foreign exchange resources and were obliged to suspend partially or wholly the service of their external debts in the creditors' currencies. But when the exchange position improved, many of the defaulters proved unable or unwilling to tax their budgets to the extent necessary for full provision of the debt service and readjustments were effected with the creditors which definitely lightened the fiscal burden of the debt charges.

In all three major periods of default which have checked the course of private lending to foreign governments,[1] some of the blame for the dénouement is attributable to issuing houses which eagerly sponsored loans to states which they knew to be very poor financial risks. Frequently these houses failed to disclose information in their possession

* This section on "Causes of Insolvency" was written by W. H. Wynne.
1. See the Introduction, *supra*, p. xx.

which would have warned the public that the borrowing government was highly unstable and financially embarrassed. In many instances their fault was still greater in that they willfully misrepresented the fiscal, economic, and political situation of the borrower, issued misleading statements as to the purposes to which the loan funds were to be put, and exaggerated the value and importance of such security as may have been assigned by the debtor for the performance of his obligations.

On not a few occasions, however, bankers floated loans to financially weak debtors avowedly to provide for military or other unproductive expenditures and in doing so served not merely their own ends but those of their governments. Such loans to the Balkan countries in particular were facilitated and encouraged by European powers anxious to gain some diplomatic advantage in the Near East over their rivals in the sphere of international politics. France and Germany took the leading part in turning loans to this purpose. Through the control they exercised over the flotation of foreign loans they buttressed political diplomacy with financial diplomacy in order to make or unmake understandings or alliances, to win potential friends and detach enemies.[2] When these economically unsound loans were defaulted, they were ready to seize the occasion to strengthen their political influence over the insolvent debtor.

High effective interest rates, often accompanied by the inducement of an issue price considerably under par, warned the cautious that in subscribing to a new foreign loan they would be taking considerable risk, but the lure of a prospective high return and appreciation of capital tempted thousands, who, when their speculative ventures failed, were disposed to represent themselves as innocent victims of the debtor's perfidy and to claim, as of right, the support of their governments in bringing the defaulter to terms.

SPECIAL CASES

These broad generalizations on the causes of default may be supplemented by a brief review of the specific circumstances that led to the débacle in a few of the best known cases of state insolvency.[3]

2. For illuminating studies of the relations between finance and diplomacy, see H. Feis, *Europe, the World's Banker, 1870–1914, passim,* and J. Viner, "International Finance and Balance of Power Diplomacy, 1880–1914," *Southwestern Political and Social Science Quarterly,* IX (March, 1929).

3. These brief outlines of the causes of particular defaults are based mainly on the case histories in Volume II of the present work.

LATIN AMERICA

Mexico. Mexico floated two sterling loans, in 1824 and 1825, to help ensure her national independence. The service of these early Mexican issues was met for a short period out of funds which the contractors retained for the purpose from the proceeds of the loans but by 1827 these funds were exhausted and Mexico defaulted on her early foreign debt before she had paid a penny for service charges out of her own revenues. Broken only for occasional short periods when negotiated settlements were carried out, the default lasted for nearly sixty years. During this period a succession of wars and revolutions made the establishment of orderly administration almost impossible and retarded the economic development of the country. Following the establishment of a strong government under President Díaz and a final settlement of the long-standing default, an era of tranquillity ensued, marked by the accumulation of a huge new foreign debt. Revolution in 1911 abruptly ended the peaceful decades and again plunged Mexico into financial and administrative disorder. Additional foreign loans proved unobtainable and in 1914 another long period of default began, interrupted only by brief temporary readjustments until 1942, when a settlement giving greater promise of permanence was effected, but at the cost to the bondholders of drastic cuts in the principal and interest to which they had previously been contractually entitled.

Santo Domingo. To maintain himself in power, the dictator Heureux supported an army of agents and spies and bribed and corrupted freely. His financial profligacy saddled Santo Domingo with a load of foreign debt which contributed practically nothing to her economic development. Upon Heureux's assassination in 1900, Santo Domingo was left with her external obligations in default and creditors of various European nationalities who were importuning their governments to intervene on their behalf. Five years of civil war ensued, which intensified the financial difficulties and made the likelihood of European intervention even greater. The crisis was resolved by the initiation of an American customs receivership in 1905. Under the financial direction of the United States, Santo Domingo's debts were readjusted. A recrudescence of internal disorder resulted in a growing interference by the United States in the country's domestic affairs, which evolved eventually into the establishment of an American military government which was not terminated until 1924. Meanwhile, Santo Domingo duly met the service charges on the readjusted old debt and floated new loans in the New York market. Notwithstanding a disastrous hurricane which swept the capital in September, 1930, and the concomitant economic troubles attributable to the world-wide depression, the Republic continued to pay punctually and in full the interest charges on its foreign debt, defaulting only on the heavy sinking fund payments. In 1940 the United States terminated the customs receivership and seven years later the Dominican Government redeemed the entire balance of its external bonded debt.

Peru. Peru's first ventures in foreign borrowing duplicated the experience of Mexico and other Latin American countries, notably Chile and Colombia. Loans raised in England in 1822 and 1825, chiefly for the purpose of obtaining munitions in order to carry on the revolutionary war against Spain, quickly fell into total default and remained so for a long period. In the case of Peru it was the discovery of guano which enriched the Treasury and enabled the government not only to settle the old debt but to embark on excessive new borrowing abroad on the security of the guano revenues. The exhaustion of the best guano deposits and the competition of artificial fertilizers sharply curtailed the government's income from guano. Left without other sources of revenue sufficient to maintain the burdensome debt charges, Peru in 1876 entered upon her second period of default. The war with Chile (1879–83) deprived Peru of the rich province of Tarapacá and was followed by three years of virtual anarchy. With the restoration of constitutional government conditions became favorable for negotiating a debt adjustment. The settlement, effected in 1889, took the novel form of cancellation of the foreign debt in return for railway and guano concessions to a British company—the Peruvian Corporation—specially organized for the purpose, in which the holders of Peru's foreign obligations acquired shares in exchange for their old bonds.

The liquidation of the old foreign debt and growing diversification of the Peruvian economy in due course paved the way for a resumption of borrowing abroad. In the twentieth century, chiefly after World War I, Peru again accumulated a substantial foreign debt. The effects of the world-wide trade depression on Peru were intensified by a succession of revolutionary outbreaks in 1930 and 1931, and in the latter year Peru joined the growing procession of defaulting states. But the world economic crisis only precipitated a default which had for some time been in the making. Excessive borrowing, promoted by issuing houses who were aware that the country was being saddled with debt charges which its revenues might prove unable to support, wasteful dissipation of much of the proceeds of the loans, and recurrent deficits on the ordinary budget all showed, to those disposed to heed such signs, that Peru was steadily traveling the road to insolvency.

Nicaragua. Political disorder, financial maladministration, inflationary issues of paper money, and the subjection of the government to a mass of claims for unpaid accounts, violation of contractual rights, and injury to persons and property combined to reduce Nicaragua to bankruptcy. The principal default occurred in 1914 when, with the consent of the creditors, all payments on the foreign debt service were suspended. A readjustment was effected in 1917 by the appointment of a mixed Nicaraguan-American commission which developed a financial plan which provided for the settlement of all claims and, following an interim period of partial cash payments, for the resumption in 1920 of the full debt service. Under terms of an arrangement concluded with American bankers in 1912 and continued by the financial plan of 1917, the collection of the Nicaraguan customs revenue and its remission for the debt service was placed under the control of an American collector-general.

World conditions placed Nicaragua in difficulties in 1932 and forced a partial suspension of sinking fund payments. A debt settlement was effected in 1937 involving some amelioration of both interest and sinking fund charges.

Venezuela. Venezuela defaulted frequently on her foreign debt—from 1834 to 1841, from 1847 to 1859, from 1864 to 1876, from 1878 to 1880, from 1892 to 1893, and from 1897 to 1905. These numerous and prolonged defaults were attributable chiefly to repeated revolutionary disturbances which drained the Treasury, retarded economic development, and gave rise to claims for injuries to the persons and property of European nationals to the settlement of which a considerable part of the foreign loan proceeds was devoted. In 1902 injuries to foreign interests resulted in a blockade of Venezuelan ports by England, Germany, and Italy as a means of enforcing redress. Claims, other than those of the bondholders of the external debt, were adjusted by mixed commissions, while the contention of the blockading powers that their claims were entitled to preferential treatment over those of other powers was referred to The Hague Tribunal. The foreign bonded debt was readjusted separately by negotiations between representatives of the Republic and of the bondholders, a settlement being effected in 1905. The discovery and exploitation of rich oil resources yielded revenues which enabled Venezuela by 1930 to complete the redemption of her old debt. Meanwhile the Republic found it unnecessary to raise further loans abroad, thereby becoming, until very recently, almost the only Latin American country without a foreign debt.

EUROPE

Turkey. In Turkey the proceeds of foreign loans were used largely to support military expenditures or to provide luxurious palaces and a horde of unnecessary retainers for autocratic and extravagant Sultans,

Domestic advances contracted at 15 to 25 per cent were liquidated by foreign loans issued at an effective yield of 10 per cent. Fiscal administration was extremely defective and tax yields were kept low through evasion or through the corruption of tax officials. Bribery and graft were encouraged by the pitifully low salaries paid to a greatly overstaffed civil service, while laxity in public expenditure was fostered by the complete absence of centralized budgetary control. These practices combined to bring about the default of the 'seventies which culminated in the imposition of foreign financial control.

Greece and Bulgaria. Greece, paralleling Mexico, defaulted on the independence loans of 1824 and 1825 while she was still fighting for her national existence and before she had been able to meet any part of the debt service out of her own resources. But the default of 1893, which resulted eventually in the institution of international financial control, was attributable less to political instability than to a combination of factors similar to those which had similar consequences in Turkey, namely, excessive borrowing applied mainly to military expenditure and the funding of floating debt, an inefficient tax system, and a lack of budgetary control. Although Bulgaria's finances were characterized by corresponding maladjustments, that country succeeded in maintaining its foreign debt service with virtually no interruption until it entered World War I on the side of the central powers. After the war, Greece and Bulgaria were both enabled to rehabilitate their finances and cope with their difficult and burdensome refugee problems through the aid of foreign loans, sponsored by the League of Nations. The defaults on these loans were occasioned primarily by the impact of the world depression but they were aggravated by the failure of both countries to effect some of the much-needed financial reforms urged upon them by the League.

Portugal. Portugal's repudiation of the Dom Miguel loan of 1832 was based on the ground that Dom Miguel was a usurper. But the Portugese default of 1892 was the culmination of a long period of heavy borrowing as an offset to recurrent deficits. Coincidentally, there was the familiar situation of an inequitable and badly administered tax system, wasteful expenditure, a defective budget system, and political corruption.

NORTH AFRICA

Egypt. In 1862 Egypt entered upon a decade of foreign borrowing. A succession of loans was raised abroad at high interest rates and substantial discounts, mainly to redeem floating debt which mounted recurrently as the result of extravagant expenditure and poor financial administration. When foreign loans ceased to be obtainable, a financial crisis ensued. Default was followed by a readjustment of the debt under the direction of a condominium of French and British advisers, succeeded in 1882 by the intervention of Great Britain, which assumed responsibility for reconstructing and strengthening the Egyptian financial system.

Section XII

THE EFFECT OF WAR
ON GOVERNMENT LOANS

GOVERNMENTAL foreign loan contracts have sometimes contained express stipulations for the continuation of payments to enemy nationals even in time of war.[1] The carrying out of such provisions has, however, been made virtually impossible by the adoption soon after the outbreak of war of trading with the enemy acts, which prohibit transmission of money or goods to or communication with enemies.

Article 296 of the treaty of Versailles established the continued liability of governments on their suspended contracts after the war by providing that accrued interest and principal were recoverable through the machinery of the Clearing Offices. With respect to government bonds, however, an exception was made for capital or interest accruing during the war to enemy nationals—or, strangely, even to neutrals—if payment during the war had been suspended, which was true of nearly all belligerent debtors.[2]

---

1. Fischer Williams, *Chapters on Current International Law*, p. 398. See the loan contract between the Republic of El Salvador and Minor C. Keith, June 24, 1922, in Hearings before the Subcommittee of the Committee on Foreign Relations, United States Senate, 68th Cong., 2d Sess., *Foreign Loans* (Washington, 1926), pp. 109 ff. (Article XI, para. 1): ". . . both principal and interest of the bonds shall be payable in time of war as well as of peace, whether the respective holders or owners thereof are citizens of a friendly or a hostile State." See also fiscal agency agreement between the Republic of Chile and Kissel, Kinnicut & Co. and Hallgarten & Co., February 1, 1927. Art. II: Fourth. "The Republic hereby pledges its full faith and credit for the due and punctual payment of principal and interest and of all amounts required for the service of the loan, in time of war as well as in time of peace, irrespective of the nationality of any holder of the Bonds . . . ." See also Colombian gold bonds of 1927, *Corp. For. Bondh. Rep.*, 1929, pp. 111–112.

2. Paul F. Simonson, *Private Property and Rights in Enemy Countries* (London, E. Wilson, 1921), p. 42; Fischer Williams, *op. cit.*, p. 360; *Brit. Yearbook*, 1920, p. 178. Austria and Hungary did not even sequestrate enemy property. German creditors, it is reported, received about ½% of their claims. National Foreign Trade Council, *Report on War Claims* (New York, 1940), p. 7.

INTEREST DURING WAR

Attention may be called to rules which have developed in exposing the debtor to liability for the payment of interest after the expiration of the due date of either coupon interest or principal. If the payment becomes due during the war when payment is prohibited by public act or the war, interest on such sum, called legal interest, is not due. Where, however, the debtor was legally privileged to make the payment before the outbreak of war, and fails to make it, interest accrues during the war until final payment is made. Since war prevents payment, the statute of limitations should not run during the war, a period of disability.[3]

NEUTRALITY

In time of war, international law imposes certain obligations restrictive of loans on neutral powers. While no rule obliges a neutral to prevent a belligerent from raising money on loans from neutral nationals, there is an obligation upon the neutral government not to make such loans. Even a state bank or government corporation may not elude the prohibition resting upon the government by undertaking such loans. There is nothing in international law to prevent a government from placing an embargo even on its private citizens to insure the national neutrality.[4] Recognized belligerents in civil war labor under somewhat

3. *Brown* v. *Hiatts*, 15 Wall. 177 (1872); *Hoare* v. *Allen*, 2 Dall. 102 (1789); *Hanger* v. *Abbott*, 6 Wall. 532 (1868); R. A. Chadwick, "Foreign Investments in Time of War," *Law Quar. Rev.*, XX (1904), 171.

4. Article 11 and Article 13 of draft convention on neutrality, published with commentary by the Research in International Law, *Am. Jour. Int. Law, Supp.*, XXXIII (July, 1939), 281, 316; Hyneman, *Am. Jour. Int. Law*, XXIV (1930), 279, 290; J. W. Garner, "The United States Neutrality Act of 1937," *Am. Jour. Int. Law*, XXXI (1937), 385, 394. This provision was also included in the 1939 act. United States lifting of the ban on private loans to belligerents had an effect in changing American neutrality. R. S. Baker, "Neutrality, 1914–15," *Woodrow Wilson, Life and Letters* (New York, Doubleday, Doran, 1935), V, 380 ff. Borchard and Lage, *Neutrality for the United States* (New Haven, Yale University Press, 1937, 1940), p. 40.

The prohibition of private loans to countries in default on their debts to the United States, decreed by the Johnson Act of 1934, had a different motivation. April 13, 1934, 48 Stat. 574, 31 U.S.C.A. § 804a; Dept. of State, *Press Releases*, No. 240 (May 5, 1934); Opinion of the Attorney General, May 5, 1934, *Am. Jour. Int. Law*, XXIX (1935), 160. By Articles 231–234 of the defunct Treaty of Sèvres, 1920, the Turkish Government agreed not to contract any loan without the consent of the Financial Commission. The coördination committee formulating sanctions against Italy, October 14, 1935, prohibited members of the League from making loans to Italy or Italians.

the same restrictions. Loans made to a successful revolutionary belligerent are binding on the state, although it has been remarked that in such a case we have the unusual situation of two belligerent parties—the constituent government and the revolutionary—both capable of binding the state. Should the revolutionary belligerent be unsuccessful, loans made to him of course are unrecoverable and are lost.

Loans to belligerents must be distinguished from loans to factions or insurgents desirous of promoting an insurrection against a friendly state. This is an illegal transaction and a breach of the neutrality laws, precluding the recoverability of the loan.[5] Difficult questions arise in the attempt to establish whether an insurgent government is actually a belligerent or recognized belligerent, and whether it is a *de facto* government binding the state. These questions are beyond the purview of the present section.[6]

MILITARY OCCUPATION

The last codified rules on this subject are those embraced in Articles 42–56 of the Rules of War following Hague Convention IV of 1907. These are themselves a product of the unratified so-called Brussels convention of 1874, enacted during the liberal period of the nineteenth century. They reflect a distinction between private property and public property which modern commentators are inclined to denominate as

5. *De Wütz* v. *Hendricks,* 9 Moo. C. P. 586, 2 Bing. 314 (1824); *Kennett* v. *Chambers* (1852), 14 How. 38; Pitt Cobbett, *Cases and Opinions on International Law,* 3d ed., II (London, Stevens and Haynes, 1909–13), 366; *Mich. Law Rev.,* XXII (1923), 118. Hyde, *International Law,* Vol. II, sec. 870. Opinion of the Law Officers as to illegality of loan to Greek insurgents, 1823, Wheaton, *Elements of International Law* (London, Stevens and Sons, 1944), p. 381.

6. The Huerta Government in Mexico contracted certain loans abroad. Those expended for state purposes were acknowledged but those expended for arms and ammunition for what were deemed the personal needs of General Huerta were repudiated by the succeeding government. The propriety of the repudiation was disputed. A settlement with creditors of 1922 leaves the matter in partial doubt, though acknowledgment is inferred. The Dom Miguel loan to Portugal of 1832 was for a long time disavowed on the ground that Dom Miguel was a usurper. The Government finally acknowledged liability for that part of the loan which the Government had received. The De Valera Government was regarded differently by Irish and American courts, the former admitting it to be the government of the Irish Free State, bound by loans made to the De Valera insurgents when seeking recognition; the American court holding that the Irish Free State was not the successor and that the bondholders were entitled to the return of their subscriptions. See Haig Silvanie, *Responsibility of States for Acts of Unsuccessful Insurgent Governments* (New York, Columbia Univ. Press, 1939), pp. 11–59; *For. Rel.,* 1922, II, 686.

partly antiquated. They are, however, the only rules we have and occupants are under the burden of responsibility should they violate them. The rules attempt to enjoin upon the occupant respect for rights of private property as incidental to respect for private persons. They permit the occupant to take over public or state property except that devoted to cultural projects, like museums, schools, public libraries, etc.

They thus permit the military occupant to take over state funds and, it is said, to accept as such the repayment of loans due the occupied state, if such repayment should be made. They do not, however, enjoin upon the occupant the duty of paying capital or interest on loans due by the occupied state. These are continuing obligations of a state which is not extinguished or of which the occupant is a legal successor.[7] The obligations presumably remain in suspense unless by good fortune the occupied country is in possession of assets abroad or if its territory is only partly occupied. Thus, Denmark, despite the military control exercised over the country by Germany during the years 1940 to 1945, made payments on its dollar bonds held in the United States under a Treasury license to disburse these funds out of Danish Government funds blocked in the United States.[8] Similarly, before December, 1941, the exiled Dutch Government, exercising its functions in London, advised holders of Netherlands East Indian loans of its readiness to pay matured coupons after it had been established that this portion of the national debt was free of enemy control.[9]

Norway serviced its dollar bonds during the war and paid them off on maturity in 1944.[10]

FORCED LOANS

This term is really a misnomer for contributions, usually in money, exacted from the local population. They may or may not be accompanied by a promise to repay but are exactions over and above taxes. The military occupant has power to demand contributions from the local popula-

7. Bonds issued by the United States, military occupant of the Dominican Republic, were recognized as binding obligations of Santo Domingo by a special agreement signed at Santo Domingo, June 12, 1924, ratifications exchanged December 4, 1925. *Am. Jour. Int. Law, Supp.* XX (1926), 53.

8. *Com. and Fin. Chron.*, CLI (July 13, 1940), 176. On payments by occupied countries, see *Corp. For. Bondh. Rep.*, 1941, p. 10.

9. *Com. and Fin. Chron.*, CLIV (November 13, 1941), 1040.

10. Cf. *ibid.*; B.I.S., *Eleventh Annual Report* (Basle, June 9, 1941), p. 109. French loans in the United States have also been serviced from licenses on blocked funds. Cf. Feilchenfeld, "Public Finance," *The International Economic Law of Belligerent Occupation* (Washington, Carnegie Endowment, 1942), p. 62.

tion. Article 52 of The Hague Regulations of 1907 provides only that contributions in kind shall, so far as possible, be paid for in cash; but, if this is not done, a receipt shall be given and the payment of the amount due shall be made as soon as possible. This is, of course, not a very compulsive prescription nor does it impose an obligation of payment on the occupant. As to money contributions, Article 49 merely provides that money contributions shall be levied only for the needs of the army or administration of the occupied territory. This is hardly a limitation on the levy of private money nor is it seriously impaired by the provision of Article 46 that "private property cannot be confiscated." It has met with objection or uneasiness by most students of the subject.[11]

Treaties in their provisions relating to forced loans vary a good deal. The Pan-American treaty of 1928, Article 4, accepted by the United States, allows them, providing they apply to the population generally. On the other hand, the Central-American Treaty of Peace and Amity of February 7, 1923,[12] exempts from forced loans the citizens of the contracting states; United States treaties with Latin American states generally provide for such exemption and exemption is also the European treaty practice. The fact that consuls are usually expressly exempted from such liability indicates that the practice with respect to civilians generally may not be uncommon.

11. Cf. Feilchenfeld, *op. cit.*, 11 ff., and index.
12. *Am. Jour. Int. Law., Supp.*, XVII (1923), 119. Article 12 of the treaty of Lausanne, 1923, prohibited Turkey from levying forced loans on nationals of allied countries doing business in Turkey.

PART IV

Bondholders' Remedies

Section XIII

BONDHOLDERS' LEGAL REMEDIES

THE peculiar nature of a contract of public loan and of the bond in which that transaction is recorded influences strongly the character of the remedy that the unpaid bondholder may invoke. Although Continental writers are prone to conclude that the contract is one governed by the principles of private law, the fact that the debtor is a state faces the bondholder with the limitations set by public law.

JUDICIAL REMEDIES IN DEBTOR STATE

Even where the debtor state may be sued in its own courts on contract, i.e., where it has given its consent to be sued,[1] the bondholders' remedy

1. Cf. discussion in *Twycross v. Dreyfus*, 5 Ch. D. 605, 36 L.T. Rep. (n.s.) 752, 755 (1877); Moulin, *La Doctrine de Drago* (Paris, 1908), pp. 86 ff.; Freund, *Die Rechtsverhältnisse der öffentlichen Anleihen*, p. 249. Professor Jèze states that the arguments of creditors against reduction of their debts are always the same, namely, that the constitution guarantees the right of property, that property includes public bonds, and that every legislative discrimination in respect of the debts is an injury to property and unconstitutional. Only in the few countries which permit the courts to set aside unconstitutional legislation is there a remedy. Others, therefore, have no distinct constitution protecting individual rights or, if they do have one, it is not judicially enforcible. Jèze, "Les Défaillances d'états," *Rec. des Cours*, LIII (1935), 399 ff.

Specific consent to a particular suit is rare. But by common law, as in many Continental and Latin American countries, general consent to sue a state or subdivision is granted by common law. In England and the United States, legislation has granted such consent in contract cases, under certain conditions. But see II, 14, n. 3: loan contract between the English firm of Montgomery, Nicod & Co. and Mexico providing that in the event of nonperformance by the (Mexican) Government of its engagements "the parties interested shall immediately have the right to claim for the losses and damages that would undoubtedly be caused to them." A lawsuit brought by the creditors against the Mexican Government after the latter's default was, however, unsuccessful. The firm's claim was, however, adjusted as a result of the intervention of the British Government. Cf. Borchard, *Diplomatic Protection of Citizens Abroad*, pp. 156, 159 ff. It was under the so-called Tucker act that the Court of Claims took jurisdiction of the gold clause cases, *infra*. In France, under a law of 1900, suit could be brought against the Government on its financial obligations before the administrative courts, but the

is not very effective. In theory, the loan is created by legislation, an act of sovereignty, and may be suspended, modified, or even repudiated by the same method, an act binding on the national courts. Thus the creditor is opposed to a sovereign who may, so far as municipal law is concerned, with ostensible legality, deprive him both of his substantive right and of his remedy. As a contract between private persons and a state, it is not governed by international law. It is commonly, although not accurately, said that the state in the exercise of its sovereign powers may regulate the execution of its own contract of loan as its public interests may seem to require.[2]

But even if jurisdiction were taken, as was the case in the suits in the Court of Claims and the United States Supreme Court on the joint resolution of June 5, 1933, suspending the gold clause in all contracts including federal loans, to obtain judgment might be difficult and execution impossible. To be sure, in the gold clause cases the Supreme Court admitted by a narrow majority that the United States had breached its contract to pay in gold of the "present standard of weight and fineness"; but with regard to an American bondholder they maintained that as the cost of living had not risen he could prove no damages by payment in a depreciated paper dollar.[3] It is not perceived why a Swiss or Dutch holder of Liberty bonds failed to sue, for he, coming from a gold standard country, could have shown a definite loss; doubtless the fear of such a suit caused Congress to pass the resolution of August 27, 1935, which denied the right of suit after January 1, 1936.[4] The inability to levy execution doubtless deters creditors from suing, even where in theory they might obtain a judgment, a mere substitution in the form of the claim.

---

government could within 4 months move to dismiss. Cf. Feilchenfeld, in Quindry, *Bonds and Bondholders, Rights and Remedies,* Vol. II, sec. 661 (b.3). Schmitthoff, "The International Government Loan," *Jour. Comp. Leg.,* XIX (1937), 190. Schoo, *Régimen jurídico,* pp. 445 ff., 456 ff.

2. Lewandowski, *De la protection des capitaux empruntés en France par les états étrangers,* pp. 24 ff. Strupp, "L'Intervention en matière financière," *Rec. des Cours,* VIII (1925), 74. While Drago and others helped to propagate the theory that a state contracts a loan in its capacity as a sovereign, *jure imperii,* and hence presumably is not bound by the obligations of contract, the theory is properly disputed. See Moulin, *op. cit.,* pp. 76 ff.; Freund, *op. cit.,* pp. 59–61; Ruy Barbosa, speech of July 23, 1907, at The Hague Conference, Actes et Discours, 60 ff.; *De Andrade v. Brazil,* Clunet, XL (1913), p. 237. Certainly a state which unilaterally changes the terms of its contract violates the contract and presumably the law; the difficulty is the practical one of enforcement of the obligation.

3. *Nortz v. United States,* 294 U.S. 317 (1935); *Perry v. United States,* 294 U.S. 330 (1935).

4. 49 Stat. 938, 74th Cong., 1st Sess.

SUITS WITHOUT CONSENT OF THE DEBTOR

In the case of the *Prince of Monaco* v. *Mississippi,* an ingenious plan was tried in the hope of avoiding the common law rule that a state could not be sued without its consent. Several Southern states had in the middle of the nineteenth century on one ground or another repudiated their debts.[5] Both state and federal courts had denied relief to the individual bondholders and even to American states which appeared as representatives of their citizen bondholders. Thereupon a plan was devised in Europe to give or sell some of the repudiated bonds to a *bona fide* sovereign who might be persuaded to sue the defaulting state, invoking the original jurisdiction of the United States Supreme Court. It is understood that the King of Spain was first selected for this test case but, when he lost his throne in 1931, the honor fell to the Prince of Monaco. Again the Supreme Court held that, although the court nominally had jurisdiction over the two parties, it would not exercise it in a case requiring the State of Mississippi compulsorily to pay its debts.[6] This fear inspired the Eleventh Amendment to the Constitution prohibiting states to be sued by a noncitizen without their consent in the federal courts, and the principle was deemed applicable to a suit brought by a foreign sovereign. The United States Government has refused to assume responsibility for the repudiated debts of the Southern states, on the perhaps valid grounds that the lender looked solely to the credit of the contracting state, an independent entity. The United States has therefore declined to arbitrate the claims.

SUITS AGAINST POLITICAL SUBDIVISIONS

In the case of municipal corporations or even the departments or provinces of Latin American countries, a somewhat broader remedy is available. Suits have been successfully brought against such departments or provinces, and, in the case of the City of Cordoba, Argentina, 7 per cent external bonds, the judgment had practical value.[7] As a matter of

5. Scott, *The Repudiation of State Debts;* Randolph, "Foreign Bondholders and the Repudiated Debts of the Southern States," *Am. Jour. Int. Law,* XXV (1931), 76; McGrane, *Foreign Bondholders and American State Debts.*

6. *Monaco* v. *Mississippi,* 292 U.S. 313, 321 (1934); see also McGrane, *op. cit.,* pp. 220–222.

7. E.g., suit by Marine Midland Trust Co., as fiscal agent, against the Department of Tolima, Colombia, for deposit of pledged revenues to be held as collateral for external twenty-year 7% bonds, until payment could be made on the bonds or a satisfactory settlement arranged. After an unfavorable decision in the lower courts, the Supreme Court of Justice handed down a decision on October 14, 1940, ordering the Department to make its deposits as from December, 1931, to July,

fact, the difficulty of suing a Continental or Latin American government or entity is generally over-stated. Greater embarrassment lies in the fact that the representative action or even the trustee's action (in the absence of express agreement with the state) on behalf of all the bondholders is not recognized.[8] Action must thus be commenced generally by a few bondholders alone, who in theory must assume the burden and the risk, whereas others may reap the benefit indirectly.

While municipal corporations in the United States can be sued on their defaulted bonds, their public property, except in New England, is by statute exempt from execution.[9] But in the New England states, the creditor of a town or other public or quasi public corporation, including

---

1938, when suit was begun. The total of the deposits would be $1,593,333 in United States currency, but the court converted this amount into Colombian currency at the parity rate in 1927 when the bonds were issued. *Com. and Fin. Chron.*, CLI (November 2, 1940), 2571.

See suit filed by White, Weld & Co., as fiscal agents, against City of Cordoba, Argentina, for payment of interest and sinking fund or coupons due in 1937 and for the attachment of revenues pledged by the city to such payment. Also suit against city for acceleration of maturity of loan, denied because not more than 50% of outstanding bonds were represented. Judgment for interest and for $1,-014,000 principal was recovered, after attachment had been granted; in April, 1939, it was announced that the judgment was ready for execution as soon as prior attachments on judgments for coupons had been satisfied. The plaintiffs expected to apply for collection of their *pro rata* share of the pledged revenues. See decisions and opinions of March 29, 1938, June 11, 1938, July 5, 1938, and July 6, 1938, and White, Weld circulars of November 19, 1937, April 14, 1938, and June 24, 1938. It was announced that further suits could be instituted for subsequently deposited bonds. *Idem*, CXLVIII (April 1, 1939), 1880. Judgment against the City for the full payment of the unpaid principal and interest on its gold bonds maturing November 15, 1937, was obtained on behalf of all bondholders who had not previously sued the municipality. *Idem*, CXLIX (November 25, 1939), 3339. The chances of successful execution of a judgment against a political entity in civil law countries are in inverse proportion to the size of the entity, city, province, or nation. Cf. E. Turlington, "Rights and Remedies of Foreign Bondholders," *Am. Bar Assn. Jour.*, XX (1934), 243. It is reported that the Argentine provinces of Buenos Aires, Mendoza, Tucumán, Santa Fé, and San Juan were ordered by the Supreme Court of Argentina, on the suit of the French Bondholders' Association, to pay in gold interest on certain prewar bonds issued in France. *Trade Inf. Bull.*, No. 656, October, 1929, "French Experience with Defaulted Foreign Bonds." Possibly such action against a nation would have been frustrated by moratoria, or prohibition of transfer, etc., but it is too much to say that such action is always "futile." Cf. A. W. Dulles, "The Protection of American Foreign Bondholders," *For. Aff.*, X (1932), 475.

Foreclosure suit against Colombia Agricultural Mortgage Bank. SEC, *Rep.*, Pt. V, p. 16, n. 46.

8. Weiser, *Trusts on the Continent of Europe*, p. 89.

9. SEC, *Rep.*, Pt. IV, pp. 16–17.

in some instances a city, may not only levy against public property, in principle, but against the private property of the inhabitants.[10] The federal municipal bankruptcy act, now sustained as constitutional,[11] would probably prevent such a privilege from becoming practical. But even in other states the bondholder is not helpless, for he can get mandamus to compel a payment from surplus funds or the levy of a tax. Such remedies have not proved very efficient.

ENFORCEMENT OF SECURITY CLAUSES

The enforcibility of a so-called pledge of revenue or security contained in many bonds of weaker countries has already been dealt with in a previous section. While the efficacy of these guaranties has not been great, especially when left to the debtor state to administer, and their inclusion in bond contracts has evoked cynical comments, security clauses have not been without value in according privileges and preferences in the reorganization of an insolvent state and in the distribution of available funds.[12]

10. *Idem*, p. 17. *Nuveen* v. *Board of Public Instruction*, 88 F. (2d) 175 (C.C.A. 5th, 1937), constructive trust for the benefit of purchaser of void bonds, noted in *No. Car. Law Rev.*, XVI (1937), 42. See list of cases noting conditions under which the writ of mandamus will be granted, in C. W. Tooke, "The Municipality and the Courts," *Municipal Year Book*, V (1938), p. 68, n. 60.

11. *Ashton* v. *Cameron County District*, 298 U.S. 513 (1936) (held unconstitutional). After change in statute, held constitutional in *United States* v. *Bekins*, 304 U.S. 27 (1938).

12. *Infra*, pp. 356–358. The Securities and Exchange Commission investigation of protective committees summarized as follows its conclusions as to the judicial enforcibility of mortgages or allocated revenues.

"The promise to allocate certain revenues to the payment of bond service ordinarily avails the bondholder little or nothing. Should the obligor nation refuse or fail to make the allocation, no legal sanction ordinarily exists to compel the obligor to comply with this covenant for the protection of its creditors.

"Nor does the mortgaging of physical property as security for the bond issues materially improve the bondholder's legal status upon default as no effective legal machinery is available to him to foreclose a mortgage or a lien on property. The only courts which have jurisdiction to enter the foreclosure decree are those of the debtor itself. While these courts may as a theoretical matter be open to the foreign bondholders to foreclose on the mortgaged property of a foreign municipal or other political subdivision of lesser dignity than a sovereign foreign government, as a practical matter the remedy cannot feasibly be pursued. In most cases the mortgaged property serves as an adjunct of the debtor in the performance of a governmental service to its citizens. Thus, for example, the security may be a governmentally owned and operated power plant. The difficulties inherent in the creditors seizing a power plant in a foreign state and operating or selling it for their benefit are sufficient to persuade the bondholders in most cases to forsake such remedy and proceed by negotiation . . . . It is apparent that any foreign

Before dealing with other forms of available remedy, some comment is necessary upon the bondholder's privilege of suing the debtor in the creditor's courts.

JUDICIAL REMEDIES IN CREDITOR STATES

The privilege of suing a debtor state on its defaulted bonds in the creditor country runs against difficulties deeply entrenched in the law. While in first instance the immunity of a foreign sovereign from suit is a matter of municipal law, nevertheless the international law rule of immunity in principle has greatly affected the municipal law in all states.

THE RULE OF IMMUNITY—NATIONAL THEORIES
AND PRACTICE

Perhaps the countries of the Anglo-American system adopt the widest degree of inherent immunity and demand an express submission before they will accept jurisdiction.[13] As this is rarely given in bond cases, the matter is in this relation of minor importance only.

The Continent of Europe, however, more impressed with the distinction between governmental activities of private law and of sovereign character, and with the fact that a bond issue is contracted under rules of private law, exhibits more disposition, though by no means a majority view, to subject states to suit on their bonds if some special facts can be alleged, such as an intention to submit to the creditor's jurisdiction, an assignment of funds or property in the creditor country as special security, a mortgage on real estate there, or some similar act implying

---

state would regard such attempt as an affront to its dignity and an interference with its sovereignty." SEC, *Rep.*, Pt. V (May 14, 1937), pp. 15 f.

13. *Schooner Exchange* v. *McFaddon*, 7 Cranch 116 (1812). *Pesaro Duff Development Co.* v. *Government of Kelantan* (1924) A.C. 797. *Lamont* v. *Travelers Insurance Co.*, 281 N.Y. 362, 24 N.E. (2d) 81 (1939). F. Deàk, "The Plea of Sovereign Immunity and the New York Court of Appeals," *Col. Law Rev.*, XL (1940), 453. Cf. Nussbaum, *Money in the Law*, p. 390; comment in *Yale Law Jour.*, L (1941), 1088.

But jurisdiction is generally assumed in the United States over government-owned corporations. *Coale* v. *Société Co-operative Suisse des Charbons*, 21 F. (2d) 180 (S.D. N.Y. 1921); *Keifer and Keifer* v. *Reconstruction Finance Corp.*, 306 U.S. 381 (1939). In England, this is less common. *Comp. Mercantil Argentina* v. *United States Shipping Board*, 131 L.T. Rep. 388 (1934).

Clauses providing that the law of New York, for example, shall be applied to the contract would hardly have the effect of subjecting the foreign state to the jurisdiction of the New York courts. It is doubtful whether express submission in the contract would be construed as a general waiver of immunity. Cf. Feilchenfeld, *op. cit.*, Vol. II, sec. 638 (e). Schoo, *op. cit.*, p. 445.

consent to the jurisdiction. This is fortified perhaps by the Belgian, Italian, and Egyptian willingness to subject to the jurisdiction not only the state itself but any state acting *jure gestionis* and by the fact that "implied consent" or voluntary submission is more readily assumed than in the Anglo-American world. Thus we find the Belgian, French, Swiss, and German courts exercising jurisdiction in certain bond cases where by contract the court inferred or assumed a voluntary submission. As the immunity is deemed not inherent in public policy, it may be waived.[14] So, a state (Antioquia) was held subject to suit in France in the person of an agent whom it had appointed with power to sue and be sued; [15] where the parties had stipulated that a certain law or certain courts were to have jurisdiction over disputes; [16] in a suit in Switzerland against the Austrian Treasury on bonds which the Austrian Government had agreed to repay in Swiss currency, provided such bonds were purchased in Switzerland by Swiss nationals; [17] where an Austrian railroad, taken over by the Austrian Government just before execution of the judgment, was sued on its Treasury bonds by a German bondholder.[18]

14. In *U.S.S.R.* v. *Chaliapine* (*Rec. Sirey*, 1937, 1, 104), the French Court of Cassation held that the Soviet Union had recognized the jurisdiction of the French courts in commercial matters and was therefore subject to their jurisdiction in such matters.

15. *Credit foncier d'Algérie*, etc. v. *Départment de Antioquia* (Trib. civ., Seine, 1922), 1 Gaz. Pal. 439, 444; *Am. Jour. Int. Law, Supp.*, XXVI (1932), 552.

16. *Rochaïd-Dahdah* v. *Gouvernement tunisien* (Trib. civ., Seine, 1888), 1 Gaz. Pal. 626; *Am. Jour. Int. Law, Supp.*, XXVI (1932), 552.

17. *K. K. Oesterreich. Finanzministerium g. Dreyfus* (Bundesgericht, 1918), 44. I. *Entscheidungen des Schweizerischen Bundesgerichtes*, XLIV (1918), I, 49, 51; *Am. Jour. Int. Law, Supp.*, XXVI (1932), 558. Yet where these conditions are not present jurisdiction was declined by the Swiss courts, even when the property of the debtor government had been attached. *Hellenische Republic* v. *Obergericht Zürich* (Bundesgericht, 1930), 56. I. *Entscheidungen des Schweizerischen Bundesgerichtes*, 237, 250; *Am. Jour. Int. Law, Supp.*, XXVI (1932), 559. In distinguishing the *Dreyfus* case, the court conditioned Swiss jurisdiction on the fact that the debt was "originated, concluded or performed" in Switzerland by the debtor or that he shall have designated a place of performance in Switzerland. Athens was the place of payment. Miss Eleanor Wyllys Allen, in her valuable work on *The Position of Foreign States before National Courts* (New York, Macmillan, 1933), p. 284, informs us that the Swiss Federal Council were so much concerned by this decision that they annulled it, July 12, 1918, and issued a decree which forbade, subject to reciprocity, the sequestration of the property of a debtor or bankrupt state and forcible measures of execution against movable property of foreign states. A legislative bill to this effect after the war failed of passage and on July 8, 1926, the decree of July 12, 1918, was repealed. The *Hellenische Republik* case is described by Miss Allen, *idem*, p. 285.

18. *Heizer* v. *Kaiser-Franz-Joseph Bahn A. G.* (*Gerichtshof für Kompetenzkonflikte*, Bayern, 1885), *Gesetz- und Verordnungsblatt für das Königreich Bayern*,

Egypt, having become a protectorate of Great Britain in 1914 and having been released from liability for the Turkish tribute by the treaty of Lausanne, contended that she was no longer liable for service of the three tribute loans, and in July, 1924, suspended payment. The bondholders thereupon brought suit in the mixed courts and obtained judgment, the opinion remarking that the refusal of pay was not a sovereign act which escaped judicial review but a breach of contract, the issue involving the interpretation of the contract and the Khedival decrees written into the 1891 and the 1894 bonds.[19]

Although Germany has adopted a wide degree of immunity over foreign states and in principle refuses to permit the attachment of funds of a foreign state, the German courts nevertheless held that Turkey had by implication submitted to the jurisdiction of the German courts and to the execution of judgment as well—a conclusion somewhat unusual—when funds were deposited in a German bank as special security for Germans furnishing credit to the Turkish Government.[20] Again, by

1885, I, 16; *Am. Jour. Int. Law, Supp.*, XXVI (1932), 619. Cf. O. Fischer, *Die Verfolgung vermögensrechtlicher ansprüche gegen ausländische staaten* (Leipzig, 1912), p. 16, citing Bekker's work on the Austrian railroad litigation. This was deemed, by way of exception, a voluntary submission to execution, because Austria had succeeded to the position of the railway after the plaintiff became entitled to judgment. Cf. *Feldman* v. *State of Bahia* (Bruxelles, 1907), *Pasicrisie Belge*, Ser. III, 1908, Pt. II, 55, suit for breach of contract to negotiate loan in Belgium; but suit on the loan would have been rejected. In *Hamspohn* v. *Bey of Tunis* (Court of Appeal of Lucca, 1887), *Foro Italiano*, XII (1887), 474, 487, a suit on a treasury note, immunity was not granted because it involved a transaction of private law, but on the ground that the parties were both nonresidents and that the obligation was both contracted and to be performed abroad. Funds in Italy belonging to Tunis had been attached. *Am. Jour. Int. Law, Supp.*, XXVI (1932), 639. Allen, *op. cit.*, 230. In the *Trutta* case, suit against Romania in Italian courts, Romanian bonds located in Rome were successfully attached. *Idem*, p. 245. They were "patrimonial," not "sovereign," property. See comment· in *idem*, p. 262. Nor was immunity maintained in *De Croonenbergh* v. *L'État ind. du. Congo, Pasicrisie Belge*, Ser. III, 1896, Pt. III, p. 252 (agent sued principal for whom he contracted loan).

19. II, 522 ff.; *Gaz. des Trib. Mix.*, XV (1924–25), 193; *idem*, XVI (1925–26), 261. The mixed courts have jurisdiction over the suit of a foreigner against Egypt, where "an established private right is claimed to be violated by an administrative act" (Art. 11). But in the special law of liquidation, Article 86 prohibited suit by bondholders (II, 611). Yet the Commissioners of Public Debt (*Caisse*) sued the Egyptian Government in 1884 for violating the law of liquidation by diverting funds used for the sinking fund from the *Caisse* to the Minister of Finance. Pending appeal from a judgment for the *Caisse*, the Government resumed payments to the *Caisse*.

20. *X* v. *Türkischen Militärfiskus* (Court of Conflicts, Prussia, May 29, 1920, No. 2714), *Jur. Woch.*, L (1921), 773; *X* v. *Türkische Reich* (Court of Conflicts, Prussia, November 13, 1920, No. 2728), *idem.*, 1478. A different view was taken

virtue of the special circumstances, the French courts held that the Bey of Tunis had submitted to the jurisdiction of the French courts suits on certain bonds issued through French banks under an agreement by which disputes arising thereunder should be settled according to French law by French courts, to which the parties agreed to submit.[21] Among the several suits brought against Dreyfus Brothers, agents of Peru and holders of a monopoly over Peruvian guano, of which some was set aside

---

in the *Ziemer* case, 1881, described by Allen, *op. cit.*, pp. 62–64. Cf. *Entsch. Reichsg. Zivil.*, XIV (1884), 430, where real property of the Republic of Peru was attached. The decisions of the 1880's led Romania, Austria, and Peru to protest to Germany against the seizure of the property of those states, whereupon in 1885 the Federal Council presented to the Reichstag a bill prohibiting German courts from taking jurisdiction over foreign states or sovereigns. The bill was defeated. Allen, *op. cit.*, p. 67. But the Weimar Constitution of 1919 made international law a part of German law (Art. 4). This had really been the case before 1919, for on several occasions German courts refused jurisdiction over foreign states, especially on loans, *Entsch. Reichsg. Zivil.*, XXII (1889), 19.

21. Trib. civ. de la Seine, April 10, 1888, Clunet, XV (1888), 670, described by Allen, *op. cit.*, p. 168. Even the establishment of a debt commission, *infra*, p. 286, did not withdraw the case from the French jurisdiction. So the submission of a case to a French arbitrator was deemed to imply a submission to the execution of the award in France. *Heirs of Ben Aïad* v. *Bey of Tunis*, Clunet, XIX (1892), 952. In the case of *Government of Morocco and Maspero* v. *Lauress, Société Marseillaise de Crédit* (Lauterpacht, *Annual Digest of Public International Law Cases, 1929–1930*, p. 116), the Court of Aix held that the circumstances of the case did not warrant a presumption that the Moroccan Government had submitted to the jurisdiction of the French courts. In the absence of an act showing deliberate intention to waive immunity, courts in the creditor state have no jurisdiction over the debtor government because "national loans floated in France by a foreign Government are political acts of sovereignty, and bondholders can cite before French tribunals neither the head of that Government nor its financial agents. The Moroccan loan of 1904 fell into this category: it was raised by the Sultan to meet public needs and for the public services in virtue of his political power and in exercise of his governmental function." In connection with the Peruvian guano loans of 1870 and 1872, the French courts took jurisdiction over suits brought by bondholders against Dreyfus Bros., agents who had floated the loans. The Court of Appeal held that as the Peruvian Government was not a party to the suit, but that Dreyfus Bros. were sued personally, the court had jurisdiction, even though Dreyfus might have recourse against the Government of Peru. But, on the merits, the Court concluded that Dreyfus had not entered into any personal engagements and that as agents of Peru they were not liable. Allen, *op. cit.*, p. 167, and II, 133.

The French courts distinguished between personal torts of the bankers and those undertaken in proper execution of their mandate as agents of a foreign government. Fraudulent acts for personal benefit, including the issue of valueless bonds or false advertising with knowledge of falsity, or statements to inspire unfounded confidence in the credit of his principal made the banker personally liable. See note to case of *Bernet et al.* v. *Herran, Dreyfus. Schreyer et al.*, April 21, 1886, Court of Cassation. Dalloz, 1886, p. 393.

as security for the loans issued, a Belgian court held Dreyfus personally liable to the bondholders for unpaid coupons because of diversion of the security in the hands of Dreyfus. The Court of Appeal of Brussels held the assumption of jurisdiction proper, inasmuch as Peru was not a party to the suit.[22] But the British courts considered Dreyfus merely an agent, not a trustee, of the Peruvian Government, hence sharing its immunity.[23]

The special nature of these cases in which jurisdiction over foreign states was assumed may alone lead to the correct inference that as a general principle it is not possible to sue a foreign state on its public bonds. Even the courts of Belgium and Italy admit this, notwithstanding their view that a bond represents an instrument of private law and that a state emitting a loan abroad cannot act in a sovereign but only in a private or corporate capacity. The various attempts that have been made to sue defaulting states in the creditor's country, even where on occasion security has been attachable, as in the case of the Peruvian guano loans, have shattered for the most part on the elementary principle that a foreign state cannot in principle, under established rules of international law, be sued in municipal courts.[24] This rule was applied by the higher French courts in a case in which the funds had been deposited in France by the Moroccan Government as a guaranty for a loan, a fact which was held not sufficient to evidence voluntary submission to the jurisdiction;[25] in a suit against Italy which had undertaken to guarantee the defaulted bonds of a private company, a case in which the Italian courts might have assumed jurisdiction;[26] in a suit against the French banks

22. *Pasicrisie Belge*, Ser. III, 1877, Pt. II, 307, cited in Allen, *op. cit.*, p. 195. II, 130.

23. *Twycross* v. *Dreyfus, supra*, n. 1. The bondholders sued Dreyfus, the bankers, claiming their own priority over Dreyfus under the bonds of 1870 and 1872. The Court held that Peru had not divested itself of the guano, so as to create a trust or equitable assignment, and that there was no fiduciary relationship between Dreyfus and the bondholders.

24. *Spain* v. *Cassaux*, Dalloz (1849), I, 5, France: basic decision of January 22, 1849, and other French decisions cited by Imbert, *Les Emprunts d'états étrangers*, p. 17; Allen, *op. cit.*, pp. 151 ff.

25. *Laurens* v. *Gouvernement imperial du Maroc*, etc. (Cour d'Appel, Aix, 1930), 1 Gaz. du Pal. 246. The lower court (Trib. civ. Marseille, 1929), 1 Gaz. du Pal. 214, 216, thought the guaranty fund represented an implied submission to the jurisdiction. See also *State of Céara* v. *Dorr*, Cour d'Appel of Colmar, *infra*, n. 40. Cf. *Lamont* v. *Travelers Insurance Co.*, 281 N.Y. 362, 24 N.E. (2d) 81 (1939).

26. Commercial Trib. of the Seine, April 11, 1867, Dalloz (1867, II), 49, note, cited in Allen, *op. cit.*, p. 166. So in a suit against Belgium arising out of the Congo State bonds, payable in gold francs in Belgium and France, *Le Temps*,

which had issued now worthless loans of the Government of Honduras, because banks were deemed not personally liable but were merely agents of Honduras;[27] in a case prohibiting a garnishment in France of Yugoslav funds as a means of obtaining payment of principle and interest on a Yugoslav loan.[28] Similar conclusions have been reached in England,[29] Germany,[30] Belgium,[31] Italy,[32] and other countries.[33] The rule is applied with special rigidity in the United States.[34]

Although there is some tendency to subject foreign governments to suit when they engage in "an industrial, commercial, financial or other business enterprise" and the action arises therefrom, the (Harvard) *Research in International Law*, Article 11, nevertheless came to the conclusion that this provision should not be construed to allow a state to be a defendant in a proceeding relating to its public debt.[35] This goes

---

October 16, November 22, 1933, cited by Nussbaum, *op. cit.*, p. 344. The Belgian courts had held the gold clause void.

27. *Bernet*, etc. v. *Herran et al.*, Dalloz (1886), I, 393, cited by Allen, *op. cit.*, p. 167. Cf. suit against Dreyfus Bros. on Peruvian loan, *supra*, pp. 128–134.

28. *Banque ottomane et Soc. fin. d'Orient* v. *Philippe*, Clunet, LVIII (1931), 1040. Cf. *Reilhac et Chabot* v. *Comptoir National d'Escompte* (Trib. civ., Seine, 1895) [(1908) 2 *Gaz. des Trib.*, II, 270], *Am. Jour. Int. Law, Supp.*, XXVI (1932), 637.

Judge André Weiss suggested in a lecture that the French courts in the future would not entertain jurisdiction of suits on loans contracted abroad by a foreign government to meet army or navy or budget expenses, but would take jurisdiction when the loan was contracted for its "domaine privé." There seems little authority for this view, and Weiss himself suggested that the "nature of the acts undertaken by the foreign State" should alone be taken into consideration. *Rec. des Cours*, I (1923), 545 ff.

29. *Twycross* v. *Dreyfus, supra*, n. 1: Clause pledged Government of Peru to reserve sums sufficient to cover interest out of the proceeds of guano; declaration sought that interest on the bonds is a prior charge on the funds and guano in defendant agent's hands. *Smith* v. *Weguelin*, L.R. 8 Eq. 198, 212 (Eq. 1869), suit to compel defendants to apply proceeds of sale of guano, pledged as security for the loan, to redemption of loan. *Wadsworth* v. *Queen of Spain*, 17 Q.B. 171 (1851). When the English creditors of Turkey threatened to attach sums due by Great Britain to Turkey, they were told by the Government that they had no case, and that the Government, if any one, had a prior claim. II, 442.

30. *Ziemer* v. *Government of Romania*, 1881, *supra*, p. 165, n. 20.

31. Civil Trib. Brussels, December 1, 1893, *Pasicrisie Belge*, Ser. III, 1896, Pt. III, 32, and Civil Trib. Brussels, April 20, 1903, *Pasicrisie Belge*, Ser. III, 1903, Pt. III, 180, cited by Allen, *op. cit.*, p. 203.

32. Cf. dictum on public loans in *Hamspohn* v. *Bey of Tunis, supra*, p. 164, n. 18.

33. *Hellenische Rep.* v. *Obergericht Zurich, supra*, n. 17.

34. *Oliver Amer. Trading Co.* v. *Mexico*, 5 F. (2d) 659 (C.C.A. 2d, 1924); *Hassard* v. *Mexico*, 61 N.Y. Supp. 937 (1899); *Mason* v. *Intercolonial Ry.*, 197 Mass. 349 (1908), *Yale Law Jour.*, XL (1931), 786.

35. *Am. Jour. Int. Law, Supp.*, XXVI (1932), 597. Heymann speaks of a grow-

rather far, for the term "public debt" is broad. The conclusion was based on practical reasons, accentuated by the demands of Señor Drago who in his famous note of 1905 [36] emphasized the argument that a public loan was an act of "sovereignty." He found support in the reasoning of the Master of the Rolls in *Twycross* v. *Dreyfus* [37] who, considering the fact that the English courts would not assume jurisdiction of a case seeking to enforce the payment by agents in England of a Peruvian loan, reached the conclusion that

these so-called bonds amount to nothing more than engagements of honour, binding, so far as engagements of honour can bind, the government which issues them, but are not contracts enforcible before the ordinary tribunals of any foreign country, or even by the ordinary tribunals of the country which issued them, without the consent of the Government of that country.

As already observed, this is not an accurate description of the legal nature of the obligation, although difficulties of judicial enforcement make it seem almost true.

But, where judicial remedies are not effective, political remedies are necessarily invoked. The extent to which these are available to the bondholder and the extent to which he has other remedies at his disposal, we shall endeavor to establish.

JUDGMENTS ON COUNTERCLAIMS

In the meantime it may be observed that, while jurisdiction will not be taken in general against a foreign state, judgments over the plaintiff government or agency may occasionally be obtained on a counterclaim.[38] In bond cases this has little practical importance.

---

ing tendency to subject foreign states to the local jurisdiction in matters of a private law character. *Archiv. civil. Prax.* (new series), I (1923), 149.

36. *Infra*, p. 271.

37. *Supra*, n. 1. Also *Crouch* v. *Crédit Foncier of England*, 8 Q.B. 374 (1873). Cf. Phillimore, *Commentaries on International Law*, II, 18.

38. *Dexter & Carpenter, Inc.* v. *Kunglig Jarnvagsstyrelsen*, 43 F. (2d) 705 (C.C.A. 2nd, 1930). While no execution could be issued on the judgment on the counterclaim, amounting to about $400,000, the judgment was diplomatically settled between the United States and Sweden for $150,000. Dept. of State, *Press Releases*, No. 210 (Oct. 7, 1933), p. 199. See also Freund, *op. cit.*, p. 258. German decision, December 12, 1905, 62 *Entsch. Reichsg. Zivil.* 165. Belgium, Trib. Civ. Antwerp, June 19, 1880, *Pasicrisie Belge*, Ser. II, 1881, 313, 316. Suit by Peru for guano shipped from island in possession of rebels; judgment on the counterclaim for damages due to restrictions placed on the free disposition of guano. Allen, *op. cit.*, p. 194.

EXECUTION OF JUDGMENTS

Moreover, while judgment may occasionally be secured, execution on the judgment through judicial processes is very rare. Most states would refuse to order execution.[39]

IMMUNITY OF MEMBER STATES OF FEDERAL UNIONS

Although the member states of federal unions do not possess sovereignty in the international sense of the term, the immunity granted to the federal government in suits on loans issued abroad occasionally also extends to the component states in cases where suit on their bonds is brought against them in courts of the creditor country.[40]

IMMUNITY OF GOVERNMENTAL AGENCIES

There is much difference of opinion as to how far government corporations or government-owned domestic corporations share this immunity from suit. We have seen that it was shared in France and England by bankers who were deemed merely agents of the foreign government. At various times the Belgian State Railroad, the Imperial Railway of Canada, the Intercolonial Railway of Canada, owned by the Crown, the

39. *V. Hellfeld* v. *Russia*, December 29, 1909, *Am. Jour. Int. Law*, V (1911), 490; *Dexter & Carpenter* v. *Kunglig Jarnvagsstyrelsen, supra,* n. 38. Opinions of experts in *ZaöRVR,* IV (1910), 309–448. Allen, *op. cit.,* pp. 76–79. Freund believes that only public property, such as embassies, war vessels, etc., is by international law free from seizure on execution, unless further exemption is accorded by municipal law or treaty. Such a limitation is doubtful, for in the forum of either the debtor or the creditor public property used for any purpose is generally exempt. *Berizzi Bros.* v. *Steamship Pesaro,* 271 U.S. 562 (1926), though attachments are occasionally allowed on bank funds until the principal issue is decided. Continental writers concede jurisdiction where the suit involves real estate owned by a foreign government. Freund, *op. cit.,* pp. 252, 257. Decision of Supreme Court, December 12, 1905, *Entsch. Reichsg. Zivil.,* 62, 165; decision of June 7, 1921, *idem,* CII, 251; December 10, 1921, *idem,* CIII, 275; April 16, 1924, *idem,* CVIII, 50. Cf. Fischer, *op. cit.,* p. 14. As to Egypt, see *supra,* n. 19.

40. *Sullivan* v. *The State of São Paulo,* 36 F. Supp. 503 (E.D. N.Y. 1941). In a suit brought by a bondholder against the State of São Paulo, one of the Federated States of the United States of Brazil, for the payment of principal and interest on its bonds, the court held that, although international law did not require such recognition, the State of São Paulo should be recognized as possessing sovereign immunity as a matter of comity and reciprocal treatment. Funds of the State within the United States territory were declared to be immune from attachment because of the interest of the United States of Brazil in these funds. See also comment in *Yale Law Jour.,* L (1941), 1088. Cf., furthermore, *State of Céara* v. *Dorr,* Cour d'Appel of Colmar, June 1, 1928, (I, 2, *ZaöRVR* 216). The establishment of a guaranty fund with French banks was interpreted as implying a voluntary submission by the State to French jurisdiction.

Finnish State Railway, the Russian Volunteer Fleet, the Lloyd Brasileiro, and the United States Shipping Board have all been deemed governmental instruments enjoying the immunities of the state itself.[41] An international convention to take this immunity away from merchant ships, though owned or operated by governments, was concluded in 1926 at Brussels and has come into force for Belgium, Brazil, Chile, Estonia, Hungary, Poland, Germany, The Netherlands, Italy, and Romania.[42] A resolution to adhere to the Brussels Convention and an amendment of 1934 was adopted at the Lima conference in 1938. Such movements will doubtless continue. Governments now by municipal statute, as in the case of the United States, submit nationally owned vessels to foreign jurisdiction, at least by way of action *in personam* with provision for the posting of bonds.[43]

The United States has at times declined to extend the jurisdictional immunity to corporations organized by foreign governments or over which foreign governments exercise control.[44] Possibly if the foreign ambassador claimed immunity for the corporation as a public instrument a different view would be taken. This happened during the Dexter proceedings when the Swedish Government failed to claim its immunity from execution until after a decision had been obtained against the State Railway on a counterclaim.[45]

INCIDENTAL QUESTIONS

It is perhaps needless to say that many incidental questions not involving the duty of the defendant government to pay have been settled by suits in municipal courts. Claims against issuing bankers,[46] claims by

41. Citations to these cases will be found in Allen, *op. cit.*, p. 9. See also Hackworth, *Digest of International Law*, II (Washington, 1941), 480 f.; *Hannes* v. *Kingdom of Romania Monopolies Institute*, 260 App. Div. 189, 20 N.Y.S. (2d) 825 (1940), and comment in *Yale Law Jour.*, L (1941), 1088.

42. See International Convention for the Unification of Certain Rules Relating to the Immunity of State-owned Vessels, signed at Brussels, April 10, 1926, and Additional Protocol, signed at Brussels, May 24, 1934. League of Nations, *Treaty Series*, Vol. CLXXVI (1937), p. 199 (No. 4062).

43. Act of June 5, 1920, c. 250, 41 Stat. 988.

44. *Coale* v. *Société Co-operative Suisse des Charbons*, 21 F. (2d) 180 (S.D. N.Y. 1921); *United States* v. *Deutsches Kalisyndikat Gesellschaft*, 31 F. (2d) 199 (S.D. N.Y. 1929); *Molina* v. *Comision Reguladora del Mercado de Henequen*, 91 N.J.L. 382, 103 Atl. 397 (1918); *Perry* v. *Norddeutscher Lloyd*, 150 Misc. 73, 268 N.Y. Supp. 525 (1934); *Holzer* v. *Deutsche Reichsbahn Gesellschaft*, 160 Misc. 597, 289 N.Y. Supp. 943 (1936), 159 Misc. 830, 290 N.Y. Supp. 181, 196 (1936); *Yale Law Jour.*, XLV (1936), 1463.

45. *Dexter & Carpenter* v. *Kunglig Jarnvagsstyrelsen, supra*, n. 38.

46. Claims against the issuing house: see *The Economist*, April 24, 1875; *idem*, January 15, 1876; *idem*, March 31, 1877 (suit brought against André before Paris Tribunal of Commerce).

agents for services rendered and for reimbursement of expenditures,[47] even certain types of suits involving priority [48] have come before municipal courts. In *Twycross* v. *Dreyfus*,[49] Jessel, Master of the Rolls, thought that, as between the terms of the prospectus and the bond, the bond controlled.[50]

SUMMARY

It will have become apparent from this section that the judicial remedies of a bondholder in the forum of either the debtor or the creditor are exceedingly tenuous and in most cases practically unavailable. Suits may occasionally be brought against issuing banks for misrepresentation in the prospectus or for other personal tort of the bankers, and occasionally we may find circumstances from which the court will conclude that there has been a voluntary submission by the defaulting state to the jurisdiction of the creditor's forum. But these cases are likely to be rare. More promising are likely to be the political and economic remedies of the organized bondholders with or without the help of their state, and these will now engage our attention.

47. II, 141.
48. II, 141–143. Expenses v. bonds, and bond v. bond.
49. [1877] 5 Ch. D. 605, 617, L.T. Rep. (n.s.), XXXVI (1877), 752.
50. See *supra*, section on the Technical Contract.

Section XIV

BONDHOLDERS' ECONOMIC
REMEDIES

IT has been shown that the judicial remedies of foreign bondholders are hardly effective. The diplomatic remedies, as we shall see, are
not reliable, for not only do most governments hesitate in principle
to protect bondholders from the unfortunate result of their investment
but the opportunity to interpose diplomatically depends on the political
relations of the investors' government with the defaulter and upon other
political factors over which the bondholder has no control. Bondholders
have therefore learned to rely mainly upon their own bargaining power
and such means of reprisal as they may through private organizations
have available to obtain redress for inexcusable defaults and make terms
of composition or adjustment they consider proper under the circumstances.

Naturally, also, bondholders have sought to introduce into the loan
contracts clauses, such as arbitration, security, pledge, priority, and
other safeguards designed to protect themselves in cases of default, justified or unjustified. Bitter experience has also taught them the advantages
of a united front and protective committees in dealing with insolvent
governments. In some countries which coöperate with bondholders either
preventively or punitively to safeguard their interests, we find that governments may close a domestic bond market to a country in default to
national bondholders. The means of redress open to a disappointed bondholder may best be examined in the light of practical experience, although
naturally remedies and opportunities for reprisal and sanctions will vary
greatly according to circumstances.

EXCLUSION FROM QUOTATION ON STOCK
EXCHANGE

In the absence of a governmental promise of protection against the
borrower's default, bondholders naturally seek to find their own means
of protection or redress. One of the most effective has been for the stock
exchanges to deny a quotation to new bond issues of the defaulting gov-

ernments, when the circumstances warrant the exchange committee in believing that bad faith, recalcitrance, or unwillingness to perform are involved. For example, the London Stock Exchange long ago adopted a rule reading as follows:

The Committee will not recognize new bonds, stock or other securities issued by any foreign government that has violated the conditions of any previous public loan raised in this country, unless it shall appear to the Committee that a settlement of existing claims has been consented to by the general body of bondholders. Companies issuing such securities will be liable to be excluded from the official list.[1]

But this rule appears not to have been carried forward into the rules of 1925,[2] although it is known that governmental authorities can influence the stock exchange committee to refuse permission to deal in such securities.[3] Neither the Securities and Exchange Act of 1934 nor the New York Stock Exchange Regulation have any provision similar to London Rule 63. The stock listing requirements by the Board of Trade of the city of Chicago provide that the application to list foreign bonds must show the past record of "defaults, scaling down of interest payment, or suspending sinking fund payments."[4]

It is a serious handicap to a country to have all or some of its bonds excluded from an exchange market, and few countries would care to incur the obloquy. The possibility of this form of reprisal is an inducement to fair dealing with the bondholders. Following the two thirds reduction of interest on Portuguese external bonds in 1892, the Continental bourses decided not to deal even in these listed bonds if the partially defaulted coupons were detached. The London Stock Exchange, however, declined to follow suit, taking the view that such action would inconvenience the bondholders more than the Portuguese Government.[5]

1. Rule 63 as printed in Melsheimer and Gardner, *The Law and Customs of the Stock Exchange* (4th ed. London, 1905), p. 179. Cf. William J. Greenwood, *American and Foreign Stock Exchange Practice* (New York, Financial Books Co., 1921), p. 560.

2. F. J. Varley, *Rules and Regulations of the Stock Exchange* (London, Effingham Wilson, 1925).

3. *The Problem of International Investment*, p. 81.

4. The Securities and Exchange Commission under Section 12 (e) and (f) requires a statement of the law under which a security for which registration is requested is not serviced according to its original terms and the "circumstances of any other failure to pay principal, interest or any sinking fund or amortization installment." 135 C.C.H., pp. 4313 ff. For the Chicago rule, see *idem*, pp. 8025, 8041.

5. *Financial News* (London), July 1, 1892. During the years 1837 to 1856, while earlier issues of Portuguese bonds remained in partial or complete default,

In the case of Turkey the bondholders of the issues of 1858 and 1862 tried to prevent the quotation on the London Exchange of the loan of 1872 because of the Porte's failure to fulfill its promise to let the Control Syndicate receive and administer the revenues specially hypothecated to their loans.[6] The loan of 1877 was denied listing until 1882, soon after the settlement of the default on the previous Turkish issues.[7]

Greece having defaulted on the 1824 and 1825 bonds, the London and Paris exchanges refused to grant any quotation to the 1833 loan of Greece, notwithstanding its foreign guarantee.[8] So in 1897, while in default, Greece could obtain no loan to meet the Turkish war indemnity, because new Greek issues were barred from European markets.[9]

Bulgaria's diversion of the 1892 loan to purposes other than those agreed on resulted in a threat, futile as it proved, to bar quotation of new Bulgarian loans until the breach was remedied.[10] Bulgaria was not at the moment especially sensitive to maintaining its credit standing. In July, 1922, the Paris Bourse suspended the quotation of Bulgarian loans because of the continuance of the "black lists," numbered bonds which had been held in countries of depreciated currencies and had been transferred to Paris to secure the benefit of a better exchange rate. Diplomatic pressure in 1924 induced Bulgaria to withdraw the black lists.[11]

The attempt of Santo Domingo to bar the Hartmont bonds from inclusion in the conversion of 1888 caused the bonds of that country to be denied a quotation on the London Exchange until 1897, when Santo Domingo yielded.[12] On the ground that no proper settlement had been made of the British bondholders' claims in 1908, the London Exchange refused quotation of the new 1908 customs bonds.[13]

While the bondholders of Mexico protested in 1874 the grant of railroad concessions and sought to prevent quotation of the bonds on the stock markets, the concessions were granted, although Amsterdam did refuse the quotation. London did not follow, notwithstanding the default on the 1851 and 1864 loans, on the ground that the railroad debtor was

the London Stock Exchange agreed not to quote any new issues of Portuguese bonds. II, 364.

6. A quotation was granted only after the Porte, in February, 1873, effected an arrangement acceptable to the bondholders. II, 405 and 409.

7. II, 424.

8. II, 287, 292.

9. II, 313.

10. II, 534, n. 18.

11. II, 546, n. 75.

12. II, 209. A portion of the proceeds of the 1879 loan was used to pay off the unconverted Hartmont bonds. II, 223.

13. The British had to take a 10% cut like the San Domingo Improvement Co. II, 261, n. 71.

a Mexican private company.[14] In 1883 the fact that the London money market remained closed to Mexico operated as a strong incentive to readjust the Mexican debt.[15]

In 1854 a bondholders' committee in England objected to the grant of a quotation to Peruvian internal bonds on the ground that they had been illegally issued.[16] But upon Peru's agreeing to raise the rate on the sinking fund of the 1853 loan, the committee dropped its objections. In 1887 the bondholders succeeded in persuading the Exchange to refuse quotations to the Chilean loan of 1887, until Chile agreed to assume a part of the Peruvian debt arising out of Chile's annexation of the province of Tarapacá whose guano had been assigned as security for the original loans.[17] In 1909 the French Government refused to permit the listing of a loan negotiated in Paris, unless Peru abandoned its *non possumus* with respect to the Dreyfus claims and agreed on a composition with French creditors.[18]

JOHNSON ACT—REPRISAL FOR DEFAULT

In an effort to prevent American private loans to countries in default on their indebtedness to the United States, Senator Johnson introduced in the Senate an act, duly passed in 1934 by both Houses, known as the Johnson Act. It read as follows:

Be it enacted by the Senate and House of Representatives of the United States of America in Congress assembled, That hereafter it shall be unlawful within the United States or any place subject to the jurisdiction of the United States for any person to purchase or sell the bonds, securities, or other obligations of, any foreign government or political subdivision thereof or any organization or association acting for or on behalf of a foreign government or political subdivision thereof, issued after the passage of this Act, or to make any loan to such foreign government, political subdivision, organization, or association, except a renewal or adjustment of existing indebtedness while such government, political subdivision, organization, or association, is in default in the payment of its obligations, or any part thereof, to the Government of the United States. Any person violating the provisions of this Act shall upon conviction thereof be fined not more than $10,000 or imprisoned for not more than five years, or both.

SEC. 2. As used in this Act the term "person" includes individual, partnership, corporation, or association other than a public corporation created

14. II, 34.
15. II, 38.
16. II, 112, n. 9.
17. II, 157.
18. II, 169.

by or pursuant to special authorization of Congress, or a corporation in which the Government of the United States has or exercises a controlling interest through stock ownership or otherwise.[19]

Attorney General Cummings, May 5, 1934, was requested by the Secretary of State to render an opinion on the meaning of "default" and "partial default" as used in the act, for the purpose of determining the countries to which the prohibition was applicable. On the basis of administrative rules, he held [20] that Czechoslovakia, Italy, Latvia, Lithuania, Great Britain, and also Canada were not in default, although they were, except Canada, in arrears in the payment of their debt, and in spite of the words "partial default" used in the act. President Roosevelt had stated on November 7, 1933, that, in view of the token payment made in that year by Great Britain, he would not regard Great Britain as in default. There was a difference of opinion in Congress on this question, Mr. McReynolds, Chairman of the House Committee on Foreign Affairs, as did the Attorney General, following the executive view. Mr. Cummings also held that private money could be loaned to the political subdivision of a country in default, that a renewal of old loans was excepted from the restriction, but that Soviet Russia was a country in default. In spite of a strong effort of the Administration after 1940 to get the Johnson Act repealed,[21] it was not until 1945, when the Bretton Woods Agreements Act [22] and the Export-Import Bank Act [23] were passed, the latter authorizing a great increase in the Bank's capital, that authority was given both banks to guarantee private loans. This is generally regarded as effecting a tacit repeal of the Johnson Act.[24]

OTHER ECONOMIC REMEDIES

The most obvious response against a breach of a loan contract is a bondholders' protest. Such protest acquires added weight if made by a committee of bondholders or by the Council of Foreign Bondholders or

19. 48 Stat. 574, 31 U.S.C.A. § 804a (April 13, 1934).

20. *Ops. Atty. Gen.*, XXXVII (1932–34), 505; *Am. Jour. Int. Law*, XXIX (1935), 160.

21. *Hearing before the Senate Committee on Finance on S. 636*, 79th Cog., 1st Sess. (1945). See also remarks of Representative Chiperfield, *Cong. Rec.*, XCI (June 19, 1945), p. A3148.

22. Chap. 339, Public Law 171, 79th Cong., 1st Sess. (July 31, 1945).

23. Chap. 341, Public Law 173, 79th Cong., 1st Sess. (July 31, 1945).

24. *Hearings before the House Committee on Banking and Currency on H.R. 3464 and H.R. 3490 superseded by H.R. 3771*, 79th Cong., 1st Sess. (1945), p. 13; *Hearings before the Senate Committee on Banking and Currency on H.R. 3771*, 79th Cong., 1st Sess. (1945), p. 17.

other recognized national group. Thus in 1894 the French, British, and German bondholders immediately protested through their committees against Greece's arbitrary abrogation of their contractual rights.[25] Again, in 1875 the bondholders protested against a uniform treatment by Turkey of secured and unsecured creditors.[26]

An unusual exemplification of bondholders' protest was the street campaign waged against Portugal by the holders of the Dom Miguel bonds. With posters, sandwichmen, and handbills they probably contributed to the failure of a Portuguese loan issue in 1890 [27]

Reprisals of various kinds have occasionally been resorted to. Thus, in 1932 the holders of Bulgarian bonds, because of their objections to the statute of April 20, 1932, impairing their rights, ordered their agent to refuse to deliver banderoles or tax certificates for tobacco to the Bulgarian officials, a refusal which threatened to diminish the public revenues through injury to the tobacco factories.[28]

The bondholders may seek to protect themselves by foresight in drafting the loan contract and especially by introducing clauses which may be invoked in the event of disputes. Among these the arbitration clause is acquiring vogue.[29] Article 17 of the agreement of 1901 between Santo Domingo and the Belgian and French bondholders provided for the arbitration of disputes.[30] Provisions for security and priority belong in this category but are so varied that they will be treated in separate sections.

In lieu of bond payments or as special security bondholders occasionally obtain in the loan contract a commitment to assign to the bondholders, in the event of default, some public utility for operation by the bondholders in the interests of themselves and the government. Naturally, only weak governments consent to such arrangement, without which, however, no loan would have been obtained. Thus, Peru assigned to the Peruvian Corporation under the Grace contract the operation of the Peruvian railways.[31] The Bulgarian loan of 1892 provided that in the event of default the bondholders could operate the railroads and, after

25. II, 308.

26. II, 418.

27. II, 363.

28. II, 567. Bulgaria threatened then to print the banderoles. The dispute was settled by a compromise. II, 568.

29. Cf. II, 229, n. 22.

30. In the San Domingo Improvement Co. arbitration agreement the Government agreed on the purchase price for the Company's rights but left to arbitration the terms of payment, including security, installments, and interest. II, 230.

31. II, 155, 171. When Peru failed to pay the subsidy due under the contract, the Peruvian Corp. refused to continue railroad construction.

two years' default, could sell the lines to pay for overdue coupons and drawn bonds and eventually for the nonamortized balance.[32]

Bondholders naturally find their best protection in an arrangement which gives them direct control of the revenues and enables them to discharge their own obligations and distribute the balance to the debtor government.

THE DEBTOR'S CREDIT

However attractive to the purchaser of a bond and however effective in particular instances these economic and other remedies of the bondholder have proved to be, the most effective sanction for the service and payment of a foreign bond in the minds of bankers is the consequence of default on a nation's credit and the effect on all credit-seeking subdivisions and even private business. By making new loans unavailable, or obtainable only at a cost commensurate with the risk involved, prolonged default may exert a depressing if not disastrous effect on the economic life of a country.[33] The fact that a defaulting state usually seeks to reëstablish first its external credit lends weight to the view of Mr. Thomas W. Lamont that the interwoven fabric of international credit and trade often gives moral considerations greater force than legal measures.[34]

32. II, 534.
33. J. A. Levandis, *The Greek Foreign Debt and the Great Powers, 1821–1898* (New York, Columbia University Press, 1944), p. 86.
34. T. W. Lamont, "Foreign Government Bonds," *Ann. Am. Acad.*, LXXXVIII (March, 1920), 123.

Section XV

PRIVATE PROTECTIVE
COMMITTEES

A FOREIGN bond default leaves the individual bondholders helpless, since in his isolated position he has no means of effective
negotiation with the creditor. Hence it was natural for the idea
of a joinder of interests and representation to develop, exemplified first
in England during the first half of the nineteenth century by the formation of protective committees of the bondholders of Spanish-American,
Portuguese, Greek, and other loans. These early committees were apparently composed solely of bondholders of the defaulted loans. The
frequency of default and the inefficiency and lack of governmental
support of the purely private committee led in 1868 to the organization
of the Corporation of Foreign Bondholders,[1] described later. In the
United States the disadvantages of the private protective committee,
only occasionally consisting of bondholders, were more acute and led
to the organization of the government-sponsored Foreign Bondholders
Protective Council, Inc., also to be discussed presently.[2]

INDEPENDENT COMMITTEES IN THE UNITED
STATES

The growing investment of United States private capital, following
the outbreak of World War I, in foreign governmental bonds, found
this country without any institutions for dealing with possible defaults.
England and the Continent, the nineteenth-century suppliers of nearly
all the capital invested in foreign bonds, had learned from experience
the importance of an orderly medium for negotiating with debtor governments on behalf of scattered bondholders the readjustment of an insolvency. Responsible organizations like the British Corporation of

1. Even after the establishment of the Corporation of Foreign Bondholders,
bondholding committees, not under the aegis of the Corporation, were occasionally
formed. Cf. the Bouverie, Hamond, and Tocqueville committees in Turkey (II,
427, 428, 433. The Croyle minority committee in Peru (II, 137).
2. See *infra*, p. 193 ff.

Foreign Bondholders and somewhat smaller bodies in other countries had demonstrated their value in protecting the interests of bondholders in the adjustment of defaults. In the United States no thought appears to have been given to this subject until about 1932, after the crashes of 1929 and 1931 had brought into default practically one third of the foreign governmental loans floated in the United States during the roseate period of the 1920's.[3] The unfortunate experience with independent volunteer committees finally led the United States Government to suggest some more formal governmental institution to assist bondholders without committing the United States Government.

Title II of the Federal Securities Act of 1933 had in fact provided for a governmental body to be financed by the United States.[4] Reconsideration of the matter persuaded the President not to bring Title II into force but to use the good offices of the Government to help organize and give prestige to the Foreign Bondholders Protective Council, Inc., a private organization financed from private contributions.

INVESTIGATION BY THE SECURITIES AND EXCHANGE COMMISSION

Dissatisfaction with protective committees in all fields of bond investment, commercial, municipal, real estate, and foreign, and especially the widespread discussion of the abuses associated with such groups led Congress to include in the Securities Exchange Act of 1934 a section, 211, authorizing the Commission to undertake a "study and investigation of the work, activities, personnel and functions of protective and reorganization committees." This study and investigation, directed by Justice William O. Douglas, then a professor of the Yale Law School,[5] covered a period of over two years and the results are embodied in a

---

3. In England the existence of the Corporation of Foreign Bondholders has not precluded the formation of independent committees. The interests of British holders of defaulted Peruvian bonds remained during the long negotiations of 1876 to 1890 in the hands of such a committee. When, in 1890, the federal government of Argentina proved unable to meet its foreign debt obligations, a committee of bankers dealt with the matter; on the three occasions on which the financial difficulties of the Brazilian Government necessitated the funding for a period of the service charges, the House of Rothschild itself concluded the arrangements; while a League Loans Committee was constituted under other auspices than that of the Corporation. But such instances are few and can be accounted for by special circumstances.

4. 48 Stat. 74; 15 U.S.C.A. § 77a.

5. Subsequently Chairman of the Securities and Exchange Commission and now an Associate Justice of the United States Supreme Court.

report of seven volumes.[6] The report is one of the ablest and most informative documents ever published in the field and, whether or not all its recommendations are ultimately incorporated in legislation, it has already served to correct many abuses. Some of these are controllable by the SEC itself and others may be administratively supervised by other departments of the government. For present purposes, our main interest lies in the disclosures concerning the operation of "protective committees and agencies for holders of defaulted foreign governmental bonds," covered by Part V of the Commission's report.[7]

The SEC investigated the organization and operation of some thirteen independent private committees created after 1932 to deal with the defaulted bonds of Salvador, Colombia, Chile, Cuba, and Peru. These represent more than half of the independent committees then functioning in the foreign bond field, and the Commission considered them and their practices representative of all similar committees.[8]

The independent committees in this country fall into three groups: (1) those organized by strangers to the issue in default, speculators, lawyers, and others desirous of assembling as many bondholders as possible and charging a fee, generally a small percentage of the face amount of the bonds, for a successful negotiation and readjustment with the debtor country; [9] (2) those organized by the issuing bankers or those who participated in the original distribution of the bonds, who may desire to save their reputations, help their clients, or be otherwise useful, also charging a fee; and (3) committees formed by the Foreign Bondholders Protective Council, Inc., analogously to those of their British counterpart, who enjoy quasi official support and standing and are in a position through superior facilities for negotiation to compete successfully with the more selfish independent committees. While the SEC began its investigation with an open mind, they reached the conclusion that the last type of committee warrants primary approval, except possibly where action for fraud or misrepresentation is to be brought against issuing bankers.[10]

6. SEC, *Rep.* See Abbreviations.

7. Cf. the review of this volume by Edwin Borchard, *Col. Law Rev.*, XXXVIII (1938), 376–383.

8. According to the SEC, *Rep.*, Pt. V, 94, the 13 committees investigated acted for some $557,000,000 of defaulted bonds, or 32% of the foreign bonds in default.

9. A fee of, e.g., 1% of the face amount of the bonds would, of course, be a much higher percentage of the value of the bonds at default prices.

10. SEC, *Rep.*, Pt. V, pp. 302, 737. The Council does not usually organize subcommittees but did so in the case of Chile and Cuba because of the existence of competing independent committees.

METHODS OF EVIDENCING REPRESENTATION
OF BONDHOLDERS

The independent committees' methods of evidencing representation of the bondholders varies. Some committees solicit the physical deposit of bonds, which ties the bondholders' hands by removing their control over the bonds and enables the committee to pledge them and establish a lien for the committee's compensation. It usually indicates the bondholders' approval of the committee's contract for services and possibly assures their assent to any arrangement for readjustment. On the other hand, the protective committee thereby assumes the obligations of a trustee. Some committees accept powers of attorney or proxies without seeking physical control of the bonds. They are then merely agents of the bondholders, not necessarily trustees. Finally, some committees merely request "registration" with the committee of the name, address, and holdings of the owner. The committee speaks for these bondholders but is not actually an agent for them. The legal relationship, if any, is usually determined by what a bondholder does in accepting or rejecting a plan of readjustment. Particular individuals or corporations may also at times represent the bondholders by consent, as in the case of San Domingo Improvement Company, which represented European bondholders in its negotiations with Santo Domingo in 1900.[11]

CREATION AND OPERATION OF PROTECTIVE
COMMITTEES

The Commission in its investigation of independent committees established certain evils associated with the unregulated voluntary operation of these bodies. The Commission found that these private committees spring into being at the initiative of persons seeking to profit from the bondholders' need of having organized representation but who have otherwise, apart from certain issuing bankers' or fiscal agents' committees, no connection with the defaulted issue, own no bonds, have little or no experience in the field, enlist a few distinguished names for façade, and then impose onerous and oppressive conditions on the bondholders, especially penalties for the withdrawal of bonds or representation from the committee.

11. In 1900 the Belgian bondholders who had been represented by the Company became dissatisfied with the arrangement by which bondholders were asked to make sacrifices, withdrew their assent to being further represented by the committee, and so notified Santo Domingo, II, 226. Cf. II, 158.

Legislation governing protective committees in a few of the American states [12] and the simple registration requirements of the SEC, where the actual deposit of bonds is solicited, hardly cover to any material extent protective committees in the foreign field. These committees practically operate without administrative or judicial control, notwithstanding their fiduciary character. Even the registration under the Securities Act when bonds are deposited insures only a disclosure of a few essential facts and hardly reaches the practices of the committee, especially not the qualifications of its personnel, its relations with bondholders, its charges and expenses, not to speak of the merits of any plan of adjustment. Practically no capital is required to launch the protective committee and legal services are offered or obtained on a contingent basis.[13] One of the major faults established by the Commission was the fact that on independent self-constituted committees would be found the representatives of interests which sometimes conflicted with those of the bondholders, e.g., short-term creditors, issuing bankers. There are no external standards to govern such trustees.

It appears that issuing bankers are prone to consider themselves especially qualified to deal with a default and resent the "poaching" of outside voluntary committees, either because they consider such committees not qualified by experience or because they are competitors or because they may inspire suits against bankers for fraud or rescission. The bondholders in the foreign as distinguished from the domestic field as a rule take no initiative in the formation of protective committees but are often in a quandary to know which of several competing committees to entrust with their representation. Hence the advertising lure of distinguished names as chairmen or members of the committees, although the owners of such names may perform little or no service on the committees. Only rarely, apparently, do members of such committees own any substantial part of the issue in default. This is true even of committees formed by issuing bankers.[14] Occasionally the issuing bankers will not organize a committee of their own but will throw their support to one of several self-constituted committees. The lack of opportunity of the bondholders to learn the character and qualifications of the committee that is soliciting the privilege of protecting them is one of the evils which

12. For an account of the actual operation of domestic bondholders' protective committees in real estate reorganizations, see comment in *Col. Law Rev.*, XXXV (1935), 905–916, and SEC, *Rep.*, Pt. III.

13. Protective committees formed by the Foreign Bondholders Protective Council, Inc. had to date not deemed the services of attorneys necessary. SEC, *Rep.*, Pt. V, p. 97.

14. *Idem*, pp. 100 ff.

the Commission found most important to correct by full disclosure.[15] The Commission favored giving the bondholders some voice in the selection of members of committees, although this seemed not to be true in the case of the committees appointed by the Foreign Bondholders Protective Council. The fear of the organizers of independent committees that bondholders could never agree on such selections and that it was better to present them with a slate did not altogether impress the Commission.[16]

The Commission found that, aside from the desire to share in fees,[17] membership on such committees is induced by a desire for public recognition, publicity, inside information; issuing bankers may in addition feel a moral responsibility for adjusting a default, a desire to "save face" or maintain business relations with the debtor government, obtain preference for other claims they may have, forestall a voluntary outside committee, make trading profits on the basis of the secret information such bankers would receive, avoid the public exposure of and a suit for negligence in issuing the loan or misrepresenting the facts to the public. The acceptance of new securities or the deposit of the old may cut off the bondholders' right to rescission. The contract often provides that the committee has a lien on the bonds deposited for its fees and expenses. The Commission pictures the uncontrolled power of these committees to fix their fees as the "sorry spectacle of fiduciaries sitting in solemn judgment on the worth of their own services." Two of the committees examined provided for arbitration of the amount of the fee at the initiative of a protesting depositor, but as to others the amount of the fee was final.[18] The Commission regarded this provision as an altogether inadequate protection for the bondholders who should have available an

15. The committees organized by the Foreign Bondholders Protective Council seemed to the Commission better qualified and hence received the approval of the Commission. *Idem,* Pt. V, p. 115. The members are appointed by the Protective Council.

16. *Idem,* Pt. V, p. 119.

17. It appears that the committees formed by the Foreign Bondholders Protective Council serve without compensation. *Idem,* Pt. V, p. 121. Even a fee of 1% of the face amount of the bonds deposited or "registered," the customary limit for the initial service, might result in a substantial return. Additional compensation may be hoped for from the debtor government or at the time the bonds are exchanged for new ones. A "finder's fee" for the promoter of the committee is not unknown. *Idem,* Pt. V, pp. 136–137.

18. Cf. financial arrangements made by the Colombian committee described in *idem,* Pt. V, p. 130. The Commission characterized the arrangement as "a syndicate which looked upon committee service as a speculative business venture." The committee is reported to have pledged the deposited bonds with a bank for a loan. *Idem,* Pt. V, p. 131.

independent review of fees and expenses. Although of the thirteen committees examined by the Commission only one, the Salvador (Lisman) bankers' committee, concluded a debt settlement and received any substantial compensation for its services, the Commission nevertheless regarded the independent self-constituted committee as an established institution, with possibilities of future development, and therefore made numerous recommendations with respect to its improvement. But the future scope of the self-constituted committee seems exceedingly limited.

SPECIAL PRACTICES OF INDEPENDENT COMMITTEES

The SEC devoted some space to an examination of the special practices of independent committees, drawing conclusions not flattering to the committees. The Commission discussed at length the practice of soliciting the deposit of bonds. Not enjoying the prestige of either the British or the American Council, deposit is often solicited both to obtain a better claim on the bondholder and to strengthen the committee's bargaining power with the defaulting country.[19] Such power is likely to be in direct proportion to the amount of bonds represented; except for one or two committees among the thirteen studied by the Commission, the amount of bonds represented by the committee was strikingly small in relation to the whole issue and most of the promoters, except the Salvador (Lisman) committee, must have lost money.

DEPOSIT OF BONDS

The actual deposit of bonds may sometimes be necessary and desirable. Such is the case when litigation with issuing bankers may become necessary, when protective committees of several countries are competing for representation of the bondholders or for preferences from the debtor, or when negotiations between such committees become necessary, and, particularly, to prevent the purchase of the depressed bonds in the open market by the defaulting country. Under such circumstances, even the British Council has on occasion found it useful to solicit and obtain the deposit of bonds. The American Council, it is said, has never requested the deposit of bonds, and neither the American nor the British Council has needed such deposits in order to negotiate effectively on behalf of national bondholders. The authority of these bodies is established by other factors, such as the public knowledge that both bodies enjoy the confidence and assistance of their governments. The deposit

19. *Idem.* Pt. V, p. 217.

of bonds gives the depositary committee control over the bonds and the authority of an ostensible owner. The SEC states that six of the thirteen committees examined solicited deposits and two solicited proxies which bound the donors to the terms of the usual deposit agreement.[20]

REGISTRATION

Registration with the committee, which was requested by three of the committees organized by the Foreign Bondholders Protective Council and by two independent committees, served merely as a list to enable the committee to keep in touch with the bondholders. It involved no representation or agency.

SOLICITING SUPPORT

Because independent committees, although not the Council or its committees, are dependent both for their bargaining power and their compensation on the support of a substantial portion, perhaps a majority, of the bondholders, the committees must be active in soliciting such support, and the SEC examined the devices employed to this end. The first

20. *Idem,* Pt. V, p. 220. The form of such an agreement, defining the powers and duties of the committee, is printed at pp. 220–221. In all, 16 committees filed with the Commission deposit agreements and the report indicates the broad powers conveyed by these agreements. In all but one case, the powers were irrevocable (p. 221). In contrast to the broad and detailed American forms, the British Council uses a short form printed on the back of the letter of transmittal (p. 222). By this power the Council is appointed the agent of the bondholder to support his claims, make demands, delegate authority to subagents, negotiate compromises, send the coupons abroad for conversion or payment, give the consent necessary in case of settlement, and to act in general as agent of the bondholder (pp. 222–223). The SEC points out that the American form is even broader in constituting the committee the sole judge of its own expenses. In England the costs may be charged against the proceeds of a settlement only on the vote of the depositors. In the United States a lien is asserted upon the deposited bonds and money may be borrowed upon them. Not so in England. In the United States but not in England a plan may be consummated without further vote of the depositors (p. 223). In the United States the typical agreement relieves the committee members from all liability except for gross negligence or willful misfeasance. In England the Council, as custodian, is bound to use reasonable care. Under the American agreement, the bonds can be withdrawn only under limited conditions. On the other hand, proxies may be withdrawn freely. The proxies are insufficient to serve as pledges of the bonds to enable the committee to raise money, as in the case of bonds actually deposited (p. 225). The SEC concludes that registration is easiest to obtain, proxies next, and deposits most difficult of all, for obvious reasons. But private committees may begin with proxies or registration and, in case of negotiation with the debtor government, seek to follow with deposits. This might often be necessary to assure compensation. The SEC approves the retention by the bondholder of his security.

is newspaper publicity, designed to convince the single bondholder that his protection lies in united action and that the committee has been formed to defend his interests against the debtor country and possibly against the issuing bankers. These announcements will be calculated to convey the impression that there is a strong chance of a favorable settlement with the debtor country. The advertisements may be followed by mailed circulars, provided the committee can obtain a list of the bondholders from the issuing bankers or other source, an extremely difficult and usually judicially unenforceable effort.[21] News accounts of the efforts made by the committee on behalf of the bondholders are printed when such publicity is obtainable. The SEC reports that the advertisements entailed expense beyond the means of most of the committees examined and that the lack of lists of bondholders placed the independent protective committees at great disadvantage as against the committees formed by the issuing bankers or fiscal agents, who have such lists, and necessarily the Council or its committees, which require no such lists. In the Cuban case, the issuing Chase National Bank, which had been unsuccessfully sued to disclose the list to the independent Coyle committee, voluntarily handed the list to the Council, considering the latter a disinterested agency. Occasionally an issuing banker may give the list to a private committee that he approves, but such grant appears to lie in the unreviewable discretion of the banker or fiscal agent who ordinarily cannot be obliged to divulge his knowledge.

The SEC also investigated the practice of soliciting the deposit of bonds on a commission basis, a practice which in the domestic field evoked serious criticism. The Commission found that in the foreign field this was less important, although two private committees had initiated the attempt and the Lisman committee on Salvador, one of the few committees that had found the enterprise profitable, had presumably selected one member because of his ability to secure the deposits of bonds.[22]

THREATENING SUITS

The Commission also called attention to the practice of some committees in threatening suits against houses of issue on behalf of the bondholders for misrepresentation of the merits of the issue. In one case

21. *Idem*, Pt. V, pp. 229, 232–234. The Lisman committee on Salvador bonds, having been formed by the issuing bankers, had a partial list of the bondholders and had facilities for getting additional names (p. 234). In the domestic field, where bondholders themselves often form protective committees, statutes may under precise conditions give courts authority to order the disclosure of bondholders' lists to majority or minority groups of predefault bondholders. Cf. New York Laws, 1936, c. 899, and *Col. Law Rev.*, XXXVII (1937), 491.

22. SEC, *Rep.*, Pt. V, pp. 248–256.

the Council was attacked as partial because it was in part financed by houses of issue. The Commission concluded that in large part these attacks on issuing bankers or their protective committees were designed to evidence the vigilance and energy of the independent committees and to furnish to the bondholder an incentive for the deposit of bonds with the committee.[23]

FIXING OF TIME LIMITS

Aside from these devices to elicit bondholders' support and deposits, the Commission found that some committees employ the device of inculcating fear in the bondholder, fear that the debtor is diverting revenues assigned to the defaulted issue; that the country is discriminating in favor of other classes of creditors or nationals of other countries; that the debtor may propose a unilateral plan which could not be successfully fought without a united front; that a nondepositor would be excluded from the benefits of a plan of adjustment. Thus time limits for deposits are sometimes fixed and while at times these are merely intended to exert pressure to file bonds, at other times they may result in actually excluding nonassenting bondholders from the benefits of the plan of adjustment. The more monopolistic and assured the committee, the more imperious it may be in fixing time limits; e.g., the Lisman issuing bankers' committee on Salvador which assembled 95 per cent of the bonds, inclusive of those deposited with their London affiliate, could afford after several extensions to close down on further deposits and make the plan applicable only to depositors. A less established independent committee, whose entire success would depend upon assembling bonds, would fix closing dates only to extend them, the purpose being to gather in as many bonds as possible. The Council, as already observed, does not solicit deposits and negotiates in the general interest of all bondholders. When it approves a plan, bondholders who accept it may offer their bonds for stamping or, by accepting new bonds or coupons or a reduction, will be deemed by the adjustment agreement to have assented to the plan. In either case the nonassenting bondholder has practically no relief, though his legal rights may not be disturbed. The result is that when a large majority of the bondholders accepts a plan, the minority is perforce obliged to follow suit. Independent committees working for fees or commissions may on occasion effect agreements making them or their fiscal agents the authorities for the exchange of new bonds or certificates for the old, and for that service may exact fees.[24]

23. *Idem*, Pt. V, pp. 256–261.
24. *Idem*, Pt. V, pp. 261–270.

COMPETITION BETWEEN COMMITTEES

The Commission called attention to the disadvantages of competition for patronage among different committees, sometimes among independent committees themselves, sometimes between independent committees and houses of issue, sometimes between both these types and the Council. This competition has generally resulted in disadvantage to all parties concerned, including the bondholder, increasing the expense and decreasing the chances of a favorable or speedy settlement. Sometimes the manifestly unfortunate results of unseemly competition have brought about a merger of independent committees or of independent and bankers' committees.[25]

While the Commission deprecated the competition of several committees seeking to adjust the same default,[26] it nevertheless concluded that possibly the independent committee may have a *raison d'être* as against the bankers' committee, with whose interests those of the bondholders may conflict. But as between independent committees and the Council the Commission was in less doubt. In spite of the charges that the Council was financed by issuing bankers, of which the most was made by independent committees, the Commission concluded that for many reasons the Council is a better protector for the bondholders, except possibly in initiating suits against the bankers for rescission—in most cases more of a threat than a justified hope. Although the Council found difficulty in its early days in determining its precise relationship to the independent committees, offering to coöperate with them yet refusing to endorse them or be dominated by them, time has established the fact that in most cases the independent committee is unnecessary to the bondholders and to the Council. The slight place that the Commission purported to allow the independent committee is too narrow to justify its formation, so that in effect the Commission endorsed the Council as an exclusive agency and discountenanced the independent self-constituted committee. The Commission did not mention the fact that the Department of State, whose good offices are often necessary, may simply decline to extend its help to an independent committee without openly opposing it. A refusal of help is an effective form of discouragement. Thus, the Council has so much prestige and official aid that there does not seem

25. *Idem,* Pt. V, pp. 271–302. For the disadvantages of competing committees, see II, 136–138, 374 ff.

26. On occasion, as in the Peruvian, Turkish, and other cases, there have been protective committees representing different bond issues which were served from the same revenues or otherwise competed. This may be unavoidable and necessary competitive protection.

much justification left for the creation of private independent bond-holders' protective committees.[27]

CONTROL OVER PROTECTIVE COMMITTEES

The Commission noted the distinction between court control of a bankruptcy in the domestic field and control or supervision in the foreign field, where it is almost nonexistent. The assets of the foreign debtor are not subject to the creditors' jurisdiction, and the readjustment and the relations between creditors' agent and principal practically escape administrative control. Yet the Commission believed that some control, legal or economic, may and ought to be exercised over protective committees, over a central agency like the Foreign Bondholders Protective Council, Inc., and over certain obnoxious practices of debtors.

BONDHOLDERS' COMMITTEES

The Commission would encourage, not discourage, committees composed of the actual owners of defaulted bonds or their representatives. While they are not as effective in negotiating plans of adjustment as a central agency like the Council, they may safeguard the rights of investors against the issuing bankers for fraud or misrepresentation and may apply vigilance to prevent short-term creditors from obtaining a preference for their claims. But, while they may not be able to prevent the natural advantages of bargaining power which the short-term creditor often possesses, nevertheless "chiselling" or undue advantage might be made difficult, thought the Commission.[28] Such committees, said the Commission, may balance the influence of houses of issue, fiscal agents, trustees under indentures, or even a central agency like the Council. They must thus serve as watchdogs on behalf of the bondholders to prevent abuses by other agencies in a position to affect deleteriously the bondholders' interests.[29] The Commission conceived these private committees as analogous to minorities in a corporation balancing the interests of a majority, offsetting the defects of monopoly control. In the light of the evils which the Commission exposed, it seems doubtful whether a bondholder, knowing these facts, would be disposed to risk the payment of two commissions or to believe that he needs protection against so disinterested a body as the Council. Still, in the light of weaknesses that even the Council might develop and with which it has been charged, some

27. SEC, *Rep.*, Pt. V, pp. 302, 737.
28. *Idem*, Pt. V, p. 738.
29. *Idem*, Pt. V, p. 739.

bondholders might be disposed to employ an investigating private committee to supervise and report on the activities of the Council.

To make these committees effective, the Commission recommended that houses of issue should not be represented on independent protective committees, because of possible or latent conflicting interests, however useful they might otherwise be to protective committees or the Council; that fiscal agents, short-term creditors, and holders of commercial credits against the debtor country, and others whose interests might conflict with those of the bondholders, including their attorneys and representatives of the debtor country, should be equally disqualified. The Commission recommended that the use of deposit agreements should be greatly restricted and the powers of committees over depositors seriously curtailed, so as to eliminate all extortionate or oppressive practices. A similar limitation on proxies and powers of attorney should be imposed, so as to obviate the abuses the investigation disclosed.[30] Finally, the fees and expenses of committees should be subject to independent scrutiny, review, and determination; trading in securities by committee members and affiliated interests should be prohibited; committees should not alone determine when bondholders may deposit or withdraw bonds, determine the amount of penalty for withdrawal, or determine who may or may not share in the benefits of the plan.[31]

METHODS TO ENFORCE STANDARDS

While there is as yet no statutory endorsement of these recommendations, there are two methods by which the standards presented can be enforced: (1) the Department of State could, as it now often does, refuse its aid to a committee that in its opinion fails to live up to the standards recommended; (2) the Foreign Bondholders Protective Council, which in the natural course of events should acquire greater prestige in the representation of bondholders and the safeguarding of their claims, will probably refuse to coöperate with a private committee which in its opinion fails to measure up to the high fiduciary standards the Commission recommends.

30. *Idem*, Pt. V, p. 740.
31. *Idem*, Pt. V, p. 741.

Section XVI

QUASI-OFFICIAL BONDHOLDERS' COMMITTEES

A GOVERNMENTAL default is quite different from any other. The creditor cannot obtain judgment against and levy execution upon a debtor government nor can he take over the management of its affairs. The functioning of the debtor government cannot be impaired, so that the creditor is perforce driven to negotiate and make such adjustments as he can. The default may be due to a variety of causes, such as war, depression, or financial mismanagement; new ones appeared in the disorganization of world trade in the early 1930's which brought in its train various restrictions on foreign exchange, transfer moratoria, and other measures, the lifting of which often requires collateral negotiations with importers and others. In many defaults, moreover, several types of obligation are affected, some unsecured, others carrying varying classes and orders of security and priority, including debts, funded and floating, internal and external, tort and contract. Any reorganization must take account of the varying quality and character of these claims. The problem is one which has engaged the attention of many bondholders' committees and, because it lies at the root of most adjustments of conflicting claims, requires the fullest consideration. The negotiators, in order to effect an adjustment likely to endure, must also be able to comprehend the needs of the debtor country so that a restoration of impaired credit can be effected and a repetition of bankruptcy avoided. All this requires knowledge, skill, experience, objectivity, and statesmanship of a high order.

Because single protective committees for a particular issue have often not had all the necessary qualifications, they have at times proved ineffective. Moreover, the conflicts of interest frequently prevailing among the holders of varying groups and series of bonds, and among other claimants, have brought about differences of policy which have been deleterious to all concerned. When they have sought governmental aid, these conflicts of interest have been hampering to successful efforts. When the issuing bankers form protective committees they are sometimes handicapped by a real or potential lack of disinterestedness or by an equivocal position between their client, the defaulting government, and the holders of the bonds.[1] They are rarely able to act promptly or on their own initiative and cannot effect that coöperation with or, on occasion, protection against foreign committees of similar character, which may be necessary. Thus, the interests of the bondholders, of the Foreign Office, and of the defaulting government combine to emphasize the importance of some central body through whom all parties can effectively deal.

THE FOREIGN BONDHOLDERS PROTECTIVE COUNCIL

The Foreign Bondholders Protective Council, Inc., with its offices at 90 Broad Street, New York, was initiated by the Department of State. The exchange and bank crash of 1929–31, followed by the great drop in the price level and the resulting depression, brought about an avalanche of defaults, both in Europe and in Latin America. Beset by the importunities of the bondholders, whose legal remedies against either the defaulting government or the issuing bankers were practically worthless, the Department of State was faced with the alternatives (1) of taking an active part in the negotiation of readjustments, an interposition which would have been often embarrassing and prejudicial to other interests of the United States, (2) of disclaiming all responsibility, as they had attempted in the circulars of 1922 [2] and 1927,[3] or (3) of adopting the intermediate course of establishing an autonomous bondholders' protective committee or council. The Administration decided upon the third course, by which it was thought that it could escape major responsibility for the conduct of the negotiations and their outcome and yet lend the weight of governmental support to the activities of the bondholders' council.

The absence of a central protective agency had stimulated a mushroom growth of private committees, either self-constituted or organized by issuing houses, which were not always as responsible or disinterested in personal gain as might have been wished.[4] This had concerned the Department, for it was often in doubt whether and when to make representations on behalf of or lend support to a particular committee.

To emphasize the private nature of the proposed new central commit-

1. For a fuller discussion of this point, see Dulles, "The Protection of American Foreign Bondholders," *For. Aff.*, X (1932), 474, at 478 f.

2. *For. Rel.*, 1922, I, 557; J. F. Dulles, "Our Foreign Loan Policy," *For. Aff.*, V (1926), 33.

3. *For. Rel.*, 1927, I, 312.

4. SEC, *Rep.*, Pt. V, pp. 507 ff., 583 ff.

tee or council, the Departments of State and Treasury and the Federal
Trade Commission invited a few prominent citizens to a meeting in
Washington held on April 15, 1932, with Government officials. The private conferees were urged to study the question of forming an unofficial
protective council on the general model of the British Corporation of
Foreign Bondholders. This committee submitted its report on May 23,
suggesting the formation of a council composed of fifteen eminent men
who would command general confidence. Their functions were originally
conceived as those of consultation and coöperation with private protective committees rather than those of initiation, direction, or control
of negotiations.[5] The committee or council was not to intervene except
in rare instances; it was not itself to form subcommittees but was to act
as an advisory body in the formation of private committees. The financing of the council, it was recommended, should come from bankers' associations and houses of issue, bondholders, foundations, and interested
individuals. Only subsequently was objection raised to financing by issuing bankers.

These plans, as we shall see, were later modified. The Foreign Bondholders Protective Council ultimately established was a nonprofit membership corporation, headed by a few high-salaried executives and an
executive committee of seven, backed by a board of directors of some
twenty men. They had with official approval to solicit the financial support of issuing bankers; they formed—in only two instances, however
—their own bondholders' subcommittees; they negotiated with defaulting governments independently of and in sharp competition with private
protective committees operating for profit; and, owing to the advantage
of governmental support, they were often able to negotiate more effectively and authoritatively than purely private committees.

Before the first recommended plan could be acted upon, Congress,
which had devoted some time to the study of bond defaults, took the
initiative in authorizing, at the suggestion of Senator Hiram Johnson,
the creation of a corporation of foreign security holders as a quasi-
governmental agency. This provision was included in an amendment,
known as Title II, to the Securities Act of May 27, 1933. As modified by
the conference of the two Houses, the directors were to be six in number.
Another amendment, which proved vital, or fatal, postponed the coming
into force of Title II until the President found it in the public interest.
Since the President never so found, Title II never came into force. Objection to so close a connection with the Government had resulted in
an Administration recommendation for revival of an unofficial council
much along the lines that the Department first contemplated. But a few

5. *Idem,* Pt. V, p. 64.

features of the proposed official "Corporation of Foreign Security Holders" deserve consideration. Its directors, disinterested persons, were to be appointed by the Federal Trade Commission. The Reconstruction Finance Corporation was to lend it $75,000 until it could be privately financed. It was authorized to organize protective committees, accept deposits of bonds, and negotiate debt settlements, provided 60 per cent of the bondholders consented, to collect and circulate documents and statistics concerning foreign securities, and, especially, to secure the adoption of clear and simple forms of bonds and just and sound principles in their terms.

Although by the act itself the United States Government disclaimed any possibility that the corporation might be considered in any way to represent the Department of State or the United States, the large official hand in the origin and financing of the corporation was calculated to make it too preponderantly governmental to be such a protective agency as the Department of State had contemplated.[6] Moreover, it was thought dangerous to make a government corporation responsible for the forms and terms of foreign bonds and pass on their merits; and conflicts of interest would probably arise when the debtor was in default both to the United States and to private investors. While the corporation was to do nothing to interfere with the policy of the Department of State, the necessary consultation with the Department to that end might create a new supposition of Department approval of the corporation's acts. Its governmental character would expose it to political pressure and convey the impression, whether disavowed or not, that the United States Government was pressing its claims, with resultant effect on the political relations of the United States with debtor nations. Its statistics, it was said, would be regarded as official, whereas figures from some foreign countries are not necessarily accurate. The conflict of private interests among different groups of creditors would result in embarrassment if resolved by a government corporation. If the corporation were unsuccessful in its mission, the Administration would be blamed by the bondholders and others. All these considerations were deemed to militate against the adoption of Title II.

With the dropping of Title II, plans were formulated under the direction of Mr. Raymond B. Stevens, then a member of the Federal Trade Commission, for the organization of a privately financed and controlled protective council. On October 20, 1933, it was announced that, on the invitation of the Secretary of State, the Secretary of the Treasury, and the Chairman of the Federal Trade Commission, some eighteen well-known persons had attended a meeting to create such a council. A press

6. *Idem*, Pt. V, p. 71.

release was issued by the White House affirming the Government's benevolent interest in the success of the Council in unifying the interests of the bondholders but disclaiming any governmental direction, control, or responsibility for the actions of the Council. It was to be an entirely independent body, functioning on behalf of bondholders but without involving the Government in its policies. It was to have "no connections of any kind with the investing banking houses which originally issued the loans," a statement which gave rise to subsequent attacks on the Council on the ground that they had actually received operating funds from bankers, including houses of issue.

On December 13, 1933, the Foreign Bondholders Protective Council, Inc., was incorporated as a nonstock, nonprofit membership corporation under the laws of Maryland. By-laws were adopted. In general its corporate powers resemble those of its British counterpart. The members of the Council are divided into three classes: full members, who are the directors and alone entitled to vote, so that the board of directors is a self-perpetuating body; contributing members, who may attend meetings of the Council but cannot vote; and founders, a few in number but not limited, both the latter groups to be elected by the first group, the directors. Contributing members pay annual dues, the founders a lump sum of $500 on election. Directors, nineteen in number, receive no compensation but are paid traveling expenses in attending meetings.

The directors operate through an executive committee of not more than seven. Mr. J. Reuben Clark, Jr., as president, until April, 1938, received an annual salary of $15,000, reduced to $7,500 from April, 1938, to December, 1939, when the salary was abolished, plus $400 monthly (from January, 1936, to April, 1938, $100) "maintenance"; the executive vice-president and secretary, Mr. Francis White, up to April, 1941, also received $15,000, then $10,000, per annum.[7] A secretary and assistant treasurer is also salaried.[8] The work of the Council is carried on by the executive committee and its officers, with occasional subcommittees like those appointed for Chile and Cuba.[9] The training of the earlier

7. When Mr. White became president, April 26, 1938, he received $16,500. This was reduced to $10,000 on April 30, 1941. November 17, 1942, he left the Council. His successor as president was Dr. W. Dana Munro of Princeton.

8. During the first 6 years of its existence, the Council's total expense account amounted to 0.0034% on the amount of interest offered to bondholders, or to 0.00027% of the face value of the bonds concerning which the Council negotiated either temporary or permanent adjustments. J. Reuben Clark, Jr., "Collecting on Defaulted Foreign Dollar Bonds," *Am. Jour. Int. Law*, XXXIV (1940), 119.

9. These subcommittees, by reason of the high standards for membership, their nonprofit character, and their limited functions as mere advisers of the negotiating executive, have fallen into disuse. The Chilean and Cuban subcommittees of the

two principal officers was diplomatic rather than financial. Mr. Clark is also a distinguished lawyer and an expert in international law. Other members of the executive committee supply financial experience. It is thus a well-rounded body. The very existence of the Council as a non-profit organization has discouraged the formation of private committees.

The financing of the Council proved embarrassing. While it was hoped that bondholders, who would permanently benefit, would contribute to its support, this would necessarily be delayed until debt settlements were effected and a beginning had to be made before then. Foundations having declined support, it was finally decided to solicit the aid of bankers, who subscribed the principal part of the $90,000 per annum which was raised during the first three years, from 1934 to 1936. About 60 per cent of this amount, the SEC found, was raised from houses of issue (numbering 30 of the 189 contributors), a fact which subjected the Council to the unfounded criticism of supposed domination by such houses. All but 20 per cent of the amounts contributed were regarded as advances to be refunded. In fact, the Council received substantial sums from several of the debtors with which adjustments were effected.[10] Down to the end of 1936 nearly $95,000 from 5 debtor nations had thus been received, partly reimbursements of cash outlays, partly contributions.[11] In one, the Province of Buenos Aires, the Council requested from the benefited bondholders voluntary contributions of ⅛ per cent of the face amount of the bonds. Similar sums were received from the benefited bondholders of other settlements, temporary or permanent.[12] These contributions from foreign debtor governments and bondholders, and founders' contributions became practically the sole source of income.[13]

The Council's *modus operandi* differs from that of the private protective committee. Instead of inviting proxies or the deposit of bonds from

Council seem to have been appointed in the early days of the Council, largely to forestall the effectiveness of competing private protective committees operating for gain. SEC, *Rep.*, Pt. V, pp. 182 ff.

10. *Idem*, Pt. V, p. 89.

11. Requests for contributions from debtors have been made by the Council on the principle that the debtor, having defaulted on its obligations, should pay some part of the expenses incident to an arrangement for the resumption of service. *Idem*, Pt. V, pp. 89, 719–722.

12. The Council receives nothing either from debtor governments or from bondholders in case a settlement is not effected, nor has it asked for contributions either from debtors or bondholders where offers of service could not be favorably recommended, as in the cases of Colombia, June, 1941, Chile, 1935, Peru, 1937.

13. The board of visitors established that in 1940 the Council had a deficit of $21,300 compared with a surplus in 1939 of $37,931. *The New York Times*, December 23, 1941, p. 35.

bondholders, it initiates the negotiations with the foreign government by virtue alone of its prestige as a semiofficial organization. Since innumerable issues were in default when it began operations in 1934, it had to deal with those deemed most likely to effect a settlement. Sometimes the initiative was taken by the foreign debtor, who would approach the Council with a proposal of settlement or readjustment.

The Council has no power and does not purport to bind the bondholders to any plan of adjustment. But its recommendation for or against acceptance of a particular plan is likely to have considerable weight with the bondholders. In the process of negotiation it may consult with the interested houses of issue, the fiscal agents, or other informed persons. Bondholders, those who may have registered their names with the Council or those who have not, usually indicate their acceptance of the recommendation by cashing the first coupon under the new plan of adjustment, by permitting the bonds to be stamped, or by exchanging old bonds for new. Nonaccepting bondholders have little opportunity for legal or diplomatic recourse against the debtor and none against the Council or their fellow bondholders. Bondholders really have little opportunity to pass upon the merits of a plan of adjustment but assenters are probably better off than dissenters, who may receive nothing on their bonds and may incur some expense, such as the withdrawal of deposited bonds from private committees.

In June, 1941, after the Department of State had apparently approved a Colombian proposal for the adjustment of two Colombian governmental or guaranteed issues, we had the unusual experience of the Council's disapproving the plan, on the ground that it was not fair or equitable enough to the bondholders.[14]

Acceptance of the plan recommended by the Council is not conditional upon payment of an assessment by the bondholders or the debtor, nor does or can the Council make any deduction to cover its fees or expenses.[15] It is usual, as in the case of the Buenos Aires settlement, to suggest to the bondholders and the debtor voluntary contributions which, in the case of the bondholders, consist of authority to the paying agent to make a small deduction from the first coupon, often ⅛ of 1 per cent of

14. In June, 1942, 4 guaranteed and 7 nonguaranteed issues were adjusted. The Dominican settlement of 1940, effected by the Department of State, was also disapproved by the Council.

15. SEC, *Rep.*, p. 367. At first the Council's request for contributions from bondholders was on a voluntary basis with respect to those adjustments which the Council was able to recommend favorably. Experience, however, showed that, while the average American bondholder was willing to and did make these voluntary contributions, the foreign holders of these dollar bonds and *arbitrageurs* were unwilling to do so.

the face amount of the coupons.[16] The debtor's contributions, also dependent upon the good will of the debtor, are probably dependent upon the character of the work entailed by the adjustment and the size of the transaction. If a private bondholders' protective committee has been formed, the bondholder may incur some obligation to that committee. The Council does not object to the formation of private committees and may consult them if in being but the existence of the Council may impress bondholders with the undesirability of incurring considerable expense by the creation of a private committee which at best would be a consultative organization for the Council. As we shall see, while this has some resemblance to the practice of the Council of Foreign Bondholders in London, the relations between the English Council and its protective committees is more intimate, members of the English Council being represented on the protective committee usually formed to deal with each default situation.

In England the Council assumes responsibility for the selection of members of the protective committee which is to act with it. The president and vice-president *ex officio* and possibly some Council members are appointed to each special committee. In the United States only two committees selected by the Council, those for Cuba and Chile, have come into existence and their function was extremely limited. The American Council thus in practice relies exclusively upon its own officers, its executive committee, and if necessary its board of directors. Additional private committees representing the bondholders are thus effectively discouraged.

While the British committees are never self-appointed but act as advisory adjuncts of the parent Council in a particular default, the American Council acts usually without special committees, declines to receive the deposit of bonds, and does not act as attorney in fact of the bondholders. On the other hand, the British Council does, though only on comparatively rare occasions when special circumstances are present,[17] request the deposit of bonds and become, in consequence, the legal representative of the bondholders. The British advisory or special committee passes upon the plan of adjustment and advises the Council whether the plan should be recommended by the Council to the bondholders. The American Council judges that matter for itself, though it may consult with a private committee that may have been organized. The English method assures harmony between Council and committee; the American method does not. In submitting a plan to the public the procedure and

16. *For. Bondh. Prot. Coun. Rep.*, 1935, p. 20. See also assortment of contributions by holders of Dominican and Chinese bonds, SEC, *Rep.*, Pt. V, p. 367, note.
17. *Infra*, pp. 209–210.

function of the two councils are essentially alike. The details of the plan are described in England by a statement to the press or at a general meeting of bondholders, where a vote, without final significance, may be taken. In the United States the Council, unless it has a register of bondholders affected, must notify them through a notice in the press. In the years of the Great Depression, most of the recommendations of both councils related to suspensions of sinking fund, suspension of the transfer of service into foreign exchange, or methods of alleviating temporarily the debtor's burden. For measures such as these a meeting of the bondholders is not convoked by the British Council. Where bonds are accepted for deposit, the settlement can hardly be accepted without convoking the bondholders, usually made a condition of the deposit agreement. In such case the plan is formally submitted to a vote of the bondholders, with conclusive results, but without fixing any quorum. British distances and the considerable size of individual or corporate holdings make a meeting of bondholders, frequently resorted to, more practical than in the United States, where such meetings have never been attempted.

The American Council, in its endeavor to work out an acceptable arrangement with the debtor government, may encounter opposition and conflict from private protective committees who have their own ideas and their own interests to protect, both by way of authority to negotiate and fees to be earned. Such a conflict of interest arose in the case of the Colombian [18] and the Cuban [19] defaults. The Council may attempt to reconcile the interests of the disputing groups without yielding its claim to priority in power to negotiate or may seek to checkmate an unwelcome private committee, as in the Cuban case.

The advantages of a centralized, experienced, permanent Council over the ephemeral, *ad hoc* protective committee are overwhelming. It is for that reason that the Securities and Exchange Commission [20] unhesitatingly endorsed the Council as the most appropriate organ for the negotiation of bond adjustments, not only in saving money for the bondholders [21] but in prompt attention to a case of prospective default, even before actual default and promptly thereafter, without loss of time, expense, or energy in organizing committees, soliciting bondholders, and appointing officers and counsel, and without the handicap of competing committees for the same or diverse defaulted issues of a debtor country. The Council

18. SEC, *Rep.*, Pt. V, 378.
19. *Idem*, pp. 298 ff.
20. *Idem*, pp. 620 ff.
21. *Idem*, Pt. V, p. 621, points out that the expenses of the Council for the first few years covering all its activities and adjustments in numerous countries were less than the expenses of the Lisman committee for the Salvador loan.

constitutes an accredited agency, having political and financial authority to receive offers or proposals from debtor governments.[22] The Council is vigilant to protect bondholders against changes in law or regulations in foreign countries, such as diminishing the security guaranteeing a bond issue, which may deleteriously affect their rights, a function which only a permanent organization speaking with some authority can perform. It has been persistent in criticizing the practice of defaulting governments in buying up at default prices and repatriating the bonds which, though having funds for purchase, they allowed to remain in default.

The Council has the advantage of cumulative experience and records and a trained personnel, and thus has opportunity for service of a kind which no *ad hoc* committee could render. Without receiving the deposit of a single bond, it may act for all and not merely for certain groups of bondholders, with full disinterestedness among possible competing groups which might singly accept an immediate advantage to the detriment of a long-run adjustment and the interests of all groups. The Council's close relation to the Government and its opportunity to speak with governmental support are advantages which no private committee could possess, notwithstanding the fact that on a few occasions in recent years, as in Santo Domingo and Colombia, the Department of State in pursuit of political objectives approved settlements or adjustments at the expense of bondholders which the Council was not willing to support or openly disapproved.[23]

Since bond defaults usually have political repercussions and are likely to affect diplomatic relations, it is a great advantage to the Department

22. See instances like Brazil, Mexico, etc., when foreign debtors approached the Council in advance of or immediately after default. The Council does not make offers or proposals to defaulting governments on its own or bondholders' initiative. The Council, in giving its reluctant assent to the agreement of November 5, 1942, between the Government of Mexico and the Committee of Bankers, stated the general policies of the Council as follows: "The Foreign Bondholders Protective Council, Inc., has not participated in any way in the negotiation of this agreement. The plan of service offered under this agreement, involving as it does a reduction of principal, cancellation of a very large part of the back interest, payment of the current interest at an exceedingly low rate, and discrimination in favor of certain issues of 'secured bonds,' involves principles which the Council has not admitted in its dealings with foreign governments. The Council could not, therefore, accept the plan as a precedent for its negotiations with other countries."

23. The Foreign Bondholders Protective Council ordinarily does not participate in negotiations concerning loans couched in currencies other than United States dollars. It felt, however, justified in acceding to the request of the Chinese Minister of Finance to join in the procedure for the settlement of the Hunkuang railway loan of 1911, a sterling loan, on the ground that one *tranche* of it has been floated in the United States with the approval of the United States Government. *For. Bondh. Prot. Coun. Rep.*, 1936, p. 265.

of State to be able to escape responsibility for the adjustment while having the assurance that the interests of the bondholders have been safeguarded by a council in which it has confidence, a condition hardly likely to prevail when only self-appointed private protective committees are in operation and making demands for diplomatic support. The embarrassment entailed by having to withhold support from a private committee representing important groups of bondholders is great and is likely to create difficulties in Congress, although the Department may be acting in the highest interests of the nation. The Department has little control over the actions of private committees, including charges exacted for their services, whereas it has some control over the Foreign Bondholders Protective Council, a control made more definite by the fact that the Council submits an accounting of its activities during the year to a board of visitors made up of State Department and SEC officials. Indeed, it was such a board which tacitly approved the rule authorizing the Council to charge bondholders ⅛ of 1 per cent on all bond adjustments.[24] Reciprocally, by virtue of the sponsored relation of the Department to the Council, the latter is likely to be sensitive to the position of the Department of State in negotiating adjustments and, in view of the diplomatic training of some of its principal executives, is more likely than a private committee to be aware of the political aspects of its activities and to heed departmental suggestions as to method or time of approach, degree of pressure, and other considerations which the Department might have in view, not only as to the best way of protecting the bondholders but of promoting or not impairing the interests of the two governments.[25] The Council constitutes an excellent coördinator of the interests of the bondholders and of the United States Government, protecting the bondholders while relieving the Government of responsibility.[26]

24. Second Report of Board of Visitors, 1939. The Council's practice of requesting contributions from debtors after a satisfactory plan of service has been negotiated has never had the approval of the SEC. SEC, *Rep.*, Pt. V, pp. 719–722. The board of visitors advised the Council that they had no comment to offer in connection with various requests for contributions from foreign debtors, although on one occasion the SEC member of that board suggested that revaluation of this procedure in future cases might be necessary lest it become by precedent a permanent procedure.

25. See considerations in the Cuban settlement, 1935. *Idem*, Pt. V, p. 631.

26. There have been criticisms of the Council, in its failure to coöperate with the existing private committees, its alleged failure to take prompt action, its failure to achieve better results for or to become the legal representatives of the bondholders in particular negotiations, etc., the alleged closeness of its connections with houses of issue and short-term creditors. These have come mostly from competing private committees, who naturally are not pleased at the minor role into

THE BRITISH CORPORATION OF FOREIGN
BONDHOLDERS

Great Britain was the first country in which the need was felt for a central body to protect the interests of the holders of defaulted foreign governmental bonds. In 1868 the Council of the Corporation of Foreign Bondholders was organized in London "for the purpose of watching over and protecting the interests of holders of foreign bonds." Inasmuch as this body has had a long and successful experience in the adjustment of bond defaults and has had the approval if not the support of the British Government, it has served as a model for other central national organizations of bondholders like the French, Belgian, German, Dutch, and, more recently, the American Foreign Bondholders Protective Council.[27]

Prior to the establishment of the Corporation of Foreign Bondholders, British holders of foreign bonds (and the same was, of course, true at that time of the relatively few bondholders of other nationalities) had no recognized means of organization for the protection of their interests. They were in many instances represented by committees which were either self-constituted or appointed by an informal meeting of holders of bonds which had gone into default; but there was in existence no institution whose object it was to represent the interests of the holders of foreign bonds in general, to represent their claims to the British Government, and to negotiate terms for the settlement of the default and the resumption of payment.

The need for such an organization was apparent, and at a general meeting of holders of foreign bonds convened in London on November 11, 1868, the following resolutions were unanimously adopted.[28]

1. That in the opinion of this meeting, the formation of a Council for the purpose of watching over and protecting the interests of holders of foreign bonds is extremely necessary and desirable.

2. That with the view of giving weight to its recommendations and a practical character to its policy, the Council should comprise some members of

---

which they have been forced by this officially supported Council. The SEC did not seem to regard these criticisms as entitled to great weight. *Idem*, pp. 632 ff.

27. The rest of this section on the Corporation of Foreign Bondholders and the ensuing brief account of the corresponding French association is reprinted from an article by William H. Wynne and Edwin Borchard, "Foreign Bondholders Protective Organizations," *Yale Law Jour.*, XLIII (1933), 281. It should be noted that the article describes the organization of these bodies as of 1933. No account has been taken of changes since then in such matters as the size and membership of the Council and its committees.

28. London *Times*, November 12, 1868.

those eminent houses who have had experience in dealing with foreign governments.

In accordance with a third resolution a committee was appointed to prepare a general plan embodying rules and regulations for the proposed Council. The report of this committee was represented to a second general meeting on February 2, 1869, and obtained complete approval.[29]

The committee took the view that one of the main advantages of the Council would be that in negotiations with debtor states it would not be hampered as issuing houses had tended to be by a sense of divided loyalty. Whenever defaults have occurred, the committee stated,

contractors have found themselves in an embarrassing situation towards the Government and Bondholders, being under certain obligations to both. On such occasions the Council will be ready to act as mediator between the Foreign Government and the Bondholders, relieving thereby the contractor from his unpleasant and sometimes equivocal position.

The Council, the committee recommended, should be composed of members of loan-contracting houses and of the stock exchange, together with private bondholders. The committee left it to the Council to determine the best method of financing the organization, but suggested that the necessary funds might be secured either: (a) from fees for services rendered to bondholders, special committees, loan contractors, and foreign governments, supplemented perhaps by annual membership subscriptions entitling subscribers to copies of the Council's publications; or (b) by raising a permanent fund large enough to yield an income sufficient to cover the running expenses of the Council.

After paying its way for three years chiefly by means of fees, the Council decided to establish a substantial capital fund by forming a bondholders' association of 1,000 members, each of whom was to subscribe for a 5 per cent bond of £100. The entire assets of the association were to be the property of the members and to remain so even after all the bonds had been repaid. The income of the association, to be derived from interest on the invested capital, from the contributions of bondholders, from fees, and from commissions on claims settled, would, the Council believed, be considerable, so that, "besides rendering invaluable services to the public," the association would be "not only self-supporting, but amply repay the members."[30] But without incorporation the liability of the members would, it was realized, be unlimited. An appli-

29. *Idem,* February 2, 1869. The report of the committee was published in pamphlet form, London, 1869. There is a copy in the library of the British Museum (8228d2).

30. Circular issued by the Foreign Bondholders Association, London, 1872. A copy is in the library of the Council of Foreign Bondholders.

cation for incorporation by Royal Charter was refused,[31] while incorporation by Act of Parliament was found impracticable.[32] The Council thereupon decided to abandon the idea of a profit-making organization and, after considerable trouble and delay, succeeded in obtaining from the Board of Trade a license under Section 23 of the Companies Act of 1867 [33] permitting the association, as one formed not for the purposes of trade or profit but for a public object to be registered as a corporation and to enjoy limited liability without having the word "Limited" added to its title.[34]

Upon its incorporation in August, 1873, under the designation of the "Corporation of Foreign Bondholders," the association returned the contributions of those who were unwilling to remain members, now that there was no longer a prospect of profits,[35] while the bonds of the continuing members were redeemed as rapidly as the growing revenues of the Corporation permitted. The whole of the original capital fund was repaid by 1885,[36] but the subscribers, in accordance with the Articles of Association, retained their certificates of permanent membership. These were transferable, the holder having the right of electing the members of the Council. As time passed, a considerable number of these certificates found their way into the hands of persons who were not "directly in-

31. "It was proposed to incorporate the Association of Foreign Bondholders under limited liability by Royal Charter. Although Her Majesty's Government had resolved in 1856 not to exercise for the future the Royal prerogative of granting Royal Charters, it was believed that an exception would be made in favor of this institution, on account of its public importance.

"The petition was presented to Her Majesty, and referred to the Privy Council, but although several ministers were in favor of granting it, the Cabinet decided against it, being unwilling to establish a precedent." *Corp. For. Bondh. Rep.*, 1872, p. 7.

32. The difficulty was explained by the solicitors to the Council, in a letter to its chairman, as follows: "On one point, which was a *sine qua non*, viz., that the liability of the Members of the Corporation should be limited, we came to the conclusion that Parliament would not sanction such a condition, and after very careful search for precedents of any such conditions having ever been incorporated in a Private Bill, none could be found, and we are of opinion that such a condition would not be likely to be permitted by Parliament." *Idem*, p. 9.

33. 30 & 31 VICT. c. 131 (1867).

34. *Corp. For. Bondh. Rep.*, 1873, p. 6.

35. The sum of £60,280 was paid in by the permanent members of the Corporation. "The amount originally fixed was £100,000, but as the Council decided to allot only one Bond of £100 to every Member, the surplus subscriptions were returned to those who had not furnished a special nominee in respect of every £100 subscribed. To a number of subscribers, who had joined the Association for different objects than the protection of the rights and interests of the holders of Foreign Bonds, their subscriptions were likewise returned." *Idem*, p. 8,

36. *Idem*, 1885, p. 5.

terested in foreign securities or in the work of the Corporation or the objects for which it was established." [37] Such holders looked with covetous eyes upon the substantial fund (amounting at the end of 1896 to about £100,000) which the Corporation had been able to build up and invest even after the repayment of the contributions of the permanent members. They clamored to have some part of this fund distributed among the certificate holders, although—as the Council was advised on the highest legal authority—any such distribution was absolutely precluded under the constitution of the Corporation.[38] As a further consequence of the acquisition by unsuitable individuals of a voice in the selection of the governing body, so critics of the Corporation alleged, the Council had come to include many members who had no knowledge at all of the type of business it had to transact.[39] Criticism of the Council was carried even further, and it was repeatedly accused during the 'eighties and 'nineties of serving limited interests at the expense of the bondholders.[40]

While no valid evidence was educed to show that the Council had in fact been influenced by any other considerations than the welfare of the bondholders, the Council decided that it would be wise to reconstitute the Corporation so as to insure that it "should in the future more directly and exclusively represent the interests of the holders of foreign and other public securities" and also remove all danger of a diversion of its surplus funds to purposes other than the public objects for which it was constituted.[41] Such a reorganization could not be effected without the authority of Parliament. The necessary bill was successfully piloted through its various stages and became law on July 25, 1898, as the "Corporation of Foreign Bondholders Act." [42] This act, therefore, is the present constitution of the Corporation, which is organized and operates in accordance with its provisions.[43]

37. Preamble to "An Act to Reconstitute the Corporation of Foreign Bondholders," 61 & 62 Vict. c. 149 (1898). Reprinted in *idem*, No. 26, 1898–99, pp. 1 ff.

38. *Idem*, No. 25, 1897, p. 21. The legal opinion of Sir Farrer Herschell and Mr. Phipson Beale, O.C. (to whom the question was referred in 1883) is printed *in extenso* in *idem*, 1893.

39. "The Corporation of Foreign Bondholders," *The Economist*, LV (1897), 1624.

40. Feis, *Europe the World's Banker*, p. 113, n.

41. Preamble to the Corporation of Foreign Bondholders Act of 1898.

42. *Supra*, n. 37.

43. The Act (Art. 10 and Second Schedule) required the Council to appropriate at least £2000 each year for the purchase and subsequent cancellation of the certificates of permanent membership. Holders of these certificates were invited to tender them for sale at a price not exceeding £100, the lowest tenders being accepted. The sum paid for these certificates averaged a little over £48 in the

While the act gave the Corporation the status of a recognized quasi-public body, enlarged (though perhaps only on paper) [44] its objects and scope, and laid down new rules and regulations for the appointment of members of the Council and for the conduct of its proceedings, it effected no significant change in the policy and methods of the Corporation. The founders had made the initial mistake of attempting to establish the institution on a profit-making basis but they quickly realized their error and then proceeded to build wisely and well. Throughout the sixty-odd years of its history the Corporation has followed much the same procedure in dealing with a default as it adopted from the outset.

The Council, or governing body, of the Corporation consists of 21 ordinary members, of whom 6 are nominated by the British Bankers' Association and 6 by the London Chamber of Commerce, while the remaining 9—of whom at least 6 must at the time of their election be *bona fide* holders of foreign bonds to the nominal amount of £5,000—are coöpted by the Council as a whole. The Council have the power to appoint additional members provided that the total number of members does not exceed 30. A body thus chosen is representative of the whole financial and commercial interests of the City as well as of the bondholders at large. The Council has included directors of the Bank of England, the chairmen of the Big Five joint-stock banks,[45] men of importance in commerce and industry or of considerable experience in public affairs.[46] The bondholding community is thus able to rest assured that, whenever the necessity unfortunately arises, its affairs will be handled by the Corporation with ability and good judgment and that the financial guidance with which it is furnished will be both competent and disinterested.

The Council acts through various bondholders' committees, associated with it under the rules and regulations of the Corporation, of each of

first redemption (May, 1899) and rose in later years to nearly par. The redemption was completed in May, 1919. *Corp. For. Bondh. Rep.*, 1898–99 to 1919.

44. The objects and scope of the Corporation are defined in Art. 4 of the Act. By paragraph (a) of this article the Corporation is authorized "to watch over and protect the rights and interests of holders of public securities wherever issued but especially of foreign and colonial securities issued in the United Kingdom." In practice the Corporation has concerned itself solely with foreign securities.

45. These are, of course, commercial banks. According to the London *Times* of November 22, 1918, representatives of the issuing houses are not eligible for membership on the Council. In this respect a significant departure has been made from the original plans for the Corporation which contemplated including such representatives in the Council.

46. Seven members of the Council retire by rotation each year but they are eligible for reëlection.

which the president and vice president of the Council are *ex officio* members and chairman and deputy chairman, respectively. When a default occurs, many of the financial institutions, jobbers, and private individuals affected usually urge the Council to take action on their behalf.[47] As soon as it is clear that there is a demand for its services, the Council first investigates the extent of the British holding. If this is comparatively small, if the interest of the British bondholders is practically identical with that of the bondholders in other countries owning the bulk of the defaulted issues, and if the latter are strongly represented, as, for example, by a committee of the Association Nationale, then the Council may take the view that it is unnecessary to have a separate British committee. In such circumstances the Council will act on its own initiative without the advice of a committee and use its influence to secure fair treatment for the minority interest it represents.

The bondholders' committees set up by the Council are more or less permanent, new members being appointed as required. When, therefore, the defaulting country is one whose financial delinquencies have on previous occasions been the concern of the Corporation, there is likely to be in existence the appropriate committee to which the matter may be referred. Should there be no committee and one be desired, the Council itself—as it has full authority to do—nominates the members. It may perhaps invite various banks and the issuing houses to make suggestions and usually calls a conference of important bondholders to consider the proposed list of members, but it is not obliged to call a general meeting of bondholders to ratify its appointments. The Council is able to select committees much more satisfactory than those which would be likely to result from the haphazard nomination and vote of a large assembly. The members need not be bondholders; they are chosen solely on the basis of their general qualifications and special knowledge. The size of the committee is determined in each case by the Council but the membership is usually small and ranges at present [i.e., as of 1933] from 4 (for Nicaragua) to 10 (for Bulgaria).

The committees are the expert advisers of the Council, not the attorneys of the bondholders. While the business of a committee is to advise concerning the negotiation of a settlement of the default, it cannot conclude a binding agreement with the government concerned. The arrangements it advises are submitted to the Council, which, in turn, if it approves, recommends them for acceptance either to a general meeting of bondholders or by a reasoned communiqué to the press where such

47. For information on many aspects of the Corporation's procedure, communicated in interviews in 1933, indebtedness is acknowledged to the then Secretary, Douglas Reid, Esq., and the Assistant Secretary, A. L. Philp, Esq.

may seem adequate. There has in practice been no real dissension between the Council and any of the committees. Harmony at all times is practically assured, since the two chief members of the Council sit on each committee—and in some instances one or more other members also —while the Council, having itself selected the members of the committee, has full confidence that any settlement which they advise is as fair and reasonable a one as it is possible to obtain. It may in fact be said that once an agreement has been recommended by a committee, the assent of the Council tends to follow as a matter of course. In the final stage —the general meeting—the bondholders, too, throughout the history of the Corporation, have usually voted their accord, either unanimously or nearly so.

Such a general meeting is, however, only a convenient and easy method of giving bondholders the means of hearing explanations of an arrangement, discussing its pros and cons, and expressing their opinions with regard thereto. The majority cannot bind the minority, and even the vote of those who are in favor of the acceptance of the arrangement has no binding force. The real acceptance comes when the bondholders send in their securities to be stamped with the new conditions or exchanged for the new bonds, or when they encash the first coupon after the new arrangement. During the years of world-wide depression the Council was obliged to agree, in respect of the external public debts of several countries, to a suspension of sinking fund, cessation of the transfer of part or the whole of the debt service from domestic into foreign currency, or to other arrangements for alleviating the burden of the debtor. These interim arrangements were rarely submitted to a general meeting of bondholders, for, as the time, purpose, and results of the meeting must be advertised all over the country, the reasoned communiqué recommending measures to deal with transitory conditions over a short period or by repetition over a series of short periods provides a less cumbrous and more elastic method.

Bondholders are not as a rule asked to deposit their bonds with the Council when the latter undertakes to protect their interests. Apart from other considerations, where the British holding is very large, the mere space required to accommodate the securities would in itself constitute a considerable problem. The request for a deposit of bonds has been made in the rare cases where a government was attempting to profit through its own default by buying up its bonds at the resulting depressed price, or in circumstances under which the exact extent of the bondholders' interest represented by the Council had to be known. Such circumstances have arisen when it has been desirable to dispel doubts expressed by the defaulting state or foreign—and perhaps conflicting—

financial interests as to the existence of a substantial British holding, or when litigation affecting the rights of the bondholders was contemplated, or when it was desired to give someone a power of attorney on their behalf. On depositing his securities the bondholder receives in exchange certificates for which the stock exchange may be asked to grant a quotation, thus making it possible for him to sell the equivalent of his holding in the market. The deposit agreement which he is required to sign is a simple and standard one, containing only five clauses. These include a provision that "any Resolution passed by a General Meeting of the Certificate holders convened by the Corporation in the manner provided by its Rules and Regulations shall be valid and binding on all Certificate holders." Having deposited their securities the bondholders concerned are thus bound individually by the vote of a general meeting, whereas they are not so bound when no such deposit is required. Bondholders who have not by prior or subsequent lodgment of their bonds or in some other way consented to a new arrangement are not, however, bound by it. Theoretically they are entitled to retain intact the rights conferred upon them by their original bonds but they have no effective means of enforcing these rights, with the result that once an arrangement has been accepted by the large majority of bondholders the small minority are practically obliged to come in, and in fact do so.

While negotiations are in progress for the settlement of a default, the bondholders may from time to time be informed of how matters are proceeding, but the Council tends to be spare with its communiqués, for these, if issued frequently, may provoke much ill-considered discussion or exacerbating criticism and thus do more harm than good.

The original charter of the Corporation provided for three classes of members: permanent members and life members, who were to qualify by a single payment of £100 and £20 respectively, and subscribing members, who were to pay £2 2s. per year. But the policy thus initiated of financing the Corporation in part by membership contributions was put into practice only for a short period and to a very limited extent. No steps were taken to invite the bondholding public at large to become life members or annual subscribers,[48] while the contributions of the permanent members—which were, in effect, loans—were all refunded, as already mentioned, by 1885. The Council defrays the expenses of its affiliated bondholders' committees and recoups its outlay when a settlement is made, together with an additional sum for the general purposes of the Corporation, either from the state concerned or, to the extent to which this proves impossible, from the bondholders concerned. Apart from the cost of such negotiations, the ordinary expenses of the Corporation

48. Five life members were, however, acquired, but no subscribing members.

amount to about £20,000 a year. Approximately two thirds of this sum are met out of invested funds and the Council looks forward to the day when it will not have to make any charge whatever to bondholders for its services. "In most cases, the expenses have been borne by the Governments concerned, and no charge has fallen on the Bondholders." [49]

At the time of the first incorporation it was contemplated that the president and members of the Council should give their services gratuitously, and for the first seven or eight years they did so. But as the business operations of the Corporation increased it was no longer to be expected that busy men of high standing and position would continue to act without remuneration, and in 1880 a modest scale of payment was adopted (though not until an opinion had been received from the Board of Trade that it saw no objection to such a course) which, with some slight modifications, was authorized under the reorganizing act of 1898. The president receives £1,000, the vice-president £500, and the other members of the Council £100 per annum. The duties of the president, in the words of the late Lord Avebury, who for twenty-five years acted in that capacity,

necessitate almost daily attention, frequent attendance at the meetings of the Council and of the twenty committees of foreign loans affiliated with it, constant communication with the Secretary and supervision of a large correspondence and of the daily work of the Council, involving most important and delicate negotiations and official communications with foreign states and others.[50]

The members of the bondholders' committees are required by the terms of the incorporating statute to serve gratuitously. But the Council is authorized, when a settlement is arrived at and providing funds are available, to pay them as an honorarium a moderate fee for each attendance at the meetings of their committee. No such fees are paid, however, to the president and vice president.

While the Corporation has the great advantage of operating under an excellent constitution, its past achievements and present influence must be ascribed in no small degree to the character and capacity of the men who have been chiefly responsible for the direction of its policy and the conduct of its activities. To the successive presidents and secretaries of the Corporation—and they have been few,[51] for a proud tradition of

49. Preface to Annual Reports of the Corporation for 1948 and previous years.
50. Evidence of Sir John Lubbuck (afterward Lord Avebury) before the Select Committee of the House of Commons on the Bill to Reconstitute the Corporation of Foreign Bondholders, quoted in *The Financial News*, May 14, 1898.
51. The secretary is the head of the small permanent staff of the Corporation. From the foundation of the Corporation in 1868 to 1933 there were only 7 different presidents and 4 secretaries.

lifelong service has been built up—the foreign bondholding community in Great Britain owes a great debt. These officers necessarily play the leading role in the negotiation of the debt settlements and, had they been less conspicuous for integrity, ability, tact, and good judgment, many defaults would have been far less satisfactorily adjusted.

THE ASSOCIATION NATIONALE DES PORTEURS FRANÇAIS DE VALEURS MOBILIÈRES

The Association Nationale des Porteurs Français de Valeurs Mobilières was founded in 1898 by the Paris Stock Exchange (Chambre Syndicale des Agents de Change) at the request of the French Minister of Finance. Its constitution [52] and practice [53] are very similar to those of the older British institution. It, too, embraces an executive council, a number of bondholders' committees, and a small permanent staff. The functions and powers of the members of the committees, their relationship to the Council and the bondholders, and the method by which they are selected are practically identical in the two organizations. Under French law, however, the members of the committees must be bondholders, while, on account of the great number of small holders of foreign bonds in France and their wide dispersion, general meetings of bondholders are seldom, if ever, called, even for the consideration of a proposed settlement. The bondholders signify their assent by encashment of the first coupon under the new arrangement. Before World War I, acceptance by holders of about two thirds of the French interest in the defaulted issues was required, but there has been no insistence since on such a proportion and even a bare majority might now be accepted. If only a minority of the coupons should be presented, the Association would probably instruct its committee to reopen negotiations, but no such situation appears to have arisen. As in England, a deposit of bonds is required only in rare and corresponding circumstances. The Association also throws the burden of providing for the expenses of its bondholders' committees upon the state whose default made the negotiations necessary, but, unlike the Corporation, its ordinary expenditure is financed partly out of annual contributions. The stock exchange is the chief contributor but modest sums are also derived from subscribing and associate members, while a small subvention is also received from the state. The Council of the Association is a much smaller body than its English

52. The *Statuts* of the Association are printed in the Annuaire of the Association for 1915–20.

53. For an explanation of the procedure of the Association, indebtedness is acknowledged to M. Barde, the Director in 1933.

counterpart, being composed of only 8 members.[54] In 1933 2 of these were representatives of the stock exchange and 2 of large commercial banks, one was an eminent professor of law, another a leading government engineer, and the remaining 2 a distinguished diplomat and a former high official in the Ministry of Finance.[55]

THE BELGIAN ASSOCIATION POUR LA DÉFENSE DES DÉTENTEURS DE FONDS PUBLICS

The year 1898 also witnessed the organization of the Belgian Association pour la Défense des Détenteurs de Fonds Publics. It is a nonprofit association governed by a central committee and has close relations to the Antwerp Stock Exchange. It is mainly a coördinating body for the several subcommittees which it appoints for special defaults as occasion requires. It functions without pay for the members, except that the Association receives gifts, accepts fees from bondholders after a successful negotiation, and collects annual dues, the amount of which is determined by the general assembly of members each year.[56]

GERMAN COMMITTEES

In Germany down to 1914 the issuing bankers organized the protection of their clients when needed. After 1918 the Government took an interest in the matter because of the problems connected with the treaty of peace. In 1927 a committee sponsored by bankers, chambers of commerce, and stock exchanges organized a special body for the protection of foreign bondholders.[57] Its by-laws were similar to those of the French Association but it did not become very active.

54. The *Statuts* of the Association provide for 9 members, but for the several years prior to 1933 the Council had only 8 members. The members are appointed for 6 years but are subject to reëlection.

55. A more detailed description of the history and functions of the French Association will be found in the article by James H. Ronald, "National Organizations for the Protection of Holders of Foreign Bonds," *Geo. Wash. Law Rev.*, III (1935), 411, at 428.

56. Ronald, *op. cit.*, p. 426. It was reorganized in 1923, under the Belgian law of June 27, 1921. By Article 199 of the decree of November 30, 1935, Belgian and foreign corporations are assimilated in their requirements for prior publicity concerning a bond issue. Janne, "La Protection des obligataires en droit belge," in *Rapports préparatoires à la Semaine internationale de droit*, No. VI, p. 49.

57. Cf. Protection of foreign bondholders in Department of Commerce, Finance and Investment Division, Special Circular 359 (1931), p. 3. The German committee was not, like the British, a corporation, but an association organized under

SWISS AND ITALIAN COMMITTEES

Swiss and Italian committees were organized by the respective associations of bankers and in Holland by the Amsterdam Stock Exchange. As the allotment of these countries was usually merely a part of an international syndicate flotation, these national committees usually coöperated with the protective committees of other countries.[58]

THE LEAGUE LOANS COMMITTEE

The term "League of Nations loans" or "League loans" was applied to the nine loans issued [59] under the auspices of the League of Nations in order to restore the financial stability of the States concerned, and to enable them to face new and unparalleled conditions. In all cases the con-

---

the civil code. In principle, the "Permanent Commission," as it was called, gave its advice only to the issuing house. The Commission took the initiative only if no issuing house existed. Ficker, "La Protection des obligataires en droit allemand," in *Rapports préparatoires à la Semaine internationale de droit*, No. VI, p. 26.

58. Ronald, *op. cit.*, pp. 432–436. Under the auspices of the Swiss Association of Bankers, protective committees have been set up for the various countries in default in Europe and South America. These committees bring the interests of the bondholders to the attention of the Swiss Government. They are represented on international bondholders' committees. Carry, "La Protection des obligataires en droit suisse," in *Rapports préparatoires à la Semaine internationale de droit*, No. VI, p. 131. Holland's stock exchange committee has several functions: (1) as a listing committee to determine whether foreign bonds may be admitted to quotation, denied generally in case of notorious default; (2) the supervision of the performance of the terms of a contract; (3) the examination of the merits of a plan of adjustment and recommendations to the exchange of steps to be taken for the protection of bondholders. It is not customary to invoke diplomatic interposition, although an exception was made in connection with the transfer difficulties which arose in Germany after 1932. Star Busmann, "La Protection des obligataires en Hollande," *Rapports préparatoires à la Semaine internationale de droit*, No. VI, p. 90. Also Hamel, *idem*, p. 10. Somewhat extended reports concerning the scope and functions of these national protective associations were filed in 1936 with the League Study Committee. Docs. I.L. 6–9.

59. These loans were as follows: 1 loan to Austria, issued in 1923 (converted, 1934), also jointly guaranteed by Great Britain, France, Czechoslovakia, Italy, Belgium, Sweden, Denmark, and Holland; 1 loan to Hungary, issued 1924; 1 loan to Estonia, issued 1927; 2 loans to the City of Danzig, issued 1925 and 1927; 2 loans to Bulgaria, issued 1926 and 1928; 2 loans to Greece, issued 1924 and 1928. L. of N. Doc. C.59.M.59.1945.11.A, *The League of Nations Reconstruction Schemes in the Inter-War Period*, p. 60. Except for the Estonia loan, all these loans went into default, Danzig in July, 1939, the others in 1932. There was, however, some subsequent service, considerably reduced, on the loans of Hungary, Bulgaria, and Greece.

ditions of the loans, their amount and the purposes to which they should be applied, were determined by the Financial Committee of the League of Nations and approved by the Council; and it was this examination and approval which inspired investors with confidence and secured their support.[60]

As to the responsibility of the League for these loans, it may be noticed that "the prospectus of each loan bore in a prominent position a statement to the effect that the loan was made under the auspices of the League of Nations and that the Council of the League had approved the issue." [61] But they were not guaranteed by the League or, except in the case of Austria, by the governments which facilitated their flotation.[62]

When the crisis of the early 'thirties brought about transfer difficulties in many countries, the so-called League loans suffered with the rest. Thereupon, in view of the prominent part which the British Government had taken in sponsoring the League loans, the Governor of the Bank of England took the initiative in calling together a protective committee, later known as the League Loans Committee.[63]

This committee assumed less powers than the Council of the Corporation of Foreign Bondholders, for it considered itself merely a negotiating agency between bondholders and the debtor government for the best protection of both the bondholders and the debtor. It had no mandate to make any arrangements binding upon the creditors. It merely tendered advice and made recommendations, and claimed for itself complete impartiality not only among the divergent interests of conflicting creditors but between the creditors as a whole and the debtor. Although organized in England and although about half the League loans were placed in the London market, the Committee claimed that its arrangements were not designed to afford preference to English bondholders but to extend to the entire issue, hence to all *tranches* of the loan wherever floated. Yet its special function necessarily was to protect League-sponsored issues, al-

60. League Loans Committee, *First Annual Report*, May, 1933, p. 6. Cf. *The Problem of International Investment*, pp. 231–234; Schoo, *Régimen jurídico*, pp. 326 ff.

61. Sir Austen Chamberlain, "The League Loans," *The Financial News* (London), February 20, 1933.

62. The Austrian League loans were defaulted in July, 1938, after the absorption of Austria by Germany. Special arrangements for the service of these loans by Germany were made in the Anglo-German transfer agreements of July 1, 1938, and August 13, 1938. *Corp. For. Bondh. Rep.*, No. 65 (1938), p. 11.

63. It consisted first of 6 Englishmen, Sir Austen Chamberlain, Viscount Goschen, Mr. A. A. Jamieson, Mr. C. Lubbock, Sir Otto Niemeyer, Sir Arthur Salter. On November 21, 1932, it was announced that 3 additional men had joined the Committee, Dr. D. Crena de Jough (Netherlands), Dr. G. Bianchini (Italy), and Mr. Eliot Wadsworth (United States).

though it disavowed any desire to obtain unfair advantage at the expense of other creditors.[64]

64. Domestic legislation in several European countries, such as Switzerland, France, Germany, Belgium, was designed to enable bondholders to unite for the protection of their interests by the appointment of a *mandataire* or agent to represent them in any proceedings against or negotiations with the debtor. In Austria the court has been authorized ever since 1874 to appoint a curator for this purpose. While this legislation applies in principle only to the bondholders of trading corporations, domestic and foreign, a French decree of November, 1935, provided that it might apply to foreign government bonds issued in France if the ministers of justice, foreign affairs, finance, and commerce so ordered. Thus far no application of this provision appears to have been made. "Décret relatif à la protection des obligataires," *Journal officiel de la république française*, Vol. LXVII, No. 259, November 4, 5, 1935, p. 11826. Cf. Weiser, *Trusts on the Continent of Europe*, p. 77, n. 99.

Among the governmental agencies for the protection of private bondholders mention may be made of the French Commission for Gold Loans (*Commissions des emprunts or*). This commission was set up by Article 18 of the law of December 23, 1933, concerning the reëstablishment of the budgetary balance. *Appendice au Recueil Dalloz, Année 1933* (Paris, 1933), p. 455.

It was composed of 3 senators, 6 deputies, 1 representative each of the ministries of justice, finance, budget, and foreign affairs. Its function consisted in the setting up of a list of all gold loans issued by foreign states, cities, or corporations on the French market within thirty years preceding the last war; it had to examine the adjustments made and to ascertain whether the agreements had been carried out; it submitted suggestions to the ministries concerned as to how the interests of French gold investments could best be safeguarded. Of particular interest in this connection was the proposal made by the Commission in their annual report for 1935 with respect to the creation of a permanent body to coordinate certain activities of the Ministry of Commerce and the Ministry of Foreign Affairs for the purpose of protecting French bondholders. Annual report of the Commission for Gold Loans. December 31, 1935. *Journal officiel de la république française, Annexe*, Vol. LXVIII, January 17, 1936, pp. 61 ff.

It was pointed out that the conclusion of a commercial treaty, in particular the granting of a concession or of other economic privileges, might furnish a welcome opportunity for the favorable settlement of a financial dispute between bondholders and a foreign government. Consequently, no commercial treaty should be negotiated and concluded without participation of the Minister of Finance, who would advise the other agencies concerned as to the measures best suited to protect the rights of private bondholders. The necessary information would be furnished by a permanent commission consisting of members of Parliament; of representatives of the ministries of foreign affairs, commerce, agriculture, and finance; representatives of certain professional groups and of bondholders' protective associations. The commission would have to keep in close touch with the course of the bond market, with bankers, and with bondholders' protective associations. It would act as a research and advisory body which, whenever commercial negotiations with foreign countries were undertaken, would have available up-to-date information with respect to the particular country seeking economic advantages from France.

Section XVII

DIPLOMATIC PROTECTION FOR BONDHOLDERS

THE nineteenth century witnessed a growing appreciation of the importance of foreign investment, including loans to foreign governments, in the competition for national prosperity and political influence. The countries of the lenders were not always great powers, as witness Belgium, Holland, and Switzerland, nor were the borrowing countries always minor powers, e.g., Russia. But on the whole the greatest capital accumulations, with resulting capital exports, occurred in the advanced industrial and trading nations like Great Britain—the world's financial center—France, Germany, and later the United States, while the most regular borrowers were the underdeveloped and more politically unstable countries of Europe and Latin America. Although, with rare exceptions, *laissez faire* dominated capital exports in Great Britain and the United States until well into the twentieth century, it soon became apparent, first in France and later in other countries, that foreign investment could be used as an instrument of policy to serve the national political interest.

The economic exploitation of backward areas, a term not invidiously employed, became a goal of imperialism, and finance the least provocative means to the end. In countries like Egypt and Turkey, the misuse of the receipts from foreign loans, the constant financial disorder, and the eventual defaults had international political repercussions which culminated in the imposition of varying degrees of foreign control over their finances. The United States was prompted by political interest to participate actively in the stabilization and control of the finances of a number of Carribbean countries. It is not always clear whether the financial control was the seed or the fruit of the political interest but certain it is that closer contact between the lending country and its investment bankers and bondholders grew apace. As governments realized the political weight of financial power they not only took more interest in directing the flow of export capital and showed more concern in its fate but, in some instances, themselves became capital investors on a grand scale, as, for instance, the British Government by its purchase of shares in the Suez Canal Company and the Anglo-Iranian Oil Company, and the United States through its authorization to the Export-Import Bank to lend up to $700,000,000,[1] a maximum subsequently extended to $3,500,000,000.[2]

ORIGINATION OF THE LOAN

It is interesting to observe how this coöperation between government and lending bank developed in the course of the nineteenth century. In general it may be said that the British Government and to a lesser extent the German Government were in the beginning reluctant to approve or disapprove private loans to foreign countries, in the belief that approval carried some kind of commitment to enforce payment or participate in its collection. As late as 1914 Sir Edward Grey, Minister for Foreign Affairs, was adjured in Parliament to block a forthcoming loan to Brazil until Brazil paid various private claims, but Sir Edward declined to interfere.[3] This abstention was expressed as a policy.[4] While undoubtedly observed with respect to countries in which Great Britain had no political interest, like South America, and while bankers were under no duty to consult the government before bringing out a loan, it is hardly to be expected that in parts of the world more vital to the British Empire the same aloofness should prevail. Without any formal requirement of government approval, investment bankers found unofficial ways of sounding out the government, especially through the Bank of England, which, prior to its recent nationalization, was a semiofficial institution with which all bankers maintained contact. Not only would they learn of political considerations which might militate against a loan but in the light of the bank's close touch with the money market they would learn whether economic considerations dictated withdrawal or delay.[5] In countries of the Near East and China, where Britain's political interests and

1. In March, 1939, the limit on loans and obligations was set at $100,000,000. The limit was raised to $200,000,000 in March, 1940, and to $700,000,000 in the following September. Eleanor Lansing Dulles, *The Export-Import Bank of Washington, the First Ten Years* (Washington, 1944), pp. 7, 11, and 13, n. 15.

2. By the Export-Import Bank Act of 1945.

3. H. Feis, *Europe, the World's Banker, 1870–1914*, pp. 109 ff. Cf. Jenks, *The Migration of British Capital to 1875*, p. 283; Jacob Viner, "International Finance and Balance of Power Diplomacy, 1880–1914," *S.W. Pol. and Soc. Sci. Quar.*, IX (March, 1929).

4. Parl. Debates, Commons, 5th Ser., LXIV, 1448. See also remarks as to French policy of M. Pichon in the Chamber of Deputies, June 7, 1907, *Journal Officiel*, Chambre des deputés, débats parlementaires, p. 1231; Schoo, *Régimen jurídico*, p. 504.

5. Feis, *op. cit.*, p. 86. Cf. *The Problem of International Investment*, chap. vii.

its relations with the governments of other foreign investors were involved, there was more frankness in exercising some voice in directing British bankers in their loan policy. Not only were checks put on banks whose loan activities in China were thought to interfere with the British-sponsored Consortium but the Chinese Government itself was threatened with Britain's displeasure if it continued such negotiations.[6]

In 1854 the British Government, in its desire to support Turkey, had permitted its recommendation of the tribute loan to be mentioned in the loan prospectus. In 1875 the bondholders waited on Lord Derby, Foreign Secretary, and maintained that this was in effect an assumption of responsibility for the merits of the loan and an implied guaranty. While this was disclaimed, the House of Commons was persuaded to move the French Government to join with the British in making representations to Turkey to secure the fulfillment of the conditions of the 1854 loan.[7]

Recklessness in the making of loans is often followed by prompt default. On occasion this has led to parliamentary inquiries, as occurred in England in 1875 and in the United States Congress during the 'thirties.[8] The English investigation in 1875, after notorious defaults in Paraguay, Honduras, Guatemala, and other Central American states, brought a reprimand for the loose and indiscriminate making of loans but a rejection of any suggestion for government supervision, since that might have given a false sense of security and have increased the government's obligation to take measures against defaulters. Instead, the stock exchange was urged to exercise better control of issues, and laws were recommended to increase the responsibility of banks and directors and to require fuller and more honest prospectuses,[9] matters now covered by legislation.

In the matter of borrowing in London by the colonies, the Colonial Stocks Act, as amended in 1900, prescribes strict conditions of eligibility with which borrowing colonies must conform.[10] In the case of governments within the British sphere of influence, the British Government would on occasion lecture the borrowing government on its weak financial system [11] or, by means of a public commission controlled in part by the British Government or its appointees, would exercise control over the expenditure of the proceeds of a loan [12] or, as in Egypt, in order to assure

6. Cf. instances of blocking loans in Turkey and China. Feis, *op. cit.*, p. 90.

7. II, 420–21. Lord Russell had expressed "great confidence" in Turkey. II, 399–402.

8. Cf. *infra*, p. 239, n. 76.

9. Feis, *op. cit.*, pp. 105 ff.

10. *Idem*, p. 93.

11. In 1841 Portugal was given a lecture on her financial system, pointing out its deficiencies and the necessary corrections. II, 370, n. 30.

12. Turkey, loan of 1862. II, 400.

the making of a loan by British bankers, offer to participate in the active management of its fiscal affairs.[13] What was originally a bondholders' receivership, under the contract, might thus develop into a receivership conducted by their home governments.[14] When backward countries went into prolonged default and foreign supervision became feasible, some government control was exercised on occasion over the terms and conditions of refunding or reorganization loans, a fiscal intervention which sometimes, as in Egypt, merged into political control.[15] Indeed, borrowing countries which fell within the ambit of the European balance of power or conflicting imperialisms were in special danger of losing their independence in whole or in part.[16] Since 1932, under the restrictions placed on foreign loans in the British market, such foreign credits as Great Britain has extended—like those granted in 1938 to Turkey and China have subserved political ends.[17]

In England economic considerations led to the Government's control of the lending market. The balance of payments had to be kept in equilibrium, yet investment abroad was not to be stopped for good but only controlled. This control was directed to the flotation of new issues. After 1918 these were permitted only with the consent of the Treasury and the Bank of England, not by statute but by "requests" from the

13. Egypt, an administration by commission of Dairal (Khedive's) lands. II, 594. But France and England disclaimed responsibility for payment of interest on the loan.

14. II, 611.

15. Cf. II, 604, where trouble with the Khedive resulted in a joint demand by Britain and France in 1879 that the Khedive abdicate. In 1892, after the Portuguese default, France intervened actively to obtain improved terms for French investors in the reorganization loans. Feis, *op. cit.*, p. 148.

The right to intervene on behalf of loan contracts may be reserved in advance. At the Lausanne Conference of 1923 between the Allies, Britain, France, and Italy, on the one hand, and Turkey, on the other, the Allies declared: "The British, French and Italian governments reserve the right to intervene by such ways and such means as they respectively may judge suitable with the object of protecting in this respect the rights and interests of their nationals." II, 497.

16. II, 595 n. 61. Lord Cromer explained England's departure in 1878 from the nonintervention policy on behalf of bondholders by stating that the "Berlin Congress was then about to sit to regulate the situation arising from the recent Russian-Turkish War." Egyptian interests became incidental to broader diplomatic considerations. It became necessary to conciliate the French and French initiative was followed. A conference of the powers in June, 1882, deliberated on joint armed intervention in Egypt. But England alone suppressed the Alexandria riots in July, 1882, and remained in Egypt as the sole occupying power. II, 615–616.

17. Edward H. Carr, *The Twenty Years' Crisis, 1919–1939* (London, Macmillan & Co., Ltd., 1940), pp. 161–162.

Bank or Treasury which, through the relations between the issuing bankers and both the Bank and the Treasury, had all the force of statute. If a banker failed to heed the verbal injunction, he would soon learn that his bills were not discounted and that in other ways he had incurred official disfavor. But the control of capital issues was not enough. Following the institution, from 1930 to 1932, of progressively tighter restrictions on new foreign issues, it was found necessary in 1933 to extend the control to cover purchases of large blocks of foreign securities by English buyers from foreign sellers. Even foreign reconversions were prohibited up to 1934, with certain exceptions. Britain's departure from gold in 1931 necessitated rigid controls for the protection of the sterling exchange rate. The character and position of a prospective borrower accordingly became an object of public interest. Control was more closely officialized in 1936 when the Chancellor of the Exchequer announced the appointment of a foreign transactions (advisory) committee who were to pass on all loan applications from public authorities and from others and transactions for raising money which might necessitate the transmission of funds outside the Empire. British capital was now officially canalized, favorable consideration being given to the countries of the sterling block, in the light of "the exchange position of Great Britain, the volume of Empire borrowing and the movement of securities between British and other stock exchanges."[18] Due to the intensification of Great Britain's balance of payments difficulties as a consequence of World War II, the export of capital is likely to be stringently controlled for an indefinite period.

Germany entered the financial market as an exporter of capital rather late. The original disposition of the Government was to refrain from interfering in the money market or with the lending banks and to adopt no legislation formalizing Government consent, as did France. Germany wished to avoid any imputation of responsibility for the merits of foreign loans and also wished to avoid giving offense to foreign governments. But, through its relations to the listing committee of the Berlin Stock Exchange, through the official Reichsbank and through the semiofficial press, it was able to make its wishes known when it so desired, and a few loans appear to have been blocked.[19] As Germany's political interests in the Near East and elsewhere grew and the Deutsche Bank and others as media of investment became instruments of the policy of expansion,

18. Cf. *The Problem of International Investment*, pp. 76–79; Schoo, *op. cit.*, pp. 123 ff.

19. Feis, *op. cit.*, pp. 163, 165; George W. Edwards, "Government Control of Foreign Investments," *Am. Econ. Rev.*, XVIII (1928), 690.

it was natural that a closer coöperation and coördination should arise between government and lenders, without formal requirement.[20] As the relatively young German economy needed husbanding, the Government's interest in private finance could not remain detached. It went even to the point of endeavoring to control the proportions between foreign and domestic securities as a means of maintaining prices for German Government bonds.[21] As the war of 1914 approached and Germany sought greater political influence in the states of eastern Europe, the German Government brought pressure to bear on German banks to make loans to Turkey, Hungary, Romania, and Bulgaria, loans some of which had been refused by the French or British banks and in the making of which even German banks had for economic reasons hesitated.[22]

The French Government was always more active than others in controlling, by legislation and by political pressure, official and unofficial, the flow of French capital exports, sometimes blocking, sometimes aiding the flotation of foreign loans, as its political interests and public policy dictated. As early as 1785 an official decree ordered the Paris Bourse to list only French Government bonds.[23] In 1823 this privilege was extended to foreign government bonds, under the supervision of the Minister of Finance. While this was said merely to regularize operations that were taking place privately, the opportunity to refuse listing to foreign bonds is a definite form of controlling both their flotation and their marketing, even though the government made it clear that in granting listing they expressed neither approval of the loan nor an intention to help investors who might suffer loss.[24] The decree of 1823 was implemented by letters of the Minister of Finance to the Stock Exchange in 1825 and 1873 and by further decrees of 1875 and 1880, all confirming the Government's power to grant or refuse listing for financial or political reasons. A law of 1907, as amended, required announcement of proposed loans in the Official Journal and laid down requirements for publicity and other restrictions upon the freedom of issuing bonds.[25]

20. Feis, *op. cit.*, p. 167; Jenks, *op. cit.*, p. 283; W. F. Bruck, *Social and Economic History of Germany* (London, 1938), p. 80.

21. Feis, *op. cit.*, p. 170. On this account the Government in 1911 prevented the listing of American railway bonds. In 1913 they restricted foreign loans not advantageous to Germany. Bonds of Mexico, including national railway bonds, were barred from listing by the Prussian Government in 1912 because the Huerta Government, unrecognized by the United States, offered a dangerous risk.

22. Feis, *op. cit.*, p. 175.

23. Edwards, *op. cit.*, p. 688.

24. Feis, *op. cit.*, pp. 119 ff.

25. E.g., appointing an agent in France who shall represent the borrower in its relations with French bondholders. Hamel, "La Protection des obligataires,"

But, in spite of frequent desires expressed in the Chamber of Deputies for Government intervention to prevent the issue of dishonest or especially hazardous foreign bonds, no administration was willing to assume such responsibility, especially as French policy often seemed to require the advance of money to countries of doubtful credit.[26] Nevertheless, M. Caillaux, as Minister of Finance, stated in 1909 that the Government considered it its function to refuse listing to foreign bonds "when it appears that French savings may be hurt by this investment." So in 1913 the Mexican bonds issued by Huerta were refused listing, as were on occasion bonds of Brazil, Paraguay, and other countries, though in the absence of fraud the faculty to refuse on economic grounds was generally disclaimed, as was the power to prevent the sale of unlisted bonds.[27] Thus the ability to prevent the issue of loans deemed inimical to French political interest, to refuse listing, and to facilitate through its connections the issue and marketing of foreign loans deemed advantageous to France gave the Government a fairly complete control of French private finance as an instrument of political power. Loans of French capital to the French colonies were facilitated by guaranties and other statutory measures.[28]

Indeed, the Government occasionally arranged the borrowing and then selected the banks to carry out the transaction, with all the aid of official and unofficial propaganda. The loans contracted in France under French Government auspices on behalf of the Mexican Government of Maximilian having been repudiated by Mexico in 1867, France undertook to reimburse the disappointed investors to the extent of about 50 per cent.[29] Perhaps such a moral obligation is an inescapable consequence of government encouragement in the flotation of a foreign loan and accounts for the caveats of the United States and other governments in distinguishing between a lack of objection and endorsement.[30]

After 1902 the French Government exerted great pressure on the Sultan of Morocco to accept certain loans, arranged the terms and the security, shut off other possible lenders, and provided for the disposition

Rapports préparatoires à la Semaine internationale de droit, No. VI, p. 11. Cf. also the remarks of Foreign Minister Pichon, loc. cit.; Schoo, op. cit., p. 504.

26. Feis, op. cit., p. 132.

27. Journal Officiel, Chambre des Deputés, débats parlementaires, January 2, 1909, December 28, 1911. France undertook in 1911–13 to refuse listing to any Chinese loan which was to be used to weaken Russia's place in China's affairs. Feis, op. cit., p. 141.

28. Idem, pp. 142 ff.

29. Cf. details in Sack, Les Effets des transformations des états sur leurs dettes publiques, p. 18. Corp. For. Bondh. Rep., No. 51 (1924), p. 271. II, 29–30.

30. II, 407, and infra, p. 231.

of the proceeds of the loans.[31] French capital loans of £400,000,000 to Russia, encouraged and stimulated by the French Government, cemented the Franco-Russian alliance of 1890, and this access of Russia to the French money market was deemed a consideration of the alliance. The loans of 1913–14 to Russia were made conditional upon an increase in the Russian military power and the building of certain strategic railways.[32] In the negotiations for certain Chinese loans of 1911 and 1913, France gave firm support to the four-power consortium, merely insisting on sufficient control for the pledged revenues and the proper expenditure of the loan proceeds.

After the war of 1914–18 France strengthened her political influence over Poland and the Little Entente by the grant of considerable loans and credits, public and private. France participated, with Great Britain and other countries, in the guaranty of the League loan floated in 1923 to enable Austria to survive.[33] It is thus apparent that the French Government frequently utilized the export of capital of its private investors as an instrument to promote political objectives, varying the weight of its support in accordance with the circumstances and the objective to be achieved.[34]

The United States experience with capital export has been relatively short, but rich, largely in losses and regrets. The internal development of the United States had absorbed practically all American and much foreign investment capital but the European war of 1914 brought foreign bond issues to the attention of a wide public, until by the late 'twenties probably 800,000 American citizens held foreign bonds. Of the nearly 5½ billion dollars thus invested, approximately one third were in total or partial default after the financial collapse of 1931; in Latin America the proportion of default was 76 per cent of the total amount loaned.[35] After the outbreak of war in Europe in 1939, defaults were necessarily aggravated.

A few foreign loans had been made before 1914, mainly among countries in the Caribbean like Santo Domingo, Haiti, and Nicaragua. Here the American political interest was considerable. Whereas the general American practice had been to take no part in the private business of Americans purchasing foreign bonds, with a consequent refusal diplo-

31. Feis, *op. cit.*, p. 141. See E. Staley, *War and the Private Investor* (Garden City, Doubleday, Doran, 1935).

32. Feis, *op. cit.*, p. 140. Carr, *op. cit.*, pp. 159 ff. Viner, *op. cit.*, pp. 2 ff.

33. *Supra*, p. 103.

34. Cf. Imbert, *Les Emprunts d'états étrangers*, pp. 8 ff.

35. The details will be found in SEC, *Rep.*, Pt. V (1937), pp. 4–7.

matically to protect the buyer against default, the peculiar necessities
of financing the indigent countries of the Caribbean and warding off
European intervention compelled a more active participation of the
United States Government not only in encouraging investment in the
bonds of those countries but in devising security safeguards like customs
receiverships to guarantee the service of the loans.[36] To assist Salvador
and the lending banks, the United States became "woven into the contract" of June 24, 1922, and agreed in a formal exchange of notes with
Salvador not only to the appointment of a receiver of customs on default [37] but also to the unusual clause that any dispute in the interpretation of the contract would be submitted to the Chief Justice of the United
States Supreme Court or, if he was unavailable, to some other federal

36. As early as 1881, Secretary of State James G. Blaine had suggested that
the United States might place an agent in charge of the pledged customs revenue
of Venezuela to pay off foreign creditors. Venezuela had defaulted and pledged
remittances to French creditors, not others. Alice F. Tyler, *The Foreign Policy
of James G. Blaine* (Minneapolis, 1927), pp. 66–79.

The Nicaraguan receiver, an official of the Philippines Customs Service, was
introduced to the bankers by the State Department. R. R. Hill, "Fiscal Intervention in Nicaragua" (New York, Ph.D. dissertation, Columbia Univ., 1933),
p. 12. Under the Knox-Castrillo convention of 1911, the President of the United
States was to approve the nomination. *For. Rel.*, 1912, pp. 1074–1075. Brown
Bros. and Seligman & Co. were persuaded to make the Nicaraguan loan of 1911
by the guarantees thus afforded. A. A. Berle, "Policy of the United States in
Latin-America," Dept. of State, *Press Releases*, No. 501 (May 6, 1939), p. 378.
D. G. Munro, *The United States and the Caribbean Area* (Boston, World Peace
Foundation, 1934), p. 243. But Morgan withdrew from the Honduran loan, also
provisionally arranged by the Knox-Paredes convention of 1911, when the convention, including the receivership, was rejected by the Honduran Congress; it was
never acted on by the United States Senate. For the Santo Domingo customs
receivers, see *infra*, p. 295. At the request of European governments the collection
of customs was extended to all the ports of Santo Domingo. II, 241–243. On the
Nicaragua debt adjustment, see *The United States and Nicaragua: A Survey of the
Relations from 1909 to 1932* (Dept. of State, Lat. Amer. Ser., No. 61, 1932),
especially pp. 28–37, 46. As to warding off European investments in Central
America, see Dexter Perkins, *Hands Off, a History of the Monroe Doctrine*
(Boston, Little, Brown, 1941), pp. 263–264, for note to Germany expressing displeasure at loans or contracts by European powers to the Caribbean coun-
tries.

37. In 1932, when the loan went into default, the United States declined to
appoint a customs receiver on the ground that the Central American treaty of
1923 prohibited the recognition of revolutionary governments, whereupon recognition had been refused to the Salvador Government. Thompson, "The Caribbean
Situation: Nicaragua and Salvador," *For. Pol. Rep.*, Vol. IX (August 30, 1933),
No. 13, pp. 147–148. SEC, *Rep.*, Pt. V, p. 407. But the British Government
pressed for the receivership contemplated in the contract. Archives, Coun. For.
Bondh. See also *Corp. For. Bondh. Rep.*, No. 60 (1933), p. 401.

judge, a clause of which the bankers took advantage, to the embarrassment of the Department of State, in drafting the prospectuses of the bonds.[38]

Minister Ewing, Tegucigalpa, Honduras, January 9, 1914, referring to the Department's dispatch No. 172, of January 14, 1913, and subsequent correspondence concerning Mr. Keilhauer's proposal for the settlement of the Honduran debt, especially in connection with the question of the Island of Zacate Grande, Bay of Fonseca, telegraphed that Keilhauer would soon arrive at Tegucigalpa to renew his proposal for a concession, which, if slightly modified, probably might be granted. Congress, then in session, seemed, said Ewing, to be less hostile; and Keilhauer might be greatly assisted by the assurance he was holding out to the bondholders that he had the backing of the Government of the United States. As the concession seemed to Ewing to be unfavorable to the United States, he requested instructions by cable as to the attitude the legation should take. February 21, Mr. Bryan replied that the Department was considering the concession and asked Ewing whether Keilhauer's agreement with the Council of Foreign Bondholders bound them to a definitely outlined plan. Ewing answered, February 26, that the agreement definitely bound the bondholders only after its approval by the President of Honduras, its acceptance by a general meeting of bond-

38. B. H. Williams. *Economic Foreign Policy of the United States*, p. 193, summarizing the bankers' (Lisman's) statement. On October 18, 1923, the Department issued a press release stating that it had no relation to the loan except to facilitate the "arbitration and determination" of disputes that might arise between the parties and the appointment of a collector of customs in case of default, and emphasized that at the specific request of Salvador and the bankers the Secretary of State had consented to use good offices to refer such disputes to the Chief Justice or another federal judge. *For. Rel.*, 1923, II, 824. Such reference was never made. The American intervention in Haiti was legalized by the treaty of September 16, 1915, which provided for American control of Haitian finances. *For. Rel.*, 1916, pp. 328–332; Millspaugh, *Haiti under American Control, 1915–1930*, Appendix, pp. 211–215.

There had been European precedents for the representations of the bondholders collecting customs or other pledges, as in Turkey, Egypt, and elsewhere. As early as 1830, Great Britain permitted her vice-consuls at Vera Cruz and Tampico to receive pledged revenues on behalf of the British bondholders but not to act "as the agents of the bondholders in the more general and extended signification of the term." *Brit. and For. St. Pap.*, XXVIII, 970 ff. But later on the British Government did on occasion permit the British consular and diplomatic service to act as agent for the bondholders or aid the Council on Foreign Bondholders to accomplish their aims. *Infra*, p. 250. Under the French loan of 1904 to Morocco, the collection of the assigned revenues was supervised by a representative of the bondholders under the official protection of the French Legation. Supervision exercised by France and Germany from 1903 to 1914 over the loans of the Imperial Ottoman Bank. II, 478.

holders, and its subsequent ratification by the Honduran Congress in connection with the grant of a concession to Keilhauer for the construction of an interoceanic railroad.

Even before 1918 the Department of State had taken an active interest in encouraging loans to China [39] and had assumed that it had the power to name the conditions of loans to Mexico and "veto" loans not meeting its approval.[40] After 1918, under the Wilson administration, it encouraged American direct investments in Mexico and elsewhere and after the war assumed an active role in facilitating American participation in foreign enterprise of all kinds. This favorable attitude of the Government had not a little to do with the flood of foreign loans made by American bankers in the 1920's, not always with that caution which might have been exhibited. There was no legislative authority for governmental control of the export of capital but in 1922 the Department of State felt itself obliged to suggest in a public statement that it would be desirable to submit foreign loan contracts to the Department of State to see whether there was any political objection to their flotation. Since there were unofficial ways of making known its disapproval, which would have interfered with the marketing of the loan and possibly forfeited such diplomatic support as the Department might have been willing to afford at the time of default, there was no trouble in securing the submission to the Department of loan contracts.

The Press Release of March 3, 1922, read as follows:

FLOTATION OF FOREIGN LOANS

. . . The Department of State can not, of course, require American bankers to consult it. It will not pass upon the merits of foreign loans as business

39. On November 16, 1916, the Department had expressed to the Continental . . . Bank of Chicago its gratification at a $5,000,000 loan to China and stated: "It is the policy of the Department now as in the past to give all proper diplomatic support and protection to the legitimate enterprise abroad of American citizens." *For. Rel.*, 1916, p. 138. Again, on October 21, 1919, it expressed similar sentiments concerning a new contract between the bank and China, and spoke of the "interests of this government in encouraging and aiding, in every proper way, the undertakings of its nationals in foreign countries." It went further and said: "This government is willing to take all proper steps to insure the execution of equitable contracts which are made in good faith." *Idem*, 1919, I, 525 ff. In referring to a proposed loan of the Pacific Development Corp. to China in 1919, it stated: "The United States Government will feel that its citizens have a right to expect from it full diplomatic support when engaged in proper activities." *Idem*, 1919, I, 552. See also *idem*, 1920, I, 605; *idem*, 1921, I, 389 ff.

The consortium agreement of October 15, 1920, provided that "whereas their respective Governments have undertaken to give their complete support to their respective national groups. . . ." *Idem*, 1920, I, 576–577.

40. Secretary Lansing in *For. Rel.*, 1917, p. 1014.

propositions, nor assume any responsibility whatever in connection with loan transactions. Offers for foreign loans should not, therefore, state or imply that they are contingent upon an expression from the Department of State regarding them, nor should any prospectus or contract refer to the attitude of this Government. The Department believes that in view of the possible national interests involved it should have the opportunity of saying to the underwriters concerned, should it appear advisable to do so, that there is or is not objection to any particular issue.[41]

The approval of the government of the lender, even in this cautious form, had value to the issuing bank, to the bondholders, and to the borrowing government. In the ten-year period from 1921 to 1931 some 12 billions in foreign loans were floated in the American market, mostly bonds, and were hence submitted to the Department of State for approval.[42] While the Department disclaimed any intention of passing on the merits of the loans as business propositions, but only to take into account considerations of national policy, it was not always easy to separate the two. For example, one of the principal grounds on which rejection was based was the failure of the foreign government to adjust its debts to United States citizens,[43] to which the Johnson Act of 1934 added debts owed to the United States, i.e., war and postwar loans.[44]

41. *For. Rel.*, 1922, I, 557. J. F. Dulles, "Our Foreign Loan Policy," *For. Aff.*, V (1926), 33 ff.; Edwards, *op. cit.*, pp. 693 ff.
The policy began in a conference between President Harding and a number of bankers in 1921; the President expressed the desire that the State Department be informed of projected issues and of subsequent developments.

42. James W. Angell, *Financial Foreign Policy of the United States: A Report to the Second International Studies Conference on the State and Economic Life, London, May 29, to June 2, 1933* (New York, 1933), pp. 99 ff. Madden, Nadler, and Souvain name the figure for the dollar bonds at over 9 billions. *America's Experience as a Creditor Nation*, p. 70. B. H. Williams, *Foreign Loan Policy of the United States Since 1933* (New York, Council on Foreign Relations, 1939), p. 3.

43. Angell, *op. cit.*, p. 106. For other grounds, see *ibid.* Loans to unrecognized governments were disapproved. *For. Rel.*, 1913, p. 457; *idem*, 1922, II, 445 (Greece); *idem*, 1922, II, 697 (Mexico). On June 15, 1922, the Secretary of State notified Blair & Co. that, in view of the assurances received from the Yugoslav Government regarding the objects and uses of the loan proceeds, the Department had no objection to a flotation of $25,000,000. There was no commitment on additional sums. *Idem*, 1922, II, 1018.
In approving a Brown Bros. loan to Nicaragua in 1913, even as to "terms," Secretary Bryan maintained that the approval committed the Department to no further action but was merely "advisory." *Idem*, 1913, pp. 1056 ff.
The Department's power to disapprove future loans was used with Ecuador as a makeweight to persuade Ecuador to pay the interest on the bonds of the Quayaquil and Quito Railroad Co. Williams, *Economic Foreign Policy of the United States*, p. 86.

44. In 1922 the Department of State protested against a proposed Romanian

In spite of the disclaimer of all concern with the economic merits of the loan, it was inevitable that investors should draw an inference that a failure to object meant approval and that approval meant support. This misunderstanding, evidenced in various ways, led to reiterated clarifications of the Department's position.[45] Whether the right to disapprove flows from the power to exercise discretion in diplomatically protecting,[46] or from an appreciation of the close relation between economics and politics, is not altogether clear. Loans to unrecognized governments were not favored, doubtless as interference with diplomacy.[47]

The ban on disfavored loans became academic after 1931, since the unfortunate defaults of that date and the economic crash in Europe foreclosed all further interest of the American money market in new foreign loans. Attention was then turned to salvaging operations. The unsatisfactory experience with competing private protective committees persuaded the Department of State to facilitate the organization of the Foreign Bondholders Protective Council. But again in 1939, as the second European war approached and the effort to obtain political allies for American policy dominated the Department of State, the good neighbor policy was expanded to include government loans to Latin American countries through the Export-Import Bank and the United States Government supply of war materials and credit under the Lease-Lend Act to belligerents and others.

No longer were government loans made conditional upon settling private debts to American citizens.[48] Under the circumstances created by World War II, this requirement had to give way to higher political considerations.[49]

DIPLOMATIC PROTECTION TO PREVENT AND REMEDY DEFAULT

The absence of effective legal remedies available to bondholders makes it inevitable that they should seek relief through economic or political

---

refunding loan of $175,000,000 until Romania's debts to the United States were settled. A debt settlement was duly signed on December 4, 1925. *Idem*, pp. 88 ff.

45. Cf. Statement of Secretary Kellogg, *The New York Times*, December 15, 1925, quoted in Edwards *op. cit.*, p. 695. Circular Instruction to Diplomatic and Certain Consular Officers Concerning Questions Arising from the Negotiation of Foreign Loans by American Bankers, December 28, 1927, *For. Rel.*, 1927, II, 312.

46. Cf. B. H. Williams, *op. cit.*, p. 96.

47. *Supra*, n. 43.

48. See *For. Pol. Rep.*, June 15, 1941, p. 83: Export-Import Bank loans to Latin America.

49. As a consequence the Foreign Bondholders Protective Council could expect little or no governmental aid in negotiating settlements.

channels. There is undoubtedly a sanction for default, if only in the loss of credit with the resulting inability to secure new loans. But if default does occur, notwithstanding the unpleasant economic consequences, the bondholders, as already shown, can endeavor to obtain relief only through the associated strength of a great number of disappointed bondholders, i.e., ephemeral or permanent protective committees in a position to conduct negotiations with the defaulting government,[50] or through the diplomatic protection of the governments of the lending nationals.

THEORY OF PROTECTION

It has been correctly observed that diplomatic protection is not a right of the bondholder but the privilege of his government, in its discretion, to extend. Diplomatic protection has a long history. It arises out of the clan theory of human society and reflects a somewhat primitive form of social organization by which an injury to any member of the clan was deemed an injury to the clan itself, to be avenged by group sanctions. In a world of motley states, subject to no superior or central law enforcement, self-help—controlled by a vast body of customary law, treaties, practice, and arbitral decisions—is not by any means the irresponsible agency it is sometimes pictured. Vattel took over the theory in a nationalistic era and justified it in modern practice by asserting that an injury to a citizen is an injury to his state, his fellow nationals, which the government has the right to vindicate. That this is something of a fiction in most cases does not alter the fact that the institution of diplomatic protection lies at the basis of modern nationalism and that no state will permit irremediable injuries to its citizens by foreign countries to go unchallenged or unredressed. If it did, it would soon lose prestige. Nor can it be said that the institution has not had social benefits, persuading weak or irresponsible states to adhere to the minimum standards of civilized administration and justice and ultimately making for some stability in international relations and some security for the foreigner.[51]

President Coolidge has been challenged for saying in 1927: "The person and property of a citizen are a part of the general domain of the nation, even when abroad."[52] In the sense in which he made the assertion—having reference to Nicaragua—the President was not incorrect. The nation has a definite interest in its citizens and in their property abroad; they add to its wealth, bear taxes if the law so requires, and are subject within limits to the national jurisdiction. The nation cannot therefore remain indifferent to their fate. Nor is the statement of Secretary Bryan in 1914 entirely untrue: "When you go abroad you have to

50. See *supra*, p. 192.
51. Cf. Borchard, *Diplomatic Protection of Citizens Abroad, passim.*
52. Angell, *op. cit.*, p. 73.

take your chances." [53] Up to a certain point, the citizen must take his chances with nationals of the country in which he lives; he is subject to its laws, its courts and institutions. It is only when he is denied justice in the international sense of that term that his own state is justified in making his grievance a national grievance, which is not the case in the matter of disappointed bondholders except under unusual circumstances, to be mentioned presently.

But by making the issue national a difficult and delicate terrain is taken; the matter at once becomes political, affecting the citizens of two or more nations and placing them in possible conflict. The decision as to what action to take in case of a foreign default is affected by the political and economic consequences of such action on the relations of the two countries and perhaps others. Hence the difficulty of laying down rules for the political conduct of states in these matters. But it can be said that in principle a bond default is not an international delinquency which the nation is called upon to vindicate in the interests of its unfortunate bondholders. Only when the default evidences bad faith, such as a diversion of pledged securities or discrimination against the national bondholders or interests, does it become more than a mere default and interposition become justified in law.[54] Other circumstances which have induced particular interventions will be mentioned in the course of this section.

LOAN CONTRACT PRIVATE

As frequently stated, a loan contract is a matter not of international law but of private law between the lender and the foreign borrowing government. Unless, as in more recent times, political considerations are importantly involved, the governments of the lenders do not concern themselves with the terms, especially the economic terms, of the loan and, even when they express "no objection" to the loan, they are careful to disclaim any responsibility for the merits of the loan or for its collection. Being a private contract, they must necessarily assume that the price paid reflects the solvency, reputation, and debt record of the borrower. Weak and unstable governments have had to sell below par and pay high rates of interest. The purchaser and his successors therefore buy with open eyes [55] and assume all the risks. The legal facts that

53. *Ibid.*

54. On the subject, generally, see Feis, *op. cit.*, pp. 154, 183. Venezuela Bond Cases, Moore, *A Digest of International Arbitration*, IV, 3648. Feilchenfeld, in Quindry, *Bonds and Bondholders, Rights and Remedies*, Vol. II, secs. 625, 632. SEC, *Rep.*, Pt. V, pp. 10 ff., 414 ff.; Madden and Nadler, *Foreign Securities*, pp. 284, 333.

55. Aided in theory by the information which the SEC is authorized to obtain and publish, as a condition of permitting the bonds to be sold to the public.

the emission was an act of sovereignty, that the debt may be subject to
economic and political vicissitudes which may cause it to be reduced or
repudiated, that the usual civil remedies are barred, that the debtor
may claim to be the sole judge of its capacity to pay interest and principal, are facts supposedly known to all parties concerned and justify
diplomatic aloofness if the debt goes into default. It is a peculiar contract
in which the creditor deals with a sovereign debtor, who in principle,
aside from the requirements of good faith, has moral, economic, and
political grounds not to appear in the public prints as a defaulter.

For these several reasons the governments of the creditors have in
principle declined to consider a default a breach of international law
or a matter of concern to the nation as a whole. They have maintained
that they would not make the mere losses of their citizens the basis of an
international claim and interpose diplomatically for their vindication
or collection. International tribunals have in general followed this view
and have declined to assume jurisdiction, in the absence of express words,
even when the protocol of arbitration provided for the settlement of "all
claims." [56]

GROUNDS FOR DIPLOMATIC INTERPOSITION

Yet, while this is the general principle, there are qualifying considerations which do induce a certain degree of governmental interposition in
many cases. The fact that public loans are not always the purely private
transactions they were once supposed to be, the fact that the abstention
from interposition has been based upon the debtor's good faith and the
absence of bad faith in default, the fact that "good offices" to bring about
an adjustment of the debt have not usually been declined, all create
modifying circumstances, which may be regarded as sufficient warrant
for some form of interposition. Indeed, the difference between good
offices and diplomatic interposition is more theoretical than practical,
the former being deemed more unofficial and without commitment in
case of rejection—the government has presumably a freer hand as merely
a go-between or mediator, without responsibility. But in practical effect
any indication of government support for the bondholder is bound to
aid him, if the debtor government feels any need for the diplomatic
friendship or good will of the government of the creditors. The grounds
and reasons upon which this support is extended, support which is entirely discretionary with the government of the creditors in the light of
its entire political relation with the debtor government and its general
political relations to other countries, will be mentioned presently.

56. On the relevant practice of governments and of arbitration tribunals, see
Borchard, *op. cit.*, pp. 308 ff.

From what has been said it will be obvious that categorical rules embodying a predictable degree of intervention in particular cases cannot be framed. The intervention that may have been accorded in a particular case has depended greatly on the nature of the political relation of intervenor and debtor government, on the nature and causes of the default, on the probable practical consequences, special and general, of intervention in that case. Nevertheless, even within this loose framework, it is of more than historical interest to examine the types of intervention that have occurred in the past, the basis of the act and the purpose it presumably accomplished. From this assembled data some general lines of law and policy may be inferrable.

POLICY OF INTERPOSITION

That government support, however slight, is of great value to bondholders hardly needs reiteration. It required only unofficial notice to debtor governments in Latin America that the State Department had a sympathetic interest in the negotiations for settlement conducted by the Foreign Bondholders Protective Council with Brazil and Cuba to persuade those governments to make useful settlements.[57] A somewhat similar relationship exists between the British Government and the Council of Foreign Bondholders.[58] The policy of the United States in

57. SEC, *Rep.*, Pt. V, pp. 389 ff., 447 ff., 618 ff.

58. See Prime Minister Chamberlain's statement in the House of Commons, February 14, 1938:

"His Majesty's Government view with the gravest concern the loss inflicted, both on individuals and on the country, as the result of defaults on Foreign Loans. They regard the whole subject as one of very great importance and I am glad to have this opportunity of making a statement upon the matter.

"The Corporation of Foreign Bondholders is an independent statutory body, which was incorporated in 1873 and reconstituted by Special Act of Parliament in 1898. The Government recognise the Council of the Corporation of Foreign Bondholders as the body entrusted by Parliament with the duty of representing the interests of the Bondholders in all matters arising out of defaults or threatened defaults by foreign Governments, States or Municipalities. The Corporation has throughout its life rendered the most valuable services, and in recent years its activities have been steadily increasing . . . . The Council have always maintained the closest contact with the Treasury and the Foreign Office and in the last few years this contact has been continuous.

"In the case of a default, or threatened default, His Majesty's Government expect the foreign Government or authority concerned to enter into negotiations with the Council. His Majesty's Government always follows such negotiations very closely and give to the Council their fullest support. Where no acceptable agreement is reached they are always prepared to consider what further steps can usefully be taken. I consider that the arrangements which I have described afford the best and most practical means of safeguarding the interests of this country in the matter." *Corp. For. Bondh. Rep.*, No. 65 (1938), pp. 8 f.

this matter was clearly stated by Mr. Sumner Welles, later Under-Secretary of State, on December 26, 1935, as follows:

It is the traditional policy of this Government that the matter of the resumption of payments on foreign government bonds in default is one primarily and initially for negotiation by the investors themselves, or organizations representing them, this Department being constantly attentive to the situation of such investors and lending its good offices to facilitate such discussions between the interested parties. Within the lines of this policy, the Department has constantly taken all action that is deemed proper and advisable in the circumstances to protect the interests of American holders of defaulted foreign securities.[59]

This view is not greatly different from that expressed by publicists and acted upon by most governments of lending bankers or nationals.[60] Lord Palmerston expressed the view of the British Government in a celebrated circular sent in 1848 to British diplomatic representatives in foreign states. He then declared: "It is therefore simply a question of discretion with the British Government whether this matter [the non-payment of public loans] should or should not be taken up by diplomatic negotiation, and the decision of that question of discretion turns entirely on British and domestic considerations." [61]

The governments of France, Germany, Italy, Belgium, and Holland are not so self-restrained or noncommittal,[62] but where loss or injury is

59. Printed in SEC, *Rep.*, Pt. V, p. 393.

60. Cf. Borchard, *op. cit.*, pp. 310 ff.

61. Phillimore, *Commentaries on International Law*, II, 9–11, and W. E. Hall, *A Treatise on International Law*, (8th ed. Oxford, The Clarendon Press, 1924). Palmerston added: "The British Government has considered that the losses of imprudent men who have placed mistaken confidence in the good faith of foreign governments would prove a salutary warning to others, and would prevent any foreign loans being raised in Great Britain, except by governments of known good faith and ascertained solvency." The policy was not rigidly observed. For other aspects of Palmerston's circular and the views of other British Secretaries of State for Foreign Affairs, see Borchard, *op. cit.*, p. 315. Phillimore explains that the "country of the lenders has a right to require and enforce the fulfillment" (*op. cit.*, II, 8). This is doubtful.

Although authorizing the British Consul General to act with the agent of Baring Brothers in collecting 55% of the customs duties of Venezuela pledged as security for the 1862 loan, when in 1864 Venezuela stopped payment of interest and retained the customs, Lord Stanley refused to say that the customs were British property or that the bankers or bondholders would be protected in its possession. He declined to take coercive measures which might involve the country in war. Jenks, *op. cit.*, p. 287.

62. On the eve of the second Hague Conference, M. Pichon, French Foreign Minister, explained in the Chamber of Deputies that, while French diplomats could not be called upon to defend every loan made abroad by French citizens, different cases demanded different treatment, and added: "It is impossible

sustained by the nationals of several countries, holding bonds, the action of their governments tends to establish a common front—although the United States has on occasion expressed a preference for abstaining from joint representations with other powers.[63] Yet, while on occasion France, Germany, or Italy can be charged with greater vigor in the protection of bondholders, the differences of policy are not likely to be great, partly because governments are not prone to permit preferences among different nationals and partly because variations, when establishable, are likely to turn on varying views of what constitutes "bad faith" or on differences in national policy in a particular case. For these reasons no effort will be made in the following paragraphs to rely upon any differences in the policies or actions of protecting nations.

METHODS AND MEASURES OF INTERPOSITION

The principal methods used in assisting nationals are the use of good offices to induce the obligor government to carry out contractual commitments, on occasion to furnish the facilities of the diplomatic or consular service to receive payment on behalf of their citizen bondholders, to bring about a readjustment of the debt of the borrower, to facilitate bondholders' or even the intervening government's control of the collection of pledged revenues, to participate in the establishment of a governmental commission for the administration of the debtor's fiscal affairs, as in Egypt and Turkey, and finally on rare occasions to use military force to insure the payment or readjustment of a debt. The occasion for the exercise of these methods has been some manifestation of bad faith on the part of the debtor, in diverting or misappropriating pledged securities, in discriminating against nationals of the intervening state or

---

systematically and in all cases to avoid coercive measures in international relations in order to satisfy pecuniary claims, particularly when these claims rest on the execution of treaties, on incontestable rights, and on interests relating to commerce, industry, and the prosperity of states, interests that are found to be injured by governments unfaithful to their promises or careless in executing contracts." *Journal Officiel*, Chambre des Députés, Débats Parlementaires, November 4, 1901, p. 2025. (Quoted in Blaisdell, *European Financial Control in the Ottoman Empire* [New York, 1929], p. 211.) Cf. also statement of June 7, 1907, *supra*, p. 218.

On the fluctuations of French policy, see Feis, *op. cit.*, pp. 146 ff.

63. The United States deemed it necessary to act alone in Santo Domingo in 1904 because of her special interest in safeguarding Latin America against intervention by European powers. In the broader sphere of international politics the interests of the United States have, of course, become global. As Secretary of State Dean Acheson put it some time ago (*New York Times* of October 2, 1946, p. 14), "Under American policy the United States has a direct interest in any question that might develop a threat to world peace."

other type of manipulation derogatory to the bondholders' interest, or where some larger responsibility was assumed for the orderly administration of the debtor's fiscal affairs, as by the United States in the Caribbean and by England or the great powers in Egypt, Greece, Serbia, Turkey, and elsewhere.

The formula adopted by the United States, Great Britain, and other countries to explain their policy of diplomatic protection is broad enough to allow the government a free hand in taking such action, if any, as it may desire. While preferring as a rule to permit the bondholders to make their own arrangements with the debtor, giving bondholders' committees sympathetic and diplomatic support, governments nevertheless no longer remain as indifferent to foreign defaults as the *laissez-faire* economics of the nineteenth century might have indicated. The growing interdependence of economics and politics in the twentieth century, the fact that defaults often had political repercussions and that governments took an increasing interest in the making and utilization of loans for economic and political reasons, gave defaults a quasi political character which foreign offices could not escape. Perhaps the United States and Great Britain may be thought to have worked out the most successful compromise among a variety of possible policies by stimulating the creation of organizations of the bondholders, the Council of Foreign Bondholders and the Foreign Bondholders Protective Council, which acquired standing and reputation by virtue of their quasi official connections, their disinterestedness and expertness in the working out of the details of bond settlements, and yet received the support of the governments as intermediaries in facilitating both their representation of bondholders and their standing as authorized and approved negotiators with defaulting governments.

PREVENTING DEFAULT

Bondholders have frequently been accorded diplomatic support in their efforts to hold the debtor government, in case of threatened departure, to the terms of the loan contract.[64] When a government has guaranteed a foreign loan or sponsored it for political purposes, it may

64. Memorial submitted by the League Loans Committee to the British Government. League Loans Committee, *Second Annual Report* (June, 1934), pp. 16 ff.

See protest of Secretary of State to Chinese Minister in Washington, October 31, 1921, against imminent default on Chinese loans. The Department had encouraged American loans to China. *For. Rel.*, 1921, I, 380 ff.

The British, French, and Italian representatives addressed a note of protest in 1932 against the failure of Greece to carry out its League obligations. II, 353. *Infra*, n. 83.

be expected to act on its own initiative. But in other instances the British and United States governments at least will lend their support, if at all, only in response to an appeal by the bondholders. Such support has been granted when the debtor government has arbitrarily violated the terms of a loan contract with respect to payment of principal,[65] maintenance of sinking fund,[66] compliance with security provisions,[67] nondiscrimination against bondholders of the intervening nation,[68] or any other significant requirements.[69] In some instances, the creditors' government has even protested against proposed default legislation, without waiting to see whether it would in fact become law, but such preventive action has mainly been taken in the case of weaker countries or countries within the national sphere of influence.

Diplomatic action has on occasion been effective in preventing reduction of the principal or interest of a debt by a forced conversion.[70] Thus British opposition killed the 1876 Egyptian conversion scheme, in spite

65. M. De Laboulaye, French Chargé, to the Secretary of State, September 5, 1924, *For. Rel.*, 1924, II, 296. Cf. British objection to increase in the Egyptian debt, 1876. II, 589.

66. Article VIII of the treaty between the United States and Haiti, signed September 16, 1915, *For. Rel.*, 1916, 330; II, 353.

67. Guatemala in 1913 alienated coffee duties, assigned to British loan, in favor of newer creditors. A British battleship induced restoration. Feis, *op. cit.*, p. 109. *For. Rel.*, 1913, p. 569.

Greece, 1913. Governments of the tenders protested against Greek sequestration of revenues collected by Ottoman Debt Administration. Feis, *op. cit.*, p. 113.

China, 1919, See identic note from the British, French, Japanese, and Russian ministers to China, March 25, 1919, protesting against the use of salt surplus revenues as security for a new loan, inasmuch as they were security for the 1913 reorganization loan. *Idem*, 1919, I, 505.

Peru, 1932. Guano Company, on Peruvian default, turned over all its receipts to the Peruvian Treasury, although a tax on guano was security for the 1922 loan. $7\frac{1}{2}\%$ loan. London *Times*, May 19, 1932.

See a similar joint protest of Britain, France, and Holland against Peruvian law of February 2, 1915, declaring national farmers to have a preferential right to guano. II, 175. Earl of Derby to Mr. Graham, Minister at Lima, March 9, 1877. Bruns, *Fontes Juris Gentium*, Ser. B, sec. 1, p. 585.

Chile, 1933. Representations against termination of export fee of 60 pesos a ton on nitrate, security for Cosach bondholders, many of whom were American. *The New York Times*, March 25, 1933.

68. British consent to the United States reorganization of Liberian debt conditional upon maintenance of "preferential rights" of the British bondholders and the payment of the outstanding British claims." Feis, *op. cit.*, p. 113.

69. Great Britain, France, and Germany supported their national bondholders in protesting the Greek Government's abrogation of contract by law of December 10, 1893. II, 308. See also intervention of 1932, II, 353.

70. II, 364, n. 6.

of the eagerness of French banks, backed by the French Government, to accept it.[71] Again, the French Government, by threat of closing the European markets to new Tunisian securities, persuaded Tunis in 1867 not to carry out the proposed conversion of its external debt which the French Government believed would be prejudicial to French bond-holders.[72]

In 1927 President Coolidge suggested that, if the Nicaraguan currency were inflated by the revolution, the American as well as foreign bond-holders would doubtless look to the United States for the protection of their interests.[73] The suggestion was not, however, put to the test. It seems, indeed, clear that, unless bad faith can be definitely shown, bond-holders cannot look for diplomatic protection against loss attributable to the inflation of the debtor's currency.

In the case of certain Caribbean countries and Liberia, foreign govern-ments having a grievance arising out of alleged violation of financial obligations have as a rule complained to the United States of the de-linquency. This practice was doubtless based on the assumption that the United States had assumed control of the finances of these countries and was, therefore, in a position to speak for them.[74]

DEFAULT

BONDHOLDERS' PETITION FOR ASSISTANCE

It is perhaps natural that the initiative for government protection in case of default should come from the bondholders affected. Being with-out an effective judicial remedy, they are constrained to rely on the diplomatic efforts of their governments or on such economic sanctions as bondholders' protective committees and stock exchanges may bring

71. II, 588–590.

72. F.O. 102/113, No. 9 and inclosure in No. 33. See also the United States protest against the Haitian effort in 1897 to reduce by one third through conver-sion the value of bonds given to United States citizens for public works. Moore, *A Digest of International Law*, VI, 729. In 1814 France was obliged to compensate British subjects, holders of French *rentes*, for losses they had suffered in the re-duction by two thirds of their holdings of the *tiers consolidé*. E. Hertslet, *The Map of Europe by Treaty* (London, Butterworths, 1875), I, 399.

73. Message to Congress, January 10, 1927. *Cong. Rec.*, 69th Cong., 2d Sess., Vol. LXVIII, Pt. II, p. 1326. House Doc. 633.

74. France complained in 1920 that after United States assurances that the November 15, 1920, coupon of the Haitian loan of 1910 would be paid, Haiti had not so announced but, on the fall of the price of the bonds in Paris, had bought them up at depressed prices. For gold clause complaint, see *For. Rel.*, 1923, II, 415. For British complaint *in re* Santo Domingo, see II, 255 ff. For British com-plaint to the United States *in re* Liberia's failure to pay coupons and request for explanation, see *For. Rel.*, 1920, III, 102.

to bear.[75] Sometimes a parliamentary inquiry, when the loan or the default is notorious or shocking, may stimulate governmental interposition.[76]

ATTITUDE OF GOVERNMENT

As previously noted, the attitudes of protecting governments may take a variety of forms, running all the way from indifference and refusal to make default a public issue down to armed intervention. Since diplomatic action is political in character, political considerations are likely to govern the decision of a state at a particular time in a particular case. Perhaps the variation of attitude can be illustrated by a few examples. In the first half of the nineteenth century Great Britain declined to intervene on behalf of the British holders of defaulted Spanish bonds, Mr. Canning stating that he did not consider it "any part of the duty of the [British] Government to interfere in any way to procure the payment of loans made by British subjects to foreign Powers, States, or individuals." [77] In 1829 the Earl of Aberdeen, while refusing to intervene

75. Feilchenfeld, in Quindry, *op. cit.*, II, sec. 644. Protest of protective committee against diversion of security for Colombian bonds. *The New York Times*, February 7, 1933. Feis, *op. cit.*, p. 102. Protest by Continental Bank against imminent default of·Chinese loan due November 1, 1921, and immediate protest to Chinese Minister by Secretary of State, *For. Rel.*, 1921, I, 380 ff. Protest against default of Cuban public works bonds, *The New York Times*, July 3, 1934; Cuban claim that they were illegally issued by President Machado denied; estoppel by attending Cuban hearing denied; default settled in 1939.

76. In 1875 a parliamentary inquiry took place concerning the defaults of certain Latin American borrowers, Honduras, Guatemala, Santo Domingo, Costa Rica, and Paraguay, when it was shown that the loans were reckless, the proceeds misused, commissions usurious, and manipulations occurred to the disadvantage of the borrowing country and the bondholders as well. Honduras, *Corp. For. Bondh. Rep.*, No. 56 (1929), p. 227; Santo Domingo, *idem*, p. 323; Costa Rica, *idem*, No. 34, p. 168, No. 56, p. 124; Paraguay, *idem*, p. 278. Feis, *op. cit.*, p. 105. In 1879 the Italian Government was frequently urged, through interpellations in both branches· of the legislature, to extend protection to holders of Turkish bonds. II, 429, n. 40. Several investigations were held by Senate committees in 1926, 1931–32, and 1932–34, to inquire into the abuses of the 1920's by New York issuing houses in floating loans to Peru, Salvador, and other Latin American countries. Hearings before the Committee on Finance on the Sale of Foreign Bonds or Securities in the United States, pursuant to S. Res. 19, 72d Cong.; Hearings before Committee on Banking and Currency, pursuant to S. Res. 84, 72d Cong., and S. Res. 56 and S. Res., 73d Cong. On the abuses of private protective committees see the hearings of the Securities and Exchange Commission in SEC, *Rep.*, Pt. V, also sec. 15, *supra*.

77. *Brit. and For. St. Pap.*, XXVIII (November 4, 1824), 961. See also Palmerston's position of abstention, October 23, 1834, *idem*, p. 966: loss "brought upon yourself by your own spontaneous act."

officially on account of a Mexican default, authorized the British Minister to second by his "good offices" on any favorable occasion "any proper representations" which the British bondholders might make to the Mexican Government through their local agents.[78] In 1830 in Greece, the Earl of Aberdeen still considered a loan a matter of a "private nature" and the request for intervention not "a matter of right," but that the British Government, "far from viewing with indifference" the interests of "numerous individuals involved in such transactions," instructed the British minister at Athens to present the bondholders' case to the President of Greece.[79]

The continued demand for some form of interposition and possibly a growing realization of the economic and political implications of foreign loans to the nation as a whole finally led to Lord Palmerston's circular of 1848, in which he still declined to consider intervention either a right of the bondholders or a duty of the government but maintained that the government was privileged, in the exercise of its discretion, to take any position or action it desired in the light of all the circumstances. Indeed, in that very year, when Mexico failed to pay to the British bondholders any part of the 15 million dollars received from the United States by the treaty of peace of Guadalupe Hidalgo, the law officers of the Crown maintained that such allocation was Mexico's legal duty and on British official representations a compromise settlement of the arrears was effected.[80] Shortly thereafter Lord Palmerston stated to a defaulting Caribbean government that

the patience and forbearance of H.M. Government . . . have reached their limits, and that if the sums due to the British Claimants are not paid within the stipulated time and in money, H.M.'s Admiral commanding on the West India Station will receive orders to take such measures as may be necessary to obtain Justice from the nation in this matter.[81]

In 1858 the British Government forced on Mexico the Otway convention by which, as a penalty for violating the rights of the bondholders under the Doyle convention of 1851, Mexico was required to raise the interest on the Doyle convention debt from 4 per cent to 6 per cent and

78. *Idem*, XXVIII (June 18, 1829), 970; Edgar W. Turlington, *Mexico and Her Foreign Creditors* (New York, Columbia University Press, 1930), p. 57.

79. *Brit. and For. St. Pap.*, XXVIII (March 25, 1830), 967.

80. II, 10–13.

81. E. Hertslet, *Recollections of the Old Foreign Office* (London, J. Murray, 1901), p. 84, quoted by A. K. Cairncross, "Did Foreign Investment Pay?", *Review of Economic Studies*, October, 1935, p. 67, also in *The Problem of International Investment*, p. 99.

to assign as security 16 per cent of the customs revenues.[82] Unable to perform the obligations of the Otway convention because Mexico's chief ports were in opposition hands,[83] the British Government then coerced

82. II, 18.

83. The diplomatic action may be directed not to the principal debtor but to the invader whose actions caused or helped to cause the default, as in Peru, after the treaty of Ancón, when the British refused to act under the 1886 agreement, merely promising diplomatic support, but the bondholders requested intervention against Chile. II, 153. In Santo Domingo, Haiti, and Nicaragua, at least during the American occupation and probably later, foreign bondholders and their governments looked to the United States, which had exerted a large measure of fiscal control, to protect their interests. II, 247, 256. In 1927 President Coolidge remarked: "It is true that the United States did not establish the financial plan [of 1917 in Nicaragua] by any treaty, but it nevertheless did aid through diplomatic channels and advise in the negotiation and establishment of this plan for the financial rehabilitation of Nicaragua." Address before the National Press Association, Hotel Biltmore, April 25, 1927, pp. 10–11.

In 1925 the United States interposed its good offices in promoting a settlement between the Government of Honduras and the British bondholders which scaled down a debt of 150 million dollars to 6 million, refunded in payments over 30 years. *For. Rel.*, 1925, II, 338 ff.

In China, the United States not only encouraged investors but expressed to the Chinese Government great concern lest a default impair China's credit. *For. Rel.*, 1921, I, 378, 384, 385. In Bulgaria after 1922, Great Britain, France, and Holland successfully exerted diplomatic pressure to persuade Bulgaria to withdraw the 1922 black lists of foreign bondholders. II, 546 f. In 1932 several governments protested the Greek default of that year. II, 353. Representations by Great Britain, France, and the United States in Athens, 1935. II, 354. In 1933, when Germany declared a transfer moratorium, Holland and Switzerland demanded a favored position for Dutch and Swiss bondholders, which they were in a position to exact in the clearing agreements because they bought more goods from Germany than they sold. *The Problem of International Investment*, pp. 99–100. A year later, the British Government, which had protested against discrimination, demanded and secured a privileged position for the British bondholders. *Idem*. In 1938 the intimation that an anti-debt campaign might be begun by the Nazi Government of Germany led the British Cabinet to make a conditional promise to support the claims of British bondholders. In answer to a question put by a member of the House of Commons to the Chancellor of the Exchequer as to whether the British Government would consider the setting up of an Anglo-German clearing procedure to enforce payment of German-defaulted postwar debts, the representative of the Chancellor stated that "some revision of the existing arrangements in regard to British holders of German long term and medium term obligations appears desirable, and . . . , if the committee of British long and medium term creditors of Germany recommend a suitable scheme, it will have the support of His Majesty's Government." February 23, 1938. *Parliamentary Debates*, Ser. V, Vol. 332, pp. 374 ff. The Department of State vigorously insisted after the annexation of Austria by Germany in 1938 that Germany, having taken over the assets, especially the security assigned to the service of Austrian loans, was fully liable for the discharge

Mexico to make the necessary appropriations for the several defaulted British debts.[84] In 1861 Great Britain, with France and Spain, intervened in Mexico by force of arms.[85] In 1866 under similar circumstances the British Government refused to intervene against Venezuela but it did instruct its diplomatic representative to make an official demand for the return of a sum sequestrated by the Venezuelan Government after having been paid to the agent of the bondholders.[86] Thus we can observe the progression of a policy over a relatively short span of years.[87]

---

of the Austrian bonds in the hands of United States citizens. *The New York Times*, April 6, 1938; Dept. of State, *Press Releases*, No. 455 (June 18, 1938), p. 694. See the claims against Chile arising out of Chile's occupation and later annexation of the guano and nitrate fields assigned by Peru as security for Peruvian bonds. II, 147 ff.

84. II, 19.

85. II, 25.

86. Secretary of State for Foreign Affairs to British chargé in Venezuela, January 31, 1866. F.O. 80/184.

87. A few examples of government action in support of particular bondholders' claims may suffice. In 1867 France undertook, notwithstanding the unhappy experience with Mexican intervention, to press the claims of the bondholders of the Tunis debt after the default of June, 1867, an interposition which had marked political results. In 1872 Bismarck demanded the repayment in particular bonds of the Erlanger loan of 1867 to the Bey of Tunis, notwithstanding the fact that the principal business of this banking firm, of German origin, was in France. In Morocco, also, the German Government insisted on France's giving satisfaction to a German firm. In 1848, the British minister in Lima was instructed to press the claims of the 1822 and 1825 bondholders for more equitable terms than had been offered by Peru. II, 110. For improvement in the terms of a settlement, see also the French intervention in behalf of investors in the bonds of the Royal Portuguese Railways in reorganization proceedings taken by Portugal. Feis, *op. cit.*, p. 148. In 1875 Great Britain, though denying any responsibility for the defaulted Turkish debt of 1854 by reason of its recommendation of the loan, promised to use moral pressure in its support, II, 420, an interposition which ultimately led to an official debt commission. In 1889 and again in 1891 the Russian Government successfully pressed Turkey to live up to the schedule of payment to Russian citizens drawn up after the Russo-Turkish war of 1877. II, 457–58. As to Russian pressure for payment of debts to the Russian Government by Turkey, see II, 456 ff., and by Bulgaria, II, 531–32.

On the other hand, in 1901, when Portugal objected to giving the bondholders representation on the Junta de Credito Publico and preferential assignment of the customs receipts, French Foreign Minister Delcassé asserted that France would exert diplomatic pressure to assure this protection to the bondholders, while denying that it constituted bondholders' control or "direct foreign intervention," as the Portuguese complained. II, 375. Diplomatic pressure was applied after Turkey's default in 1875 to force her to agree to a bondholders' syndicate to administer the revenues as security for the bonds. See II, 418. German diplomatic pressure on behalf of its bondholders induced Portugal to pass the law of May, 1893, establishing the Junta de Credito Publico. II, 373.

The injection of so many collateral factors in each situation might make the action of governments seem more opportunistic and unpredictable than it is, but the position announced by Lord Palmerston in 1848 and Mr. Sumner Welles in 1935 is still approximately accurate. Intervention is not a matter of bondholders' right or government duty, but government privilege in the light of all the circumstances [88]—unless, indeed, as Mr. Cruchaga Ossa, the Chilean member of the Committee of Experts, insisted at the Lima conference of 1938 (the right of intervention having been abandoned at the Montevideo and Buenos Aires conferences of 1933 and 1936 and equality of treatment with nationals being the ultimate claim that a foreigner may make under Article 9 of the Montevideo convention on the Rights and Duties of States) the right of interposition even on behalf of private claimants including bondholders has been surrendered on this continent.[89] This position is not concurred in by other members of the Committee of Experts, nor has it Conference support, but it is likely again to be advanced.

The right reserved to the French Government under the loan contract of 1902 between Bulgaria and French bankers to notify to the Bulgarian Government the selection of a bondholders' delegate was designed to indicate France's readiness to protect French investors. II, 538. See also Allied representation to Turkey at the Lausanne Conference that its bondholders would be protected. II, 497.

88. A rare example of declining diplomatic protection by the United States in advance because of the supposed greed of the American lending bankers, a denunciation of the bankers, and an apology to the defaulting foreign government, Bolivia, is to be found in the remarks President F. D. Roosevelt is said to have made to President Peñaranda of Bolivia in 1943 on the occasion of the latter's visit to the United States. Judging from the subsequent default of Bolivia, the high rate of interest, 8%, was what an impecunious debtor might have expected, though an 8% commission might appear exorbitant. As reported in a press dispatch to *The New York Times*, May 8, 1943, p. 1, col. 2, the following remarks were made by the President at a press conference.

President Roosevelt repudiated what he considers acts of financial exploitation in Latin America during the Coolidge era when he announced at his press conference today that he had apologized to General Enrique Peñaranda, the Bolivian President, for an American loan made to Bolivia more than fifteen years ago.

The President told of the apology in discussing the visit to the White House this week of General Peñaranda, and said that if he had anything to do with it money would never be lent to a foreign country at the high interest and commission rates which figured in the loan he had in mind.

Mr. Roosevelt explained to his press conference that years ago, in 1926 or 1927, some Americans sold to the Bolivian Government through supersalesmanship the idea that it needed a loan. A bond issue was floated in this country at 8 per cent interest and an 8 per cent commission, according to the President, so that Bolivia got only 92 per cent of the proceeds.

Of course, President Roosevelt declared, Bolivia was unable to pay either the interest or the principal.

89. See Borchard, "The 'Committee of Experts' at the Lima Conference," *Am. Jour. Int. Law*, XXXIII (1939), 276 ff.

But, since abuses of foreign intervention led (1) to the Calvo clause in constitution, law, and contracts, providing for a maximum of equality between foreigner and national and a repudiation of diplomatic interposition, (2) to the Drago Doctrine rejecting the use of force in the collection of bond claims—always a rare phenomenon and never present in isolation from other grounds—and (3) to the novel doctrine advanced by the Mexican Government of President Cardenas in 1938 that confiscation (of agricultural land) may be adopted as a national policy toward foreigners provided nationals are equally despoiled—it is submitted that the foreigner, not the Latin American government, is now abused. The Mexican oil expropriation of 1938 succeeded by virtue of American restraint and acquiescence due to the outbreak of World War II and the concomitant desire to cultivate Mexican good will and support. The Cardenas doctrine, accompanying a sentimental economic nationalism and desire for emancipation from foreign influence, could sustain repudiation as a principle and deny the right diplomatically to protect the despoiled foreigner. Growing economic nationalism has led in other Latin American countries and elsewhere to similar violations of property rights held by foreigners which, added to other unfavorable circumstances, has been a deterrent to new private foreign investment in such lands.[90]

FACILITATING SETTLEMENTS

Apart from the cases where a particular claim is advanced because of aggravating circumstances,[91] such as a default in bad faith [92] or outright repudiation,[93] governments take account of the difficulties of their

90. See Introduction, *supra*, p. xxxviii.

91. Cf. French intervention to secure settlement with Serbia for cancellation of a railroad concession. M. Simitch, *La Dette publique de la Serbie* (Paris, 1925), chaps. viii and xvii. See also N. S. Petrovitch, "Les Emprunts et la dette publique du royaume de Serbie," *Revue de Science et de Legislation Financières*, IV (1906), 70–71; and the *The Economist*, October 26 and November 23, 1889.

92. See *supra*, p. 126.

93. Russia's repudiation of American loans to the Czar was made a ground by Secretary Hughes and his successors to 1933 for refusing recognition to the Soviet Government. Secretary Hughes, quoted by James Brown Scott in *Am. Jour. Int. Law*, XVII (1923), 296. Although Mr. Litvinoff agreed with President Roosevelt on November 16, 1933, to settle the American claims after recognition, Soviet Russia has failed to do so. On the repudiation of the debts of the southern states of the United States, see Randolph, "Foreign Bondholders and the Repudiated Debts of the Southern States," *Am. Jour. Int. Law*, XXV (1931), pp. 63, 75. Repudiation was deemed an international delinquency by the experts on codification of international law, The Hague, 1930, and the countries replying to their questionnaire. League of Nations, *Conference for the Codification of International Law. Bases of Discussion: Responsibility of States*, L. of N. Publications, Doc. C. 75. M. 69. 1929. V, pp. 59 ff., 62 ff. See also *Am. Jour. Int. Law, Supp.*, XXIV

bondholders in effecting settlements with the defaulting government and freely use their good offices to aid and facilitate such private settlements.[94] In the latter part of the nineteenth century the Council of the Corporation of Foreign Bondholders received the moral support and sometimes the diplomatic help of the British Government in effecting settlements. The Foreign Bondholders Protective Council in the United States in the negotiation of its settlements received the diplomatic support of the Department of State in a variety of ways, called "unofficial" but manifesting clearly the Department's interest in a fair settlement and its willingness to impress the defaulting government with the desire of the United States that a settlement be arrived at through the Council.[95] Thus it actually discouraged competing private protective committees by withholding its important support on the alleged ground that negotiations of the private committee were premature.[96] Yet it did not hesitate to bring together the Lisman committee and the Salvador Government after the 1932 default, while pointing out that the Foreign Bondholders Protective Council was founded "with the encouragement of this government, with the view of providing a central and disinterested agency to

(1930), 54, 55. The *Research in International Law* provides, Article 11, that the state cannot be made a respondent in any proceeding relating to its public debt. *Idem,* XXVI (1932), 597 ff.

94. Where governments themselves take a direct part in the settlement of a default, their purpose is either to prevent the debtor from resorting to unilateral action or to enforce certain terms of the plan considered to be in the best interest of their nationals. Thus, the issuance of a decree by the Brazilian Government putting into force the so-called "Niemeyer Plan" for the adjustment of Brazil's foreign debts was withheld pending examination of the plan by the Department of State which had requested time for its study on the ground that at first glance the plan seemed to deal unfairly with the Brazilian dollar bond issues. *For. Bondh. Prot. Coun. Rep.,* 1934, p. 27. When in November, 1937, the Brazilian President, after the execution of his *coup d'état* establishing the Estado Novo, announced over the radio his intention to suspend the service of the external debt, pressure was brought by various foreign governments, so that the threatened unilateral action was not taken. *Corp. For. Bondh. Rep.,* No. 64 (1937), pp. 29 ff.

95. SEC, *Rep.,* Pt. V, pp. 28, 391, 393, 395, 412, 446, 461. Cf. White House statement, October 20, 1933, quoted in Turlington, *Am. Bar Assn. Jour.,* XX (1934), 242. There were times, as in Santo Domingo (1940) and Colombia (1941), when the Council not only received no help from the Department of State but was opposed by the Department of State for political reasons.

96. See, e.g., the attitude toward the Nye or Coyle protective committee for the defaulted public works bonds of Cuba, *idem,* 395. As to competing bondholders' committees for all or different bonds and the protesting or defaulting government's power to distinguish between them, see II, 138. The government may of course undertake to give support to one loan as against another. France gave support to the four-power consortium loan as against the never-issued currency loan of 1911 or the reorganization loan of 1913.

protect the interests of holders of foreign securities in default." [97]

Emphasizing the quasi-official character of the Council, the Department of State in 1937 organized a board of visitors which supervised the work of the Council and made for a time annual reports commenting upon it and the settlements it effected.[98] In 1940 the Department went further in the effort to adjust the Colombian debt default, for which there were three separate private committees besides the Council. Beginning in 1939 the Departments of State and Treasury and the Federal Loan Administrator met in New York with representatives of the Colombian Government and the Council "in the hope of finding some common ground of adjustment." After pointing out what Colombia had done in the way of partial payment to meet the default, the Department of State announced that these public officials had acted as "friendly intermediaries to assist the parties in reaching an agreement" but then expressed the opinion that "the offer of the Colombian Government constitutes a fair effort on its part to adjust its obligations." [99] The implication is all too plain.

Such government support of bondholders in effecting a settlement, especially where political interests were at stake in controlling the settlement, has a long background in European experience. To mention but a few: The Tunisian settlement of 1870 had the support of the French and British governments. The British minister in Central America [100] in 1909 endeavored to effect a settlement of the Honduran default along lines which had been approved by representatives of the British bondholders.[101] Great Britain actively promoted the Egyptian settlement before 1879, when more direct government intervention and finally political control came into effect.[102] In 1876 the Earl of Derby, although reluctant to assist the bondholders against Peru notwithstanding their claim that

97. SEC, *Rep.*, Pt. V, pp. 412, 447.

98. Cf. second report of the board (1938), in *Com. and Fin. Chron.*, CXLIX (July 15, 1939), 347.

99. *Dept. of St. Bull.*, IV (January 4, 1941), 12 ff. See also *Com. and Fin. Chron.*, CLII (January 4, 1941), pp. 8 ff. Gantenbein, *Financial Questions in United States Foreign Policy*, p. 185, as to the general policy of the United States Government to lend its good offices to facilitate discussions between the parties; B. H. Williams, *Foreign Loan Policy of the United States since 1933*, p. 29. In 1867 the British Consul General in Tunis invited the British residents to participate in the conversion of the internal debt. F.O. 102/79.

100. Mr. Lionel Carden.

101. Coun. For. Bondh., Archives.

102. II, 584, 594. See also the threat that Chinese default would lead to customs receivership and "forcible interference in the financial and even the political affairs of China." United States chargé to the Secretary of State, July 11, 1913, *For. Rel.*, 1913, p. 185.

their guano security was being turned over to French creditors, finally agreed to instruct the British minister at Lima "unofficially" to assist the bondholders to bring their case before the Peruvian Government.[103] In 1883 the British Government, in connection with Mexico's attempt by law to repeal the 1851 and 1857 adjustments with the bondholders, inquired whether the bondholders were willing to surrender their claims and on refusal helped to effect an adjustment in 1886.[104] Turkey was pressed in 1877 and in later years to fulfill her engagements to the bondholders and as recently as 1927 in response to diplomatic pressure resumed negotiations after a default.[105] In 1901 the Portuguese Government, after diplomatic efforts by France, appointed a representative to come to a settlement with the bondholders.[106] In the Honduran debt settlement of 1909, the governments of Great Britain and the United States took an active part by conducting negotiations on behalf of the bondholders.[107]

In 1931, taking advantage of Yugoslavia's desire to float a stabilization loan, the French Government intervened at the request of the bondholders to compel a settlement of the earlier default.[108] The Ottoman Debt Council, with the help of the British and French governments, sought to persuade Yugoslavia to assume her share of the Ottoman public debt as part of a general settlement of the Yugoslav external debt.[109] It is natural in a case of state succession that the new division of the old debt should be controlled not only by the bondholders but by the official representatives of the successor states who are to become the novated debtors, as in the case of the break-up of Austria-Hungary.[110] Finally,

103. Feis, *op. cit.*, p. 106.

104. II, 41.

105. II, 421, 499.

106. II, 374.

107. *For. Rel.*, 1912, p. 550; *Corp. For. Bondh. Rep.*, No. 56 (1929), p. 229. See, however, with regard to the role of a government in negotiations for the adjustment of debts the letter of the Acting Secretary of State, November 27, 1933, quoted in Memorandum of the Foreign Bondholders Protective Council on the Haitian Dollar Bonds and Treaty Provisions Thereto of October 28, 1940, p. 26: "Your letter urges that a new treaty be drafted looking to the discontinuance of financial Control at the same time the Marines are withdrawn, or before, and to an adjustment of the Haitian debt. In the first place, this Government has no power to negotiate an adjustment of the Haitian debt, which, as stated above, is largely held by private individuals, citizens of this country, of Haiti and of other countries."

108. Dette Publique réportie de l'Ancien Empire Ottoman, Rapport sur le second exercice (1930–1931), p. 32.

109. *Corp. For. Bondh. Rep.*, No. 64 (1937), p. 71.

110. The Innsbruck protocol of June 25, 1923, by which questions connected with the service of Austrian and Hungarian debts were settled, was concluded be-

the effort of Greece in 1932 unilaterally to reduce its interest obligations met with the resistance not only of the bondholders but of the British, French, and United States governments and the League Loans Committee, which over a period of years, after urging Greece to send a delegation to London, endeavored to persuade Greece to come to an agreed arrangement of its debt.[111] In these matters, especially where the nationals of several countries are affected and the issue becomes political, it is common to make joint representations, partly to lend weight to the diplomatic effort and partly to avoid a conflict of interest and policy among the various bondholders and their governments.[112]

Where political interests are at stake the governments themselves, sometimes over the heads of the bondholders, may seek to effect a settlement with the defaulting debtor.[113] It is clear that the United States took an active part in effecting the financial reorganization of Santo Domingo, Haiti, and Nicaragua [114] as an incident of its quasi-political control of the countries during the period of occupation, an arrangement which operated to the advantage not only of the bondholders but of the governments concerned, even if it did incur the hostility of certain groups and of some Latin American opponents of the United States.

---

tween bondholders' committees and the representatives of the successor states. See text of the protocol in *idem*, No. 51 (1924), pp. 87 ff.

111. League Loans Committee, *Fourth Annual Report*, 1936, pp. 16–17. *Corp. For. Bondh. Rep.*, No. 61 (1934), pp. 231–232; *idem*, No. 64 (1937), p. 43. The Council of Foreign Bondholders complained in 1938 that all the efforts of the bondholders and their governments have been unavailing to bring the Brazilian default to an end. *Idem*, No. 65 (1938), p. 12. See the Brazilian offer of settlement, 1943, recommended to the bondholders as acceptable by the Foreign Bondholders Protective Council, *For. Bondh. Prot. Coun. Rep.*, 1941 through 1944, p. 156.

112. II, 312, 315. Germany took the lead in protecting the bondholders of the default in the peace negotiations with Turkey, 1894 and 1898. II, 604, 613. Germany protested the arrangement of 1911.

113. The German representatives at the conference which settled the terms of peace between Turkey and Greece took the initiative in bringing sufficient Greek revenues under international control to assure service of the Greek foreign debt. Feis, *op. cit.*, p. 184.

In 1902 the French Government, not the bondholders, made the settlement with Portugal. II, 375. There were political reasons for the acceptance of the English committee.

In 1881 it was France which determined the new financial organization of Tunis.

114. See, for Santo Domingo, II, 242 ff.; for Nicaragua, *For. Rel.*, 1916, p. 916, and *Corp. For. Bondh. Rep.*, 1917, pp. 247–268; for Haiti, *For. Bondh. Prot. Coun. Rep.*, 1935, p. 122.

FINANCIAL COMMISSIONS

As will be seen presently,[115] bondholders' governments have in several instances taken an active part in the reorganization of the finances of a defaulting state through the establishment of financial commissions.

OTHER GOVERNMENTAL PROTECTIVE SERVICES

In France, and to a lesser degree in some other countries, the government has exercised a form of control over the flotation of foreign loans which has enabled it, when it saw fit, to impose conditions calculated to protect bondholders.[116] Thus, when Serbia in 1901 tried to sell on the Paris Bourse the unified bonds, the French Government gave its consent only on the condition that the French representative on the monopolies administration should be the official representative of the French Government.[117] When the French bondholders of the Tunis debt were threatened by the Bey's intention to convert the external bonds, they obtained the aid of the Government, which stopped the Bey by threatening to close the European markets to Tunisian loans.[118] In 1874, while the notorious Hartmont loan was in default, it was doubted whether France would permit the flotation of a new Dominican loan.[119]

Governments which assist in placing a debtor state's finances in order are likely to participate by treaty or otherwise in laying conditions designed to insure the fulfillment of a loan contract.[120] This has happened on the part of the United States in connection with its effort to support or arrange with private bankers the refinancing of Nicaragua, Santo Domingo, and Haiti. Under the Knox-Castillo convention of 1911, Nicaragua agreed to appoint a collector general of customs from a list of names prepared by the fiscal agent of the loan and approved by the President of the United States.[121] In Santo Domingo and Haiti the measures of supervision assumed a character both general, redounding to the benefit of all bondholders, and specific, in treaty protection of a particular loan. The general measures took the form of the establishment of a United States customs receivership in both Santo Domingo and Haiti. By the treaty of 1907 with Santo Domingo, the United States was authorized to appoint a

---

115. *Infra*, p. 291.

116. Feis, *op. cit.*, Pt. II, *passim.*

117. Simitch, *op. cit.*, pp. 424–428.

118. L.J., January, 1869, *Affaires de Tunis*, pp. 172, 175.

119. II, 204. The French Government may also prohibit the quotation of foreign government bonds on the exchange. Cf. Portuguese bonds of 1902, II, 381.

120. See *infra*, p. 295.

121. *For. Rel.*, 1912, pp. 1074–1075.

general receiver of customs to collect the customs duties until the extinction of the bonds issued under the treaty, with a provision that during the life of the loan public debts should not be increased or import duties modified without the consent of the United States. This receiver was continued under the treaty of 1924.[122] Under the treaty of September 16, 1915, between the United States and Haiti, an American receiver-general of customs and financial adviser was set up, the public expenditures were controlled, and the public debt limited. By the executive agreement of August 7, 1933, further agreements were made with regard to the budgetary allocation of certain revenues.[123]

By way of specific protection for the bondholders of certain loans, mention may be made of the customs administration sinking fund bonds issued by the Military Government of Santo Domingo in 1922. Not only were the customs duties to be collected by an official appointed by the United States but the issue was to be a direct lien on such duties. A somewhat similar provision was included in the loan contract for the bonds of 1926.[124] The contract for the Haitian customs and general revenues bonds of 1922 provided that Haiti "hypothecates such revenues, and authorizes the General Receiver . . . to set aside from the hypothecated revenues the sums required to be remitted pursuant to the provisions of the bond contract." [125]

Somewhat related to this form of governmental preventive protection was the refusal of the interallied commission in Bulgaria to reduce the reparations debt until Bulgaria made some changes in her trade policy, arrested the progress of inflation, and gave security for future payments.[126]

There are numerous services that governments have performed for the benefit of national bondholders which deserve special mention. Notwithstanding the traditional reluctance of the British Government to intervene on behalf of holders of the bonds of defaulted foreign governments, it nevertheless authorized British diplomatic and consular officers, e.g., in Guatemala and Colombia, to act as agents of the bondholders and collect the sums due them.[127] The British and French governments

122. After a temporary suspension commencing in 1931, the collection of all customs duties by the receivership was resumed in 1934. In 1940, the receivership was finally abolished. II, 277.

123. Angell, op. cit., pp. 26 ff.; R. L. Buell, "The Caribbean Situation: Cuba and Haiti," For. Pol. Rep., IX (June 21, 1933), pp. 90–92.

124. Corp. For. Bondh. Rep., No. 64 (1937), pp. 482, 483.

125. For. Bondh. Prot. Coun. Rep., 1937, p. 455.

126. II, 549 ff.

127. Feis, op. cit., p. 105. Permission was given to the British Consul-General in Venezuela to act as the agent of the contractors of the 1862 loan for the pur-

have on occasion extended diplomatic support to such officials in the performance of their duties as bondholders' agents [128] and to those persons who were appointed as members of the Egyptian, Turkish, and other debt commissions.[129] Mr. J. Reuben Clark has testified that the British Government goes further in the diplomatic support of the Council of Foreign Bondholders, by permitting its foreign service to act as agents of the Corporation, than has the State Department in thus assisting the Foreign Bondholders Protective Council.[130]

That debtor governments are not unaware of the interest which the governments of bondholders take in a default is evidenced by the fact that the diplomatic representatives of these governments of the creditors are addressed by the debtor, sometimes in advance of bondholders' representations, with an explanation of the reasons for the default, an at-

---

pose of forwarding to them the sums payable out of revenues assigned by Venezuela for the service of the loan. The loan prospectus stated, however, that the agreement between the bankers and the British Consul-General was of a strictly private character entailing no responsibility on the part of the British Government, and this view was expressly confirmed in 1867 by Lord Stanley, then Secretary of State for Foreign Affairs, who refused after default to concede to the bondholders any claim arising out of the services of the Consul. In a letter to Messrs. Baring, Lord Stanley made the following statement: ". . . I need scarcely remind you that whatever part Mr. Orme [The British Consul-General] was allowed to take in such matters was subject to the condition that the arrangement between you and Mr. Orme was of a private character, and that it involved no responsibility on the part of His Majesty's Government." Archives, Coun. For. Bondh.

To execute the agreement between Santo Domingo and the French bondholders in 1901, the French Government permitted a representative of the Foreign Office to act for two years as agent of the French creditors. II, 234.

128. A case where diplomatic protection is accorded to the agent of the bondholders is reported in II, 234. The French Government permitted an official of the Ministry of Foreign Affairs to act for two years as the agent of the French creditors under the contract of June, 1901, and this official was accorded constant support by the diplomatic representative of his country at Santo Domingo.

129. See II, 593, 596. A step further in the direction of genuine financial control through a foreign government may be seen in certain measures of the French Government for the purpose of securing bondholders' rights through governmental interference. Brodbeck, *Internationale Finanzkontrollen und ihre Politischen Grenzen* (Berlin, Junker & Dünnhaupt, 1935), pp. 9 ff. In 1901 the French Government permitted an official of the Ministry of Foreign Affairs to act for two years as the agent of the French creditors of the Republic of Santo Domingo. II, 234. The fact that the nomination of this agent was officially recognized by the Dominican Government, while not amounting to an actual exequatur, nevertheless indicated the intention on the part of the Dominican Republic to treat the French agent as a person vested with governmental authority and not merely as the representative of a group of private bondholders.

130. SEC, *Rep.*, Pt. V, p. 448.

tempt to justify it, or a promise of efforts to make early reparation.[131]

The protecting government may by various forms of diplomatic pressure seek to bring about the resumption of payment on a defaulted debt or to obtain special security for its payment.[132]

The protecting government may extend its aid in facilitating a transfer of the necessary funds to meet a bond obligation in the creditor state.[133] In 1881, under provocation of Turkey's failure to apply the surplus revenues of Cyprus to the service of the guaranteed loan of 1855, Great Britain herself seized that surplus and applied it directly to the benefit of the bondholders.[134] In the period since 1931, when so many countries were obliged to suspend payments of their foreign debts, a few creditor countries in a position to do so have made levies for their national bondholders upon the trade balances of debtor countries. The principal device of this kind was the clearing agreement with the debtor country.[135]

The power of the French Government over the listing of securities on the stock exchange, exercised in England by the stock exchange itself, has been used to compel foreign governments to perform their obligation either under the issue excluded or on some other contract. This power was used in the cases of the Portuguese loan of 1902 and the Serbian loan of 1895.[136] In 1901, when Serbia sought to sell certain bonds on the Paris

131. Cf. Argentina, 1833. Foreign Minister to British chargé, September 11, 1833. *Brit. and For. St. Pap.*, XXVIII (1839–40), 1014.

Chile, 1827, 1829. Foreign Minister to British Consul-General, October 2, 1827. *Idem*, p. 1015. Cf. also note of March 2, 1829, *idem*, p. 1020, and Palmerston's message to the bondholders, *idem*, p. 1027.

132. See action of Italian minister in Santo Domingo, 1903. II, 235. United States on behalf of San Domingo Improvement Co., getting Puerto Plata customs and control at Monte Cristi. *Idem*, pp. 245–246.

Collective pressure of many powers procured in November, 1872, a Venezuelan decree setting aside 5.2% of customs receipts for the payment of the "diplomatic debt." See *The Venezuelan Arbitration before The Hague Tribunal, 1903*, S. Doc. No. 119, 58th Cong., 3d Sess., p. 757.

133. In 1830 the Secretary of State for Foreign Affairs, at the request of the committee of Mexican bondholders, authorized the British Vice-Consuls at Vera Cruz and Tampico to "undertake the office of receiving and remitting the money set apart for the payment" of interest on foreign bonds. II, 7 f., 12, n. 23. A. H. Feller, *The Mexican Claims Commission, 1923–1934* (New York, Macmillan, 1935), pp. 11 ff.

134. II, 442.

135. See *infra*, n. 153.

136. II, 381. Simitch, *op. cit.*, pp. 321 ff. The action of the French Government was based (according to *L'Economiste Français*, June 1, 1901, p. 790) on its desire to await a demonstration of the ability of the Autonomous Monopoly Administration to assure the service of the unified bonds; the French Government was also displeased by the return of ex-King Milan to Serbia in 1897 and his participation in the political affairs of the country.

Bourse, the French Government gave its approval only on condition that the French representative on the Autonomous Monopoly Administration should be the official delegate of the French Government.[137] It permitted the quotation of a Bulgarian loan in 1902 only on condition that Bulgaria pay off all arrears due on the eastern Roumelian annuities, under the Ottoman Debt Administration.[138]

Other forms of reprisal have been known. France threatened Morocco in 1909 that the banks would withhold financial aid unless the loan proposals of that year were accepted.[139] When France blocked the Hope and Blackmore project in Tunis in 1868, the French minister said that any arrangement would be contingent on settlement of the issues concerning the financial commission.[140] The British Government protested in 1879 against the conclusion or execution of a contract between the Peruvian Government of Pierola and the Dreyfus Company on the ground that it would constitute a gross violation of the rights of the bondholders.[141] A most unusual case of reprisals—on private property—on account of a bond default occurred in the United States in 1934 by the passage of the Harrison Resolution of that year. Although Congress had in 1928 passed the Settlement of War Claims Act authorizing the return to their legal owners of 80 per cent of the German private property sequestrated by the United States in 1917, and although most of this 80 per cent had already been returned by the Alien Property Custodian, the Harrison Resolution stopped payments on the small balance due to several private owners, the return of whose property had been delayed by tax disputes, by litigation, and by administrative red tape.[142] A decision of the Supreme Court upholding the constitutionality of this withholding of property whose return had already been authorized was put on the questionable ground that the property had already been confiscated by the United States and that its return was an act of grace, subject to conditions.[143] This decision misinterpreted the acts of Congress sequestrating

137. Simitch, *op. cit.*, pp. 424–428.

138. II, 538, n. 46. In 1914 the French Government pledged itself to refuse listing to any loan which might be so employed in China as to weaken Russian influence in China's affairs. Feis, *op. cit.*, p. 141. In 1909 France refused to permit the listing of a Peruvian loan unless Peru abandoned this *non possumus* with respect to the Dreyfus claim and agreed to a compensation with its French creditors. II, 169. French ban against listing of securities of South Spanish Railroad because of discrimination against French bondholders. Feis, *op. cit.*, p. 149.

139. L.J., *Affaires du Maroc*, V, 1908–10 (1910), No. 249.

140. F.O., 102/115, No. 764.

141. II, 135–136.

142. See editorial by Borchard in *Am. Jour. Int. Law*, XXX (1936), 108.

143. *Cummings et al.* v. *Deutsche Bank und Disconto Gesellschaft*, 300 U.S. 115, 57 S. Ct. 359 (1937).

the property and unnecessarily injured the public record of the United States and the essential conditions of foreign investment.[144] The "freezing orders" of the Roosevelt administration beginning in 1940 were based on the desire to keep American funds out of the hands of the German Government or its nationals and is a reprisal not relevant to the present discussion.

Governments may assist their bondholders by embodying in treaty form the terms of a debt settlement effected by the bondholders with the defaulting government. This occurred in Portugal after the settlement of 1902, thus making any breach in the performance of the conditions of the agreement an international offense.[145] Such treaty arrangement has also occasionally been the form in which an agreement for the payment of claims over a period of years was carried into effect.[146]

There are other forms of reprisal and coercion which have been exerted by the governments of creditors. One is the breach of diplomatic relations when the debt service is suspended or the debtor refuses to enter into a settlement. A few illustrations may be given. The British Government withdrew its ambassador from Mexico in 1938 on the occasion of the oil expropriation.[147] In 1868 the French agent in Tunis severed his relations with the Bey of Tunis because he refused to issue the decree agreed upon with the powers for the appointment of a financial commission.[148] In 1860 Great Britain broke off diplomatic relations with the Miramon Government in Mexico because it had seized from the British Legation 660,000 pesos assigned to the bondholders of the London debt.[149] When in 1861 Juárez issued his decree suspending service on the foreign debt for two years, the French Government broke off diplomatic relations and the British minister recommended the same course and the use of force and the seizure of customhouses to compel payment of the assigned revenues, a course which was pursued.[150] Joint action to prevent the importation of products of the defaulter into the creditor countries has also been recommended.[151] With the growing predilection for economic sanctions on the part of governments seeking what they call "collective security," there is

144. See editorial by Borchard in *Am. Jour. Int. Law*, XVIII (1924), 523, reprinted in *Cong. Rec.*, Appendix, January 7, 1942, pp. A 36–38.

145. II, 382.

146. As, for example, agreement with Mexico of November 19, 1941, for the settlement of the general claims, U.S. Dept. of State, *Treaty Series*, No. 980. II, 94.

147. This was followed by a dunning note concerning other claims, which Mexico purported to resent, whereupon the breach occurred.

148. L.J., *supra*, n. 118, p. 176.

149. II, 21.

150. II, 24.

151. "Sir N. Grattan-Doyle asked the Secretary of State for Foreign Affairs whether, in view of the national losses caused by foreign Governments defaulting on loans raised for developing their countries, he will ask the United States,

no telling how far economic pressure—much more practical than political pressure in this field—may ultimately go. As the London study group, dealing with the problem of foreign investment, maintained in their 1937 report, the fact that some countries are in a much stronger position than others to apply economic sanctions or pressures will induce a serious modification of the principle that all holders of a loan should be treated alike and is likely to have profound effects on the trends of international investment.[152]

CLEARING SYSTEMS

A device of direct debt collection by the creditor countries is the institution of a system of forced clearing of commercial transactions with the debtor country, whereby payments due to the debtor on trade account are used to satisfy his obligations toward the creditor country.[153] It was applied by Great Britain when Germany, in June, 1934, declared a mora-

France, and Holland to join with this country in refusing to admit the products of those defaulting countries until an acceptable debt rearrangement has been reached, with a view to assisting the rehabilitation of international trade created by foreign loans; as, although this may result in temporary loss of export trade to the creditor countries, it will compel debtor countries to feel the effect of their debt repudiation on their own trade?

"Sir J. Simon: I agree with my hon. Friend that in cases of default it is desirable for His Majesty's Government to act, so far as possible, in co-operation with the other creditor countries concerned, and this is the existing practice. The appropriate action to be taken to defend the interests of British bondholders is a matter for consideration in each case in the light of all relevant circumstances. I do not, however, consider that a proposal on the lines suggested by my hon. Friend would be likely to achieve the results desired." *Parliamentary Debates*, Ser. V, Vol. CCCXXXII, House of Commons, February 21, 1938, pp. 18–19.

152. *The Problem of International Investment*, p. 99.

153. "According to the terms of a clearing agreement, importers in each country pay into a special office (usually the Central Bank) all sums due for imports. From the funds thus received, each clearing office pays exporters for goods shipped to the other country. Provision is also usually made for the use in the creditor country of part of the in-payments to liquidate frozen commercial and financial claims against the other party, since their immobilisation was the immediate cause of the introduction of clearing agreements. Sometimes, as in the Swiss-German agreement, payments for tourists' expenditures are also covered, as well as other special items. In most agreements a definite percentage of balances not required by the creditor nation to pay for exports is reserved for the liquidation of blocked claims, while another portion is put at the free disposal of the debtor." P. T. Ellsworth, *International Economics* (New York, Macmillan, 1939), p. 409.

The process began with a statute in England, Debts Clearing Office and Import Restrictions Act, 24 & 25 Geo. V., c. 31 (1934), providing for compulsory clearing, but on protest this was not made operative. Nussbaum, *Money in the Law*, p. 506. It led to the agreement with Germany, which was followed as a model by other creditor countries.

torium on all long-term and medium-term debts, including the Dawes and Young loans, and led to the conclusion of the Anglo-German transfer agreement of July 4, 1934, whereby the German Government undertook to pay the full interest in sterling on Dawes and Young bonds.[154] The remedy of forced clearing is, of course, available only to countries having an unfavorable trade balance with the debtor. Moreover, experience has shown that economic pressure of this kind—which was used in 1934 by Holland and Switzerland—is likely to disrupt the trade relations between the countries concerned. For this reason, the League Loans Committee, when asked to press for the imposition of trade clearings on defaulting debtors, declined to adopt the proposal, holding that the injury to the bondholders' interests as a result of the damage to the economy of the debtor country would far outweigh any possible benefit temporarily accruing to the bondholders from such forcible means of collection.[155]

Mr. J. Reuben Clark in his article, "Foreign Bondholdings in the United States," [156] remarks:

A third respect in which the situation of the European bondholders' associations differs from that of the Council is found in the fact that since the War the European countries have abandoned the international principle of conduct obtaining among nations before the War—namely, that governments would not normally interpose, even their good offices, in behalf of their nationals holding foreign government bonds, so that, in violation of that principle, they now not only make representations upon behalf of such interests, but even impose coercive measures—such as compulsory clearings—against debtor governments to compel the adequate service by these debtors of their long-term obligations held by the nationals of the coercing state.

The American Government still adheres to the old rule, though rendering to the Council within that rule, the maximum assistance it considers proper.

We may next consider the international offenses of a diversion or misuse of pledged revenues and the exercise of discrimination against national bondholders, recognized bases of diplomatic intervention.

154. Feuerlein and Hannan, *Dollars in Latin America*, pp. 34 f.; Harris, *Germany's Foreign Indebtedness*, pp. 60 f.; *Corp. For. Bondh. Rep.*, No. 61 (1934), p. 35; B.I.S., *Fifth Annual Report* (May, 1935), p. 59; Schoo, *op. cit.*, pp. 911 ff. The agreement of July 4, 1934, embodying a clearing arrangement, differs from that of November 1, 1934. See *supra*, p. 132.

155. *Third Annual Report* (June, 1936), p. 11. On clearing agreements and their economic effects in general, see Ellsworth, *op. cit.*, pp. 407 ff.; *Enquiry into Clearing Agreements*, League Study Committee Report, II. Econ. and Finan. 1935. II.B. 6.

156. *Am. Jour. Int. Law*, XXXII (1938), 439, 443.

MAINTENANCE OF SECURITY

In order to make a loan attractive to issuing banker and bond buyer, borrowing countries with poor credit standing have usually had to pay a high effective rate of interest, give special security—such as a hypothecation of certain revenues—or both. The more precarious the government or its debt record, the better the security demanded. Since security, therefore, plays such a part in creating the loan, it is obvious that bondholders and their governments will seek to prevent its diversion or dissipation, even though the bondholders do not control it and its maintenance depends on the good faith of the borrowing government.

Governments are thus observant to prevent security from being diluted or weakened by having to support loans additional to those for which it was originally assigned [157] or from being diverted to other purposes or other bondholders than originally agreed upon. The ground advanced is that the diversion is a tortious breach of contract, since revenues already assigned are beyond the power of disposition of the borrower, whether or not a bondholders' collector has been appointed. Thus, various diversions of Peruvian guano, often used as security for Peruvian loans, evoked the resistance and protest of creditor powers.[158] The French and German ambassadors protested the repledging in 1899 of state railway receipts already pledged to the 1895 loan of Austria and succeeded in obtaining a substitution of the match and cigarette paper monopoly receipts.[159] Turkey on several occasions undertook to divert security but the effort always met with resistance and a readjustment if not desistance.[160] Greece after the second Balkan war attempted to

157. In 1868 France objected on this account to a proposed loan by an English firm to Tunis.

China, 1921. United States protest against use of salt tax for other loans and weakening authority of inspector of security. *For. Rel.*, 1920, I, p. 636. See also *idem*, 1921, p. 392.

Ecuador, 1920. Opposing increase in public debt of Ecuador which might jeopardize United States held bonds. *Idem*, 1920, II, 179.

158. British protest against Dreyfus contract, depriving bondholders of security. France declined to join, preferring to support Dreyfus. II, 136.

But while the Peruvian dollar loans continued in default after 1932, the British guano-secured loan was serviced. II, 193.

159. Y. Zivkovitch, *La Garantie des emprunts publics du royaume de Yougoslavie*, pp. 66–67. In 1894 a fund made up of assigned revenues in the hands of a Serbian official, representative of the foreign lenders, was raided by Serbia to pay overdue salaries. After protest, Serbian banks paid bond coupons. *Daily News* (London), April 13, 1894; *The Times* (London), April 28, 1894; *The Economist*, April 28, 1894.

160. Cf. II, 407, 412, 419.

sequester the revenues collected by the Ottoman Public Debt Administration but the powers persuaded her to desist.[161] Italian pressure in 1903 to collect the claims of sufferers in the Santo Domingo revolution resulted in a protocol promising payment, secured by 5 per cent of the customs revenue, an assignment which the French and Belgian bondholders successfully resisted.[162] Ecuador on several occasions undertook to divert the security pledged to the bondholders of the Guayaquil and Quito railroad but got out of the difficulty by desisting, by offering new security, or by a reorganization of the loans.[163] China on similar attempts was called to account by the powers.[164]

Guatemala affords an instance of diversion of assigned taxes without much success for the disappointed creditors. Although the coffee duties had been pledged to the 1895 British loan, the Guatemalan Government first arbitrarily withdrew the security and then for fourteen years defaulted on the interest, although the coffee duties were greatly in excess of the bond requirements. Both the bondholders and the British Government were unsuccessful in restoring the security or having payments resumed and finally sought United States good offices to persuade Guatemala to arbitrate. The United States made it a condition of their assistance that the bondholders agree to a conversion, a change which the Council of Foreign Bondholders considered derogatory to their interests.[165] Finally in 1913, after Guatemala made an attempt to alienate the coffee duties, Great Britain dispatched a warship to Guatemala and secured a restoration of the diverted coffee duties and a settlement of the default.[166]

Lord Derby in 1876 objected at the request of the bondholders against the failure of the Egyptian Government, under the proposed debt unification plan of May, 1867 to make any allowance for the special security assigned to the bondholders of the 1862 and 1864 loans.[167] Diplomatic pressure failed in Portugal in 1893 to secure priority for the external bondholders after the decree of 1892 but did succeed in reviving the Junta de Credito Publico to receive and disburse the assigned revenue.[168] The French political encroachment on Morocco between 1902 and 1912 was partly explained by anxiety to protect the prior liens of French bond-

161. Feis, *op. cit.*, p. 113.

162. II, 235.

163. *Corp. For. Bondh. Rep.*, No. 56 (1929), pp. 145, 147.

164. *For. Rel.*, 1919, I, 505.

165. Memorandum from the British Foreign Office, London, January 28, 1913. *For. Rel.*, 1913, 566.

166. *Supra*, p. 237, n. 67.

167. II, 589.

168. II, 373.

holders.[169] In 1923, in an exchange of notes between the United States, on the one hand, and Ecuador and Great Britain, on the other hand, the Secretary of State warned against the conclusion of any loan contract between Ecuador and the Ethelburga Syndicate which might require an assignment of customs revenues already assigned to the Guayaquil and Quito Railroad and its bondholders under an earlier contract.[170]

Any local law which purports to release from its lien property whose revenues had been set aside as security for a foreign loan is likely to be protested in advance of passage by the country whose bondholders would be deleteriously affected.[171] Even a removal of the customs collection from its present depositary may be regarded as a breach of the contract and of the security protection of the bondholders.[172]

Perhaps the most striking diplomatic controversies have arisen in connection with political changes occurring in the debtor country which affect the security assigned to the service of a foreign loan by the attempt of a new régime or a conquering country to appropriate the security in whole or in part. An established security may therefore be impaired not by act of the debtor but by a third country over which neither he nor the creditor has any direct control. Thus, Lord Salisbury in a circular to the powers objected to the treaty of San Stefano, 1877, by which Russia exacted an indemnity from Turkey deemed prejudicial to the British bondholders of the Turkish debt. He thereupon succeeded in writing into the treaty of Berlin, 1878, a reallocation of the sources of some Turkish revenues and of their destination and got Russia to agree to respect prior hypothecations so as to give preference to secured loans.[173] Thence also came the recommendation to the Porte of the establishment of an international financial commission. Britain protested the preference given to the short-term Galata bankers in 1880, holding that the security thus affected was a prior lien of the British bondholders of the 1862 loan.[174] When Bulgaria objected in 1881 to the use of the Bulgarian tribute for private creditors but maintained that the Russian indemnity had prior claim, Britain entered into a diplomatic refutation of the contention.[175]

169. The French bondholders were practically the sole creditors of Morocco.

170. For. Rel., 1923, I, 934, 938, 939.

171. Secretary of State Hughes to minister in Bolivia, December 19, 1923. For. Rel., 1923, I, 451.

172. Haiti, 1915. For the controversy between the Banque and the Haitian Government, see idem, 1914, pp. 345–382; idem, 1915, pp. 496–521; see also Millspaugh, op. cit., pp. 22–24.

173. II, 426; Phillimore, op. cit., p. 13.

174. II, 430–31.

175. II, 440.

One of the most interesting cases in diplomatic history involved the conquest and annexation by Chile in 1883 of the Peruvian province of Tarapacá, the nitrate and guano of which province had been assigned by Peru as security for certain French and British loans—some held by American citizens. The foreign offices of the creditors' nationals at first took the view that having taken the security Chile came under a legal obligation to assume a part of the Peruvian debt secured thereon. This claim was gradually diluted to a demand that equity rather than law required an assumption of a proportion of the Peruvian debt. Chile finally made an agreement with the countries of the bondholders and undertook to assume a share of the debt, leaving to an arbitration with France certain questions of priority.[176]

In 1932 and 1935 the Department of State apparently declined to take action with respect to the diversion by Salvador and Cuba of the security assigned to the service of the defaulted bonds of those countries.[177] In the case of Salvador, the explanation is to be found in political reasons, the nonexistence at time of default in 1932 of a recognized government and the creation of the Foreign Bondholders Protective Council in addition to the Lisman committee. In the case of the Cuban Public Works there were also competing protective committees and the Department considered the time inopportune to protest at the demand of the Nye-Coyle committee. Diversion of security provided a major ground for bondholders' complaint against the Colombian default of 1932 [178] but there is little evidence that the Department of State was impelled by that fact to change its general attitude of allowing the Foreign Bondholders Protective Council to work with the private protective committee to readjust the matter.[179] While diversion of security affords a special ground for diplomatic protest,[180] it is no guaranty that political considerations which dictate nonintervention will be materially modified by that fact.

DISCRIMINATION

Discrimination against nationals is one of the customary grounds of diplomatic intervention. Yet there is some question whether a country is

176. See details in II, 137, 147–151, 157, 161, 164.
177. SEC, *Rep.,* Pt. V, pp. 407, 415, 417.
178. *The New York Times,* February 7, 1933.
179. See *supra,* p. 246.
180. On the effects of diversion of security, see J. Reuben Clark, Jr., "Foreign Bondholdings in the United States," *Am. Jour. Int. Law,* XXXII (1938), 439, 443, quoted in Hackworth, *op. cit.,* V, 626.

bound by international law not to discriminate among nationals of different countries, where there is some justification therefor, such as, under a régime of clearing agreements, the existence with some creditor countries, but not with others, of an unfavorable balance of trade.[181] The real ground justifying intervention is an unfair or unjustified discrimination among nationals. But, whether excused or not, nothing produces so immediate a diplomatic protest as actual discrimination in the treatment of nationals of the protecting state by a foreign debtor, and in this respect equality of treatment may be said to be an unwritten financial tradition and practice.

On the other hand, it would be inaccurate to say that equality of treatment between citizens and aliens, or what is called "national treatment," is the limit of obligation that can be exacted from a foreign debtor. If the national treatment is so grossly unfair or below what is called the standard of civilized justice, foreign nations will not consider themselves barred from officially claiming an international delinquency, as did Secretary Hull in connection with the expropriation without adequate compensation of agricultural land in Mexico,[182] notwithstanding the contention of Mexico that Article 9 of the treaty concluded at Montevideo on the rights and duties of states provided that equality of treatment was the limit of national obligation. Secretary Hull countered by remarking, in effect, that this did not contemplate equality of mistreatment.

Moreover, a sharp distinction must be made between external and internal loans, although some writers go further and would give the issuing state sovereign authority to change the terms of all its loans by municipal law.[183] But this cannot be true as a matter of law where a contract between the state and aliens provides for payment in foreign currency. Writers affirm the power of the state to reduce or to revalorize a state debt by legislation and to subject aliens in this respect to the same treatment that nationals must tolerate on an internal obligation expressed in terms of local currency. Obviously, all residents of the state are subject to local vicissitudes and if the unit of currency changes value foreign holders of the currency or of internal loans can claim no preferen-

181. Feilchenfeld, in Quindry, *op. cit.*, II, secs. 656(b), 652(g).
182. Dept. of State, *Press Releases*, No. 354 (July 21, 1938); *Press Releases*, No. 398 (August 25, 1938). Convention between the United States and Mexico of November 19, 1941, U.S. Dept. of State, *Treaty Series*, No. 980, concerning the final settlement of the claims. II, 94.
183. Strupp, "L'Intervention en matière financière," *Rec. des Cours*, VIII (1925), p. 67. Marburg, "Enteignung im Völkerrecht," in Strupp, *Wörterbuch des Völkerrechts* (Berlin, 1929), III, 828.

tial treatment.[184] It was on this ground that Austria defended its imposition of a tax on the coupons of its public debt.[185]

Measures directed exclusively against aliens, when not justified on a recognized ground, fall into an entirely different class.[186] So do measures which favor one group of aliens over others, or give preference to internal creditors over external, or to short-term over long-term creditors, or to one bond issue over another. On several occasions diplomatic protest has been made against the payment of domestic creditors before foreigners were paid, especially where the pledged revenues gave priority to the latter.[187] Mexico by decree of July 25, 1930, ended what she claimed was the preferred status of foreign creditors, to all of whom, domestic and foreign, she was in default.[188] A Danzig decree of 1939 providing for the conversion of three municipal loans into Danzig gulden was accompanied by an official assurance that the decree applied only to Danzig nationals and foreign residents of Danzig.[189]

A more vigorous protest is usually made if the nationals of other countries, theoretically in the same debt position, are given preference by a debtor in the payment of interest or principal, or the establishment of security.[190] The protest may be made to the debtor or to the foreign country whose nationals receive preference. Thus, under the Dominican

184. Decision of the German Supreme Court, February 2, 1926, Entsch. Reichsg. Zivil., CXIII, 42. As to conversion of 3% loan of 1901, see decision of German Supreme Court, January 27, 1929, *Jur. Woch.*, 1927, p. 1843.

185. The Austrian Foreign Minister refused to concede the privilege of diplomatic interposition on the part of foreign states. *Staatsarchiv*, XV, 159; Bruns, *Fontes Juris Gentium*, Ser. B, sec. 1, p. 1269. The Spanish coupon tax of 1898 did not apply to the 4% external loan. Freund, *Die Rechtsverhältnesse der öffentliche Anleihen*, p. 243.

186. Cf. Secretary of State to Mr. Parker, February 6, 1917. *For. Rel.*, 1917, p. 1007.

187. Santo Domingo, 1903. French-Belgian bondholders successfully protested against payment of internal floating debt creditors. II, 234. In 1922 the United States, British, French, and Japanese bondholders objected to China's giving preferred treatment to holders of internal loans, by confining "surplus customs revenue" to internal bondholders only. *For. Rel.*, 1923, I, 525.

188. *Corp. For. Bondh. Rep.*, No. 60 (1933), p. 38. Manes, *Staatsbankrotte* (3d ed.), p. 67, states that foreigners were better treated by Prussia than nationals, between 1806 and 1815, foreigner creditors being paid after 1812, nationals only after 1815. The alleged discrimination by Czechoslovakia and Yugoslavia against foreign bondholders when they separated their currencies from that of Austria (*ibid.*) was not intentional but resulted from the fact that these countries were prohibited for a certain period from sending their currency out of the country, even on domestic bonds held abroad.

189. *Com. and Fin. Chron.*, CXLVIII (May 20, 1939), 2978.

190. SEC, *Rep.*, Pt. V, p. 417. Scroggs, "Foreign Treatment of American Creditors," *For. Aff.*, XIV (1936), 345.

debt settlement arranged with the help of Professor Hollander in 1906, the English bondholders alleged that they had been treated unfairly as compared with the French and Belgian bondholders. The United States Government maintained that the complaint of the English bondholders was not well founded, but the latter, through the Corporation of Foreign Bondholders, persisted in their contention. In 1908, when a new Dominican customs loan was issued as part of the debt readjustment plan, the Corporation successfully opposed its quotation on the London Stock Exchange.[191] The German minister protested Admiral Caperton's actions in Haiti in 1915 on the ground that no provision was made for payments due to German interests, until Haiti was requested by the American chargé to state that German creditors would receive the same fair treatment as all foreign interests.[192] Although no foreign creditor in the absence of agreement has a right to demand preferred treatment,[193] there are occasions when preferred treatment for secured creditors is called for by the terms of a reorganization or is demanded under contract as a condition of consent to a new settlement.[194]

The extraordinary restrictions on transfers which were a phenomenon of the 1930's brought in their train several situations in which discriminatory treatment of American bondholders was evident. Dollar bonds issued or guaranteed by European governments were in default in 1934 to an amount of about 600 million dollars. The most notable case of this discrimination occurred in Germany, where the default of 1934, involving over 300 million dollars, was based on an alleged lack of foreign exchange. Germany undertook to deny residents of Germany foreign exchange for the payment of all nongovernmental loans but permitted the borrowers to make payment in Reichsmarks into a special account with the Reichsbank. As to the Dawes and Young loans, the German Govern-

---

191. II, 254–257, 261, n. 71. See also protest of Italy and Belgium against preference to San Domingo Improvement Co. II, 246.

192. *For. Rel.*, 1915, p. 520. See also French protest to both Chile and Peru against Elias-Castellon protocol, allegedly for benefit of English bondholders only. II, 161.

France having protested to Great Britain in 1902 that a seizure of the Venezuelan customs would prejudice French interests, both France and Belgium were given assurances to the contrary. But the intervening powers did obtain from The Hague Court a 30% preference for their diligence in bringing Venezuela to account. Case of Great Britain, *Venezuelan Arbitration of 1903,* pp. 761, 1252.

In 1869 Italy and Great Britain protested against preference to France in Tunis.

The Foreign Bondholders Protective Council in negotiations with Buenos Aires influenced by concurrence of French and British creditors and good debt record of Argentina. SEC, *Rep.,* Pt. V, pp. 380–381.

193. Feilchenfeld, in Quindry, *op. cit.,* II, sec. 656(a).

194. Feis, *op. cit.,* p. 113: Britain to United States *in re* Liberia reorganization.

ment from July, 1932, to December, 1934, paid half in dollars and half in blocked Reichsmarks; in 1935 the German Government announced that interest would be paid at a reduced rate, the one from 7 per cent to 5 per cent, the other from 5½ per cent to 4 per cent.[195] The balance of the interest was deposited in Reichsmarks in Germany but could be sold or cashed at stated reduced rates.

The vigorous American protest against this treatment of American bondholders was based on three grounds: (1) that the British, French, and Dutch *tranches* of the Dawes and Young loans were paid in full, whereas the American *tranche* was paid at a reduced rate, notwithstanding that the loan was a single loan based on a global security; [196] (2) that the action of Germany was unilateral, without consultation with the creditors; and (3) that there was evidence that German debtors were obtaining the dollar exchange to buy in their depreciated bonds on the American market.[197] The German Government undertook to meet the charge of discrimination by stating that the British, French, Swiss, and Dutch governments had unfavorable balances of trade with Germany and threatened to seize the surplus as a fund from which to pay their national bond creditors, whereupon Germany was forced to enter into clearing agreements—without consultation with the American bondholders—by which the foreign exchange owned by German nationals in those countries could be used to satisfy bondholders. The United States having a favorable balance was unable to take advantage, even had they seen fit to do so, of this device. So the discrimination remained unredressed, except that the clearing agreements themselves collapsed after a time.[198] The United States complained of the fact that Great Britain, France, and Holland utilized their unfavorable trade balance solely for the benefit of their own nationals.[199]

Similar difficulties were encountered with other European countries. Portugal in 1924 provided by decree that the interest on certain gold bonds was to be paid in depreciated currency, except that British holders

195. *For. Bondh. Prot. Coun. Rep.*, 1935, p. 119.

196. *Idem*, 1937, p. 345.

197. The full details of these complicated transactions, varied every few months, appear in the SEC, *Rep.*, Pt. V, pp. 419 ff. The diplomatic correspondence is also summarized or reprinted.

198. *Supra*, p. 256.

199. SEC, *Rep.*, Pt. V, pp. 9 ff., 435 ff. This case had a curious feature in that the British Government first joined in the Dutch and Swiss protest against discrimination and then demanded discriminatory treatment for British creditors, waiving in 1934 the establishment of a clearing office in return for a German agreement to pay full interest on the Dawes and Young bonds in beneficial ownership of British holders on June 15, 1934. See *Corp. For. Bondh. Rep.*, No. 61 (1934), p. 35. The arrangement, in force for six months, was periodically renewed.

in Great Britain were to be paid in sterling. The United States successfully protested against this discrimination against American citizens.[200]
Romania after March, 1934, while making no dollar payments on its
dollar bonds, paid other foreign creditors in their proper currencies, in
some cases offering a bonus of 10 per cent.[201] The Department of State
objected to a Hungarian plan which announced a list of priorities which
might have proved discriminatory against holders of dollar bonds.[202]
The Department was able, through the efforts of the Foreign Bondholders Protective Council, to obtain from Brazil in 1933 an improved
status for the dollar bondholders under the Niemeyer plan which, by
its classifications of external bondholders, gave the British bondholders
a considerable advantage. The Department succeeded in persuading
Brazil to defer announcement of the plan and of the implementing decree
and then effected a modification of the plan.[203]

The fact that foreign governments, after the United States went
"off" gold early in 1933, paid their dollar bonds in paper and not in
gold afforded no basis for protest on the part of the United States, which
itself paid its debts in paper, although some debtors, like the French
cities, honored their bond obligations as written.[204]

Governments not infrequently protest not to the debtor but to a competing creditor government to prevent a discrimination against or impair-
ment of the interests of the bondholders of the protesting government.
Thus, when Italy in 1871 sought to secure concessions from the Bey of
Tunis, Britain and France protested.[205] When the British Foreign Office
contemplated, as alleged, an approval of foreclosure proceedings by the
Council of Foreign Bondholders against the Guayaquil and Quito railroad, the Department of State undertook to defend Ecuador and to
present the grounds on which foreclosure was deemed detrimental to
the American bondholders and the railroad and disadvantageous to all
creditors.[206]

Governments may protest to the debtor against a preference shown

200. Portugal agreed to pay principal and interest to American holders in
pounds sterling. The correspondence is printed in Hackworth, *op. cit.*, V, 627.

201. *For. Bondh. Prot. Coun. Rep.*, 1937, p. 692.

202. SEC, *Rep.*, Pt. V, p. 435.

203. *Idem*, Pt. V, pp. 386 ff., 417 ff.; *For. Bondh. Prot. Coun. Rep.*, 1934, p. 27.

204. Belgium offered to pay its dollar bonds in gold, if the bonds were presented
for stamping within four days of April 30, 1933, a condition which presumably no
American holder could fulfill, though some European holders could. This discrimination might be said in reality to place most Europeans at the same disadvantage as Americans. Scroggs, *op. cit.*, p. 436.

205. Britain and France regarded these concessions as contrary to debt adjustments previously approved by the three powers.

206. *For. Rel.*, 1919, II, 194.

to one group of creditors over another and may seek to alter or remove inequalities. So a creditor government may itself make distinctions between different types of bondholders it will protect or between bondholders and other creditors.[207] This is a matter within the discretion of the protecting government. Not all the creditor governments may give their diplomatic support to the same type of creditors. Thus, in 1878 in Egypt, the German, Austrian, and Italian governments were supporting the judgment creditors, whereas Britain and France were supporting primarily the bondholders.[208]

PUBLIC BONDS BEFORE ARBITRAL TRIBUNALS

Bond cases have been submitted to international tribunals on several occasions. Very little light is thrown upon the subject by the results of these arbitrations, except as by their dicta the commissions express the opinion that governments have the *right* to press the claims of bondholders of a foreign debt, though they generally admit that in practice such claims are not diplomatically presented. As a general rule, however, jurisdiction has been declined—usually for the reason that governments are not in the habit of presenting such claims diplomatically and because of the unwillingness of commissions to assume that they were intended to exercise jurisdiction in the absence of express words in the protocol.[209] It has been so held even where the protocol provided for the settlement of "all claims." [210] The Colombian bonds decision, rendered by Sir Frederick Bruce, Umpire, was severely criticized by Commissioner Little in the Aspinwall case before the United States–Venezuelan commission of December 5, 1885. He held, with Commissioner Findlay (Andrade dissenting), that the inclusive term "all claims" embraced bond claims.

207. II, 589 ff.: Egypt; bonus to Treasury bill holders. II, 331: Greece; funding loan in 1898 accorded discriminatory treatment and improvement, effect of protest.

208. France *in re* Haitian loans, *Précis historique des faits relatifs à l'emprunt d'Haiti et des derniers arrangements financiers conclus entre le gouvernement haitien et le comité des porteurs de titres du dit emprunt* (Paris, 1849), 94 pp. France in Peru, 1880, supported the Dreyfus claim in preference to the bondholders. II, 146. But France denied any distinction between bondholders and other creditors having a lien on the same guano.

209. Overdue Mexican coupons, *Du Pont de Nemours* (U.S.) v. *Mexico*, July 4, 1868. Moore, *A Digest of International Law*, IV, 3616. Opinion by Wadsworth; Zamocona concurred. See dictum of Thornton, Umpire, in *Widman* (U.S.) v. *Mexico*, July 4, 1868, *idem*, p. 3467.

210. Colombian bond cases, *Riggs, Oliver, Fisher* (U.S.) v. *Colombia*, February 10, 1864, *idem*, pp. 3612–3616. In the case of Gibbes before the 1857 and 1864 United States–Colombian commissions (*idem*, pp. 1398, 1410) an assigned bond was the subject matter of the claim; the jurisdictional question does not appear to have been raised.

This case constitutes one important exception, prior to the Venezuelan arbitrations of 1903, to the general rule that jurisdiction over bond claims is not exercised by international commissions.[211]

Before the Venezuelan commissions, sitting at Caracas, four bond claims were presented, with various decisions. In the case of the Compagnie Générale des Eaux de Caracas (Belgium),[212] Venezuelan bonds payable to bearer had been issued to the corporation for certain public works. From the decision it would seem that the general rule of nonenforcement of bond claims may be held not applicable where the bonds are issued in payment of property rights transferred to the government. Although many of the stockholders were not Belgians, an award was made with the peculiar provision that the money should be deposited in a Belgian bank and the bonds paid on being turned in. The production of the bonds naturally was made a necessary condition for the making of an award, so where, in the case of Ballistini (France),[213] the original bonds were not produced, the claim was dismissed, Paul, Commissioner, in a dictum giving expression to the usual rule of the nonenforcement of bond claims before international commissions. In the case of Boccardo (Italy),[214] where national bonds were delivered to claimant in payment

211. Venezuelan bond cases, *Aspinwall, Executor of G. G. Howland et al.* (U.S.) v. *Venezuela*, December 5, 1885. *Idem*, pp. 3616–3641. This claim was dismissed by the mixed commission under the convention of April 25, 1866. The findings of this commission were reopened because of the alleged fraud of the arbitrators. Under a strict construction of the protocol, Bates, Umpire, dismissed the Texas bond cases before the British–United States commission of February 8, 1853. *Idem*, p. 3594. One reason was that they had not been treated by Great Britain as a subject for diplomatic interposition. The decision is criticized by John Westlake, *International Law* (Cambridge, The University Press, 1910), I, 77–78, citing Dana in Dana's Wheaton, s 30, n. 18. Jurisdiction was exercised by the Mexican commission of 1868 over a stolen bond, *Keller* (U.S.) v. *Mexico*, July 4, 1868 (Moore, *op. cit.*, p. 3065), on the ground of fraudulent destruction of specific property having a definite value and certain assurances by the Government. See also *Eldredge* (U.S.) v. *Peru*, January 12, 1863. *Idem*, p. 3462. The failure to fulfill the obligations of a bond issued for supplies was held not an "injury to property" by the United States–Mexican commission of 1868 (Manasse case, *idem*, p. 3463), although the failure to pay for supplies furnished under contract had been so construed.

212. *Compagnie Générale des Eaux de Caracas* (Belgium) v. *Venezuela*, March 7, 1903. J. H. Ralston, *Venezuelan Arbitrations of 1903* (Washington, Govt. Printing Office, 1904), pp. 271–290. Hackworth, *Digest of International Law*, V, 628.

213. *Ballistini* (France) v. *Venezuela*, February 27, 1903. Ralston, *op. cit.*, pp. 503–506. Hackworth, *op. cit.*, p. 627.

214. *Boccardo* (Italy) v. *Venezuela*, February 13, 1903, cited in note to Ralston, *op. cit.*, p. 505 (not reported). See, however, the brief statement given by Mr. Ralston in his address before the International Law Association, *Twenty-fourth Report*, pp. 193–194.

for articles furnished and were never transferred by him, judgment was rendered on the authority of the Aspinwall case before the Venezuelan commission of 1885. The fourth case, Jarvis (U.S.),[215] was dismissed because the service and the supplies for which the bonds were issued (by a temporary dictator of Venezuela) were furnished to an unsuccessful revolution, which had not been recognized by the Government of the United States, and hence presumably they were not valid obligations of Venezuela.

In the case of Canevaro (Italy) against Peru,[216] Italy based its claim upon the fact that Peru had refunded its internal debt by issuing consolidated bonds at a greatly reduced rate and that bonds of this internal debt held by Italian subjects by assignment were thereby unlawfully reduced in value. The Permanent Court of Arbitration at The Hague supported the contention of Peru that the internal debt did not become external by its assignment to aliens and that alien transferee-holders were in no better position than national holders of the bonds. The Court held that the "financial measures" (in this case the Peruvian debt law of 1889, reducing the rights of creditors) "taken inside a country do not affect the acts concluded outside and by which the government has appealed directly to foreign credit." In this case the certificates were "created at Lima and payable at Lima, in compensation for a payment made voluntarily in behalf of the Peruvian Government." [217] This was held not to be impaired by the fact that the certificates were payable in pounds sterling.[218]

Various claims of French and other citizens and corporations against Chile, based upon bonded indebtedness guaranteed upon guano deposits ceded by Peru, were submitted to the tribunal sitting at Lausanne, the awards upon which were rendered July 5, 1901.[219] By the protocol of February 2, 1914, between France and Peru, it was agreed to submit to arbitration the claim of the widow Philon-Bernal and other bondholders of the loan of 1870.[220]

215. *Jarvis* (U.S.) v. *Venezuela*, February 17, 1903. Ralston, *op. cit.*, pp. 145–151.

216. *Canevaro* (Italy) v. *Peru*, April 25, 1910. *Am. Jour. Int. Law*, VI (1912), 746, 752.

217. *Idem*, p. 750.

218. Georg Schwarzenberger, *International Law* (London, Stevens & Sons, 1945), p. 26.

219. Descamps and Renault, *Receuil international des traités du xxᵉ siècle*, pp. 188 ff.

220. Clunet, XLI (1914), 1440–1442.

MILITARY ACTION

It cannot be said that military action in support of bondholders is now or ever was an important phase of international relations. Against smaller countries, particularly of Latin America during the nineteenth and early twentieth centuries, European countries have occasionally dispatched warships, and the display of force, while not necessarily collecting money, has brought about an agreement of settlement.[221] The threat of force was implicit in the agreements with Santo Domingo, Haiti, and Nicaragua to protect the customs receiver and in all three cases military occupation over a considerable period took place—in Santo Domingo over the eight years from 1916 to 1924.

Aside from the military protection promised and given by the United States to customs receivers in certain Caribbean countries and the intervention which occurred in those countries in the early twentieth century, as an incident of temporary political control of disorganized local governments, the cases which are usually considered as examples of military intervention in support of bondholders are rare. In fact, even they are not exclusively illustrations of military protection of bondholders but involve other types of claimants as well. Armed forces have been landed by the United States and other countries on numerous occasions to protect citizens against immediate danger to their life and property, but these are not within the scope of the present study.[222]

DISPLAY OF FORCE

Instances where a display of force was employed to support a demand for pecuniary reparation of a bond default, in addition to those already mentioned in Santo Domingo and Guatemala, may be the dispatch in 1892 of a French battleship to Santo Domingo to support the French-owned Banque Nationale against the unjustified demands of the local government, and the threat in 1903 that the customs would be taken over

221. Italy in 1903 sent her minister at Habana to Santo Domingo in a warship and obtained the Government's signature to a protocol for the resumption of payment on claims, and obtained certain security. II, 235. Again in 1905, after the United States Senate failed to ratify the treaty with Santo Domingo, Italy and Belgium demanded a resumption of payments and Italy sent a warship. *Idem*, p. 246. The United States in 1905 sent a warship to enforce its demand for the control of the customs at Monte Cristi. *Idem*, p. 246. Great Britain in 1913 sent a battleship to persuade Guatemala to restore the coffee duties which had been diverted to new creditors. *Supra*, p. 258, and Feis, *op. cit.*, p. 109.

222. United States Solicitor of the Department of State, *Right to Protect Citizens in Foreign Countries by Landing Forces*, Memorandum (3d rev. ed., Washington, 1934, Dept. of State Publication No. 538).

to assure payments to French bondholders.[223] A British warship in 1913, produced in Guatemala a restoration of the diverted coffee duties and a bond settlement.[224]

ARMED INTERVENTION

The two most notable examples, however, are Mexico in 1861 and Venezuela in 1903, and neither of these presents a clear case. In the period between 1851 and 1861 Mexico had repeatedly defaulted on promises to make payments on its loans and to apply certain customs revenues to the purpose. In addition, tort claims of various kinds remained unsatisfied, while Mexico found herself involved in the preliminaries and aftermath of the Juárez revolution of 1857. The presence of British and French warships had exerted some influence to obtain temporary accords and promises not only for British but also for Spanish interests. When finally the Mexican Congress in 1860 refused to sign an accord which looked more conclusive, Sir Charles Wyke, the British minister, advised his Government to seize and administer the customs houses and he was instructed to use naval force to obtain bond interest, an assignment of pledges, and payment of the Laguna Seca claim for reparation.[225] Joint intervention thus took place, but when it became clear that France had greater ambitions and sought to overthrow the Juárez Government and substitute Maximilian as Emperor the British and Spanish withdrew.[226]

Perhaps the most striking case is that of the blockade of Venezuela by Germany, Great Britain, and Italy in 1902–03. Venezuela had suffered a disastrous revolution in 1898 lasting more than two years. Since foreigners had largely helped to develop Venezuela, they and their property had considerable representation in Venezuela and sustained losses during the revolution. The claims arose out of injuries to person and property, some tortious, some merely civil war losses, breaches of contract, and, as to Great Britain, claims for seizures of British ships. Only in September, 1902, did the British bondholders ask that their demands for a settlement with Venezuela be joined to the other claims and pressed. To various offers of arbitration the dictator Castro either replied that these were matters for the Venezuelan courts or else advanced counterclaims. His dilatoriness and recalcitrance finally persuaded the three powers to give him an ultimatum, blockade La Guiara and Puerto Cabello, and seize the customhouses there until Castro proved willing

223. II, 238, Feis, *op. cit.*, pp. 146 ff.
224. *Supra,* p. 258.
225. II, 16, n. 5, 24 ff.
226. II, 27 ff.

to arbitrate the debatable claims and settle the less controversial for cash. All that he was asked to do for the bond claimants was to sign an agreement accepting bondholders' terms for the gradual liquidation of the debt. President Theodore Roosevelt had doubtless encouraged the intervening powers by his statement that the Monroe Doctrine was not designed to enable the Latin American countries to escape their legal obligations or sanctions for offenses, so long as intervention did not result in the permanent occupation of American territory.[227]

At all events, the intervention in Venezuela, which lasted from December, 1902, to February, 1903, less than two months, had the desired effect. United States Minister Bowen was entrusted by Castro with the conduct of the negotiations in Washington on behalf of Venezuela, small cash payments were made for what the intervening powers considered their first-line claims, arbitration commissions were established not only for the claims of their nationals but also for those of the United States, France, Holland, Belgium, and Spain, and a bond settlement was concluded.[228] When the intervening powers demanded priority for the payment of their claims, the United States protested; but, in an arbitration held at The Hague in 1904 between those powers and the United States, their right to a preferential payment of 30 per cent of their claims was recognized on the ground that they had incurred the expense of an intervention which resulted in benefits to others as well.[229]

THE DRAGO DOCTRINE

Curiously, out of this intervention in which bond claims played a negligible part, Dr. Luis Drago, Argentine Foreign Minister, advanced his contention, known as the Drago Doctrine, that "the public debt [of an American state] cannot occasion armed intervention, nor even the actual occupation of the territory of American nations by a European Power." [230] Since a public debt of a state had never as an isolated motive

227. President Roosevelt in his message of 1901 had said: "We do not guarantee any state against punishment if it misconducts itself, provided that punishment does not take the form of the acquisition of territory by any non-American power." Cf. Secretary Hay in *For. Rel.*, 1903, p. 5.

228. J. H. Ralston, *The Law and Procedure of International Tribunals* (Stanford University, Calif., Stanford University Press, 1926; Supp., 1936). The text of the agreement between Venezuela and the bondholders is given in *Corp. For. Bondh. Rep.*, No. 32 (1904), pp. 446–455.

229. The Ruhr invasion of 1923 is sometimes cited as an illustration of the policy of collecting money by force and of the futility of the effort. Schoo, *op. cit.*, p. 507. In fact, that invasion pursued political objectives.

230. Cf. discussion of the origin and development of this doctrine in Borchard, *Diplomatic Protection of Citizens Abroad*, pp. 308 ff.

brought about an armed intervention, unless we include in this classification the doubtful cases of Egypt and Turkey—certainly Venezuela affords no illustration—Dr. Drago's Doctrine had little support in the facts. This is especially true when it is realized that Dr. Drago expressly stated that he did not intend his "doctrine" as a defense "for bad faith, disorder, and deliberate and voluntary insolvency," even though the factual existence of these limiting conditions may be subject to a difference of opinion. Dr. Drago made no reference to diplomatic interposition generally nor to pecuniary claims arising out of contract or tort generally.

But, since Dr. Drago made a direct reference to the Monroe Doctrine, to which he appended his corollary, since some writers, ever since Palmerston's circular, had debated the question whether breach of a government's contractual obligation to an alien might not properly be made the subject of diplomatic interposition if not intervention, since The Hague Conference was to meet in 1907 to regulate as many questions of law as possible, Dr. Drago's demand received world-wide discussion hardly warranted by its lack of novelty or practical importance. Secretary Root instructed the American delegation to support a resolution distinguishing between bad faith and good faith in the nonperformance of contracts, deprecating the use of force for the recovery of contract debts, and placing reliance upon peaceful methods.

THE PORTER PROPOSITION

These proposals resulted in a convention, known as the Porter Proposition,[231] by which the signatories agreed not to have recourse to armed force for the collection of contract debts unless the debtor state refused or neglected to reply to an offer of arbitration, or, after accepting the offer, prevented any *compromis* from being agreed on, or, after the arbitration, failed to submit to the award. The Porter Proposition evoked several reservations which would prohibit diplomatic intervention except for denial of justice. It may be said that the Proposition is objectionable in that it conditionally sanctions the use of armed force in a class of cases in which the United States and, on occasion, other powers have declined, as a matter of policy, to interpose diplomatically. Again, when a country defaults, it does not as a rule deny the validity of the debt but asserts its inability to discharge it or meet its obligations under the contract. There is therefore nothing to arbitrate, unless it be its capacity to pay, which is not usually a subject of arbitration.

Viewed objectively, therefore, the Porter Proposition may not mark any advance. It failed to solve any practical problem. Perhaps that is one

231. *Idem*, p. 319.

reason why it has never been invoked and why several of its signatories have since 1907 denounced their adherence to the convention. In any event, it may probably be said that armed intervention for the collection of bond obligations is not likely to occur. If such intervention does occur, it will most probably have political objectives, to which economic considerations are secondary.

PART V

Financial Control

Section XVIII

FINANCIAL CONTROL

THE protection of bondholders' rights through private or semi-official committees, diplomatic representations, refusal of stock exchange listing to new loans of a defaulting country, or judicial action involves no interference with the sovereignty of the debtor. Other protective measures have, however, in many instances been adopted which have involved such interference in varying degree. These measures have sometimes taken a relatively mild form, as, for example, the assignment to foreigners under a loan contract of limited powers of supervising the expenditure of the loan proceeds or the collection and transmission of pledged revenues. Occasionally, following the grave default of an economically weak country, a type of foreign financial control has been imposed which has encroached materially upon the political independence of the debtor.

LEGAL BASES

Protective measures of this nature require for their institution specific title under international law.

In the absence of contractual agreements with the debtor government,[1]

---

1. Bondholders are sometimes specifically authorized under the terms of loan contracts to institute measures of financial control in case the debtor defaults. The contract of the 6% gold loan of 1920 of the Republic of Poland provided that in the event "of any interruption in the service of the loan, a representative of the bondholders may administer the railways in their interest" and that "the gross receipts from the railroads will be deposited in the Bank of Poland for the service of the loan." Madden and Nadler, *Foreign Securities*, p. 179. In the 1922 loan contract between the Government of Salvador and a group of American bankers, it was stipulated that in the event of a default for thirty days the fiscal agent was entitled to require the establishment of a customs administration and the appointment of a director-general of customs for the collection of the customs. The text of the contract is given in Robert W. Dunn, *American Foreign Investments*, pp. 222–247. Under the terms of the 1911 Costa Rica conversion bonds, the Government consented to the appointment by the issuing bankers, in the event of default for thirty days, of a customs agency having the sole right to collect customs by means of certificates. The contract of the Costa Rica gold loan of 1911 gave the representative of the bankers the right, after default for 60 days, to take over the

financial control may legally be imposed on an unwilling debtor only for just cause. Neither the imminence of default nor actual default of itself entitles foreign states to impose financial control on the debtor. Such action is warranted only when foreign creditors are illegally treated, especially if they are discriminated against in favor of national creditors or if certain categories of creditors are preferred to others, or when special funds assigned as security to the payment of certain debts are diverted or suppressed—in short, when bad faith may be considered the moving cause of the nonpayment.[2]

Financial contròl may be exercised by the bondholders through their agents and representatives, by foreign states, or by agencies acting on

---

administration of the assigned revenues. *Corp. For. Bondh. Rep.*, No. 56 (1929), pp. 126–127. A sort of "negative Calvo Clause" in the loan contract, viz., an express authorization to invoke the diplomatic interposition of their governments, may form the legal basis for financial intervention and control. The contract between the Government of Santo Domingo and the San Domingo Improvement Co. authorized—indeed, obliged—the company "in case of default or for any other manifest necessity, to request the Governments of Holland, Belgium, England, France and the United States to designate a citizen bondholder for each country as a member of an International Financial Commission." II, 215. For an unsuccessful attempt to carry out this provision, see II, 220 ff. The arrangement between the Government of Nicaragua and the Council of Foreign Bondholders of May 25, 1912, provided that the Government was "to recognize the right of the Bankers and the Council to apply to the United States for protection against any violation of the provisions of the Arrangement." *Corp. For. Bondh. Rep.*, No. 56 (1929), p. 264. Cf. Schoo, *Régimen jurídico*, p. 485.

2. Borchard, *Diplomatic Protection of Citizens Abroad*, pp. 310 ff. See also Strupp, "L'Intervention en matière financière," *Rec. des Cours*, VIII (1925), 8 ff., 40, 51, 94. Intervention is permissible only if authorized by the general principles of international law with respect to international responsibility. Strupp, *Intervention in Finanzfragen* (Leipzig, 1928), pp. 83, 97: Interference with the affairs of a foreign state is legally justified only when the state undertaking such diplomatic or military intervention derives its title from the general principles concerning international delinquencies. Oppenheim-Lauterpacht, *International Law*, I (6th ed., rev. London, Longman's Green, 1944), 256, n. De Lapradelle and Politis, *Rec. des Arb. Int.*, II (1923), 548: Intervention is legitimate if the debtor state abuses its autonomy and inflicts unjustified injury upon its creditors. Madden and Nadler, *op. cit.*, p. 358. As to the question whether the assumption of a guaranty of a loan by third states creates a right to interfere with the financial affairs of the debtor state, either on the part of the guaranteeing powers or for the benefit of the bondholders, see *supra*, section on Guaranteed Loans, p. 106. An instance where participation in an interventionist action against China was refused by the United States is recorded in *For. Rel.*, 1913, p. 133: While insisting on protection for the interests of its nationals, including adequate guarantees for the leaders and efficient supervision of disbursements, the United States Government was not prepared to join in any coercive steps designed to compel China's acceptance of any particular proposal as to advisers.

behalf of both the bondholders and their governments. If exercised by bondholders, financial control rests on an agreement between the debtor state and private individuals; it may become a matter of international law only if the rights of the bondholders under the agreement are violated in such manner as to involve the international liability of the controlled state and to result in diplomatic intervention by the bondholders' governments.[3] Where foreign states participate in the control, either jointly with the bondholders or alone, the matter lies clearly within the sphere of international law. To prevent any one state from gaining preponderant influence within the controlled state, financial control has usually been established by concerted action on the part of several powers.[4]

BONDHOLDERS' CONTROL

APPROVAL OF ADMINISTRATIVE ACTS

Bondholders' control in its least oppressive form has simply debarred the debtor from doing, without previous consent of the bondholders, certain things which might be prejudicial to their interests. Thus, the Bulgarian Government, under the loan agreement of 1902 with a group of French bankers, undertook not to modify the laws and regulations governing the imposition and collection of certain revenues unless previously approved by the bondholders.[5] Similarly, in order to insure the

3. Fischer Williams, *Chapters on Current International Law and the League of Nations*, pp. 258, n. 3; 259; 349. Strupp, "L'Intervention en matière financière," pp. 11, 40; H. M. Alvares Correa, "The International Controls of Public Finances" (Dissertation, Leiden, 1926), p. 3; Schoenborn, *Rec. des Cours*, XXX (1929), 173. Those agreements are sometimes vested with an international character by the fact that the governments of the bondholders take notice of them. This was the case with the Serbian bond adjustment of July, 1895. See Perm. Ct. Int. Just., Ser. C., No. 16–111, p. 335. The Turkish decree of Mouharrem, establishing the Ottoman Debt Council, was a "bilateral agreement between the Imperial Government and its creditors. In addition, it had an international aspect, for, by Article XXI, the Ottoman Government was required to communicate the Decree without delay to the Powers." II, 451, 486, and *infra*. See also A. M. Andréadès, "Les Contrôles financiers internationaux," *Rec. des Cours*, V (1924), 52.

4. Oppenheim-Lauterpacht, *op. cit.*, p. 256, n.; Andréadès, *op. cit.*, pp. 7, 100; B. H. Williams, *Economic Foreign Policy of the United States*, p. 176; Borchard, *op. cit.*, p. 314; Brodbeck, *Internationale Finanzkontrollen und ihre politischen Grenzen*, pp. 36 ff.; N. Kaasik, *Le Contrôle en droit international* (Paris, 1933), pp. 103, 355; L. Dupuis, *Le Contrôle financier de la dette publique Ottomane* (Paris, 1908), p. 9. When financial control was imposed upon Egypt in 1876, a number of governments at first shared in the control. II, 591 ff. On the other hand, the preponderant financial influence of France in Tunis and Morocco led to the establishment of French protectorates over these countries.

5. II, 538, n. 46.

stability of the Bulgarian currency in which the loan was to be serviced, no modifications were to be made in the laws then in force regulating the fiduciary issue of the National Bank of Bulgaria and no more silver money was to be coined without the approval of a delegate of the bondholders.[6] The borrowing power of the Government of Morocco was in effect subjected to the control of a group of French banks with which the loan was contracted by a clause in the contract of the 1904 loan providing for the consent of the contractors before a certain portion of the customs duties could be pledged as security for future loans.[7] As a precautionary measure against governmental interference with the yield of customs revenues through individual exemptions and reductions, the Dutch banking house of Westendorp and Company, in its loan contract of 1888 with the Government of Santo Domingo, reserved to itself the right of consent to "privileges of any description whatsoever" which the Government might wish to grant in the matter of customs duties.[8] In view of the legal uncertainty of a governmental engagement to surrender certain rights of sovereignty to foreign private individuals or corporations, the promise on the part of a debtor government to subject certain administrative measures to the previous approval of its creditors has little practical value unless implemented by some legislative act making such control a part of the debtor's municipal law.

INSPECTION OF BOOKS

Holders of secured loans are sometimes accorded the right to inspect the books and accounts kept by the agencies in charge of the pledged revenues. This form of control is less conspicuous than the method of direct collection of revenues by agents of the bondholders and may prove no less effective; it is therefore preferred where national susceptibilities must be spared. The British minister in Mexico, instead of insisting on the collection of the customs duties in Mexican ports through British commissioners, was satisfied with the inspection of the customhouse books and papers by consuls and bondholders' representatives, believing that these agencies would exercise "the real *bona fide* powers of interventors, without outraging the national feelings."[9] The trustees of Peruvian loans, secured on the guano deposits of the country, were permitted to inspect the accounts and business documents of the private company to which a concession for the exploitation of guano had been granted.[10]

6. *Ibid.*
7. Art. 32.
8. II, 207.
9. II, 25, n. 29.
10. II, 125.

PARTICIPATION IN FINANCIAL AGENCIES

A more direct form of control consists in the participation of bond-holders in decisions of regular financial agencies of the debtor. Thus, Article 3 of the contract between the Government of Santo Domingo and the San Domingo Improvement Company of January 28, 1893, provided for the appointment and removal of customs officials by common accord between the Minister of Finance and a representative of the issuing house, the latter, at the same time, being made director of the régie or Caja de Recaudacion, an agency in charge of the collection of the customs dues of the Republic.[11] A British subject was appointed chairman of the Imperial Ottoman Bank of Turkey.[12] The State Bank of Morocco, set up by the Conference of Algeciras, was placed under foreign management.[13]

In view of the inseparable organizational ties between the central government and its regular instrumentalities, a more effective control is assured if the administration of the public debt is entrusted to independent boards or commissions in which the bondholders or their representatives take a more or less active part. In a note announcing the establishment of an autonomous administration of certain state monopolies the proceeds of which were pledged as security for foreign loans, the Serbian Government declared that this agency was to be "independent of political control and in part directly representative of the creditors."[14] It was composed of the Governor and Vice-Governor of the National Bank of Serbia, two Serbs appointed by the Minister of Finance, and two representatives of the bondholders.[15] The issuers of the 1922 loan to Peru were granted the controlling interest, as trustees for the bondholders, in the Guano Administration Company of Peru, a semiofficial agency for the administration and collection of the pledged guano revenues.[16] A Mexican law of October, 1830, provided that the customs revenues were to be delivered to two commissioners, one nomi-

11. II, 207, 214, n. 12. See also Dunn, *op. cit.,* p. 344: Bondholders demanded the right to appoint the collector-general of the customs.

12. II, 411.

13. Andréadès, *op. cit.,* p. 36; Strupp, *Intervention in Finanzfragen,* p. 23.

14. Simitch, *La Dette publique de la Serbie,* pp. 273–274; Andréadès, *op. cit.,* p. 74.

15. Publications Perm. Ct. Int. Just., Ser. C, No. 16–111, pp. 327–334, Art. 6; Andréadès, *op. cit.,* p. 73. The foreign members were legal representatives of the bondholders. The administration functioned like a private corporation. Foreign governments took official notice of the arrangement, thus vesting it with an international character.

16. II, 175, 183. See also the proposal by the Greek Government in 1897 to give the bondholders a majority representation on the administration council of the Greek Monopoly Co. II, 314.

nated by the Government, the other by the bondholders.[17] Under the terms of the trust agreement between the Republic of Bolivia and the Equitable Trust Company of New York of May 31, 1922, a permanent fiscal commission for the purpose of supervising and fiscalizing "the collection of all taxes, revenues and income of the Nation" was established. It consisted of three commissioners, to be appointed by the President of the Republic, two of them upon recommendation of the bankers.[18] The Portuguese Junta de Credito Publico, set up by a law of May, 1893, for the purpose of receiving and disbursing the revenues assigned as security for the consolidated bonds, was composed of five members, all Portuguese; one was named by the Chamber of Peers, one by the Chamber of Deputies, one by the Government, and two by the bondholders.[19] The contract for the Turkish loan of 1858 provided for the institution of a commission to superintend the collection of pledged revenues. Its president was the Minister of Finance; two of its members were named by the Government and two by the contractors of the loan. Obstruction of the work of the commission by the Porte soon caused the discontinuance of its activities.[20]

DIRECT COLLECTION OF SERVICE MONIES

The example of the last-named commission shows that financial control through representation on independent agencies may be rendered ineffective if the debtor government retains a preponderant influence in those commissions. Bondholders have an adequate safeguard against default only when they are granted administrative powers which enable them to receive the service monies directly within the debtor country without interference on the part of the government. Since it involves severe restrictions on sovereign rights and may even be considered by the debtor as incompatible with its national dignity,[21] such surrender of

17. II, 8, 13.

18. Margaret A. Marsh, *The Bankers in Bolivia* (New York, Vanguard Press, 1928), p. 156.

19. II, 373. See also *supra,* section on Secured Loans, p. 91, n. 58.

20. II, 397.

21. The Mexican Government in 1859 protested against a British demand for the appointment of agents of British bondholders at Mexican customhouses as being "in the greatest degree humiliating to their dignity." II, 19, n. 13; 25, n. 29. The institution of a régie for the collection of revenues, half the members of which were to be chosen by the bondholders, was declared by the Greek Government in 1895 to be "an attack upon its dignity." II, 312. See also Andréadès, *op. cit.,* pp. 60, 72; Levandis, *The Greek Foreign Debt and the Great Powers, 1821–1898,* pp. 85–86; Hyde, *Am. Jour. Int. Law,* XVI (1922), 539; Lippert, *Handbuch des internationalen Finanzrechts,* pp. 1035 f. Yet, to placate the bondholders, the Greek Finance Minister on June 14, 1895, proposed to Parliament the creation of

administrative functions to foreign individuals is not easily granted [22] and may assume various forms. The least painful method from the point of view of the debtor government seems to be the granting to bondholders of a concession to operate one of the public services of the country, the proceeds of which have been assigned to the service of the loan. Thus, the management of railroads and steamship lines, the construction and administration of a ship canal, the exploitation of guano deposits, the administration of salt, tobacco, and alcohol monopolies have been surrendered to foreign creditors who exercise their control either directly as concessionaries or through private corporations in which they hold the controlling interest.[23] While in all these cases the government still retains supervisory authority, it may go a step further and divest itself entirely of its public powers with respect to certain branches of its fiscal administration. A comparatively mild form of direct collection is the sale of customs certificates, tax stamps, or tobacco banderoles by the issuing bankers to the taxpayers or governmental agencies.[24] Under the terms of the 1902 loan the French Government notified Bulgaria of the appointment of a bondholders' delegate in Sofia thus emphasizing her readiness to lend diplomatic support to the bondholders' participation in the financial administration of Bulgaria.[25] More serious from the standpoint of the political independence of the debtor government is the collection of

---

a Greek public debt commission to administer the collection of certain revenues. Levandis, *op. cit.*, p. 84.

22. When the Sultan of Morocco, upon request by French bondholders, increased the powers of French financial controllers, opposition of the natives against the new measures caused serious disturbances. L.J., *Affaires du Maroc*, III, 1906–1907 (1907), Nos. 324 and 519. On the other hand, the turning over of customhouses or revenues to foreign financial agents was not always regarded as a hardship by Latin American governments. Santo Domingo's President Morales in 1904 welcomed such institution. II, 241.

23. II, 536, 543 (tobacco export monopoly to be formed under bondholders' control); II, 300, 309 (administration of salt, petroleum, matches, etc., monopolies through a company to be formed by the loan contractors); II, 31 ff. (offer by the Mexican Government to bondholders of a concession for the construction of a ship canal across the Isthmus of Tehuantepec); *The United States and Nicaragua: A Survey of the Relations from 1909 to 1932* (Dept. of State, Lat. Amer. Ser., No. 61, 1932), pp. 17–18; II, 110, 115–116, 137, 141, 142, 155, 161, 171, 174, 178, 183.

24. The following may be mentioned as examples: Honduras, *Corp. For. Bondh. Rep.*, No. 53 (1926), pp. 246–249 (sale of invoice stamps to exporters by the National City Bank of New York); Bulgaria, II, 538 (tobacco banderoles manufactured abroad and sent to the bondholders' delegate in Sofia who sold them to the Bulgarian Minister of Finance and remitted the proceeds to be applied to the service of loans); Salvador, loan contract of June 24, 1922, Art. 7, Dunn, *op. cit.*, pp. 222–247.

25. See II, 538.

public revenues by foreign agents on the spot, where direct contact with the nationals of the debtor country may cause frictions harmful to the smooth functioning of the debt service machinery. In view of such injurious effects, contrary to the very purpose for which it is created, financial control through some form of direct collection of revenues by agents of the bondholders has been resorted to only in exceptional cases.[26] Its chief example is the Ottoman Debt Council.

THE OTTOMAN DEBT COUNCIL

Even prior to its establishment in 1881, Turkey had experienced the institution of revenue collection by certain creditors under the terms of various loans.[27] The creation of the Ottoman Debt Council was the corollary of a comprehensive settlement between Turkey and her foreign creditors. It was embodied in the so-called Decree of Mouharrem which gave the debt adjustment its final form. Though issued as a municipal law, the decree was in the nature of a bilateral agreement between the Turkish Government and its foreign creditors.[28] The Council of Administration, as the Debt Council was officially called, was composed of representatives of the foreign bondholders; positions in the service of the Turkish Government or official connections with the military, consular, or diplomatic representations of foreign governments in Turkey were incompatible with membership in the Council. In its capacity as representative of the bondholders, the Council was charged with "the administration, collection, direct encashment, for the account of the bondholders and by means of its agents, of the revenues and other resources" ceded to it.[29] It organized its own revenue-collecting service

26. See II, 114, n. 12, 200, 240, 245. As to European controllers in Moroccan ports, see Andréadès, *op. cit.*, p. 36.

27. In 1879 a group of Constantinople bankers agreed to grant loans to the Turkish Government in exchange for a pledge of the customs of the harbor of Constantinople. They placed their own agents in the customhouses to collect the portion of the customs due to them. II, 429. Later the Turkish Government leased to the bankers for ten years the tax on spirits, the duty on stamps, the silk tithes of certain districts, and the fish tax of Constantinople. All these taxes were collected by the lessees. II, 430.

28. II, 451, 486; Andréadès, *op. cit.*, p. 52; Strupp, "L'Intervention en matière financière," *Rec. des Cours*, VIII (1925), p. 25; Donald C. Blaisdell, *European Financial Control in the Ottoman Empire* (New York, Columbia University Press, 1929), pp. 90, 102 f. From the fact that the decree was "communicated" by the Turkish Government to the powers signatories of the treaty of Berlin, a number of writers have concluded that the agreement was vested with an international sanction, entitling the powers to immediate intervention in case of a violation of its provisions. See *idem*, pp. 103 ff. The case has never become practical.

29. *Idem*, p. 95. The belief held by the Turks that the Council, although composed of representatives of European bondholders' syndicates possessing no offi-

which in 1881 employed over 3,000 agents.[30] Not satisfied, however, with collecting what the country was willing and able to pay, the Council endeavored to increase the yield of the revenues under its control by efficient administration and by improving the industries with which it was concerned. Thus, it took steps to combat phylloxera, developed an export trade in salt, and promoted better methods in agriculture.[31] The Council was so successful in its operations that the general credit standing of the Turkish Government profited from its measures. Also the security of foreign capital was increased, risks were reduced, and profits enhanced.[32] Turkey's changed political and territorial status under the treaty of Lausanne profoundly affected the debt administration. After years of protracted negotiations, an agreement to replace the decree of Mouharrem was reached between the Turkish Government and its foreign creditors in June, 1928, under the terms of which the Turkish Government regained full financial sovereignty. It took over completely the Debt Council from the administration and collection of the assigned revenues. The Council survived under the name of "Debt Council" (Council of the Repartitioned Public Debt of the former Ottoman Empire) but it was obliged to shift its seat to Paris and was reduced to little more than a trustee and transfer agency.[33] In 1940 the Council's remaining functions were taken over by the Turkish Government on the ground that, due to the war, the Council was no longer able to perform them. The matter soon ceased to have any practical importance, for in 1944 the Turkish Government redeemed the entire residue of its share of the Ottoman public debt.[34]

CONTROL BY PRIVATE AND PUBLIC AGENCIES (MIXED TYPE OF CONTROL)

Perhaps the best example of the mixed type of control where the burden was shared by bondholders and governments was the control

cial connection with their respective governments, was in fact the semiofficial agency of the European governments whose nationals composed it had no foundation in the facts. *Idem*, p. 181. The Council had a legal personality of its own and, therefore, became owner of the revenues collected by its agents. *De Neuflize* v. *Deutsche Bank et al.*, Franco-German Mixed Arbitral Tribunal, October 29, 1924, *Rec. des déc.*, IV, 794 (798). See also Andréadès, *op. cit.*, pp. 45 f.

30. Blaisdell, *op. cit.*, p. 1.

31. II, 466. See also Andréadès, *op. cit.*, p. 48.

32. Blaisdell, *op. cit.*, p. 152; II, 461.

33. *Corp. For. Bondh. Rep.*, No. 55 (1928), pp. 369 ff. See also Blaisdell, *op. cit.*, pp. 204 ff. A so-called "Bondholders Council" for the holders of loans other than the unified debt and the lottery bonds was abolished under the agreement of 1933. II, 512.

34. II, 515, 516.

instituted in Tunis in 1869.[35] Its organization reflects an attempt to strike a balance among the interests of the private investors, the debtor government, and the intervening foreign powers. The international control consisted of two commissions which functioned either separately or together. (1) The executive committee, a Franco-Tunisian organ, was composed of three members, two Tunisians and one French inspector-general of finances, the latter appointed by the French Ministry of Foreign Affairs. It was charged with the general financial administration of the regency. (2) The members of the commission of control were elected by the private holders of the Tunisian internal and external debt, among them two Italians, two Anglo-Maltese, and two French representatives. Its function was to supervise the activities of the executive committee whose decisions needed the approval of the commission of control before they could be carried into effect. The two agencies together formed the so-called "Financial Commission" which administered the customs duties, the market tax, and certain other revenues. The international control in Tunis ceased to exist when France, in 1881, established an outright protectorate over the country.

INTERNATIONAL GOVERNMENT CONTROL
CLASSIFICATION

The assumption of exclusive or at least preponderant control by foreign governments over the financial administration of the debtor marks the final stage in the evolution of financial intervention. The eminently political character of this institution accounts for the great variety of the forms of control, which defy reduction to a definite type. There is no single and uniform type of financial control; each case must be taken by itself. Says Andréadès: "One may say of international financial control what has been said of the protectorate: There are protectorates, but not one protectorate." [36] Respect for the political traditions of the debtor state may influence the nature and extent of the control.[37] The form adopted in a particular case is often expressive of political rivalries among powers having stakes in the debtor country concerned rather than the result of objective thought as to the methods best suited to serve the proposed end.[38] Despite great varieties, a classi-

35. Strupp, *Intervention in Finanzfragen*, pp. 16, 17, 19, 23; Andréadès, *op. cit.*, p. 35.

36. *Op. cit.*, pp. 5, 97; see also p. 12.

37. II, 321. Direct collection by the international control was out of the question in a highly democratic country like Greece; the task was therefore allocated to the Greek Société de Régie.

38. This is particularly obvious in the case of the Tunisian control of 1869. Andréadès, *op. cit.*, pp. 15, 16; see also II, 321 ff.: The inclusion of representatives

fication of the various forms of international government control is possible if the historical evolution of this institution and the geographical distribution of its major instances are considered.

Financial control through foreign governments was first developed during the second half of the nineteenth century by European nations with respect to certain North African and Balkan states where extraordinary indebtedness coupled with incompetent administration threatened to inflict heavy losses on foreign bondholders. The main characteristic of this so-called "European type" was the joint participation of several powers in the control; it was exercised either by one organ as representative of the intervening states, like the International Financial Commission in Greece, or by a number of agencies in which the bondholders as well as the debtor government had a voice, like the Tunisian control council. The "American type" of financial control was created by the United States for the purpose of administering the finances of certain Central American states; it was characterized by the fact that only one creditor nation, namely, the United States, was involved, a fact which made it possible to evolve a unified system of control applicable to all debtors alike. The most recent type was the control exercised by the League of Nations with respect to loans issued under its auspices after World War I to various smaller European nations.

THE EUROPEAN TYPE

Purpose. European financial control was initiated by concerted action of the principal European powers since the countries where the foreign intervention occurred, like Egypt and Greece, had long been the object of political rivalries among those powers. The primary purpose, therefore, of placing the financial administration of such a country under competent foreign supervision was the maintenance of the political status quo by collective action which would prevent the country from falling prey to one single foreign power and would preserve it as a political entity through the stabilization of its finances and the adoption of sound budgetary methods. This objective of pure power politics, together with the desire on the part of the intervening states to secure regular returns on the investments of their nationals, marks European financial control as an instrument primarily designed to safeguard the interests of the intervening states and their subjects; benefits accruing to the debtor were a welcome, but by no means essential, by-product of its operation.[39]

---

of Russia, Austria and Italy among the members of the International Financial Commission was attributable to political considerations, for hardly any of the Greek debt was held by citizens of those countries. Furthermore, Meyer Balding in Niemeyer's *Zeitschrift*, XXVI, 416.

39. Andréadès, *op. cit.*, p. 7.

Reasons. The immediate reasons for subjecting the financial administration of debtor countries to interference on the part of the great powers
of Europe varied. The establishment of foreign financial control in Tunis
in 1869 and in Egypt in 1880 was the result of defaults arising out of
gross mismanagement and financial extravagance on the part of the native
rulers; the countries whose nationals had been the principal victims of
these defaults succeeded in impressing upon the debtors the necessity
for a thorough reorganization of their finances under the guidance and
constant supervision of foreign governmental representatives, who not
only were to administer certain revenues of the controlled states but
were also to be accorded a decisive voice in the general fiscal policy of
the debtors in question.[40] In other instances, such as Morocco, 1902, and
Serbia, 1895, the institution of financial control became the very means
of avoiding bankruptcy. When these two countries needed new loans to
overcome their financial difficulties, they were able to place them on the
principal European money markets only after they had consented to
transfer part of their financial administration to certain independent
agencies under foreign governmental control.[41] An altogether different
case is that of the Greek control of 1898. It was established after the
Graeco-Turkish war of 1897 by the European Concert, which acted as
mediator between the belligerents. Impoverished by war and already in
default on the foreign debt, Greece was saddled with an indemnity liability which she could not possibly meet without outside financial help.
Upon the insistence of Germany, a clause was inserted in the peace
treaty between Turkey and Greece providing for the creation of an
international commission of representatives of the European powers
to administer Greek revenues for the benefit of existing creditors and to
assure the prompt payment of the war indemnity.[42]

Legal Bases. As regards the legal bases of the various financial controls, the Greek control of 1898 deserves special attention in view of the
fact that one of the parties to its creation, namely, Turkey, had no connection whatever with the proceedings. When the German Ambassador
at Constantinople first suggested the introduction into the peace preliminaries of a clause protecting the rights of the holders of Greek bonds

40. *Idem*, at pp. 15, 25.

41. Simitch, *op. cit.*, pp. 424–428; Andréadès, *op. cit.*, pp. 35, 72.

42. II, 313, 316; Andréadès, *op. cit.*, pp. 58, 61 ff.; Levandis, *op. cit.*, pp. 88 ff.;
Madden and Nadler, *op. cit.*, p. 343; see also *Die Grosse Politik der Europäischen
Kabinette, 1871–1914*, Vol. XII, Pt. II (Berlin, 1922–27), p. 431. A proposal
for a Greek Régie was rejected by the creditors in 1895; negotiations proceeded
and a tentative agreement was reached in February, 1897, allowing for foreign
participation in the régie, when the outbreak of the war with Turkey threw the
whole arrangement into limbo.

and providing for the establishment of an international commission of control, the majority of his colleagues objected on the ground that the question of control in Greece could not properly form the subject of a stipulation between Turkey and the powers.[43] Germany, on the other hand, maintained that, in order to achieve the evacuation of Greek territory by Turkish troops, Greece had to be provided with means to enable her to pay the war indemnity. The only way to do this was by establishing an international financial control.[44] Since the Greek Government, by invoking the mediation of the great powers in the conflict with Turkey, had placed the interests of Greece in the hands of the mediating powers, the latter—so Germany argued—had a right to impose upon Greece the principle as well as the mode of the proposed control without being obliged to ask the consent of the Greek Government.[45] In addition, the German Foreign Secretary pointed out that in view of the strongly expressed public opinion in Germany it would be impossible for any German Government to neglect the interests of holders of Greek bonds, many of whom were German.[46] The other mediating powers, Great Britain, France, Italy, Austria-Hungary, and Russia, finally acceded to the German proposal which in substance became Article 2 of the peace treaty of 1897.[47] While the principle of the international financial control thus rested on an international agreement, a Greek municipal law, namely, the law of control of March 10, 1898, regulated the specific powers and functions of the international commission.[48] It embodied in its provisions a plan elaborated by six delegates of the mediating powers for the settlement of the Greek debt and for the future control of Greek finances.[49] Even the liquidation law, however, was a sovereign act of Greece in appearance only. Article 38 provided that it could not be modi-

43. II, 313; Levandis, *op. cit.*, p. 93; see also *Parl. Pap.* (1898), CVII, Turkey No. 2 (1898), Correspondence Respecting the Negotiations for the Conclusion of Peace between Turkey and Greece Nos. 166, 175, 203. Andréadès, *op. cit.*, p. 61.

44. *Parl. Pap.*, Turkey No. 2 (1898), No. 184; Levandis, *op. cit.*, p. 94.

45. *Parl. Pap.*, Turkey No. 2 (1898), Nos. 277, 285.

46. *Parl. Pap.*, Turkey No. 2 (1898), Nos. 277, 275. See also No. 188.

47. II, 316; Levandis, *op. cit.*, p. 97. The clause reads: "Greece will pay to Turkey an indemnity of 4,000,000 Turkish pounds. The necessary arrangement, in order to facilitate the rapid payment of this indemnity, will be made with the consent of the mediating Powers in such a way as not to jeopardize the vested rights of the holders of the bonds of the Greek Government. To this purpose an international commission consisting of representatives of the mediating Powers will be established."

48. II, 317.

49. *Ibid.;* see also Strupp, *Intervention in Finanzfragen*, p. 18: The Act was "transformation of international law into Greek municipal law." Madden and Nadler, *op. cit.*, pp. 167, 170.

fied without the consent of the powers.[50] Thus, the final decision in all matters concerning the international control lay with the foreign powers.

A similar picture is presented by the procedure adopted by the European Concert in establishing financial control over Egypt. The first step consisted in coördinating the views of the five European powers—Great Britain, France, Germany, Austria-Hungary, and Italy—with respect to the reorganization of the Egyptian finances by means of an international convention. On March 31, 1880, the five powers agreed upon the appointment of a "commission of liquidation" which was to be sent to Egypt to investigate the situation on the spot and to submit proposals for a final settlement. The contracting parties undertook to accept in advance and without reservation the conclusions which the commission might reach in the course of their investigation.[51] Next came the transformation of the international agreement into Egyptian municipal law by the Khedivial decree of March 31, 1880, which authorized the functioning of the commission on Egyptian territory.[52] The recommendations of the commission finally were included in the law of liquidation of July 17, 1880; the Caisse de la Dette Publique lost its private character and became an independent international organ.[53] The law, though promulgated by the Khedive, was in fact an international instrument; it was binding upon Egypt as well as upon the powers with respect to its subject matter, namely, the readjustment and administration of Egyptian finances.[54] Its subsequent modifications were all the result of previous agreements among the controlling powers.[55]

In other instances of financial control of the European type, the international legal foundation was less clear or was altogether lacking. The reason for the absence of specific international agreements among the creditor states prior to the establishment of the control was usually a desire on the part of the powers to spare the susceptibilities of the debtor nation involved. Thus, the Autonomous Monopoly Administration in Serbia rested entirely on Serbian municipal law. Its creation, however, was notified to the powers whose nationals were holders of Serbian bonds, and the powers took official note of the fact. In addition, the Serbian

50. II, 317.

51. II, 600. Kaufmann, *Das internationale Recht der egyptischen Staatsschuld*, pp. 76 ff.

52. II, 600. Kaufmann, *op. cit.*, p. 76.

53. Andréadès, *op. cit.*, p. 27; Kaufmann, *op. cit.*, p. 138.

54. Strupp, *Intervention in Finanzfragen*, p. 18; Brodbeck, *op. cit.*, pp. 9 ff.; Kaufmann, *op. cit.*, p. 79. The passage of the law was notified to other powers, like the United States and Russia, who declared their assent by formal diplomatic act.

55. Kaufmann, *op. cit.*, pp. 102 ff.; II, 618, 620.

Government informed the French Government that it considered the conversion law of 1895, in which the rights of the bondholders had been defined, as fully binding as any contract of international public or private law.[56] The "legal" basis of the Tunisian control was a decree issued by the Bey at the request of the French Government while a French man-of-war was moored in the roadstead of Tunis.[57] France's control over Moroccan finances resulted from her treaty of protectorate with the Sherifian state.[58]

Organs. The organs of financial control of the European type were, as pointed out above, international commissions representing the controlling powers and charged with the administration of the finances of the debtor. No uniform type of international organ for the performance of such task, however, was developed; neither the composition of the various commissions nor their functions were alike. The most simple as regards its general legal character was the type represented by the international commission of control for Greece.[59] Its six members were representatives of the foreign powers; it was the common organ of the signatories of the treaty of 1898.[60] Although their nomination was notified to the Greek Government, the commissioners stood in no legal relationship whatever to the latter. A Greek official was allowed to attend the meetings of the commission in an advisory capacity. The members of the commission enjoyed the same rights as the staffs of the various legations accredited to Greece. The commission appointed and dismissed its own executive agents who, in the exercise of their functions, enjoyed the protection accorded to officials of the state. It decided by the majority of votes—a remarkable deviation from the rule of unanimity otherwise prevalent in international organizations.[61] The duties assigned to the commission were threefold. (1) It was the legal representative of foreign bondholders in Greece and exercised rights and privileges granted them under the terms of various loans, e.g., the right to demand payment in

56. Publications of Perm. Ct. Int. Just., Ser. C, No. 16–III, p. 335; Andréadès, *op. cit.*, p. 74.

57. Strupp, *Intervention in Finanzfragen*, p. 22; Andréadès, *op. cit.*, p. 15.

58. See *Laurens and Société Marseillaise de Crédit* v. *Government of Morocco and Maspero*. France, Court of Cassation, November 20, 1934. Lauterpacht, *Annual Digest of International Law Cases, 1933–34* (London, 1940), p. 171.

59. See the Greek law of control of March 10, 1898, *Brit. and For. St. Pap.*, XC, 403 ff. For a detailed description of the organization and functions of the Greek financial control, see Murat, "Le Contrôle international sur les finances de l'Egypte, de la Grèce, et de la Turkie" (Thèse, Paris, 1899), pp. 101 ff.; see also Andréadès, *op. cit.*, pp. 62 ff.; Levandis, *op. cit.*, pp. 102 ff.; II, 320 ff.; Strupp, *Intervention in Finanzfragen*, pp. 17 ff.

60. *Idem*, p. 18; Levandis, *op. cit.*, p. 105.

61. Oppenheim-Lauterpacht, *op. cit.*, I, 227.

gold. (2) It administered, through the medium of the Greek Société de Régie, the revenues assigned to the service of the public debt, namely, the state monopolies (salt, petroleum, matches, playing cards, cigarette paper, Naxos emery), the stamp and tobacco taxes, and the customs duties collected at the Port of Piraeus. (3) It supervised the public services which produced the assigned revenues. In this capacity it received periodical and detailed reports from the administrative agencies in charge of those services; it could demand the removal of officials whose conduct gave rise to justified complaints.[62]

Altogether different in legal nature as well as in the scope of its functions was the international organ instituted for the control of the finances of Egypt, namely, the Caisse de la Dette Publique.[63] While the Greek commission of control was the representative organ of the controlling powers and, therefore, subject in all its actions to their will, the Caisse enjoyed a position of complete independence both from the foreign states and the Egyptian Government. This freedom from outside interference was the result of a unique procedure in appointing and removing the members of the Caisse. The foreign commissioners were designated by their respective governments and nominated by the Khedive; they became thereby Egyptian state functionaries. However, neither the Khedive nor the controlling powers could, by unilateral action, remove a commissioner from office before the termination of the statutory five-year period of his appointment. The necessity of concurrence by the two parties with regard to his removal afforded the individual commissioner a position of independence both from the debtor government and from political pressure of his home state.[64] The Caisse therefore was characterized as an international organ with a legal personality of its own.[65] Professor Kaufmann, whose writings on the subject are authoritative, has likened it to a trustee in bankruptcy. He says:

A certain independence of the trustee in bankruptcy both from the creditors and the debtor is a necessary prerequisite for the performance of his task which consists in looking after the interests of both parties alike . . . . The Caisse is able to fulfill its double function [of protecting the debtor

62. See Politis, "Le Contrôle international sur les finances helléniques et ses premiers résultats (1898–1901)," *Rev. Générale*, IX (1902), 5. In 1937 the international financial commission protested against the promulgation of the Greek decree-law of March 31, 1937, regarding the modification of alcohol taxation without the previous consent of the commission as required by Article 38 of the law of 1898. *Corp. For. Bondh. Rep.*, No. 66 (1939), p. 300.

63. See Murat, *op. cit.*, pp. 58 ff.; Strupp, *Intervention in Finanzfragen*, p. 18; Andréadès, *op. cit.*, pp. 26 ff.; Kaufmann, *op. cit.*, pp. 135 ff.

64. Murat, *op. cit.*, p. 60; Strupp, *Intervention in Finanzfragen*, p. 18.

65. *Idem*, p. 14; Kaufmann, *op. cit.*, p. 137, n. 4.

State as well as the creditors] because it is organized in such a fashion as to constitute an organ independent of both interested parties.[66]

The scope of its duties exceeded that of the Greek commission of control. While it shared with the latter the task of representing the bondholders in their rights against the debtor government and of administering the revenues assigned to the service of the public debt, the Caisse, in addition, took an active part in the general fiscal administration of the debtor country. The raising of new loans and alterations in the laws governing the collection of the hypothecated revenues required the previous consent of the Caisse. Disputes between the Egyptian Government and the administration of railroads, telegraphs, and the port of Alexandria with regard to the question whether or not an expenditure should be considered as ordinary or extraordinary to be referred to the Caisse, whose decision was binding upon the parties. As the result of political changes, the Caisse was abolished by agreement between the British and Egyptian governments of July 17, 1940.[67] Sums designed to be paid on foreign bonds were in future to be deposited (one half three months in advance of the due dates) in a "special account" with the National Bank of Egypt, which was to effect the actual debt service.

Summary. International government control of the European type has on the whole been successful in that it has benefited debtor and creditors alike. Judged by their practical results, no definite conclusion can be reached as to whether control through an independent commission, endowed with an international legal personality of its own, as in the case of Egypt, is to be preferred to the Greek type where the control organ was the direct representative of the intervening powers. While the latter method guaranteed the prompt and efficient execution of the wishes of the controlling states and, therefore, seemed to be preferable from the bondholders' point of view, the purpose of financial control, to secure both the debtor's and the creditors' interests, appeared to be more appropriately served by an organ independent of both interested parties. In view of the political nature of the institution, the particular circumstances of each case rather than theoretical preferences ultimately determine the choice of the more appropriate method.[68]

66. *Idem,* p. 137; Kaufmann, *Les Commissaires de la dette publique egyptienne et le droit international* (Cairo, 1896), pp. 6 ff., 20 ff., 25; see also Strupp, *Intervention in Finanzfragen,* pp. 14 f.; Andréadès, *op. cit.,* p. 27.

67. II, 631.

68. See Andréadès, *op. cit.,* pp. 15 ff.; Strupp, *Intervention in Finanzfragen,* pp. 21 ff.

THE AMERICAN TYPE

Reasons. The establishment of financial controls in the western hemisphere was an immediate outgrowth of the Monroe Doctrine. Excessive borrowing of Central American and Caribbean republics on European money markets led to defaults and brought close to American shores the menace of intervention by European governments for the purpose of protecting the investments of their nationals. This situation caused considerable alarm in the United States. In his message to the Senate of February 15, 1905, President Roosevelt declared that "under the Monroe doctrine, the United States can not see any European power seize and permanently occupy the territory of one of these Republics." [69] He added, however, that "those who profit by the Monroe doctrine must accept certain responsibilities along with the rights it confers." In other words, the United States felt a moral obligation to prevent American republics from defaulting on their bonds, thus eliminating a source of legitimate grievances on the part of European bondholders and their governments. The means to achieve this end was the institution of financial control over certain American debtor nations.[70]

Methods of Control. Fiscal readjustment in the debtor countries where some measure of financial control by the United States was imposed necessitated, in most instances, the flotation of a new foreign loan. The customs receipts, constituting as a rule the debtor's principal revenues, were the standard security pledge for the service of the loan. The customs administration was placed under the control of authorities closely associated with the United States Government, who received the revenues and applied them to the payment of interest and sinking fund. In addition, there were in some cases control over customs rates (usually in the form of a veto power),[71] supervision of internal revenues,[72] public debt limitations,[73] and supervision of some part of the expenditure of public monies.[74]

69. Moore, *Digest of International Law*, VI, 518; see also *Am. Jour. Int. Law*, V (1911), 1051.

70. For a detailed account of American financial intervention in Latin America, see Angell, *Financial Foreign Policy of the United States: A Report to the Second International Studies Conference on the State and Economic Life, London, May 29 to June 2, 1933;* D. G. Munro, *The Latin American Republics* (New York, D. Appleton-Century, 1942), pp. 588 ff.

71. In Santo Domingo, Haiti, Nicaragua, Liberia. Angell, *op. cit.*, pp. 36 f., 65 f.

72. In Haiti, Nicaragua, Liberia. *Ibid.*

73. In Cuba, Santo Domingo, Haiti, Liberia. *Ibid.;* see also *For. Aff.*, 1913, p. 466, note of the Secretary of State to the Secretary of War of March 10, 1913; B. H. Williams, *op. cit.*, pp. 56, 200.

74. In Cuba, Haiti, Nicaragua, Panama, Liberia. Angell, *loc. cit.*

In the appointment of the authorities in charge of the financial control, a varying degree of influence on the part of the United States Government manifested itself. Under the Dominican treaty (article 1) the general receiver of customs and his assistants and other employees of the receivership were appointed outright by the President of the United States.[75] Under the terms of the unratified Honduran and Nicaraguan treaties (article 4), the fiscal agent of the loan was to prepare a list of persons, which, after approval by the President of the United States, was to be presented to the other contracting government, and one of the persons on the list appointed collector general of the customs by the government whose customs were to be collected and administered.[76] The legal significance of the difference between these two modes of appointment has been stated by Mr. Finch as follows: [77]

. . . when the customs officials are appointed by the President of the United States, such appointment constitutes them American officials; but when Honduras and Nicaragua do the appointing, albeit their choice is confined to a list which has been approved by the President of the United States, the appointees bear Honduranean and Nicaraguan commissions and are therefore Honduranean and Nicaraguan and not American officials.

Under the treaty of 1916 with Haiti, an American receiver-general of customs and a financial adviser were set up; five treaty services were established and some two hundred Americans were placed in the administration.[78] In 1922 a high commissioner was appointed to supervise and coördinate the administrative work. Under the influence of the good neighbor policy developed by President Roosevelt after 1933, the financial control over Haiti was the first to be modified. By the agreement of August 7, 1933, there was substituted in the place of the receiver general and the financial adviser an American fiscal representative to collect the customs revenues in behalf of Haiti's creditors rather than of the United States.[79] The customs receivership of Santo Domingo was abolished by the convention between the United States and the Dominican Republic of September 27, 1940,[80] under which the two governments agreed to name a bank as sole depository of the debt service charges and

75. II, 259, 263; Angell, *op. cit.*, p. 22 ff.; *Corp. For. Bondh. Rep.*, No. 64 (1937), pp. 479, 482, 484.

76. *Am. Jour. Int. Law*, V (1911), 1047 ff.

77. *Idem*, p. 1048.

78. Angell, *op. cit.*, p. 26.

79. Madden, Nadler, and Sauvain, *America's Experience as a Creditor Nation*, p. 272; Gantenbein, *Financial Questions in United States Foreign Policy*, p. 192, n.; Ludwell Lee Montague, *Haiti and the United States, 1714–1938* (Durham, N.C., Duke University Press, 1940), pp. 274–276.

80. II, 277 ff. Text of the agreement and exchange of notes in United States Dept. of State *Treaty Series*, No. 965 (1941).

an official to act in the bank as the representative of the bondholders. A year later the receivership of the Haitian customs was also terminated [81] and replaced by an arrangement similar to that instituted for the Dominican Republic.[82]

THE LEAGUE OF NATIONS TYPE

General Character. The various financial controls set up during the postwar period by the League of Nations over some of the minor European states differ in two fundamental respects from the earlier European and American types of control. While international financial control in prewar Europe and in the Americas was primarily designed to protect existing bondholders and other investors, the principal purpose of the control measures instituted by the League of Nations was the reorganization of the economic life and the stabilization of the currency of certain countries which had suffered from the war, as the necessary prerequisite for the flotation of new foreign loans which those countries would have been unable to raise without the support of powerful external authority.[83] The League system excluded the possibility of the control's

81. U.S.–Haitian agreement signed September 13, 1941. *Exec. Agree. Ser.* 220.

82. In the light of the above developments nothing more than mere historical interest can be attached to a proposal submitted in 1927 to the American Institute of International Law by Ruiz Moreno of Argentina with respect to a uniform type of financial coöperation to be applied in all cases where American sovereign states found themselves under the necessity of suspending, wholly or in part, the service of their public debts. Draft convention submitted by Isidoro Ruiz Moreno to the American Institute of International Law, Session of Montevideo, March, 1927. See Isidoro Ruiz Moreno, *Economia y finanzas contemporaneas,* pp. 223 f. In case of financial distress, the debtor state was to request the coöperation of the other states of the American continent whose representatives were to meet with those of the bondholders and of the debtor state in the capital of the latter for the purpose of establishing the bases of the future debt service and the payment of arrears. The agreement was to determine among other matters the form of financial control to be instituted over the debtor state by an international commission and the powers of the latter, the pledges that the debtor state was to be required to give, and the financial reforms to be introduced as part of the reconstruction program. The international financial control, as a rule, was to be collective and was to be organized in such a way as not to affect the political independence or territorial integrity of the controlled states. None of the controlling powers was to enjoy special privileges and favors which may compromise that independence or integrity.

83. Brodbeck, *op. cit.,* pp. 14 ff.; II, pp. 348, 552; League Loans Committee, *First Annual Report,* May, 1933, p. 6; Memorial from the League Loans Committee (London) to the Council of the League of Nations, July 18, 1932, *idem,* p. 22; Madden and Nadler, *op. cit.,* pp. 339 f.; Oppenheim-Lauterpacht, *op. cit.,* I, 256, n. See generally L. of N. Doc. F. 1696 (1944), *The League of Nations Reconstruction Schemes in the Inter-War Period.*

being used as an instrument for the political purposes of a single power or a group of powers. The League's control was therefore essentially financial rather than political in character.[84] It must be noted that all of the controlled states were themselves members of the collective body in whose name and under whose authority the control was exercised.

Establishment and Methods of Control. The League type of control was first established over Austria by the so-called Geneva protocols signed on October 4, 1922, between the British, French, Italian, Czechoslovakian, and Austrian governments.[85] It is significant that the initiative was taken by the state in need of financial assistance. Its appeal to the League, not a request on the part of the controlling body, furnished the legal basis for the League's action. The Austrian Chancellor himself, when he first apeared before the Council of the League, offered to accept control as a condition of assistance.[86] He became a member of the so-called Austrian committee to whom part of the preparatory work had been entrusted. Other aspects of the problem were dealt with by the financial and economic committees and the legal advisers of the League. The result of their investigations, which also extended to an examination of conditions on the spot, was a plan for an international loan from private sources with specific security on definite revenues, the setting up of a control mechanism, and a guaranty by certain of the powers, mainly Great Britain, France, Czechoslovakia, and Italy. Both the scheme for the financial reconstruction of the controlled state and the rules governing the organization and functions of the control authorities were embodied in a series of diplomatic instruments signed under the auspices of the League by the assisted state and those member states whose nationals contributed to the flotation of the loan. The participation of two groups, namely, the League of Nations and a smaller group consisting of states where the money was actually raised and which also undertook to guarantee service and redemption of the loan, was reflected in the organization of the control authority. It consisted of two organs: a commissioner-general appointed by and responsible to the Council of the League, and a committee of control of the governments guaranteeing the loan. The commissioner-general who was to reside in Vienna was charged to insure that the necessary reforms and economies in the ad-

84. Fischer Williams, *op. cit.*, pp. 386, 389. J. Saint Germès, *La Société des Nations et les emprunts internationaux* (Paris, 1931), p. 147.

85. See, for the text, Fischer Williams, *op. cit.*, p. 390, n. See also Plesch and Domke, *Die österreichische Völkerbundanleihe.* On the general subject of League controls, see L. of N. Doc., 11 Econ. and Finan. 1930. 11.16. *Principles and Methods of Financial Reconstruction Work undertaken under the Auspices of the League of Nations.*

86. Fischer Williams, *op. cit.*, p. 386.

ministration of Austria were carried through; he also controlled the expenditure of the proceeds of the loan. His functions ceased in July, 1926, when the Financial Committee of the League assumed control over the expenditure of the balance of the loan.[87] The control committee was to protect the interests of the guaranteeing powers; it had the right to require from the commissioner-general periodic statements as to the progress of the reforms. In case of insufficiency of the mortgaged revenues it could demand the assignment of additional security. The control committee had no right to communicate directly with the Austrian Government; its suggestions and requests had to be addressed to the commissioner-general. Thus, the representative of the League "intervened between the Austrian Government and its creditors."[88] Special arbitral functions were assigned to the Council of the League. In the event of any difference as to the interpretation of the protocols and in case of abuse of the loan proceeds, the parties to the protocols could appeal to the Council, whose opinion and decisions they agreed to accept.[89] A similar organization was provided by the terms of the Austrian (consolidation) loan of 1933. The functions of the League were performed by a representative and an adviser to the Austrian National Bank, while the committee of control assumed the same duties with respect to the new loan which it exercised under the protocols of 1922.

Procedure and forms of control for the remaining League loans (none of which, however, carried foreign government guaranties) followed more or less closely the precedent set by the Austrian example. Under the terms of the state loan for Hungary of 1924, a commissioner-general of the League and a committee of control were appointed to supervise the budget. Both organs, however, acted only during a short period of reconstruction. They were replaced by trustees for the bondholders who were nominated by the League. In case the security for the loan fell into jeopardy, they had a right to require that the full control of the budget be reëstablished and the commissioner-general restored to power. The decision in such case rested with the Council of the League which acted by majority vote.

The control scheme in the case of the Greek Government refugee loan of 1924 differs from the other instances in two respects. (1) The service

87. League of Nations, *The Financial Reconstruction of Austria*, p. 276; Max Winkler, "The Investor and the League Loans," *For. Pol. Assn., Information Service*, IV, Special Supplement No. 2 (June, 1928), p. 18; *The Problem of International Investment*, pp. 231, 239.

88. Fischer Williams, *op. cit.*, pp. 389 f.

89. *Idem*, p. 389, n. 1, justly remarked that the task here assigned to the Council of the League was open to criticism as the Council was organized for political and administrative work rather than for the functions of a judicial tribunal.

of the loan was placed in the trusted hands of the International Financial Commission which since 1898 had been in control of the revenues assigned to meet the service of the Greek external debt. (2) The Greek Government had no direct power to dispose of the proceeds of the loan. The so-called "Greek Refugees Settlement Commission," a body international in its composition and independent of the Greek executive, was charged with the work of settlement and, for that purpose, received the proceeds of the loan.[90]

The central features of the League schemes for the economic and financial rehabilitation of war-impoverished countries were: (1) the institution of financial control upon request of the state to be assisted; (2) participation of the latter in the elaboration of the program of financial reconstruction; and (3) exercise of the control not by creditors or their governments but by organs representing the interests of the bondholders as well as those of the international community at large. These principles may yet afford some guidance for future foreign lending.

90. *Idem*, p. 406, described the general function of the Settlement Commission in the following terms: "This body corporate enters into financial operations and is utilised not only for giving a guarantee to the subscribers to a loan for the proper application of their money, but also in order to provide a security for the bonds and in effect to strengthen the financial position as a borrower of the Greek Government itself."

PART VI

Readjustment of Governmental Defaults

Section XIX

READJUSTMENT
OF GOVERNMENTAL DEFAULTS

PREVIOUS sections have discussed the nature and relative efficacy of the various means by which holders of foreign government bonds have sought to protect their rights in the face of threatened or actual failure of the debtor to perform his contractual duties. It has been seen that bondholders can rarely, if ever, bring suit against a defaulting foreign state, that diplomatic support has not always been available to them, and that the imposition of financial control, except in a comparatively mild form, requires governmental action which has been taken in comparatively few cases and then, generally speaking, only when consideration for bondholders' contractual rights was accompanied by political motives.[1] For the adjustment of their difficulties with foreign governmental debtors, bondholders have had to depend mainly on the activities of their protective committees. Through negotiations conducted by the latter, a distressed debtor state has usually had to be induced to continue or resume payments by some alleviation of its foreign debt burden.

DEFINITION

As the term indicates, the readjustment or settlement of public debts is essentially a procedure for terminating a default by substituting new terms for the existing obligation which, for one reason or another, can no longer be fulfilled. In the negotiation of a readjustment plan the debtor government seeks to place its indebtedness on a basis more in accord with its capacity to pay and with changed economic and possibly political conditions, and the creditor tries to obtain as favorable a settlement as he can, including guaranties, against a recurrence of the default.[2] The settlement has in some instances been effected in conjunction with

1. *Supra,* pp. 277 ff.
2. Some readjustments have provided for an eventual return to the terms of the original contract.

the establishment of foreign financial control through which an attempt has been made to reorganize the financial practices of the debtor state.[3]

REASONS FOR READJUSTMENT

Defaulting governments have usually been impelled to negotiate a settlement with their creditors mainly because, until this was accomplished, they could not obtain new loans which they urgently needed for financial readjustment or economic development.[4]

UNILATERAL AND NEGOTIATED SETTLEMENTS

Readjustment plans have not always been the outcome of negotiations between the defaulting debtor and representatives of the bondholders acting with or without the support of their governments.[5] Such plans have sometimes been imposed on the bondholders by unilateral action of the debtor.

"Readjusting" a debt by unilateral action means that the debtor, without consulting the bondholders or their representatives, draws up a plan modifying the original contract as to service, and offers it to the bondholders for "acceptance," the understanding being that those who refuse the offer will receive no payment whatsoever.[6] The plan has usually

3. As, for example, in the financial interventions in Egypt, Greece, and Morocco.

4. However, to promote the political aims embodied in the good neighbor policy, the United States made loans, through the Export-Import Bank, to Latin American countries while they were still in default on their old foreign bond indebtedness. "The willingness of the issuer to negotiate with representatives of the bondholders and eventually to agree to readjust its default generally has two motivations: a desire to restore the prestige and reputation of the nation and a desire to borrow more money." SEC, *Rep.*, Pt. V, pp. 31 ff. In 1879 political as well as financial motives impelled Greece to readjust the 1824–25 revolutionary loans. II, 285. Forced by the closing of the London money market, the Portuguese Government in December, 1855, effected a settlement with the British bondholders. A new issue of the Government was then admitted to the exchange for quotation. II, 364; see also Manes, *Staatsbankrotte*, p. 78. The settlement of the 1822–25 defaults enabled Peru to borrow abroad again. II, 112.

5. Numerous examples of government support to their nationals in the negotiation of a settlement with a defaulting foreign state may be found *supra*, pp. 244–248.

6. "The mechanics involved in the consummation of a unilateral plan are essentially simple. The obligor nation enacts a decree or makes a formal pronouncement that debt service is scaled to the amounts specified by the debtor or that the original covenants of the loan are otherwise modified. The debtor nation will further provide that a bondholder may accept the new arrangement by cashing his coupon at the reduced rate or by otherwise accepting the treatment accorded

been made effective by the issuance of a municipal decree. While numerous individual loans have thus been extracontractually converted into new issues at reduced rates of interest,[7] instances where the whole external indebtedness of a government has been readjusted unilaterally by legislative action of the debtor are comparatively rare. A recent and striking example of such unilateral readjustment of a country's external debt was the Chilean decree law No. 5580 of January 31, 1935.[8] It established a plan for the service of Chile's external bonds, interest and amortization, in substitution for the service arrangement originally stipulated. Its principal features were: (1) the assignment to the debt service of certain levies from the nitrate and copper industry, namely, governmental revenues especially suited for this purpose because they produce most of the country's foreign exchange needed for actual payment and because they are free from the political vicissitudes ordinarily affecting the finances of governments; (2) the division of these revenues into two equal parts, one to be utilized for the service, the other for the retirement of the bonds; (3) the execution of the plan by an independent agency, the "Autonomous Institute for the Amortization of the Public Debt of the Republic of Chile." [9] A further provision in the law to the effect that acceptance of the payment of a coupon in the manner established by the plan shall extinguish the original responsibility of the debtor was strongly protested by bondholders' organizations, and their repeated warnings against accepting the plan caused the Chilean Government to issue, on June 11, 1938, a decree setting forth that Law No. 5580 in no wise purported to affect or modify the original obligation of the bonds insofar as the capital owed was concerned but merely established a new service ar-

him under the plan. This acceptance is at most one of form only as the plan proposed by the government either explicitly or impliedly states that the alternative to the reduced bond service specified will be no payment whatsoever. It is a take-it or leave-it proposition." SEC, *Rep.*, Pt. V, p. 34.

7. The conversion by the Ecuadorean Government of the government debt into railway bonds was forced upon bondholders by the retention of pledged revenues. The 6% internal debt of Venezuela (largely held in Europe, particularly in France) was by Venezuelan decree of January, 1906, converted into 3% internal bonds. *Corp. For. Bondh. Rep.*, No. 33 (1905–06), pp. 437–438. The 1870 and 1872 bonds of Peru were compulsorily converted. II, 124.

8. English translation of the decree in *For. Bondh. Prot. Coun. Rep.*, 1936, p. 230; also SEC, *Rep.*, Pt. V, p. 463, n. 862.

9. The "Autonomous Institute" was set up by the Chilean decree of September 9, 1932. Text in *For. Bondh. Prot. Coun. Rep.*, 1935, p. 103. By placing the revenues and the payment of interest and amortization in the hands of an autonomous organization, creditors "are given the fullest possible assurance and guaranty of the proper operation of the plan." Memorandum of the Chilean Special Financial Commission with Respect to Law No. 5580, *For. Bondh. Prot. Coun. Rep.*, 1935, pp. 38 ff.

rangement in lieu of the old one.[10] Law No. 5580 served, unaltered, as the basis for the payment of Chile's external obligations until March, 1948, when an agreement was concluded with representatives of the bondholders, for the institution of a new debt settlement plan.[11]

While doubts regarding the legal validity of a unilateral debt settlement may be overcome by the subsequent assent of the bondholders— usually expressed by the act of cashing coupons at the reduced rate— the practical wisdom of this method of adjustment, from the point of view of the debtor, remains questionable. The main purpose of the debtor in readjusting a default is, after all, to reëstablish confidence in its financial integrity, and it is manifest that a settlement negotiated on the basis of a free exchange of views by both parties will produce better and more stable results than a plan imposed by unilateral action. Or, in the words of the Foreign Bondholders Protective Council when urging the Chilean Government to discuss its proposed debt settlement with representatives of the bondholders: [12]

Experience indicates that joint examination and discussion between bondholders and Government frequently brings about by mutual accommodation advantages to each without undue detriment or hardship to either. It would be most unfortunate if anything should be done which would justify the bondholders in feeling that their legitimate rights and interests had been ignored and sacrificed without full opportunity to present their views.

It is, of course, conceivable that a debtor government is perfectly willing to settle its default and arrange new terms by discussing them with its foreign creditors but is prevented from doing so by circumstances beyond its control. Thus, Turkey, while agreeing in principle to settle the default of 1875 through negotiations with her creditors, had to give up this plan because of the wars with her Balkan satellites and with Russia during the following years when she was fighting for her very existence.[13] In

10. As the result of negotiations between the Foreign Bondholders Protective Council and the Chilean Government, the latter on June 11, 1938, published Decree No. 1730, clarifying the scope of Law No. 5580. Following the issuance of this decree, the Chilean Government applied for listing of the assented bonds on the New York Stock Exchange, which was accorded in October, 1938. *For. Bondh. Prot. Coun. Rep.*, 1938, pp. 13 ff.; see also *Corp. For. Bondh. Rep.*, No. 65 (1938), p. 31.

11. See, for a detailed history of the Chilean debt adjustment through unilateral action, SEC, *Rep.*, Pt. V, pp. 462 ff. Details of the new plan are given in *Corp. For. Bondh. Rep.*, No. 75 (1948), pp. 24–28.

12. Telegram sent by the Council to the Chilean Minister of Finance, October 31, 1934, *For. Bondh. Prot. Coun. Rep.*, 1934, p. 56c. See also, for a similar statement, the telegram sent by the Council on August 22, 1934, to the President of Colombia, *idem*, p. 94.

13. II, 418, 421.

the absence of special circumstances of this kind, however, the method best suited for settling a default situation to the mutual benefit of all parties involved remains the exchange of views by discussion and negotiation, and experience shows that it has actually been followed in the great majority of all debt settlements.

PRELIMINARY EXAMINATION OF THE DEBTOR'S POSITION

Since the primary objective of a debt settlement is the adjustment of the payments to the "actual position of the debtor," [14] the first step in any such procedure should be a preliminary investigation into the economic and financial conditions of the debtor country in order to ascertain what it can reasonably be expected to pay, both as regards the revenues of the government and its capacity to transfer them into foreign currency. Careful investigations of this kind have sometimes been made. Thus in the case of the financial reorganization of Egypt by the great powers of Europe a commission was sent to Egypt to investigate the situation on the spot and to submit proposals which the contracting powers undertook to accept in advance.[15] Again, when countries which had obtained League loans seemed likely to default or had actually defaulted, the Council of the League was in many instances called upon to investigate and report on the local economic and financial situation in order to provide both debtor and creditor with an objective guide in the negotiation of new terms of debt service.[16] Where such first-hand investigation is not feasible, it would seem desirable for the creditors, as was done by the holders of Brazilian bonds in the United States and on the Continent of Europe prior to the formal opening of negotiations with the defaulting debtor government in 1937, to arrive at an estimate of the

14. League Loans Committee, *Second Annual Report,* June, 1934, p. 9.

15. II, 606. The commission went so far as to reduce a payment made to Halim Pasha, uncle of the Khedive, from £60,000 to £15,000. The German representative objected to this procedure with the warning that the powers, which had agreed in advance to accept the law of liquidation, might refuse to accept such a confiscation or denial of justice and that the matter should have been referred to the mixed courts for decision.

16. The services which the Financial Committee may perform in this respect are described by the League Loans Committee in its *Second Annual Report,* June, 1934, p. 7, as follows: "The Financial Committee examine the situation of the debtor countries; they establish the facts of the debtor's position objectively and afford a sound basis on which both creditors and debtors can judge the degree of temporary relief which the debtor requires. This is clearly more satisfactory to all parties than if the creditors were compelled to rely solely on ex-parte statements by the debtor."

debtor's paying capacity and to reach an agreement among themselves as to the policy to be adopted in the negotiations.[17] If the debtor's will to honor his obligations is obviously lacking or cannot be ascertained as a guiding element in judging the fairness of his request for relief, some objective criteria for the determination of his paying capacity must be resorted to. They may be found in disinterested studies of the economic situation of the debtor country by such bodies as the League of Nations;[18] sometimes statistics and information available from the debtor government's own agencies may present facts which are at variance with the picture drawn by the debtor for the purpose of proving his inability to fulfill his external obligations.[19] In general, the particular situation of the debtor at the time of the settlement, as judged from all the circumstances, will furnish the proper clue for a fair estimate of what the debtor can reasonably be expected to pay.[20] Such a situation will hardly remain stable; it may grow worse or better. If worse, the debtor will demand a revision of the debt settlement in accordance with the depressed state of his economy. If better, the benefit of revision will be asked by the bondholders. In fact, they have frequently maintained their right to share, and the debtor's corresponding duty to let them participate, in the latter's increased prosperity.[21] Sometimes this right is expressly recognized in

17. *Corp. For. Bondh. Rep.*, No. 64 (1937), p. 29.

18. Reference to such studies was usually made by remarks such as: "The bondholders' representatives have carefully examined the situation of the debtor country in the light of information which has been made available by the League of Nations." League Loans Committee, *Third Annual Report*, June, 1935, p. 38. (Bulgaria); *Fifth Annual Report*, September, 1937, pp. 42 (Bulgaria), 61 (Hungary); *Corp. For. Bondh. Rep.*, No. 65 (1938), p. 24 (Bulgaria).

19. See *idem*, No. 64 (1937), p. 44. The Greek delegation "did not accept the interpretation of various figures put forward by the Council, which figures incidentally were taken from official Greek sources and also refused to admit certain official statements made by the Minister of Finance and the Department of Agriculture."

20. See statement of March 20, 1939, by the Foreign Bondholders Protective Council to the holders of Costa Rican dollar bonds, *For. Bondh. Prot. Coun. Rep.*, 1938, p. 335. Also *Corp. For. Bondh. Rep.*, No. 66 (1939), p. 26. *Idem*, p. 39. League Loans Committee, *Fourth Annual Report*, August, 1936, p. 16. *Corp. For. Bondh. Rep.*, No. 64 (1937), pp. 43, 52 f. *Idem*, No. 65 (1938), pp. 56 f. *For. Bondh. Prot. Coun. Rep.*, 1937, p. 229; *Corp. For. Bondh. Rep.*, No. 65 (1938), pp. 37, 59. *Idem*, p. 40.

21. See Sir Austen Chamberlain's article on "The League Loans" in League Loans Committee, *Second Annual Report*, June, 1934, p. 24. See, furthermore, the exchange of letters between the Greek Finance Minister and the League Loans Committee on the question of Greece's capacity to pay 50% of interest due instead of 35% as proposed by Greece. *Third Annual Report*, June, 1935, pp. 43 ff. See also *Fourth Annual Report*, August, 1936, pp. 9 ff. Also p. 42, reply of Sir

the settlement through a stipulation entitling the bondholders to increased payments in case conditions improve.[22]

On occasion it has been clear that a foreign debt settlement was not likely to endure unless it was made part of a scheme for readjusting the entire indebtedness of a country, domestic as well as foreign.[23]

SCOPE OF THE SETTLEMENT

Debtor governments have sometimes, but not always with success, tried to limit the scope of the negotiations. During the negotiations between the Greek Government and bondholders' organizations in London in 1937, the Greek delegation insisted that their offer for the resumption of the debt service constituted the maximum obligation Greece was prepared to assume and that it was made on the understanding that further discussions should take place within the limits thus imposed. The Council of Foreign Bondholders and the League Loans Committee thereupon

---

Austen Chamberlain to the Greek Finance Minister, February 18, 1935. *Sixth Annual Report,* June, 1938, p. 8. *Corp. For. Bondh. Rep.,* No. 65 (1938), pp. 20 f. Bosch, *De Staatsschulden in het internationaal Recht,* p. 193, suggests the insertion in debt adjustments of a clause cancelling the original obligation. No duty would then exist to let the bondholders share in a future improvement of the debtor's finances.

22. The first instance of a "prosperity" clause is offered by the so-called "plus values" system of the Greek settlement of 1896. The bondholders were given the right to participate in the surplus which the revenues assigned to the service of the debt might in future produce in excess of the sums needed to pay the minimum rate of interest. II, 310, 312, 335 f. The operation of the system was suspended after 1932. See *Corp. For. Bondh. Rep.,* No. 66 (1939), pp. 285 f. See also II, 337, 346. Under the terms of the Colombian settlement of 1873, bondholders were to receive 5% interest as soon as the customs receipts reached the sum of $3,000,000. *Corp. For. Bondh. Rep.,* No. 61 (1934), p. 148 (Colombia, 1873). *For. Bondh. Prot. Coun. Rep.,* 1934, p. 60. The proposal by Greece for a permanent settlement in 1933 provided for increased payments according to an "index of prosperity," *Corp. For. Bondh. Rep.,* No. 60 (1933), p. 35. *Idem,* No. 58 (1931), p. 98. Arrangements providing for a gradual increase in the rate of interest payments will be discussed *infra;* see n. 79.

23. Hence Mexico, in 1883 as well as in 1922 and during the following years, looked to the settlement of the whole debt as the only satisfactory way out. See II, 39, 66 ff. The debt adjustment of federal states should include the national debt as well as the debt of the constituent states. The Mexican readjustment of 1922— which failed to work—applied to all external federal loans, bonds of the City of Mexico and of the states of Vera Cruz, Tamaulipas, and Sinaloa, for which the Government had assumed responsibility. II, 67. The Brazilian Government agreed to the inclusion of the debts of the State of Bahia in the scheme embodied in the decree of February 8, 1934. *Corp. For. Bondh. Rep.,* No. 61 (1934), p. 21.

both refused to enter into discussions "the limits of which had been arbitrarily fixed in advance." [24] On the other hand, a debtor government, as in the case of Chile in 1935, has occasionally put itself in a strong bargaining position by embodying its offer to foreign bondholders in a domestic law. When the president of the Foreign Bondholders Protective Council inquired whether the commissioners of the Chilean Government who had come to negotiate with the Council upon the Chilean debt were authorized to make a settlement beyond the terms of Law No. 5580 of January 31, 1935, he received the categorical answer that the commission had no authority to change or go outside the terms of the law and was limited by its provisions.[25] The principle of national sovereignty has also been invoked by a debtor government to deny a request by bondholders that it refrain from determining future debt payments short of full service before the bondholders have a chance to examine the economic situation of the country and to discuss the matter with the government.[26]

THE DEBTOR'S INITIATIVE

Bondholders, though vitally interested in forestalling unilateral action by which debtors may try to fix arbitrarily new terms for the debt service to the disadvantage of their creditors, have occasionally insisted that the debtor take the initiative in submitting suggestions for the settlement of the debt. Thus, during the negotiations in 1937 between the Greek Government on the one hand and the Council of Foreign Bondholders and the League Loans Committee on the other, both agencies

24. *Idem*, No. 64 (1937), p. 54; League Loans Committee, *Fifth Annual Report*, September, 1937, pp. 20 f.

25. See *For. Bondh. Prot. Coun. Rep.*, 1935, p. 38; the Chilean delegate, however, suggested that without changing the law it might be possible so to interpret some of its provisions that it would be possible for the Commission and the Council to agree on a proposal acceptable to both parties. *Idem*, p. 76.

26. See the reply of the President of Colombia to a telegram sent by the Foreign Bondholders Protective Council, September 8, 1934. *Idem*, 1934, pp. 95 f.: "I do not suppose that bondholders can justly consider that their legitimate rights and interests have been ignored or sacrificed without having had full opportunity to present their case, by the mere fact that the Government of Colombia does not agree to your suggestion to reserve any decision as to what can or cannot be paid as service on the external debt until the Foreign Bondholders Protective Council has had an opportunity to discuss said report with the Government with a view to reaching an agreement regarding what the Government can pay . . . . the Government could not bind itself in the manner you suggest to restrict its freedom of action to discuss in Congress none of the measures that may affect the service of the external debt of Colombia, not even to accept the conclusions that the Congress may wish to take in connection therewith."

maintained, when asked by the Greek delegation to submit suggestions with regard to Greece's future payments, that "it was not for the creditors to make to the debtor proposals involving any reduction of service"; [27] they urged the Greek Government to bring the default to an end by making an offer for the payment of current coupons which they could recommend to the acceptance of the bondholders.[28]

PARTIES TO THE PROCEDURE

SECTIONALISM

The question as to the parties to a readjustment procedure is complicated by the fact that the foreign loans of a debtor state are usually floated in the money markets of various countries. Bondholders are likely to form national groups and to press their claims in disregard of the common interest. "Sectionalism" among them destroys the unity of purpose and action which alone promises ultimate success. The history of debt adjustments offers a number of instances showing how the conclusion of satisfactory arrangements was delayed by lack of solidarity among various sections of foreign bondholders. The plan submitted in 1875 by C. F. Hamond for the settlement of the Turkish debt was accepted by the English bondholders but rejected by the French group, and it was only several years later that an agreement between the two principal national groups made it possible for the creditors to come to terms with the Turkish Government.[29] Similar difficulties arose in 1901 during negotiations between Portugal and her foreign creditors. Proposals by the debtor government that seemed acceptable to the Continental bondholders were deemed unsatisfactory by the British committee until it eventually yielded to its opponents.[30] Disagreement in 1894 among the English bondholders on the one hand and the French and German committees on the other may have delayed the readjustment of the Greek debt.[31]

While the creation, in the various countries, of central agencies for the protection of bondholders and a policy of coöperation designed to promote the mutual benefit of all groups of creditors without distinction of nationality or place of issue, such, for example, as adopted by the League

27. *Corp. For. Bondh. Rep.*, No. 64 (1937), p. 42; see also League Loans Committee, *Seventh Annual Report,* July, 1939, p. 9: ". . . the responsibility clearly lies with the Greek Government and not with the creditors for submitting proposals which might form a basis for agreement."

28. See League Loans Committee, *Fifth Annual Report,* September, 1937, p. 20.

29. See II, 425, 427–28, 434; see also II, 469.

30. II, 374–375.

31. II, 304 ff.

Loans Committee since its inception,[32] tends to lessen the dangers arising from "national sectionalism," divergence of interest among the various classes of creditors will practically always assert itself during debt adjustment negotiations. To overcome its deleterious effects, bondholders should bear in mind the following statement made by the Chase National Bank in its capacity of trustee of the Danzig Port and Waterways Board gold bonds.[33]

In such a situation [where the combined claims of different groups of bond creditors represent a burden which, if unmodified, is too great for the debtor to bear] no group is inclined to grant a concession unless all other groups make corresponding concessions to the end that the aggregate of concessions may meet the assumed abilities of the debtor. In such a situation no group of creditors can successfully deal with its debtors wholly in disregard of other groups of creditors.

THIRD PARTIES

The parties to an adjustment procedure are normally the debtor government on the one hand, its foreign creditors on the other. However, in view of the importance of a debt settlement for the whole economy of the debtor country, third parties who have some interest or stake in the economic rehabilitation of the debtor may sometimes participate in the procedure. Thus, after the failure of the Hartmont loan to Santo

32. League Loans Committee, *First Annual Report*, May, 1933, p. 8: ". . . the Committee has been at pains to develop friendly relations with all the interests concerned and to promote cooperation not only between all the classes of creditors but with the debtors themselves; for it has realised that this cooperation, while it will benefit others, must benefit the League Loan bondholders in the first place." *Idem*, p. 29: "The Committee think it important to remove a misapprehension which appears to have arisen abroad that it is concerned with protecting the interests of only the British bondholders of League Loans. Although about half the total of League Loans issued was placed in the London market, it was at the time made clear, as it remains true to-day, that all the tranches of any League Loan wherever issued rank equally and enjoy the same rights and privileges. Any action which the Committee may take to secure the maintenance of the status of any particular League Loan or to protect the interests of bondholders, in any particular loan, will be for the benefit of the bondholders of that loan generally, without distinction of nationality of the bondholders or the place of issue of any tranche." The representative sent by the American General Advisory Committee of Peruvian Bondholders to Peru in 1937 to discuss with the Government a resumption of the external debt service kept in touch with the British Minister so that the interests of the holders of sterling bonds should also be protected. *Corp. For. Bondh. Rep.*, No. 64 (1937), p. 73. In 1944 Peru declined to negotiate a settlement with Mr. Rogers of the Protective Council in New York. *For. Bondh. Prot. Coun. Rep.*, 1941–44, p. 756.

33. *Idem*, 1937, p. 288.

Domingo in 1869, European concessionaires tried to negotiate a settlement with the country's foreign bondholders in order to reëstablish the credit of Santo Domingo and thereby to enable it to raise new capital which was needed for the development of their concessions.[34] Issuing houses, not formally representing the holders of specific issues, have often tried to participate in the negotiations. In 1919 an International Committee of Bankers on Mexico was organized for the purpose of studying the situation in Mexico and preparing for such action as might be feasible with a view to inducing the Mexican Government to resume payments on its bonds.[35] Supported by the unofficial backing of the governments of France, Great Britain, and the United States, the committee in 1922 succeeded in concluding with the Mexican Government an agreement embodying a plan for the adjustment of the entire external indebtedness of the country; the plan was accepted by the great majority of the bondholders and made operative, only to be suspended two years later.[36] British and French bankers took a leading part in laying the groundwork for the conversion of the Egyptian debt in 1875.[37] When Honduras in 1909 asked for a refunding loan, the banking house of Morgan and Company, which had accepted the bid, first entered into negotiation with the British bondholders in an attempt to induce them to consent to a reduction of their claims.[38]

Instances may also be found, however, where the debtor government has insisted on direct negotiations with the bondholders to the exclusion

34. II, 204. Other instances: an American syndicate, styled the "Honduras Syndicate," who were the successors of the Honduras Railway Co., concluded a contract with the Government for the building of the railway, the settlement of the foreign debt, and the establishment of a bank charged with the collection of the customs. *Corp. For. Bondh. Rep.*, No. 56 (1929), p. 228 (Honduras, 1897). In 1876 the Khedive of Egypt asked Sir George Elliot, a member of the firm of contractors for the port of Alexandria, to submit a plan for the consolidation of the debt.

35. II, 66; Turlington, *Mexico and Her Foreign Creditors*, pp. 276–278.

36. For details of the 1922 agreement and subsequent debt readjustments, see II, 66 ff.

37. Mr. Goschen, formerly of the firm of Fruhling and Goschen, joined with M. Joubert, director of the Banque de Paris et des Pays-Bas, in a trip to Egypt for the purpose of presenting new plans to the Khedive. II, 590. An example of the decisive part taken by bankers in the settlement of a specific debt is offered by the conversion in 1895 of Serbian loans, which was the result of negotiations between the Government and bankers who had no mandate from the bondholders. The latter were left no alternative but to accept the arrangement. Simitch, *La Dette publique de la Serbie*, p. 321.

38. *Corp. For. Bondh. Rep.*, No. 36 (1909), p. 16. See also the agreement between the Republic of Nicaragua and the bankers, of February, 1915, concerning the service of the 1909 loan. *Corp. For. Bondh. Rep.*, No. 42 (1915), p. 239.

of bankers.[39] If the debt settlement includes bonds of a railroad company under public management or guaranteed by the government, the participation of the company as an interested party appears justified.[40] Where a country has been placed under receivership or financial supervision by a foreign power, the local representatives of the controlling state have often taken the initiative in negotiations designed to bring about a new settlement of the debt situation.[41] Similarly, the League of Nations, on the ground that sponsorship of loans imposes a certain responsibility for their fulfillment, participated, through its Financial Committee, in the readjustment of League loans in default.[42]

39. In a statement made by the Foreign Minister of Brazil on his return from a visit to the United States, March 23, 1939, he declared that the scale of payments and other conditions for the resumption of payments on the foreign debt "would be discussed by the Brazilian Government directly with the bondholders, not with the bankers." *Com. and Fin. Chron.*, CXLVIII (March 25, 1939), 1723. As to conflicting activities of bankers and bondholders' representatives, see the testimony given by J. Reuben Clark before the SEC with respect to the São Paulo dollar *tranches*. The Council of Foreign Bondholders was trying to keep the general service on the São Paulo loans low because the proportion issued in dollars was small, whereas the payment of available exchange on the British and Dutch *tranches* would reduce the exchange available for payment of dollar *tranches* of other parts of the Brazilian debt. The banking house of Speyer & Co. wanted to get a high service on the São Paulo loan because it had issued the dollar *tranches*.

40. See, for example, the settlement of the debt signed at Quito on September 30, 1908, by the Government of Ecuador, the Guayaquil and Quito Railway Co., and the Council of Foreign Bondholders. *Corp. For. Bondh. Rep.*, No. 35 (1908), p. 156. The Ecuador National Railway Co., holding the concession for the completion of an important railway in Ecuador under a government guaranty, offered to give £15 in fully paid railway shares in respect of each £100 new consolidated debt bonds. The bondholders consented to this proposal. *Idem*, No. 19 (1891), p. 110.

41. In 1923 an arrangement was made between the Government of Liberia and the American receiver-general of customs at Monrovia under which, in addition to the punctual payment of interest, the current sinking fund was to be resumed and the arrears of the past 7 years gradually made good. *Corp. For. Bondh. Rep.*, No. 56 (1929), p. 240.

42. See League Loans Committee, *First Annual Report*, May, 1933, p. 15, negotiations of the Financial Committee of the League of Nations with the Greek Government in February and March, 1932; *Second Annual Report*, June, 1934, p. 7: General functions of the Committee in connection with the adjustment of financial difficulties of the debtors of League loans. Once a debt settlement is concluded, a court may not disturb it. See the judgment of the Egyptian Mixed Appellate Court in the case of *Negrosso* v. *Egyptian Government*, February 15, 1936.

REPRESENTATION

DEBTOR GOVERNMENT'S ORGANS

The debtor government negotiates with its creditors, as a rule, through its regular organs in charge of its financial affairs, like the Ministry of Finance or Treasury officials. Sometimes, however, special commissioners have been appointed for this purpose. If the negotiations are to be conducted with foreign bondholders' organizations abroad, the sending of special agents instead of the acting Minister of Finance may be desirable as a simple matter of administrative expediency.[43] Since a debt settlement is likely to affect the political as well as financial interests of the state, the appointment of a special commission representing the various aspects of governmental policy may be advisable in order to insure proper coördination between the various departments of the state. The composition of the special commission appointed by the Brazilian government in 1939 to confer with bondholders' representatives on Brazil's debt situation clearly exemplifies the advantages of such procedure. Its members were officials of the Foreign Office and of the Ministry of Finance, and a liaison officer between the Ministry of Finance and the Bank of Brazil.[44]

BONDHOLDERS' REPRESENTATIVES

Representation of bondholders in a debt settlement, though generally exercised by the national agencies established for the express purpose of safeguarding the interests of foreign bondholders,[45] has occasionally been entrusted to particular individuals or corporations, as in the case of the San Domingo Improvement Company, which represented European bondholders in the negotiations with Santo Domingo in 1900.[46]

43. In 1900 Spain sent representatives to London to negotiate with the Council of Foreign Bondholders. *Corp. For. Bondh. Rep.*, No. 28 (1900–01), p. 361. In 1903 Dr. Angel Ugarte was sent to Europe by the Government of Honduras as special commissioner in connection with the settlement of the debt. *Idem*, No. 31 (1903–04), p. 223. A special commissioner negotiating on behalf of the Government of Venezuela with the British Council in 1873 failed in his efforts. *Idem*, No. 1 (1873), p. 42. In 1924 an arrangement was effected between the financial agent of the Government of Paraguay and the bondholders' committees. *Idem*, No. 51 (1924), p. 311.

44. *Idem*, No. 66 (1939), p. 18.

45. See, for particulars, the section on Protective Committees. With regard to the functions of the League Loans Committee, see its Memorial to the Council of the League of Nations, July 18, 1932, *Second Annual Report*, June, 1934, p. 18. See also SEC, *Rep.*, Pt. V, p. 30.

46. II, 226. Although the trustees of a loan are as a rule precluded by the nature of their duties as prescribed by the trust deed from coöperating in a procedure de-

CONCLUSION OF THE AGREEMENT

The actual negotiations are conducted either orally among the representatives of the various parties or by exchanging memoranda.[47] They result, as a rule, in drawing up an instrument which sets forth in detail the terms of the new arrangement. The manner in which such agreements may obtain binding force depends on the mode of representation. If the loan contract provides for a legal representative of all the bondholders by whose decisions they are to be bound, the signature attached by the representative to the agreement will suffice to create a binding obligation on behalf of the bondholders.[48] But loan contracts rarely, if ever, name beforehand the persons or agencies authorized to represent the bondholders in debt settlement negotiations. A foreign bondholders' protective committee acts, as a rule, on its own initiative and, even in case bonds belonging to an issue to be readjusted are deposited with it, it merely exercises the functions of a *negotiorum gestor;* as the result of the negotiations, it frames the agreement which it may or may not recommend to the bondholders for acceptance. The latter accept it,[49]

---

signed to modify the original contract, certain actions on their part, like advice submitted to protective committees on the situation of the debtor country, may have some bearing on starting adjustment negotiations and determining their results.

47. With regard to the role of memoranda in adjustment proceedings for fixing the final terms, see the procedure followed by Danzig and Hungary in 1938 with respect to League loans. In order to lay down the conditions of future service of the loans in terms which both the governments and those bondholders who accepted the new arrangements would recognize as binding, formal memoranda were prepared, one for each loan, in which the necessary deviations from the provisions of the original general bonds of the loans were defined. The memoranda were signed by the respective governments; their acceptance by the bondholders was then recommended by the League Loans Committee. See *Sixth Annual Report,* June, 1938, pp. 10, 12, 33 ff.

48. See, for example, the settlement reached for payment of City of Cordoba (Argentina) 7% external gold bonds of 1927. The committee for holders of City of Cordoba gold bonds notified the holders of certificates of deposit that its Argentine counsel had succeeded in negotiating a settlement with the city for the benefit of all bondholders. *Com. and Fin. Chron.,* CXLIX (July 8, 1939), 186. See, furthermore, League Study Committee Report, p. 20, and Annex II, "Note on the Machinery Required in Case of the Appointment of a Legal Bondholders' Representative in an International Loan Contract," *idem,* p. 32.

49. Sometimes the debtor requires the assent of a certain percentage of bondholders to make a debt settlement plan effective. Thus, the plan for the readjustment of the external debt of the Republic of Panama of 1940 was to become operative when so declared by the Republic on or before October 25, 1940, after the holders of at least 80% of the principal amount of 5% bonds should have assented to the plan by depositing their bonds under the plan. See *Dept. of St.*

either explicitly or—as happens most frequently—by simply encashing their coupons on the basis of the new terms. Debtors sometimes fix a time limit within which assent by the individual bondholder must be given if he wishes to participate in the advantages offered under the new scheme.[50] The service effected under the new arrangement is considered as representing full payment of the contractual sums.[51] Another method of concluding a readjustment agreement consists in the subsequent acceptance by the bondholders of an originally unilateral act of the debtor.[52] Sometimes the procedure for bringing about future modifica-

---

Bull., February 8, 1941, p. 163. The commission of inquiry for the settlement of the Egyptian debt recommended in its final report that the arrangement should be made obligatory through the assent of a majority of creditors, since experience had demonstrated that a minority even numerically insignificant could always exercise an influence prejudicial to the general interests concerned. II, 602. Bondholders may approve of the bases of a plan but may reject details. That happened in the case of the 1878 proposals by Mexico. II, 33–34. See also Bosch, *op. cit.*, p. 108.

50. Thus, Panama extended the period for accepting the debt adjustment plan of 1940 from October, 1940, to February, 1941, because of conditions resulting from the war in Europe which had prevented many holders of 5% bonds from declaring their assent in time. *Com. and Fin. Chron.*, CLII (January 25, 1941), 604; see also *Dept. of St. Bull.*, February 8, 1941, p. 163.

51. See, for example, the announcement to holders of City of Porto Alegre (Brazil) 7½% gold bonds of 1925 to receive payment of 13% of the July 1, 1938, coupon: "It is pointed out that pursuant to the provisions of the Presidential Decree of the United States of Brazil, such payment, if accepted by the holders of the bonds and coupons, must be accepted in full payment of such coupons and of the claims for interest represented thereby." *Com. and Fin. Chron.*, CLII (January 4, 1941), 32; *idem*, CLII (February 1, 1941), 748. Similarly, the Greek Government declared that the payment of the coupons under the service agreement is to be considered *eo ipso* as an acceptance on the part of the bondholders that the whole settlement of the loans during the following years will be effected in exactly the same manner as during the first year of the operation of the plan. See League Loans Committee, *Third Annual Report*, June, 1935, p. 47; *Fourth Annual Report*, August, 1936, p. 46. However, equality of treatment of holders who had accepted the payments with those who had retained their coupons in the hope of achieving better terms was subsequently promised. The Greek Minister of Finance notified the fiscal agents abroad that "such an acceptance will not prejudice the rights of the bondholders towards any further payment whatsoever which might eventually be agreed upon." See *idem*, pp. 47 ff.

52. Mention has already been made above (*supra*, pp. 305 ff.) of the Chilean Decree No. 5580 of January 31, 1935, and its provision that acceptance of the decree by encashing coupons under its terms shall extinguish the original responsibility of the debtor. The Chilean Government maintained that "under the present Plan the new obligation is like the original obligation, the result of bilateral contract between an obligor and a bondholder. It is a new contract resulting from the offer, pursuant to law 5580, and the acceptance thereof by the bondholders." Memorandum of the Chilean Special Financial Commission, March 22, 1935,

tions is provided in the agreement itself.[53] Since the execution of the agreement on the part of the debtor state involves a series of administrative actions by its various organs, it is customary for debtor governments to confirm the obligations assumed under the new arrangement by incorporating the latter in a law enacted by the legislative branch of the government, thus emphasizing the binding character of the settlement.[54]

For. Bondh. Prot. Coun. Rep., 1935, p. 52. The Foreign Bondholders Protective Council at first took the position that the acceptance of the Chilean decree would mean consent on the part of the bondholder in the "destruction of his bond contract," which would become "null and void as a bond; thereafter the bond seems to be nothing more than a mere certificate that its holder is entitled to receive any funds distributed under the law, either as it now stands or as it may be hereafter amended"; the bondholder gets "some sort of unilateral undertaking the terms of which may be changed [by the Government] at will, without giving to the holder of this document any legal basis for objection or complaint against the Government." *For. Bondh. Prot. Coun. Rep.*, 1936, pp. 203, 236, 251 ff.; *idem*, 1937, p. 18. Later, however, the Council held it to be the proper interpretation of Law 5580 to apply it "only to coupons cashed under it and not to the bond itself," which remained intact. *Idem*, 1937, p. 190. This interpretation was adopted by Chile and was embodied in the decree of June 11, 1938. *Supra*, n. 10. There are other instances of the acceptance by bondholders of unilateral debt adjustments; e.g., the Mexican decree of 1850 for the conversion of the external 5% debt into new 3% bonds and the liquidation of arrears was accepted by the bondholders and the conversion carried out in 1851. II, 13. In July, 1894, the Congress of Ecuador passed a law suspending the payment of interest, changing the security for the service, and reducing the maximum rate of interest to 4%; it was accepted by the bondholders unconditionally in 1895. *Corp. For. Bondh. Rep.*, No. 23 (1895), p. 110. The assent of as many bondholders as possible to an adjustment scheme is often sought in order to avoid the impression of a compulsory action on the part of the debtor.

53. The agreement between the Guayaquil and Quito Railway Co. of Ecuador and the holders of the special series bonds in 1900 stipulated, *inter alia*, that holders of three fourths of the bonds outstanding should have the power at any time to modify or waive any of the provisions of the agreement, their assent to be given by a deposit of the bonds, and the minority to be bound thereby. *Corp. For. Bondh. Rep.*, No. 28 (1900), pp. 114 ff. Under the arrangement of December 11, 1926, between Bulgaria and foreign bondholders, the Bulgarian Government and the committees representing the holders could negotiate a revision of the arrangement by mutual agreement, if the situation should improve or grow worse. II, 569. The Foreign Bondholders Protective Council sought to improve the Niemeyer Plan for Brazil by securing a provision that "in any future review of the situation, there would be a consultation with the representatives of the principal creditor groups." *For. Bondh. Prot. Coun. Rep.*, 1934, p. 28. The offer made by Greece in 1933 to end her default provided that future arrangements for the service of the external debt were to be discussed with the Council of Foreign Bondholders and the League Loans Committee before drawing up the budgets for those years. *Corp. For. Bondh. Rep.*, No. 66 (1939), p. 277.

54. The arrangement of 1924 between the Government of Uruguay and the Council of Foreign Bondholders regarding certain questions as to the application

TEMPORARY AND PERMANENT AGREEMENTS

Two general types of debt settlement can be distinguished: those of a temporary nature [55] and those designed to adjust the indebtedness of the state on a permanent basis. The advisability of adopting one or the other scheme in a given case has always been the subject of much controversy and bickering among the principal parties to the procedure. The debtor naturally seeks to take advantage of the depressed condition of his finances by demanding a permanent reduction of his liabilities to the level of his existing capacity to pay. For the same reasons, creditors are opposed to a definitive settlement based on what they consider to be only a passing stage in the debtor's economic life. It has been the settled policy of bondholders' protective committees in recent years to resist the desire of debtors for a permanent adjustment of their indebtedness and to arrange instead short-term settlements subject to revision as they fall due for renewal, thus enabling both parties to adapt their respective rights and duties to changed economic conditions.[56] It is in keeping with

of the sinking fund on the consolidated debt of 1891 was authorized by legislative decree of January 15, 1925. *Corp. For. Bondh. Rep.*, No. 52 (1925), p. 433. An agreement between the Turkish Government and the representatives of bondholders concerning the exchange of Ottoman bonds in 1933 was approved by the Grand National Assembly of Turkey. II, 510. A debt settlement between the Republic of Nicaragua and the Council of Foreign Bondholders was reached in October, 1917, and approved by Congress in November. *Corp. For. Bondh. Rep.*, No. 44 (1917), pp. 247 f. Ratification by subsequent legislative act of the debtor may also be refused. Thus, various arrangements between Portugal and foreign bondholders between 1897 and 1901 were refused ratification. *Corp. For. Bondh. Rep.*, No. 56 (1929), p. 290.

55. Viz., valid only for a restricted period of years, e.g., for $2\frac{1}{2}$ to 5 years, or from year to year. Madden, Nadler, and Sauvain, *America's Experience as a Creditor Nation*, p. 298. A period of 6 years was held to be too extended for a temporary settlement. *Corp. For. Bondh. Rep.*, No. 65 (1938), p. 39 (Costa Rica).

56. The policy of the League Loans Committee in this respect was laid down in its *Second Annual Report*, June, 1934, p. 8, in these words: ". . . certain of the debtor countries have shown a desire to make a 'definitive' settlement now—that is, to scale down permanently the rate of interest or even the amount of their League Loans. The League Loans Committee have always resisted such proposals, which they consider premature at this stage. They do not believe that in present conditions and uncertainties, particularly as regards price levels, it is yet possible to arrive at a final solution of the problem of the foreign indebtedness of those countries. Any permanent settlement which might be made now would almost inevitably turn out to be unfair either to the creditors or to the debtors. At best this would be unsatisfactory; and not improbably the settlement might quickly become unworkable." The Foreign Bondholders Protective Council has from the first taken the position "not to discuss in these times of depression any permanent adjustment of any foreign government's obligations because the Council believes that

this general policy that bondholders' protective committees have consented to a permanent settlement where the economic and financial position of the debtor showed a reasonable measure of stability, both as regards revenue and capacity to transfer.[57]

Bondholders' committees often have their own views as to what the debtor's economy can justly bear, both at present and in the future, and their agreement to make the adjustment a permanent one is held out to the creditor as a *quid pro quo* in return for an offer which corresponds to this estimate of the latter's capacity to pay.[58] Another reason for granting permanency to a debt settlement has been found in the increased security attached to bonds to be issued under the new scheme. Thus, the Foreign Bondholders Protective Council declared in 1935 that, although

---

such adjustments should be left until the world has returned to a condition more nearly normal." *For. Bondh. Prot. Coun. Rep.*, 1934, p. 99; see also *idem*, 1935, p. 11; also *idem*, pp. 74, 97; and Gantenbein, *Financial Questions in United States Foreign Policy*, p. 179. SEC, *Rep.*, Pt. V, p. 380. Remarks by Mr. Kempner on the Greek settlement before the Council of the League of Nations, April 15, 1932, Pt. I, *Official Journal*, 1932, p. 1034.

57. Thus, permanent settlements were made with Danzig and Hungary in 1937. League Loans Committee, *Fifth Annual Report*, September, 1937, p. 11: "Hitherto the Committee have declined to conclude permanent arrangements for the service of the League Loans of the various countries with whom they have to deal, but this year they have made exceptions to that practice in two widely divergent cases. They have always maintained, and still maintain, that no permanent arrangement can be concluded until the economic and financial position of the debtor, which must also be related to the rest of the world, shows a considerable measure of stability. They are satisfied that the requisite conditions exist both in Danzig and Hungary." With respect to the situation of Greece in 1939, the League Loans Committee declared: "Both the Bank of Greece reserve and the exchange situation in Greece have improved during the last few years and neither from the budget aspect nor that of transfer does there appear to be any serious obstacle to the conclusion of a reasonable permanent settlement of the external debt." *Seventh Annual Report*, July, 1939, p. 10.

58. The negotiations of the Council of Foreign Bondholders and the League Loans Committee with the Greek Government since 1936 frequently raised this question. Both agencies declared that ever since August, 1936, when they agreed to discuss the possibility of arriving at a permanent settlement, they had emphasized that whether such a settlement could be reached must depend on the adequacy of the terms offered by Greece; if the Greek Government wished to obtain some permanent reduction in the bondholders' claims they must foster the good will of their creditors; and the necessary prelude to the consideration of a permanent settlement was the payment of a reasonable percentage. League Loans Committee, *Fourth Annual Report*, August, 1936, p. 18; *Fifth Annual Report*, September, 1937, pp. 11 f., 18 f.; *Corp. For. Bondh. Rep.*, No. 64 (1937), p. 55. The Greek Government declared its willingness to make an effort to increase the percentage paid on the bond service in return for a permanent settlement. League Loans Committee, *Fourth Annual Report*, August, 1936, p. 17.

the moment was not the proper one to make long-term permanent debt settlements, an exception had been made in the case of Buenos Aires because the Province was able and willing to offer the bondholders as security for their new bonds revenues collected by the Federal Government and paid into the Bank of the Nation and by the latter remitted to the paying agents in New York without passing through the Province's Treasury.[59]

SUBSTANTIVE PRINCIPLES

Turning now from the procedural aspects of the readjustment problem to a discussion of the principles of debt settlements, attention must once more be called to the fact that such settlements are the result of a compromise between two conflicting interests: on the one hand, there is the desire of a debtor government, either in actual or imminent default, to alleviate the burden of its past indebtedness by an arrangement with its foreign creditors for the purpose of raising new funds or of avoiding acknowledged insolvency; on the other hand, the creditor, while realizing the futility of insisting on the specific performance of his contractual rights, seeks to obtain as large a salvage of his investment as possible.

"CAPACITY TO PAY"

The primary question which is likely to dominate the entire adjustment procedure concerns the debtor's capacity to pay. Unless steps are taken to insure an impartial investigation of the facts of the situation, debtor and creditor are apt to entertain widely divergent views on the matter. In the first place, doubts are sometimes expressed by creditors as to whether the question of the debtor's capacity to pay may be raised at all in an adjustment procedure affecting debts incurred by a government toward foreign private investors. It has been argued that a government's capacity to pay actually depends primarily on its will to pay. A government, through the exercise of its taxing power, has the whole wealth of the nation, including the private wealth of all its nationals, to draw upon for the fulfillment of its financial obligations, and only in case the taxing power has reached the point of exhaustion can there be any question about the debtor's capacity to pay.[60] The principal answer to this argument is the oft-repeated maxim that no sovereign state can be

59. *For. Bondh. Prot. Coun. Rep.*, 1935, pp. 11 f., 18; see also Madden, Nadler, and Sauvain, *op. cit.*, p. 305.

60. *For. Bondh. Prot. Coun. Rep.*, 1936, pp. 7 f.; *idem*, 1937, pp. 6–11. See also Feilchenfeld, in Quindry, *Bonds and Bondholders, Rights and Remedies*, II, p. 210; Gantenbein, *op. cit.*, p. 180.

asked to sacrifice essential national interests to the performance of its loan contracts.[61] The precise question, however, is what, in a given case, constitute necessary expenditures for national purposes. Is it "the welfare of the debtor nation, as determined by itself" that must take precedence over foreign debt payments? Shall the debtor country be permitted not only to improve the standard of living of its citizens but also to maintain its political power and influence through expenditures on armaments before it can be required to live up to its financial engagements toward foreign bondholders? The answer to these questions is not to be found in any legal rules or accepted standards of justice.[62] It depends on the particular circumstances of each case where the line between bad faith and indispensable needs of the debtor is to be drawn.

Reputation as an honest debtor gained through a previous record of

61. See SEC, *Rep.*, Pt. V, p. 32. "Obviously, the debtor nation must continue to exist and discharge its essential governmental functions and its foreign trade cannot be destroyed. Proper recognition must necessarily be given to these considerations by the bondholders' representatives. To attempt to insist upon too drastic a reduction of internal expenditures, the levying of too onerous taxes or the allocation to bond service of too excessive an amount of foreign exchange is to invite an early recurrence of default." The American debt funding commission, in its report of 1925, interpreted the principle of "capacity to pay" as follows: "While the integrity of international obligations must be maintained, it is axiomatic that no nation can be required to pay to another government sums in excess of its capacity to pay. The commission on its settlement with Great Britain . . . has adhered to the principle that the adjustments made with each government must be measured by the ability of the particular government to set aside and transfer to the United States the payments called for under the funding agreement." *For. Bondh. Prot. Coun. Rep.*, 1935, pp. 39 f. In a statement to its foreign creditors, the Province of Buenos Aires declared that, if the full service of its foreign indebtedness were paid, it could not carry on "the elementary necessities of government and, of course, if the government did not function, there would not in the chaos that would ensue, be revenues and the bonds could not then be paid even as much as the Province was offering." *For. Bondh. Prot. Coun. Rep.*, 1935, p. 14. In a letter of August 7, 1934, from the Dominican minister in Washington to the Secretary of State, it was stated that the proposal made by the Dominican Republic to the Foreign Bondholders Protective Council for the service of its external debt "was prompted by an earnest desire to preserve the credit of the Dominican Republic and to preserve compliance with its obligations to foreign bondholders to the utmost degree, consistent only with its paramount duty to preserve the functions of government under the unprecedented conditions of world-wide depression from which the government and people have suffered." *Idem,* 1934, p. 64. The report of the experts on the Mexican situation in 1928 admitted that there was need for social reforms, which could not be ignored, but insisted that to make provisions for the debt service was equally necessary. II, 77 ff. "Capacity to pay" in debt adjustments is judged ultimately by measures of expediency and political feasibility rather than by a purely economic yardstick.

62. Cf. Feilchenfeld, in Quindry, *op. cit.*, pp. 210 f.

fair dealing and respect for the plighted word may prove to be an important factor in favor of a debtor government in financial distress.[63] So, where a debtor shows earnest willingness to end his default by some sort of service even in the face of adverse economic conditions, creditors are likely to accept his proposals more readily than those of a persistently recalcitrant debtor.[64] Such willingness may, in particular, be presumed if the offer made by the debtor meets the views formed by the bondholders on the basis of their own independent investigations into the debtor's economic and financial situation.[65]

ALLEVIATING THE DEBTOR'S BURDEN

The current financial burden upon the debtor government resulting from its foreign loans consists in the payment of interest and sinking fund at regular intervals and the transfer abroad of the sums due; added thereto are in case of default the accumulated arrears of the monies owed but not paid at the due dates. A change in any one of these items—rate of interest, amount of principal, time and manner of payment, transfer abroad—may have the effect of alleviating the burden on the debtor. The devices actually used in debt settlements to achieve this end differ greatly.

Conversion. The debt charges on a loan—foreign or domestic—may sometimes be reduced by conversion. As part of the plan of settlement, holders of the defaulted bonds have sometimes been required to exchange them for (that is, to convert them into) new bonds.[66] As compared with

63. See, for example, the statement by the League Loans Committee with regard to Danzig and Estonia. *Fourth Annual Report*, August, 1936, p. 8. See also *For. Bondh. Prot. Coun. Rep.*, 1935, p. 111, and the various references to the "good will" of debtor governments, evidenced, *inter alia,* by the introduction of financial reforms or by accepting advice of independent organs for improving their financial condition, in the statements by the League Loans Committee recommending acceptance of proposals submitted by these governments. League Loans Committee, *First Annual Report*, May, 1933, pp. 36, 38, 44; *Second Annual Report,* June, 1934, pp. 9, 14, 15, 24, 31, 34, 41.

64. *For. Bondh. Prot. Coun. Rep.*, 1936, p. 707. *Idem*, 1938, p. 1130. *Idem,* 1937, p. 565. See also League Loans Committee, *Fifth Annual Report,* September, 1937, p. 10.

65. See, for example, the statement of the League Loans Committee with regard to an offer by Hungary. *Idem,* p. 10. Similarly, with regard to an offer by Danzig, *idem,* p. 11.

66. Conversion operations have of course often been undertaken by debtors in good credit standing where no question of remedying a default is involved. If, by the time when the debtor may legally redeem an outstanding bond issue, interest rates have fallen to a rate below what they were when the bonds were issued, the debtor may be able to transfer his indebtedness into the new bonds with a saving

the old bonds, these may bear a lower rate of interest, represent a lower nominal capital, or both. In some instances the debtor's acceptance of an arrangement for terminating the default has enabled him to float a new loan out of which he could both effect the conversion and obtain free funds for other uses. Where this has been possible the bondholder has usually been given the option of exchanging his old bonds for new ones at a stated discount or of redeeming his old bonds for cash at a stipulated percentage of their face value. If interest rates in the loan-issuing countries are at a relatively low level it may prove possible for the debtor to obtain the new loan at a lower rate of interest than that to which the old bonds were entitled and to benefit in this way also. On some occasions a debtor government which has found it difficult to obtain the foreign exchange requirement for the service of its foreign bond issues has offered an inducement to bondholders to convert their external bonds into internal ones payable in domestic currency.

Consolidation and Unification. Similar to conversion in its effect of alleviating the service charges on current debts is the financial operation of consolidating or unifying the indebtedness of a country. It consists in creating a single debt into which all or a certain amount of the existing debts are merged. Its purpose is to give those debts a uniform rate of interest and to facilitate their administration.[67] The process may result in the reduction of interest payments or sinking fund, or both, of individual loans; it may operate to the benefit of those who receive a higher percentage under the new arrangement than under their old contract.[68] Both methods have been used in some of the major debt adjustments of modern times for the purpose of assisting a defaulting debtor or one in danger of default in his efforts to reorganize and stabilize his financial situation.[69]

---

in interest charges. The old bonds may be retired by cash redemption out of the proceeds of the new loan or, if their holders prefer, converted into the new issue.

67. See Von Eheberg, *Finanzwissenschaft,* p. 621. Like conversion, consolidation and unification are available to countries with well-ordered finances as a means of alleviating debt charges under favorable economic conditions.

68. See, for example, the unification of the Turkish debt in 1903 which gave the bondholders a higher rate of interest and, in addition, a more desirable bond. II, 471. The bondholders sacrifice, however, the possibility of a more advantageous rate of redemption.

69. See the settlement of the defaulted loans of Costa Rica in 1885: A new consolidated external debt for £2,000,000 was created; the principal of the old debts was reduced by one half, the surplus bonds to be used to pay the interest for the first two years. Costa Rica, 1885. The Egyptian decree of May 7, 1876, provided for the unification of the debt. All issues were to be unified into one general debt whose bonds were to bear interest at 7% on the nominal capital and were to be redeemable in 65 years at half-yearly drawings. The holders of the floating debt received a bonus of 25% in new bonds; the holders of the 1862 and other loans

Reduction of Principal and Interest. The simplest way for the debtor
to effect a permanent reduction of his financial obligation is, of course,
an outright cut in the amounts due under the terms of the loan contract,
whether service charges or principal. Being the most drastic encroachment upon bondholders' contractual rights, such a measure must appear
to be justified by special considerations if it is to become part of a readjustment scheme acceptable to the creditors.

In some cases debtors have claimed and obtained the reduction of the
principal on the ground that the face or nominal value of the capital was
grossly in excess of the proceeds actually realized by them from the
transaction.[70] Thus, the holders of certain loans, which the Turkish Government had floated in England and on the Continent and for which it
had received as low as £25, £18, £16, and in one case £11 per £100, consented to the reduction of the capital to the "real issue value"; the question arose, however, as to how to determine this value, whether on the
basis of the prospectus price or of the average price realized by the Turkish Government from the sale. It was finally decided to take the mean
between the figures arrived at by the two modes of calculation.[71] Similarly, the redemption value of Portuguese foreign bonds was reduced
under the settlement of 1902 to approximately the original issue price,

received either no bonus or a slight one. Under the law of liquidation of 1880, the
balances of the 1864, 1865, and 1867 loans were converted into a unified debt at
£133½%. II, 608, and *Corp. For. Bondh. Rep.*, No. 56 (1929), p. 166. Portugal
in 1902 issued a new 3% consolidated debt for the conversion of the external 3%
consolidated debt, of the 4% debt of 1890, and of the 4½% debt of 1888–89.
Idem, p. 291. Under the terms of the settlement of the Tunisian debt in 1870, the
various loans were converted into one single common stock, reducing the interest
and cutting the capital from 160,000,000 frs. to 125,000,000 frs. As to the
Turkish unification of 1903, see II, 463–471. The proposal for a settlement of
the Venezuelan debt in 1879 was based on a conversion of the external and internal debts into one single external debt. Pending the arrangements for conversion into unified bonds, the external bondholders agreed to accept 3% on their
4% bonds. *Corp. For. Bondh. Rep.*, No. 7 (1879), p. 64. In 1903 the external and
internal debts of Venezuela were converted into a unified issue. *Idem*, No. 32
(1904–05), pp. 446–455.

70. For example, of the five loans of 1862, 1864, 1866, 1868, 1873, for which
Egypt incurred an indebtedness of £55,000,000, only £35,000,000 was received, and
on this Egypt had up to 1875 paid back in interest and sinking fund £29 million,
when £45,734,000 still remained outstanding. From a return of the Egyptian Ministry of Finance, cited in the *Bullionist*, Dec. 16, 1878.

71. II, 484, 502, 503, 504. The Greek Government suggested in 1936 as a
basis for a permanent settlement of its default on the League loans that the
capital value of the loans should be written down to the average market price in
1931 and that on this reduced amount interest at 3% should be paid with sinking fund spread over 90 years. The proposal was rejected by the bondholders'
representatives. League Loans Committee, *Fourth Annual Report*, August, 1936,
p. 18.

the government thus undertaking to repay only about what it had actually received.[72] In 1885 the Government of Santo Domingo offered to recognize the claims of the Hartmont bondholders to the extent of the sum received by it.[73]

In determining whether or not the debtor's claim for a reduction of the principal to the sum actually received is justified, the reasons for the discrepancy between the face value of the loan and the proceeds realized by the debtor must be examined.[74] The sale of a bond at a substantial discount from the face value means that the real interest rate, i.e., the rate on the money actually invested, is appreciably higher than the nominal rate. The high real interest rate reflects the risk in the investment. The reduction of the principal to the issue price in such a case would mean that a debtor of very low credit standing in effect borrowed at the same real interest rate as a debtor of high credit standing; no compensation for risk by way of interest rate would be obtained. Furthermore, where the fact that the debtor received only a small portion of the issue price was due to fraud or its equivalent by the issuing houses, no legal justification is apparent for mulcting the bondholders by reducing their claim for principal to an amount well below that which they actually paid for their bonds.

The scaling down of the Greek debt of 1824–25 to about one third of its nominal value in 1867 was based on the ground that the Greek territory was then only one third of the size of the original Greek provinces which had revolted against Turkey in 1821 and had been granted a loan by British financiers for the continuation of their struggle.[75] It is, however, an obvious fact that wealth and ability to pay may be far from proportionate to the size of the territory.

In Particular: Rate of Interest. With regard to the slashing of the contractual rate of interest, debtor governments frequently maintain that they are entitled to take such a step if interest rate levels have considerably decreased since the time the loan was issued. It is true, world conditions or the plight of the debtor at the moment of floating the loan may force him to accept service rates which, compared to later conditions, may

72. II, 377 ff.

73. II, 205 ff.

74. Debtor governments have sometimes sought to justify the reduction of principal by the contention that many of the present holders of the bonds bought them for very little. But since the low price was caused by the debtor's default he cannot legally claim a right to benefit from his breach of contract; many of the bondholders may still be the original purchasers or their legatees; speculation is an element in security transactions generally.

75. II, 285, 287. See also the paragraphs bearing on State Succession, II, 487–488. It may, however, be said that there is a general tendency in debt adjustments to maintain the principal of loans intact. SEC, *Rep.*, Pt. V, pp. 33 f. The Foreign Bondholders Protective Council seeks to adhere to this rule as a principle.

seem exorbitant. However, as pointed out by the Foreign Bondholders Protective Council, the fall in the rate of interest constitutes a risk which the borrower must take and, just as the lender may not ask for an increase of service payments if interest rates should in the meantime rise, so the borrower cannot claim to be released from his promise to pay the contractual rate because of a general decrease in interest rates.[76] Since a fall in market rates of interest during the life of a loan does not entitle a debtor to refuse fulfillment of the terms of the loan contract, his unilateral reduction of the contractual rates of interest constitutes default. Nevertheless, creditors have frequently had to accept a reduction of interest payments in order to terminate a default.[77] They have, however, tried to restrict the cut to an amount which seemed to them reasonable,[78] and, in many instances, they have succeeded in having the settlement provide for a graduated increase over the initial rate.[79]

76. See also *For. Bondh. Prot. Coun. Rep.*, 1937, p. 28: "Because interest rates may have fallen since the bonds were originally issued gives no legal or moral right to a government unilaterally to reduce interest on its bonds."

77. In the Costa Rican debt settlement of 1897, the interest on "A" bonds was reduced to 3%, on "B" bonds to $2\frac{1}{2}\%$. An offer by Danzig in 1937, by which the rate of interest on 7% loans was to be reduced to 5%, on $6\frac{1}{2}\%$ loans to $4\frac{1}{2}\%$, and on the 6% loans to $4\frac{1}{2}\%$, was recommended by the Council of Foreign Bondholders for the acceptance of bondholders. *Corp. For. Bondh. Rep.*, No. 64 (1937), pp. 13 f. In the Greek settlement of 1897–98, the initial interest was fixed at 43% of the original interest for the monopoly loan, and at 32% for the other loans. In the railroad reorganization of Salvador, interest on both classes of bonds was cut from 6% to 5%. Turkey and her creditors agreed in 1876 to reduce the interest on the 1854 loan from 6% to 5%, and on the 1871 loan from 6% to $4\frac{1}{2}\%$. Mexico in 1942 agreed to pay about 1% interest for 20 years of default in interest and principal. II, 97.

78. A reduction of interest from $7\frac{1}{2}\%$ to 4% proposed by the Peruvian Government in 1938 on the guano loan of Peru was declared by the Council of Foreign Bondholders as "too great," especially in view of the "special security and status" of the loan. *Corp. For. Bondh. Rep.*, No. 65 (1938), p. 56. So, a proposal by Costa Rica to redeem interest coupons at the rate of 1% for a period of 3 years and $1\frac{1}{2}\%$ during the following 3 years was rejected by the bondholders as not being "possible to consider." *Idem*, p. 39. See also *Com. and Fin. Chron.*, CXLVIII (March 25, 1939), 1699. A cut in the interest of the original loan of 6% to 3% of a new conversion loan of Colombia was declared by the Protective Council as "entirely out of line with what Colombia can do and not in consonance with her position as a credit risk." *Idem*, CLII (June 7, 1941), 3573. See, however, the readjustment of the 1875 loan of Haiti in 1880 when the interest rate was reduced from 8% to 5% and again in 1885 from 5% to 3%. The adjustment plan of El Salvador of 1935, accepted by the British Council of Foreign Bondholders, permanently reduced the interest rate from 8% to 5% on the Series A bonds and from 7% to $3\frac{1}{2}\%$ on the Series C bonds. Madden, Nadler, and Sauvain, *op. cit.*, p. 306.

79. The Brazilian Government in 1934 offered generally a rising schedule of interest averaging in 1937 about $3\frac{1}{2}\%$ for its own obligations but less for bonds

SINKING FUND

In debt settlements involving a reduction of interest, bondholders have usually insisted that payments for interest should take precedence over those for sinking fund; in other words, that sinking fund requirements should be met only after the prescribed interest payments have been assured. They have also generally maintained that the bulk of the readjusted debt service should go to interest rather than to sinking fund.[80]

of the political subdivisions. Gantenbein, *op. cit.*, p. 159. The Province of Buenos Aires in 1935 agreed to a plan providing for the reduction in interest rates from 6%, 6½%, 7% and 7½% to 4⅛%, 4¼%, 4⅜%, and 4½%, respectively, during the years 1936–38, with no provision for sinking fund. The interest rates increased by ¼ of 1% in 1939 for all issues. Madden, Nadler, and Sauvain, *op. cit.*, p. 305. According to the explanations given by the Government of Chile, the proposal to allot the entire fiscal revenues from the nitrate and copper industry to the service of the foreign debt assured a gradual increase in payments since there was reason to believe that a revival in world trade would restore these sources of revenue to the average level of the period from 1921–30. See the Memorandum of the Chilean Special Financial Commission concerning Law No. 5580, March 13, 1935. *For. Bondh. Prot. Coun. Rep.*, 1935, p. 43. The offer made by the Chinese Minister of Finance and Railways in 1936 to the holders of the Tientsin-Pukow Railway loans of 1908–10 and recommended for acceptance by a committee of the Bank of England provided that the interest should be 2½% for 1936–38 and 5% (the contractual rate) thereafter. Young, "China's Financial Progress," *For. Pol. Rep.*, XIV (April 15, 1938), 34. Under the convention of Paris settling the Colombian default in 1861, the interest on active bonds was 2% from 1860 to 1866, and 3% afterward. Under the scheme proposed by the Greek Minister of Finance in 1894, the full original interest would have been attained in 68 years. II, 310. Under the Greek law of control, a gradual increase in the payment of interest was assured. II, 335. The arrangement with Liberia in 1898 provided for the reduction of the interest rate to 3%, rising every 3 years thereafter to a maximum of 5%. *Corp. For. Bondh. Rep.*, No. 26 (1898), p. 240. The new bonds issued by Paraguay in 1885 in exchange for the outstanding principal of the two old loans were to carry interest of 2% and 3%, respectively, for the first and second 5 years, and 4% thereafter. *Idem*, No. 12 (1884), p. 91. The reduction to 50% of the service agreed upon between Portugal and representatives of French, German, English, and Dutch bondholders in 1892 was to be only temporary, and payment was to be progressively increased after 5 years until the original rate was reëstablished in 1926. II, 371. For a period from April 1, 1934, to April, 1937, coupons on the Romanian 4% loan were paid at 50%, 53% and 55%, respectively, and on all other loans at 25%, 35%, and 42% of their face value. The interest rate for the Spanish debt converted in 1851 was 1% for the first 4 years, rising by one quarter every second year to 3%. *Corp. For. Bondh. Rep.*, No. 56 (1929), p. 343. The system of the so-called "plus values" of the Greek law of control of 1898, under which the percentage of interest and sinking fund to be paid to the bondholders increased in proportion to the rising yield from monopolies pledged as security for the debt, deserves particular attention in this connection. II, 335 ff.

80. Madden, Nadler, and Sauvain, *op. cit.*, p. 301: It would seem that strict standards of good faith require issuers in partial default on interest to apply

Thus, the Foreign Bondholders' Protective Council objected to the Chilean Government's debt readjustment plan of 1935 (embodied in Chilean Law No. 5580) mainly because the revenues assigned to the service of the debt were equally divided between interest and amortization.[81] The Council of Foreign Bondholders similarly contended in 1938 that an offer to pay 2 per cent for sinking fund as against 4 per cent interest (in settlement of the default on the 7½ per cent guano loan) was disproportionate.[82] Debt readjustments have frequently provided for easing amortization charges either by the partial or complete suspension of sinking funds for a number of years [83] or by an extension of the period

---

their entire resources to payment of interest until the default is corrected. *Corp. For. Bondh. Rep.*, No. 66 (1939), p. 39: The question of resumption of sinking fund payments by Guatemala was to be discussed only if full interest payments were assured. Article 8 (b) of the general bond of the Bulgarian 7½% stabilization loan of 1928 provides that monies are to be set aside for sinking fund only after the necessary funds for the payment of the full amount of interest have been duly assembled. League Loans Committee, *Second Annual Report*, June, 1934, p. 28. Under the Turkish debt settlement embodied in the decree of Mouharrem, payment of a minimum interest rate of 1 per cent was to be assured before any allocation was made to amortization. II, 448.

81. See *For. Bondh. Prot. Coun. Rep.*, 1935, pp. 73–74; SEC, *Rep.*, Pt. V, p. 466; the Chilean special financial commisison tried to justify its proposal to devote half the revenues from the nitrate and copper industry to the payment of interest and the other half to the sinking fund by pointing out that the purchase of Chilean bonds on the market would have the automatic effect of increasing the rate of interest payable with respect to the smaller amount of bonds which would thereafter be outstanding. *For. Bondh. Prot. Coun. Rep.*, 1935, p. 44. However, as pointed out in *The Times* (London), February 4, 1935, the practical result would be that the debtor would profit by its own default. The smaller the rate of interest that may be forthcoming, the heavier would be the depreciation in the bonds and the greater the profit at the bondholders' expense.

82. The Council was, however, "unable to induce the Peruvian government to increase or amend this offer." *Corp. For. Bondh. Rep.*, No. 65 (1938), p. 56.

83. See, in general, Madden, Nadler, and Sauvain, *op. cit.*, p. 300. Instances of the suspension of sinking fund: Argentina, 1933 (sinking fund service on all external and internal loans to be suspended for a period of 3 years commencing January 1, 1933); Bulgaria, 1926 (sinking fund suspended for another 6 years with power in Bulgaria to buy bonds for amortization, II, 553); Greece, 1932 (sinking fund to be suspended for the current fiscal year); Hungary, 1937 (redemption of the League loans to recommence in 3 years, League Loans Committee, *Fifth Annual Report*, September, 1937, p. 14); Salvador, 1933 (sinking fund payments to be suspended—assigned revenues to be used to pay interest on bonds, *Corp. For. Bondh. Rep.*, No. 60 (1933), pp. 396–400); Turkey, 1928 (amortization to be suspended for the first two years if Turkey so desired, II, 504); Yugoslavia, 1937 (amortization to be suspended during a certain period, but ultimate payment date not to be extended—amortization to be increased after the end of the period of suspension, *Corp. For. Bondh. Rep.*, No. 64 (1937), pp. 83, 86 f.)

of redemption.[84] In a few cases an adjustment of this nature has been sufficient to enable the debtor to maintain the debt service without a concurrent reduction in interest charges.

ARREARS

Debt settlements, at least those made after prolonged default, have seldom provided for the payment of arrears in full.[85] Arrears have usually been partially [86] or almost entirely [87] canceled. Moreover, the debtor has rarely been able to make any appreciable cash payments. Consequently arrears have, as a rule, been liquidated by their conversion, occasionally at par [88] but generally at a substantial discount,[89] into long-term bonds,

84. See, for example, the offer made by Nicaragua in 1937—the final maturity date of the bonds to be extended—*idem*, p. 68; Poland's offer of 1937 in respect of the sterling *tranche* of the stabilization loan—amortization period to be prolonged to 1967—*idem*, p. 21; the proposals negotiated by the League Loans Committee with the Hungarian Government with respect to the state loan of 1924 provided for a postponement of the final redemption of the loan by the operation of a reduced sinking fund. League Loans Committee, *Sixth Annual Report*, June, 1938, p. 54.

85. See League Loans Committee, *Third Annual Report*, June, 1935, p. 10. Young, *op. cit.*, pp. 33 ff.

86. Under an arrangement with Ecuador in 1855, £1,000,000 of arrears of interest were converted into £400,000 bonds; of the balance of the arrears, £400,000 were cancelled. *Corp. For. Bondh. Rep.*, No. 27 (1900), p. 85. Under the Costa Rican settlement of 1897, arrears of interest were to be liquidated at 50%. *Idem*, p. 75.

87. As under the debt settlements of 1942 and 1946 with Mexico. II, 96 and 101.

88. The payment program of the Chinese Minister of Finance, *supra*, n. 79, provided for the immediate payment of arrears of interest on various loans. In the 1885 settlement of the Costa Rican loans of 1871 and 1872, fully paid shares in the Costa Rica Railway Co. were to be given at £22 10s. for the arrears on each £100 old bond. *Idem*, pp. 73–74. In 1920 Haiti paid in full arrears of amortization and interest on the French loans. The agreement for settlement between Honduras and her creditors of 1926 provided for the redemption of the arrears of interest by payment in 60 half-yearly installments beginning in 1927. *Corp. For. Bondh. Rep.*, No. 61 (1934), p. 277. The purpose of the Salvadorean bond issue of 1923 was to provide for cash payment of interest arrears on the loans of 1908 and 1915. *Idem*, p. 410. Under the settlement with Turkey of 1876, all arrears were to be paid in full. II, 423 ff.

89. The settlement in 1927 of the Hungarian 3% "Iron Gates" loan provided that arrears coupons from 1919 to 1926 were to be met in one payment out of the net proceeds of the navigation tax in the "Iron Gates" sector collected during the same period. The distribution amounted to about 17% of the arrears. *Corp. For. Bondh. Rep.*, No. 61 (1934), p. 99. Claims registered in respect of the 70% interest unpaid by Greece from 1894 to 1898 were paid off in 1902 at the rate of 1 shilling on the pound. *Idem*, p. 222. Panama's readjustment plan of 1941 provided for the payment of interest in arrears on the 5% bonds at the rate of 4% per annum. *Com. and Fin. Chron.*, CLII (March 29, 1941), 1993.

which, in some instances, have not even been interest bearing. In a number of cases, such arrears bonds have subsequently been defaulted, so that bondholders have in fact recovered comparatively little from their unpaid coupons.

STRENGTHENING OF SECURITY

In order to insure that the readjusted debt service will be regularly paid, bondholders have frequently succeeded in obtaining under a settlement stronger security in the form of an assignment of additional or more productive revenues. When in 1935 the Chilean Law No. 5580 concerning the readjustment of the foreign indebtedness of the country was submitted to the bondholders, the Government pointed out that the revenues from the copper and nitrate industries which had been assigned to the service of the debt produced most of Chile's foreign exchange and that

in substituting substantially all of the foreign exchange revenues of Chile for revenues which produce only a return in pesos, the practical situation of the holder of a secured foreign currency obligation has been improved rather than impaired, even though the amount of such foreign exchange revenues may be less than the theoretical value in foreign currency of a sum in pesos which cannot be transferred abroad.[90]

Other instances where the service of foreign debts was improved by the assignment of new and more profitable security are found in the debt settlements of Turkey in 1878,[91] Portugal in 1902,[92] Morocco,[93] and a number of Central and South American countries.[94] The modification of

90. Memorandum of the Chilean Special Financial Commission, March 22, 1935, *For. Bondh. Prot. Coun. Rep.*, 1935, p. 53. See also the contract between the Turkish Government and the representatives of the holders of the Ottoman debt of 1928, under which the interest had to be paid in the most appreciated currency mentioned in the original loan contracts. II, 500.

91. Decree of Mouharrem, II, 507, revenues of Cyprus, Anatolia, and Roumelia, of tobacco from Samsoun, and from salt mines assigned as special security.

92. II, 377 ff.

93. Under the financial adjustments of 1909–11.

94. Province of Mendoza (Argentina), 1938 (assumption by the Government of the Argentine Republic of responsibility for the full service of the readjustment bonds. *For. Bondh. Prot. Coun., Rep.*, 1938, p. 77). Ecuador, 1908 (the Government not to constitute any charge in the future on the customs revenues to the prejudice of the bondholders' rights). Honduras, 1926 (guaranty for the payments under the new agreement is the revenue from the 3% consular service which is to be collected by means of special stamps sold to exporters through the National City Bank). Mexico, 1846 (as compensation to the bondholders for the reduction in the amount of their claims, the tobacco revenue and the duty on silver exports were hypothecated for the debt service); II, 10; 1884 (10% special security in

the original conditions of issue of the state loan of Hungary, 1924, and the Free City of Danzig tobacco monopoly loan of 1927 was accompanied by the establishment of a special account with the national banks of the two debtor countries to which sums equal to the proceeds from the revenues charged as security for the loans were to be credited; both governments undertook to use these monies for the purchase, at stated intervals, of the foreign currency required to meet the service of the loans.[95] In some readjustments the bondholders' security has been greatly strengthened by the establishment of some type of control over the administration and/or collection of the assigned revenues. The various forms of control which have been instituted and the results of their operation have already been sufficiently discussed.[96]

REVERSION CLAUSE

As a rule, the debt settlement has the effect of substituting new terms for the original loan contract; municipal decrees sometimes specifically provide for the surrender by bondholders of their former rights if the plan is accepted.[97] This exposes the creditors to the dangerous position of having to deal with the debtor on a less favorable basis if the latter fails

---

return for reduction in interest and of principal of arrears. II, 38). Nicaragua, 1895 (a special tax of at least $1 per quintal of coffee exported was to be the security for the service until the redemption of all bonds and certificates); 1911 (when the American bankers agreed to purchase Nicaraguan Treasury bills, they required that the bills were to be a lien on all export and import customs duties). Peru, 1886 (the Peruvian railroads were given to a bondholders' corporation, along with other resources, for a period of 60 years); 1907 (security for payments was a first charge on sugar consumption tax, the railroad concession was extended for 17 years). Venezuela, 1876 (additional security to the bondholders through 8% preference shares of the La Guayra and Caracas Railroad).

95. See memorandum published on behalf of the Hungarian Government, September 28, 1937. League Loans Committee, *Sixth Annual Report,* June, 1938, p. 50; memorandum published on behalf of the Free City of Danzig, September 21, 1937. *Idem,* pp. 35 f.

96. *Supra,* p. 286.

97. Under the Colombian decree of July 17, 1940, a surrender by the bond-holders of their rights, if the adjustment offer is accepted, is required. *Com. and Fin. Chron.,* CLII (January 4, 1941), p. 8. A "temporary adjustment" leaves the framework of existing treaties intact. League Loans Committee, *First Annual Report,* May, 1933, p. 9. See also the offer by China in 1936 which provided that "all provisions of the original contract remain unchanged except insofar as the carrying out of this offer gives effect to other specific provisions." *For. Bondh. Prot. Coun. Rep.,* 1936, p. 268. With regard to the controversy between the Protective Council and the Chilean Government concerning the legal effect of the acceptance of the debt service under Law 5580, see *supra,* nn. 10, 52.

to execute the new arrangement.[98] To avoid this danger, it has become customary in recent times to insert in the settlement plan a provision to the effect that the bondholders immediately revert to their original position in the event of the failure on the part of the debtor government to carry out the new terms.[99]

EQUITIES

In the absence of settled principles and fixed standards for the adjustment of public debts, the circumstances of the individual case will largely determine what both parties may accept as a fair and just settlement. Bondholders' protective committees whose function it is to examine offers

98. See the remarks of the Foreign Bondholders Protective Council with respect to the Chilean Law No. 5580. *For. Bondh. Prot. Coun. Rep.*, 1936, pp. 203, 236, 251 ff.

99. Such a "reservation clause" appeared as early as 1881 in the Turkish settlement of that year. See II, 450 ff., and the interesting diplomatic history behind the clause which was resisted by Turkey because of the "humiliating" anticipation of a future failure on the part of Turkey to honor her obligations. In the memorandum submitted, in 1937, by Danzig to the various bondholders' committees concerning the future service of the League loans and recommended for acceptance by the bondholders, it was stipulated that "in the event of any default occurring in the future service of the bonds of the loan pursuant to this Memorandum, or, so far as they are applicable, the provisions of the General Bond, the modifications specified in this Memorandum will immediately cease to be operative and the conditions for payment of interest and redemption specified in the General Bond will again become fully operative." League Loans Committee, *Sixth Annual Report*, June, 1938, pp. 34, 36; see also *Fifth Annual Report*, September, 1937, pp. 13 f., 50. See also *Corp. For. Bondh. Rep.*, No. 64 (1937), pp. 38 ff.; *idem*, No. 66 (1939), pp. 30 ff. *For. Bondh. Prot. Coun. Rep.*, 1937, p. 280. The arrangement of 1897 with Costa Rica for the payment of the defaulted loan of 1885 provided that if the new arrangement should not be carried out for a period of 6 months the rights of the bondholders under the old 1885 arrangement should be revived. *Corp. For. Bondh. Rep.*, No. 61 (1934), p. 169. The offer submitted by the Government of Peru in 1938 to the holders of bonds of the $7\frac{1}{2}\%$ (guano) loan of 1922 contained a provision to the effect that "should the Government for any reason fail to carry out any of the conditions of this offer, all the rights to which the bonds are now entitled shall be reacquired automatically." *Corp. For. Bondh. Rep.*, No. 65 (1938), p. 58. In the announcement of January 19, 1939, by the Republic of Uruguay to the holders of certain loans, it was stated that "in the event of the failure on the part of the Government to comply with any of the terms of these offers in respect of the assented Bonds of the Loans to which these offers relate, the rights originally attaching to such Bonds shall revive and the conditions of the relative offer shall cease to have effect." *Idem*, No. 66 (1939), p. 54. For a similar clause, see Bulgarian arrangement of 1926, *idem*, No. 56 (1929), p. 93.

submitted by debtors frequently state specific reasons why a certain proposal should be accepted or rejected. This practice may gradually lead to the building up of standards to which debtors and creditors alike will be forced to conform. The objections raised by the Foreign Bondholders Protective Council against the Chilean Law No. 5580 concerning the country's financial rehabilitation present a good example of a reasoned argument against a debtor proposal,[100] while the statement issued by the Council with regard to an offer by Poland in 1936 well summarizes the considerations that may be advanced in support of acceptance of such proposal.[101] Some of these considerations have already been mentioned in the preceding pages; for example, the subjective attitude of the debtor toward his default, his "paying capacity," the ratio to be maintained between the rate of interest and sinking fund payments, etc. It seems a fair conclusion from the majority of modern debt adjustment plans that the insertion in the plan of a "most favored debt" and "reversion" clause now belongs to the standard requirements for such arrangements. Sometimes the acceptance of an offer made by a debtor

---

100. See the summary in *For. Bondh. Prot. Coun. Rep.*, 1935, pp. 73–74. These were the "essential points that seem of importance in any adjustment that might be made of the external public debt [of Chile]:

"1. Plan might be statutory plan instead of an understanding or agreement with the bondholders [as in the case of Brazil].

"2. This plan should provide for,—
    (a) Definite but limited period of service.
    (b) Definite amount of annual service for the limited period, each bond issue to have the same proportionate ratio to full service.
    (c) Bulk of service to go to interest.
    (d) Normal application pursuant to bond contracts of whatever amortization service is provided.
    (e) Bond obligation to remain unchanged, except as to coupons affected by the Plan and partial amortization for the period.
    (f) Service of past due coupons.
    (g) Equitable adjustment on pesos already accumulated for service of certain issues."

See also *idem*, 1938, pp. 14 ff.

101. "In determining the reasonableness of this Polish offer bondholders will have in mind:

"That the Government of Poland is showing a will to make some service;

"That the bond obligation is to be unaffected by an acceptance of the Polish offer except as to the three coupons for which service is provided;

"That while the cash offer is to be for a partial interest service only, there is to be an offer of full interest service in Funding Bonds—the transfer of the funds for serving such Bonds (principal and interest) to be free from any and all Polish exchange restrictions;

"That the Polish Government paid the full service (interest and amortization) on its obligations during the most trying years of the depression; and

"That the Polish Government pleads as justification for the offer it is now to make the compulsion of a national situation resulting from causes it can neither control nor remedy."

Idem, 1936, p. 707.

after negotiations with bondholder organizations is urged upon the bondholders simply because it is "the best obtainable." [102] A settlement based on such resigned appraisal of the situation will hardly serve as a precedent for future arrangements. However, where an adjustment is characterized as being both fair to the debtor and "consistent with the broad equities and long-view interests of the bondholders," [103] it is likely to provide useful guidance in the negotiation of other settlements, where similar circumstances are present.[104]

The successful conclusion of a satisfactory debt adjustment will in

102. See, for example, *Corp. For. Bondh. Rep.*, No. 64 (1937), pp. 20, 73: Many attempts have been made to get the offer improved, but without success, and the Council therefore felt that, while the offer was an extremely disappointing one, there was but little likelihood of better terms for these coupons being obtainable. League Loans Committee, *Third Annual Report*, June, 1935, p. 16 (as there was no way of finding out about Bulgaria's transfer capacity, acquiescence in the offer submitted by Bulgaria was recommended); *Fourth Annual Report*, August, 1936, pp. 13 f., 29, 33; *Sixth Annual Report*, June, 1938, p. 9: ". . . in the past few years there have been occasions when the Committee have been led to recommend bondholders to accept temporary payments rather because they were the best obtainable than because they considered them completely adequate." Holders of the Santo Domingo Hartmont bonds realized in 1888 that they could not secure as favorable a settlement as that suggested in 1885 or 1886 and therefore agreed to accept £20 in the new bonds for £100 of the old. II, 209. The specific economic condition of a country as affected by circumstances such as an earthquake or depression may cause bondholders to relent and to accept adjustment offers. See II, 560 ff.

103. Letter of the Foreign Bondholders Protective Council to the Secretary of State advising him of the results of its study of the Dominican debt situation, August 15, 1934. *For. Bondh. Prot. Coun. Rep.*, 1934, p. 63: ". . . the proposal of the Dominican Government seems to the Council fair to the Dominican Republic and its people and consistent with the broad equities and long-view interests of the bondholders. . . ." See also *idem*, 1935, p. 111; *idem*, 1936, pp. 266, 268, 350 ff.; *idem*, 1938, p. 19.

104. See League Loans Committee, *First Annual Report*, May, 1933, p. 36 (40% transfer by Bulgarian Government considered fair); *Second Annual Report*, June, 1934, p. 14; *Fifth Annual Report*, September, 1937, p. 11 (they consider that the proposed new level of both interest and amortization was reasonable and they therefore recommend the settlement proposed by the Danzig Government to the acceptance of the bondholders); *Eighth Annual Report*, August, 1940, p. 8 (the Committee considered that under the conditions created by the war these proposals [by the Greek Government] were not unreasonable). Letter of the Foreign Bondholders Protective Council to the Minister of Finance of the Province of Buenos Aires. *For. Bondh. Prot. Coun. Rep.*, 1935, pp. 18 f.: ". . . a plan which as a whole and under all the circumstances involved in the situation seems to it fair and reasonable both to the holders of these securities and to the Province"; *idem*, 1936, p. 554: ". . . now that economic conditions have improved, it was not felt that cutting this interest to 3% for seven years and to 3½% thereafter could be recommended to the bondholders as just and equitable." The Colombian offer of 1940 for the adjustment of certain dollar obligations was considered by the De-

itself do much to restore the debtor's credit standing.[105] But its lasting effect will depend on the manner and spirit in which it is executed. While the very essence of a debt settlement is the adjustment of the debtor's financial burden in accordance with his present condition, and future prospects, unforeseeable events in world politics and economics may again frustrate the efforts of even the most conscientious debtor to live up to his new engagements.[106] Disputes between creditors and debtor with regard to the performance of the plan may lead to new defaults. A "reversion clause" of the type mentioned above will safeguard the creditors against losing their legal rights in case the debtor fails to carry out the plan. A more constructive remedy against such contingency, however, is provided by a clause submitting future disputes to arbitration. Its practicability was demonstrated when a controversy between Turkey and her foreign creditors over the execution of the decree of Mouharrem was settled by an arbitral award rendered under the terms of the decree.[107]

While "equity" is the touchstone and goal of all readjustments, differences of opinion necessarily arise between the conflicting views, though not the long-run interests of debtor and creditor. An assumed conflict of interests and differences of judgment as to the debtor's present and future debt-paying capacity account for the variety of adjustments in debt settlements.

---

partment of State as a "fair effort on the part of the Colombian Government to adjust its obligations." *Dept. of St. Bull.*, IV (January 4, 1941), 12 f. When the San Domingo Improvement Co. protested against reductions under the 1907 agreement, it was persuaded by the Department of State to accept the settlement because it was deemed to be "reasonable." II, 254.

105. *Corp. For. Bondh. Rep.*, No. 64 (1937), pp. 10 f., 33. As in Greece after 1900 and Mexico after 1894.

106. Influence of the war on Bulgaria's capacity to transfer. II, 564. Failure of the Mexican oil revenues forced readjustment of the debt settlement. II, 76. Partly because of adverse economic conditions (especially in the silver industry), a new readjustment of Mexican indebtedness became necessary in 1931. II, 82–83. The financial plan of Nicaragua of 1917 worked successfully until 1932 when world conditions caused suspension of sinking fund payments on the 1909 loan and of payments on the customs bonds of 1918. A change in the coffee situation of Salvador was not considered sufficient by the Council of Foreign Bondholders to justify reduction of service payments. *Corp. For. Bondh. Rep.*, No. 64 (1937), p. 81. Depression necessitated further adjustments in the payments of Serbia in 1933. Association Nationale, Communication No. 371 (October 14, 1933).

107. See II, 464. A dispute between the Greek Government and the International Financial Commission in 1926 on the subject of converting the plus values from drachmas into gold francs was settled by arbitration in 1927. II, 341; *Corp. For. Bondh. Rep.*, No. 61 (1934), p. 228. Under the protocol between the United States and the Dominican Government, arbitration for the settlement of disputes was provided, *idem*, No. 56 (1929), p. 326. See also Weiser, *Trusts on the Continent of Europe*, pp. 89 f.

Section XX

PRIORITIES AND PREFERENCES

WHEN a debtor state in financial distress ceases to perform its obligations arising from foreign loans, bondholders often rudely awaken to the fact that their claim to satisfaction has to meet the competition of other creditors, domestic as well as foreign, who seek to obtain preferred payment out of available assets. Even among themselves, bondholders are likely to demand preferential treatment because of the special nature or particular merits of their respective claims.[1]

THE PRINCIPLE OF EQUALITY

Fairness and justice in the adjustment of public debts require that all bondholders be treated alike. The principle of equality, however, does not signify uniformity of treatment. As will appear presently, the grading and grouping, according to their intrinsic merits, of claims with respect to the utilization of the available assets of the debtor have, in fact, been expressly recognized in some of the major debt adjustment plans.[2] All

1. For a typical instance of an internecine struggle among bondholders seeking to get for themselves or to prevent others from obtaining preferential treatment, see II, 421 (with respect to the tribute loans of 1854, 1871). When a few foreign bondholders sued the Egyptian Government before the mixed courts, the powers who had set them up had to step in and prevent further suits lest some creditors jeopardize the chances of the whole group. II, 601, 611. The question of priorities is sometimes left open for future litigation. II, 141, 142–144. Cf. Schoo, *Régimen jurídico*, pp. 413 ff.

2. Under the so-called Niemeyer, as well as the Aranha, Plan for the adjustment of the indebtedness of Brazil, bonds were classified into grades, each grade having its own percentage of service. See SEC, *Rep.*, Pt. V, pp. 386 f.; *Com. and Fin. Chron.*, CL (March 16, 1940), 1654. By the Innsbruck protocol of 1923 for the settlement of the debts of the successor states of Austria and Hungary, loans were divided into gold loans, foreign currency loans, and railway loans for the determination of the service rate. *Corp. For. Bondh. Rep.*, No. 61 (1934), p. 97. The Egyptian law of liquidation established three classes of floating debt creditors (privileged creditors, creditors holding debts secured by pledges, ordinary creditors). II, 608. In the Greek adjustment of 1898, loans were grouped according to their original security (monopoly loan, railway loans, *rentes*). II, 329. Under an agreement of

that the principle implies is that preferential treatment shall not be accorded to particular classes of bondholders without valid cause. A differentiation between bondholders according to their nationality has always been considered as one of the chief instances of illegal discrimination.[3] On the other hand, the better treatment of loans issued as a result of a funding operation and entailing sacrifices to the holders of the earlier

1915, the Salvadorean Government undertook to use funds for the service of its debt in the following order: (1) interest on new bonds; (2) interest on old bonds; (3) balance to amortize new bonds. *Corp. For. Bondh. Rep.*, No. 42 (1915), p. 28. As to the groups of loans formed under the terms of the decree of Mouharrem, see II, 447 ff. The principle of a uniform rate of payment for all external loans such as adopted by the Chilean Law No. 5580 was assailed by the Foreign Bondholders Protective Council: "The view of the Council was expressed against the provision of a flat rate of interest; the Council has asked that all be treated proportionately." *For. Bondh. Prot. Coun. Rep.*, 1935, pp. 84 f.; *idem*, 1936, p. 236; *idem*, 1938, p. 14: under (3), a flat rate of interest is offered instead of each issue receiving the same proportionate rate of the full service. Under a recent offer, Colombia promised its foreign creditors 50% of interest, while serving internal bonds and short-term credits in full. The Protective Council protested against this discrimination. *Com. and Fin. Chron.*, CLII (June 7, 1941), 3573.

3. Gantenbein, *Financial Questions in United States Foreign Policy*, p. 187. Cf. Schoo, *op. cit.*, p. 442. The question was raised when Germany discriminated against American holders of the Dawes and Young loans. See, for example, the letter of the Foreign Bondholders Protective Council to Dr. Hjalmar Schacht, July 12, 1934. *For. Bondh. Prot. Coun. Rep.*, 1934, p. 90: "To serve the Dawes and Young bonds held by the nationals of other countries and to decline to serve the bonds held by Americans would constitute the grossest discrimination and would be violative of every principle of justice and fair dealing." See also *idem*, 1938, p. 566. Belgians were discriminated against in the conversion of Santo Domingo loans in 1897; they were appeased by the appointment of a Belgian inspector and deputy in the personnel of the customs régie. II, 222. The San Domingo Improvement Co. bonds held in England received in the settlement of 1907 less favorable terms than the bonds held in France and Belgium. II, 255. As to the practice of discrimination, see Feis, *The Changing Pattern of International Economic Affairs*, p. 75: The extent to which many debtor countries up to the outbreak of the war sustained the practice of equality as between the investors of different countries has been, considering all the difficulties, rather remarkable. Thus, it will be found that Europe west of the Rhine, the Scandinavian countries, Italy, Poland, Austria and Hungary in the main, Japan, the British dominions, and almost every country of Latin America have made conscientious efforts to accord equality as between bondholders of different nationality in regard to payments on long-term loans and investments. See also *For. Bondh. Prot. Coun. Rep.*, 1937, p. 22: The Polish Government was making serious efforts to avoid discrimination between bondholders of different nationality, such as had been practised by other governments, either voluntarily or under pressure of various creditor groups and their governments. Under the arrangement made by Bulgaria in 1925, existing black lists of bondholders, II, 546, n. 75, were canceled and discrimination owing to nationality, resulting from recouponment, was limited to 3 years. *Corp. For. Bondh. Rep.*, No. 61 (1934), p. 120.

issues has been held permissible on the ground that the holders of such funding bonds should not be asked to make new sacrifices on an equal footing with other creditors.[4] So, preferences sometimes accorded to the national debt of a state over the obligations of its political subdivisions have been regarded as justified by the necessity of protecting primarily the national credit without which the credit of subsidiary political organizations would not be sound.[5] Explicit stipulations in a loan contract granting priority rights provide, of course, the strongest title to preferential treatment.[6]

THE "MOST-FAVORED DEBT" CLAUSE

As a logical consequence of the principle of nondiscrimination, a provision which may be called the "most-favored debt clause" has made its appearance in individual service arrangements and debt adjustment plans of recent years. It is designed to extend automatically to the adjusted debt all the advantages which the debtor government may in the future grant to any one of its outstanding external obligations.[7]

4. See *Corp For. Bondh. Rep.*, No. 64 (1937), p. 36; *idem*, No. 65 (1938), p. 10: The European associations agreed that funding bonds should receive preferential treatment over other loans. In the Greek settlement of 1897, the 1893 funding loan was classified under Group I. *Idem*, No. 61 (1934), pp. 222 ff.

5. See *For. Bondh. Prot. Coun. Rep.*, 1934, p. 28: The Council was not in a position to challenge either the wisdom or the propriety, first, of classifying into groups the various Brazilian external debt obligations and, second, giving preference in matters of exchange to national federal obligations over state and municipal obligations. See also *Corp. For. Bondh. Rep.*, No. 65 (1938), p. 10: loans issued by the central government to enjoy priority of transfer over provincial and municipal issues.

6. See, for example, *Corp. For. Bondh. Rep.*, No. 65 (1937), p. 77: In the case of the 4% external loan of Romania of 1932, which enjoys a contractual priority, the percentage of interest payments was increased from 60% to 65% and a further amount of £19.455 per annum was placed at the disposal of the bondholders.

7. In an agreement with the Foreign Bondholders Protective Council, the Polish Government declared that the principle of nondiscrimination means that, if for any reason more favorable treatment should be accorded by Poland to any one of its outstanding external obligations, then the same treatment will be extended to all Polish obligations covered by the adjustment plan. *For. Bondh. Prot. Coun. Rep.*, 1936, pp. 706 f. The clauses usually take one of the following forms: "The Bulgarian Government undertakes that, if it accords more favorable terms to any other foreign obligation due from or guaranteed by the Bulgarian State, it will accord at least as favorable terms to the League Loans." League Loans Committee, *Third Annual Report*, June, 1935, p. 30; *Fifth Annual Report*, September, 1937, p. 18. "If at any time, any Bond of any external issue of Bonds of the Government of Peru existing at the date of this offer, should receive more favorable treatment than that accorded to the present issue, equal conditions shall immediately be accorded to all Bonds to which this offer, when accepted, relates." Offer by the

THE PRINCIPLE OF DIFFERENTIATION

While the private law of bankruptcy is governed by the principle of equality of claims in the distribution of the debtor's assets (*par condicio creditorum*),[8] differential treatment of the holders of foreign government bonds in case of default is the ordinary rule. The reason therefor lies in the semipolitical nature of government loans and in the great variety of forms and purposes for which such loans are issued. The preference accorded to the guaranteed loan of 1833 in the Greek settlement of 1898 was due to the political pressure exercised by the guaranteeing powers against Greece rather than to any intrinsic merit setting the loan apart from others contracted by Greece.[9] An argument frequently advanced to justify discrimination concerns the quality of the claim as expressed in the nature and value of the security behind it. When the Brazilian Government issued its decree of February 5, 1934, dividing the holders of Brazilian bonds into certain classes for the full or partial payment of interest and sinking fund, it was announced that "owing to the difference in the quality of the securities it would have been out of the question to treat all the securities alike. The Brazilian Government recognize this, and have graded the securities in an order of priority."[10]

Government of Peru to the holders of bonds of the 7½% (guano) loan of 1922, November 16, 1938. *Corp. For. Bondh. Rep.*, No. 65 (1938), p. 58. "If at any time any Bond of any issue now outstanding to which these offers do not apply . . . or any Bond in respect of which these offers might have been but have not been accepted should receive treatment more favorable as regards service or otherwise than the treatment extended by these offers such more favorable treatment shall be forthwith extended to all Bonds in respect of which these offers have been or shall be accepted. In determining whether treatment is more favorable regard shall be had to the original rights attaching to the Bonds to which such treatment is extended." Announcement by the Republic of Uruguay, January 19, 1939. *Idem*, No. 66 (1939), pp. 53 f. "The Republic also agrees in the Conversion Bonds that if it shall hereafter find it necessary to obtain any loan by giving security or lien or charge upon any of its assets or revenues the new Conversion Bonds shall *ipso facto* share in such lien or charge equally and rateably with such other debt." Statement of the Foreign Bondholders Protective Council with respect to certain Uruguayan bonds, August 1, 1938. *For. Bondh. Prot. Coun. Rep.*, 1938, pp. 1072, 1078, 1084. For other instances of most-favored-debt clauses, see League Loans Committee, *Second Annual Report*, June, 1934, pp. 31, 38; *Fifth Annual Report*, September, 1937, p. 42; *Sixth Annual Report*, June, 1938, p. 14; *For. Bondh. Prot. Coun. Rep.*, 1937, p. 711.

8. Dölle, "Konkurs," *Rechtsvergleichendes Handwörterbuch*, V, 120 ff. This is subject to exceptions, for commercial codes—serving as a model for the Egyptian settlement of 1880—recognize the priority of claims of labor, sustenance, etc.

9. II, 321 f. See also Feilchenfeld, De Maury Elrick, and Judd, "Priority Problems in Public Debt Settlements," *Col. Law Rev.*, XXX (1930), 1115, 1129.

10. *The Times* (London), February 8, 1934.

In Article 4 of the Bulgarian debt adjustment agreement of 1925 it was explained that "the committees of holders agree to establish between the service of the various loans a distinction considered as founded on the existence or non-existence of guarantees and on the nature and yield of the securities which have been respectively allocated to them by the contracts of issue." [11] Under the contract of June 13, 1928, between Turkey and representatives of the bondholders for the settlement of Turkey's share of the Ottoman public debt, the unified bonds received preferential treatment within a group of loans entitled to an option of payment in sterling because of "the special character of their contractual guaranties and the reduction effected in the capital of the Series Bonds at the time of the unification." [12]

SPECIAL REASONS FOR DIFFERENTIATION

Sometimes the significance of a loan for the economic or political life of the country may provide the reason for granting it a priority or preference. Thus, the League Loans Committee claimed priority for the postwar loans issued under the auspices of the League, on the ground that these loans had been devoted to the economic and financial rehabilitation of the countries concerned.[13] The preferential treatment of the float-

11. II, 548, n. 76.

12. II, 500–501.

13. See League Loans Committee, *Second Annual Report,* June, 1934, pp. 9, 16–22 (the Committee have felt bound to emphasize that the League loans "form part of a powerful and useful reconstruction machine" and that the debtor countries "would be acting both far-sightedly and fairly if they accord special treatment to the League Loans"); *Seventh Annual Report,* July, 1939, p. 10 (Greece's League Loans "are entitled to consideration in the very front rank of the Government's liabilities"). The Austrian Government declared that the priority of the 1923 guaranteed loan as compared with all other Austrian external loans would "on all occasions be faithfully observed." League Loans Committee, *First Annual Report,* May, 1933, p. 32. When Hungary in 1931 declared a transfer moratorium for her external debt, she specifically exempted from it the $7\frac{1}{2}\%$ League loan which thus took precedence over all other Hungarian obligations. *Idem,* pp. 18, 43; see also *Fifth Annual Report,* September, 1937, p. 10 (maintenance of the prior position of League loans in arrangements with foreign long-term creditors). In an article in the *Times,* Sir Austen Chamberlain, Chairman of the League Loans Committee, claimed special treatment for League loans because they saved the countries concerned from complete economic and political collapse. League Loans Committee, *Second Annual Report,* p. 25. A better treatment for British loans to Chile was claimed by *The Times* (London), February 4, 1935, on the ground that "the bulk of Britain's claims represent loans made at low rates, for national purposes of a constructive character; they exist as an integral factor in Chile's gradual economic development over a century."

ing gold debt in the unified internal debt of Greece in 1898, which allowed the banks of the country to resume their normal activities, was prompted by the need for the reëstablishment of financial order in Greece, for which this aid to the banks paved the way.[14]

The same position may be said to be held by loans made to insolvent states after the readjustment of their indebtedness for the purpose of assisting them in the discharge of obligations assumed under the new settlement plan.[15] Similarly, because of their importance for the stability of the national economy of the debtor country, a privileged place in the scale of readjusted debts has frequently been obtained by bonds issued for the construction and maintenance of railroads in undeveloped countries [16] and by claims of local contractors or foreign concessionaries aris-

14. II, 333.

15. The Brazilian Government continued full service on its three funding loans on the ground that those bonds were issued in readjustment of defaults. Madden, Nadler, and Sauvain, *America's Experience as a Creditor Nation*, p. 302. The Greek funding loan of 1898 was placed in Group I and accorded priority with respect to participation in the "plus values." II, 331. In the 1930 agreement with respect to the Mexican debt, Series A bonds, issued to replace existing secured loans, were to have a prior claim on pledged revenues. II, 81. The payments to be made pursuant to the conversion arrangement of 1897 with respect to the Costa Rican debt were to be preferential to those of any future loan. *Corp. For. Bondh. Rep.*, No. 56 (1929), p. 125. Under the Argentine legislation of 1934 with respect to the readjustment of the dollar and sterling loans, the readjustment (dollar) bonds were given a first charge on the revenues collected by the National Government under the unification law and the income tax law. Institute of International Finance, Bull. No. 83, January 3, 1936. Under the arrangement adjusting the 1915 default of Salvador, the old debt service was to be resumed after August, 1919, and the funds were to be used to pay (1) interest on the new bonds; (2) interest on old bonds; and (3) amortization of the new bonds. *Corp. For. Bondh. Rep.*, No. 42 (1915), p. 28.

16. The Mexican Government in 1890 gave a preference to the payment of railway subsidies over all other obligations, the reason being that with the growth of railway mileage the economic and financial position of the country became stronger and its power to pay its creditors, therefore, greater. II, 49. Under the terms of the arbitral award between the Ecuadorean Government and the Guayaquil and Quito Railway Co., the sums required for the annual service of the railroad bonds and for the expenses of the service were made a "first and preferred obligation on the total receipts of the custom house." The Ecuadorean Government agreed not to establish "any obligation whatever against said revenues to the prejudice of the bondholders' rights." *For. Rel.*, 1923, I, 934 ff. Under the Peruvian contract with Raphael the funds available for the bondholders were applied first to the arrears and service of the Pisco Railway loan of 1869. The holders of this loan were recognized as having a prior claim throughout. II, 124, 163, n. 32. While Turkey was paying only one third of its assigned revenues to the Debt Council in Turkish currency, she paid the regular amount for the service of the Anatolian Railway bonds in Swiss francs. II, 508.

ing out of the operation of public utilities.[17] In general, it could be argued that those who lend their money for the express purpose of preserving the normal functioning of the economic life of the debtor are in the position of creditors, who have taken action to protect the assets of the common debtor against deterioration and to whom, for this reason, special consideration is due.[18] Even such economic factors as a favorable balance of trade or payment between the debtor and a particular creditor country [19] or the average market value of various loans [20] have been made the basis for differentiations with regard to the apportionment of available assets among the creditors. The priorities accorded to certain loans under the scheme of liquidation of the Turkish indebtedness in 1881 were based on such considerations as their chronological order, special hypothecations connected with each issue, the particular circumstances under which they were raised, the degree of credit that Turkey had at the time of the floating of the loans and therefore the justification that the bondholders had in lending their money, the fact that in later loans

17. See the Greenfield claim in the Egyptian debt settlement of 1880. II, 609, n. 25. Harbor dues payable to concessionaires were considered preferred obligations in the agreement of April 1, 1900, with respect to payment of Dominican debts. II, 226, n. 3. The claim of a German concern which had constructed harbor works at Tangier was accorded preferential treatment in the Moroccan settlement of 1909.

18. See the Case of Great Britain, "The Venezuelan Preferential Claims Arbitration of 1903," U.S. Sen. Doc. No. 119, 58th Cong., 3d Sess., p. 766. Reference is also made to the case of salvage where "a similar principle is applied by the general law maritime, which is part of the law of nations. It is well established that (in this case) a later creditor is preferred to an earlier on the ground that the safety of the ship has been secured by his advance. . . ." See also Counter Case of Great Britain, *idem*, p. 983: "The creditor who takes action to protect his interests is entitled to priority over another creditor who does not choose to enforce his rights. *Vigilantibus, non dormientibus subvenit lex.*" The Hague Court of Arbitration awarded the blockading powers preferential satisfaction out of the 30% of the customs revenues of La Guayra and Puerto Cabello set aside by Venezuela for the payment of foreign claims. Scott, *The Hague Court Reports*, pp. 441 ff.

19. With respect to the Brazilian Government's debt plan of February, 1934, it was complained that the American bondholders, by the forceful presentation of their view, had secured better treatment than the English bondholders, and that the English bondholders had suffered in consequence. *The Times* (London), February 10, 1934, remarked: "This is true, but the balance of payments between the United States and Brazil is much more favorable to Brazil than the trade balance with this country, and on that account alone the American bondholders could present a much more powerful claim than the British bondholders."

20. The allocation of priorities in the settlement of the Tunisian debt in 1870 was not based on the usual analysis of origin and nature of each loan but rather on the average market values. Sometimes the amount of a loan may contribute to securing it preferential treatment. Thus, the smallness of the Pisco-to-Yca loan had much to do with securing it priority. II, 182.

mention was made of the fact that provision must always be made for the service of prior loans.[21] Sometimes the mere chronological priority of a loan, as distinguished from later salvage loans, is held sufficient justification for granting it also a prior rank in the allocation of the payments to be made by the debtor on its foreign indebtedness.[22] The contract is crucial; only silence or conflicting provisions present difficulty.

PREFERENCES GRANTED

Among the preferences that have been granted, the following may be noted: preferences as to the amount of the claim, the time of paying interest as well as principal,[23] the allocation of certain revenues to the service of the loan,[24] the assignment of new security,[25] and the transfer of the service abroad by preferred assignment of foreign exchange.[26]

21. II, 448–49.

22. In the proceedings of the Turkish debt commission, it was recognized that the first claim to certain revenues (silk, fish, etc., taxes) belonged to the holders of earlier foreign loans and that it would be impossible to remove this clear priority. II, 436 ff. Sometimes earlier creditors are favored, sometimes later ones obtain priority. The decision probably depends on the need of the debtor. *The Times* (London), December 26, 1876, thought that the Egyptian decree of November, 1876, was objectionable. The earlier promises should have been given preference because the later ones were given subject to them and with notice of them. See also the remark in *Corp. For. Bondh. Rep.*, No. 64 (1937), p. 10: "Another point which should also receive attention in the future is the position of loans contracted by a Government which already has a fairly heavy burden of debt and which, as a consequence of this additional burden, cannot continue to meet the service of the whole debt. It cannot be denied that many countries now in default would have been able to continue to meet their debt obligation had they not added to the existing burden by fresh and unwise borrowing. The President of the Canadian Chamber of Commerce is reported to have observed that 'It seems very unfair that the last straw of Debt which breaks the camel's back should rank on the carcass equally with the first load which the camel was well able to bear,' a statement which puts the point concisely."

23. Under the terms of the Egyptian law of liquidation, preferences as to the amount of the payment were granted to the so-called privileged floating debts (debts secured by mortgages, state employees, working men, pensioners) which were fully recognized and paid in specie. A preference in time was accorded to debts secured by pledges which were paid immediately in return for a reduction in amount. II, 608–609.

24. For instance, in the final settlement of the Dominican debt in 1907, a first charge on the customs was given to the bankers.

25. The awards of the Nicaraguan Claims Commission of 1911 were met partly in cash, partly in bonds secured on a surcharge upon customs duties. In the Egyptian settlement, the Rothschild loan of 1878 was given a mortgage on the property of the Khedive.

26. In connection with the Brazilian decree of February 5, 1934, concerning the payment of the Brazilian foreign debt, it was announced that "Grade I (of the

Priorities are sometimes expressly stipulated in the loan agreement [27] or agreed upon in a settlement reached by the debtor with his creditors.[28] In other instances, classifications of claims are made by the debtor himself and, if based on reasonable grounds, have not been objected to by the creditors.[29]

The usual case of state insolvency does not involve the taking over and distribution of a fixed amount of assets among creditors, as is the case in bankruptcy proceedings of an individual or corporation, but

securities) will comprise the Funding Loans of the Federal Government . . . in respect of which foreign exchange for the full service will be provided. Grade II will consist of the São Paulo Coffee Realisation Loan of 1930, for which sufficient exchange will be allocated to maintain payment of interest in full . . . . In respect of the loans included in other grades no sinking fund payments will be transferred . . . ." *Times* (London), February 8, 1934. In the settlement of 1902, the external bondholders of the Portuguese debt were conceded priority over the internal (II, 377) with respect to security. In a statement regarding the moratorium legislation of 1931, the Hungarian Government listed certain issues which were to receive priority in assigning foreign exchange. See Dulles, "The Protection of American Foreign Bondholders," *For. Aff.*, X (1932), 481.

27. II, 66 f (priorities accorded in the De la Huerta–Lamont agreement); II, 259 (the terms of the 1906 loan with Kuhn, Loeb & Co. provided for the following priorities: expenses of receivership, interest on bonds, sinking fund, cost of purchasing and redeeming bonds to be retired); II, 537 ff. (the loan contract of 1902 [Art. 28] provided that the new lenders should decide in what order old debts should be discharged). The general bond of the Yugoslav Mortgage Bank bonds contained a clause fixing the order of appropriation of monies collected by the fiscal agent in case of default, expenses incurred by enforcing the indenture ranking first. *For. Bondh. Prot. Coun. Rep.*, 1936, p. 831. The charges established by the Dreyfus contract of August 17, 1869, on the net proceeds of the Peruvian guano were mentioned in each subsequent loan. II, 165.

28. The method of establishing priorities in debt settlements may vary. In the Egyptian readjustment procedure, the commission of liquidation of 1880 was to sit as a sort of bankruptcy court; all parties affected by the reorganization were to be heard. Since in the course of the Tunisian settlement of 1870 the various loans were unified into one common stock, the only method for applying different effective rates of interest to various classes was to effect the conversion at varying rates.

29. By the Brazilian Decree 7774 of September 15, 1893, priority of bondholders over other creditors of governmental subdivisions was created. Hamel, "La protection des obligataires," *Rapports préparatories à la semaine internationale de droit*, VI, 3. See also the Brazilian decree of February 5, 1934. The Government of Peru, after Dreyfus had suspended the debt service in 1873, issued a decree declaring that the holders of the 1870 and 1872 bonds had a preferential hypothecation over all the guano of Peru. II, 121. While municipal decrees may create priorities, they may also destroy them, subject to obligations *contra*. The Peruvian decree of January 7, 1880, which provided for the consolidation of all the outstanding Peruvian loans into one and thereby effectively abolished any priorities which might at one time have existed, was upheld by Chitty, J. See *Corp. For. Bondh. Rep.*, No. 11 (1883), pp. 75–78. Also, II, 142 ff.

consists almost always in apportioning shares of future revenues to various claimants according to a system of priority. Although the actual granting of preferences seems to be dictated by the peculiar facts of each case,[30] certain claims have recurrently been acknowledged as meriting preferential treatment.

INTERNAL NEEDS, ADMINISTRATIVE EXPENSES

A first charge on all its revenues exists in favor of the state itself for the satisfaction of its legitimate needs.[31] "The debtor State must continue

30. Feilchenfeld, in Quindry, *Bonds and Bondholders, Rights and Remedies,* Vol. II, sec. 656(a).

31. Feilchenfeld, *et al.,* in *Col. Law Rev.,* XXX (1930), 1115; Sauvaire, *Procédure employée en droit international contre les états qui ne remplissent pas leurs engagements,* p. 39; Von Bar, *The Theory and Practice of Private International Law,* p. 1104: "The State has a kind of *beneficium competentiae* to a large extent: it must in the first place support itself, and the payment of debt only stands in the second line." See also *supra,* section on Readjustment. Recognition of the first charge for indispensable needs of the debtor state is often urged as serving the bondholders' own interests. See League Loans Committee, *Second Annual Report,* June, 1934, p. 9: It is right to "subordinate the immediate claims of the League Loans holders to the wide issue of the reconstruction of each debtor country" and "to produce sounder budgetary conditions even at temporary cost to the bondholders." *For. Bondh. Prot. Coun. Rep.,* 1936, pp. 8 f.: In the establishment of public works enabling the state to function in a manner adequate to the meeting of its obligations "the bondholder himself is vitally interested because if he is to be paid there must be a stable and prosperous debtor State." See also the declaration of the Hungarian Government of July 1, 1932. League Loans Committee, *First Annual Report,* May, 1933, p. 43: The securing of the country's internal order and maintenance of the normal course of economic life are important interests of the creditors. When the United States took over the administration of the finances of Haiti, 75% of the gross revenues were pledged for the public debt. The State Department ruled that the maintenance of the Haitian Government should be a first charge on the fund. *Hearings on Haiti and Santo Domingo,* 67th Cong., 1st and 2d Sess., 1922, II, 1429. The Peruvian decree of 1931 stopped the service on the national loan of 1927 on the ground that the "indispensable public services" of the Republic did not permit the continued service of the loan. II, 189. The Mexican Minister of Finance to the Mexican Minister for Foreign Affairs, February 22, 1833. *Brit. and For. St. Pap.,* XXXVIII, 974 f.: "If [the President of the Republic] has not been able to perform all that he could have wished, it has arisen . . . because the resources of the public Treasury being inadequate to the expenses indispensably requisite to the existence of the nation and to pay its debts. . . . An arrear of many months of the pay of the employees and a multitude of persons who have a claim to salaries and pensions from the public Treasury, an enormous debt contracted during the last year and all the current expenses which cannot be postponed . . . such are the embarrassments with which His Excellency the President found himself surrounded on taking charge of the executive power . . . when it is impossible to pay at once all the creditors of the nation, or to meet all the exigencies of the State, it is also impossible to satisfy the claims of the foreign bondholders."

its activities." [32] However, the question what, in a given case, constitute the expenditures necessary for the continued functioning of the debtor as a state is largely a question of fact to be decided according to the circumstances of the situation.

Only a few general principles can be deduced from the nature of the case and the relevant precedents. In many instances the need for meeting their indispensable public expenditures has been advanced by debtor states as the very reason for default on their external debt, and readjustment proceedings usually begin with an investigation into the debtor's budget with a view to determining the expenses necessary for the maintenance of its administrative machinery. While every claim that can reasonably be classified as pertaining to the essential public services should partake of the privilege of preferential treatment, it seems only fair that "no sacrifice must be required of the creditors before every reasonable sacrifice has been made by the debtor." [33]

Some outlays for educational institutions, road construction, and other public improvements may be essential and justifiable but, to the extent that expenditures for these purposes may properly be regarded as a luxury rather than a necessity, they would not seem entitled to priority over obligations arising out of external indebtedness.[34]

This principle was expressed in the frequent suggestions made by the Agent General for Reparation Payments to the German Government as to the need for reducing expenditure for certain public services in the interest of the foreign debt service.[35]

Among claims against the public treasury of the debtor which have constantly been held to enjoy priority over the foreign debt service because they must be met if orderly government is to be maintained, are

32. Fischer Williams, *Chapters on Current International Law*, p. 327. See also SEC, *Rep.*, Pt. V, p. 32.

33. Report of the Egyptian Commission of Liquidation, April 8, 1879. See also Secretary Hull's note to the German Government protesting against Germany's transfer moratorium of June 27, 1934. *For. Aff.*, XIII (1934–35), 11. It has generally been judged that it is the obligation of a debtor government to so direct its policies that sums required to meet external obligations receive priority over all but essential needs of the government.

34. The Commission appointed by the powers in 1897, to investigate the financial situation and debt paying capacity of Greece, reported that in its estimate of the needs of the Greek Government during the next five years it had not allowed anything for either "extraordinary expenses" or "for the execution of great public works, such as the improvement of the ports and the construction of new railways." The Commission added that, in its opinion, "any enterprise likely to increase sensibly the budget expenses should be postponed until the finances of the country [had] attained a stable equilibrium."

35. Report of the Agent-General of November 30, 1926, p. 38; June 10, 1927, pp. 25 ff., 51 ff. See also Harris, *Germany's Foreign Indebtedness*, pp. 4 ff., 14.

the salaries of state officials and employees. In *Keller* v. *Egyptian Government,* the Egyptian Mixed Court laid down the general rule that "according to the universal principles of law and equity the employees of the State should take precedence over the creditors of the Public Debt." [36] When Mexico in 1923 permitted federal employees to remain in part unpaid in order to meet the annuity of the De la Huerta-Lamont agreement, much public protest was aroused.[37]

Settlements involving a material scaling down of the foreign debt burden, such as the Turkish readjustment of 1881, may be regarded as indirectly involving recognition of the debtor's prior right to sufficient revenue to maintain the functions of the state.

In the Dominican, Nicaraguan, and Haitian settlements it was provided that, after the payment of the charges of the foreign loans out of the customs revenues, the balance was to be turned over to the governments. It would appear that in these settlements technical priority upon the customs revenues was given to *other* than internal governmental expenses. A substantial balance, however, seems to have been obtained in the administration of the revenues and the governmental needs were met in all cases. There were, of course, other sources of revenue, apart from customs, which were reserved to the government.

In the postwar treaties with Germany, Austria, Hungary, Bulgaria, and Turkey no mention was made of the priority of governmental charges as against reparations payments. Impliedly, however, such a reservation would seem to have been made in the execution of the treaties. The repeated admonitions of the Agent-General for Reparation Payments that certain expenditures of the German Government could not be justified, implied that Germany was free to appropriate at least the sums essential for ordinary budget expenditures.

By a broad interpretation of the principle that claims affecting the political or economic stability of the debtor country should have preference over the fulfillment of external loan contracts, the so-called trade debts and short-term credits have frequently been brought into the class of preferred obligations. Though it is true that there exists "no doctrine in international law which supports the position that short term claims be paid or settled before the readjustment of the long term indebtedness be even considered," [38] yet there is noticeable a general tendency in debt

36. Egypt No. 2 (1879), p. 101. The commission of inquiry immediately gave priority to claims of the employees of the Egyptian Government. II, 608.

37. II, 74.

38. SEC, *Rep.,* Pt. V, pp. 558 f. Mr. Schoepperle, of the National City Bank, had stated before the committee investigating bondholders' protective committees that, according to "traditional international policy," short-term loans have preference over long-term ones.

settlements as well as in governmental measures, for example, in allocating foreign exchange, to accord short-term credits and those arising out of international trade a preferential treatment over long-term debts. This does not flow from any priority formally granted by the government at the time the credits were advanced but in most cases results from the fact that the national economy of the debtor is based to a material degree on the continuation of its international trade and consequently "non-payment or settlement of its trade credits may have a much more immediate and direct repercussion on the welfare of the government and its citizens than does the continuation of the default on its long term debt." [39]

Furthermore, since short-term credits are usually advanced by banks for the purpose of assisting the government in meeting an emergency situation, default on such loans may result in closing this source of financial aid in future crises. To avoid this threat to its normal functioning, a debtor government is vitally interested in satisfying its short-term creditors in preference to holders of the funded debt. [40] Thus, while the settlement of the Greek debt in 1898 reduced by about two thirds the initial interest on external bonds, it subjected the internal floating debt to little or no sacrifice. [41] The suspension of payments by Mexico in 1928 expressly excluded the short-term banking loans. [42] In the readjustment of the Egyptian public debt in 1876, the creditors of the floating debt were accorded the most favorable treatment. [43] These creditors were

39. *Idem*, pp. 563 f. See also League Loans Committee, *Second Annual Report,* June, 1934, p. 9: "The League Loans Committee have never urged that the service of the League Loans should be accorded any such priority as to impede the current service of trade debts, which, the Committee recognise, constitute an essential part of the economic structure of the countries with which they have to deal." Article by Sir Austen Chamberlain, Chairman of the League Loans Committee, in the *Financial News*, February 20, 1933 (League Loans Committee, *First Annual Report*, p. 28: "As to short-term credits, the Committee has always recognized the necessity of maintaining the machinery of genuine commercial transactions which are required to support daily economic life." H. V. Hodson, "Debts and Defaults," in Toynbee, ed., *Survey of International Affairs, 1932* (London, Oxford University Press, 1933), pp. 80 f.

40. The Galata bankers justified their actual, if not legal, priority by stating that the money they had lent was a matter of life and death to Turkey. II, 428, 437.

41. II, 332.

42. II, 79.

43. II, 588–591. *The Times* (London) of January 16, 1877, suggested that the funded debt creditors were the general public who had no means of pressing their claims, whereas the floating debt creditors were the "haute finance" of Europe, possessing great influence and standing. However, the first installment of the loan obtained from the Rothschild group in 1878 was used for the payment of interest due to the holders of the unified debt. The holders of the floating debt protested

mainly French bankers who held large portfolios of Egyptian Treasury bonds and were able to press their claims effectively despite the objections of other classes of creditors. When Chile in 1934 planned to give priority to short-term bondholders, efforts were made by foreign bondholders' committees to achieve a settlement without such priorities.[44]

INTERNATIONAL LAW DEBTS

A privileged and preferred position among claims against a debtor state is held by obligations owed by the debtor to one or more foreign countries. The reason for preferring interstate debts to claims arising out of contractual relations between governments and private individuals lies in the difference in the legal consequences resulting from such breach of contract. While mere default on a governmental loan contract with private individuals is not a breach of international law and becomes a matter of international concern only if the home state of the injured creditors, invoking an exceptional ground, espouses their claim and brings diplomatic pressure upon the defaulter, nonpayment of a debt incurred by one state toward another amounts to an international delinquency exposing the wrongdoer to the appropriate sanctions of international law. Again, by virtue of the principle that a state cannot be required to sacrifice its independent existence to the preservation of its credit with private nationals of another state, no objections can be raised against a debtor state's fulfilling its international law obligations, in times of financial difficulties, in preference to obligations owing to foreign individuals.

Since interstate debts find their origin mostly in war or in the effects of war, the question of priorities is usually settled in the instruments dealing with the political and economic reconstruction of the belligerent countries. As a rule, prewar rights and interests of private individuals remain intact. Neither reparations nor war indemnities imposed upon the vanquished may take precedence over the fulfillment of existing obligations. During the negotiations of the Congress of Berlin and in later diplomatic acts with respect to the war indemnity to be exacted from Turkey, Russia conceded the prior rank of hypothecations specially granted by Turkey to private creditors before the war.[45] Similarly, Turkey, when demanding a war indemnity from Greece after the latter's defeat in the Graeco-Turkish war of 1897, recognized that the vested rights of the foreign creditors of Greece should not be disturbed by her

---

against this "flagrant breach of contract" and sought diplomatic protection which was refused. Egypt No. 5 (1879), p. 4.

44. *For. Bondh. Prot. Coun. Rep.*, 1934, p. 56a.

45. II, 427, 439–440.

indemnity claims.[46] The German war reparations were made a direct charge against Germany but, by Article 253, all prewar mortgages or charges in favor of allied and associated powers or their nationals were expressly recognized as subsisting and unaltered by the reparations provisions.[47] However, obligations subsequently contracted by Germany were subject to the prior charge of reparations.[48] Similarly, an express action on the part of the Reparations Commission was necessary to release the revenues of the Austrian and Hungarian governments from the charge of priority placed upon them in favor of the payment of reparations in order to enable both governments to use those revenues for the service of loans issued by the two countries under the auspices of the League of Nations.[49] Other claims arising in connection with a war and its aftermath, to which priority over contractual obligations has occasionally been granted, include the costs of the military occupation of a country after a war or the expenses of international commissions set up in the vanquished state for the performance of certain supervisory tasks.[50]

A creditor government may, of course, renounce or waive its own priority in favor of its creditor nationals having private claims against the debtor state. In the case of the inter-Allied loans, especially the war debt owed by Great Britain, France, and Italy to the United States Government, the United States permitted the debtor governments to honor private debts of all kinds and accepted default for the inter-governmental debt.

The claim of a guarantor state for reimbursement by the debtor state which has defaulted on a loan guaranteed and, consequently, paid by the

46. II, 315 ff.

47. See Boyden, "The 'Priority Question,'" *For. Aff.*, VI (1927–28), 373; Feilchenfeld, "Reparations and German External Loans," *Col. Law Rev.*, XXVIII (1928), 300. In the Moroccan settlement of 1909, existing claims held by individuals or firms were preferred to the war indemnity.

48. The German external loan of 1924, issued as part of the Dawes Plan, was specifically granted priority by the transfer committee and the reparations commission over all reparations and transfers. Boyden, *op. cit.*, p. 370. Arts. 132 and 138 of the treaty of Neuilly between Bulgaria and the Allies preserved all rights and security created or guaranteed by the Bulgarian Government before August 1, 1914. II, 566 ff. The treaty of Sèvres recognized the revenues hypothecated to bondholders by permitting them to remain under the control of the Ottoman Debt Council. II, 485.

49. Fischer Williams, *op. cit.*, p. 402.

50. Under Art. 135 of the treaty of Neuilly, the cost of the military occupation of Bulgaria was given priority over the service of prewar Ottoman debt and reparations. II, 549. The abortive treaty of Sèvres between Turkey and the Allies established priority for the expenses of the International Financial Commission and the costs of the Allied forces on Turkish soil. II, 485.

guarantor is necessarily based on the international agreement containing the guaranty promise and, therefore, is in the nature of an international obligation enjoying priority over private debts. Thus, Great Britain was within her rights when, having fulfilled her guaranty promise toward the holders of the Turkish guaranteed loan of 1855, she applied the revenues from Cyprus to the payment of her claim for reimbursement against Turkey, in priority to the bondholders whose claims rested on contract.[51]

EXPENSES CONNECTED WITH THE EXECUTION OF DEBT SETTLEMENTS

The necessity to establish and maintain administrative machinery for the purpose of carrying out a readjustment plan in the interest of the debtor as well as of the creditors places expenses connected with such machinery in the category of preferred obligations. The practice of adjustment procedures is uniform in recognizing the preferential position of these expenses, regardless of whether they are incurred for the maintenance of agencies charged with the general execution of the plan or whether they apply merely to the collection of certain revenues pledged as the principal security for the service of the external debt. The administrative expenses of the Turkish Council of the Public Debt were deducted from the revenues collected for the service of the foreign indebtedness; [52] those of the international control commission for the Greek debt were a first charge upon the proceeds of the revenues assigned for the service of the debt.[53] Likewise, the costs of the receiverships set up in Santo Domingo, Nicaragua, and Haiti under treaties with the United States were paid out of the customs receipts in advance of all other claims; the expenses of administration and collection of the customs themselves ranked ahead of the service charges of foreign bonds.[54]

51. II, 441–42. The assertion of Feilchenfeld, et al., op. cit., p. 1129, that the guarantor, if he received no security to protect him from loss through his guaranty, is entitled to no better treatment in his claim for reimbursement than an ordinary unsecured creditor, seems to be in contradiction to the thesis of the authors that international law claims enjoy preference over others. Feilchenfeld's great service to this field of study is not underestimated.

52. II, 503. Blaisdell, European Financial Control in the Ottoman Empire, p. 95.

53. Greek law of control of March 10, 1898, chap. ii, 4. Brit. and For. St. Pap., XC, 405; II, 317 ff.

54. II, 238, 259; Corp. For. Bondh. Rep., No. 44 (1917), p. 254–268; For. Rel., 1916, pp. 328–332; idem, 1917, pp. 1127 f. Sometimes expenses for bondholders' committees rank prior to the claims of the bondholders themselves. See II, 142–145. Services and expenses of the bondholders' committee were a first charge on a fund from the proceeds of guano used as security for bondholders' claims.

TORT CLAIMS

In the few cases where claims arising out of governmental liability for injuries done to the person or property of alien nationals had to compete with contractual debts of the government, the former were granted priority over bondholders' claims almost as a matter of course. In the Venezuelan arbitration of 1903, the United States agent maintained: "The claims of first rank, in justice, are those for wrongs done by violence to persons and property." [55] By the protocols signed at Washington in 1902 for the settlement of various claims against Venezuela, those in respect to certain outrages on subjects of the three blockading powers were placed ahead of other claims and were satisfied at once.[56] The proceeds of the Egyptian guaranteed loan of 1885, which impaired the execution of the law of liquidation and against which bondholders had protested, were used principally to pay off in full the Alexandria riot claims of 1882.[57] Under the terms of the Doyle convention of December 4, 1851, between Great Britain and Mexico, British claims arising out of denial of justice or injuries to persons and property received preferential treatment; [58] the awards rendered by the Mexican-American Claims Commission of 1868 in favor of American claimants against Mexico were paid regularly by the Mexican Government, notwithstanding complete default on its bonded debt.[59]

Apart from the fact that tort claims against a foreign government, if reduced to an award or incorporated in diplomatic settlements, are in the nature of international legal claims and therefore, as stated above, entitled to priority, the reason for preferring them to contractual obligations of the debtor government in the classification of its debts lies in the difference in their origin. While bondholders enter into contractual relations with foreign governments "with their eyes open" and are assumed

55. See the Case of the United States, "The Venezuelan Preferential Claims Arbitration of 1903," *U.S. Sen. Doc. No. 119,* 58th Cong., 3d Sess., p. 442.

56. See Madden and Nadler, *Foreign Securities,* p. 351. See also Case of Venezuela in "The Venezuelan Preferential Claims Arbitration of 1903," *U.S. Sen. Doc. No. 119,* 58th Cong., 3d Sess., p. 225: "The British claims against Venezuela . . . were capable of classification. Those on account of the recent cases of unjustifiable interference with the liberty and property of British subjects, including the shipping claims, would rank first. Claims for injury to British property during the late revolution . . . would come next; and, in the third place, the claims of bondholders." See also the British Blue Book, No. 1 (1903). "The Venezuelan Preferential Claims Arbitration of 1903," *U.S. Sen. Doc. No. 119,* 58th Cong., 3d Sess., p. 725.

57. II, 620.

58. II, 14 ff.

59. II, 40, n. 28.

to be fully aware of the chances of nonpayment of the loan, a tort claim arises from wrongful acts against which the injured person was entitled to expect that the foreign government itself would protect him. The absence, in tort claims, of the speculative element commonly involved in the subscription to foreign bonds justifies the preferential treatment of the former and explains why governments are more prone to take diplomatic action on behalf of tort claimants than for the protection of the interests of bondholders.[60]

AWARDS OF CLAIMS COMMISSIONS

There have been few debt settlements where any issue arose as to the treatment of awardees of claims commissions as against the holders of defaulted bonds. The cases examined below throw some light on this priority question.

In the Egyptian settlement there were two series of awards of private claims. In the first place, there were the private claims reduced to judgment before the mixed courts prior to 1880, which were paid 30 per cent in cash and 70 per cent in privileged bonds. While treated less favorably than the tribute owing to Turkey and other "privileged" creditors, salaries and pensions in arrears, trust funds held by the state for orphans, and sums deposited in the state treasury, the judgment creditors received compensation in full. The foreign bondholders meanwhile suffered severe reduction in interest and postponements in amortizations. The second group of claims arose out of the disturbances in Alexandria in 1882. The awards of the International Indemnity Commission were paid in full out of a loan floated for this and other purposes and secured ahead of the old foreign bonds.

The Russian private claims arising out of the Turco-Russian war were afforded no special status at the Congress of Berlin; in fact, Russia expressly recognized the validity of security given by Turkey for loans. The sums adjudicated were apparently not secured upon any special revenues but were a direct obligation of Turkey and were supposed to be paid off as soon as submitted for payment to the Turkish Treasury. The delays and misunderstandings which arose out of these payments gave rise to the Russian indemnity arbitration before The Hague Tribunal, whereby Russia was denied interest on the sums in arrears. All the claims were met, however.

In the Greek case, Turkey expressly denied any right to disturb the "vested rights" of creditors of Greece. The rapid payment of the private

60. Borchard, *Proc. Am. Soc. Int. Law,* 1932, pp. 163, 165 f.; Feilchenfeld, *et al., op. cit.,* p. 1139; D. W. Morrow, 'Who Buys Foreign Bonds?" *For. Aff.,* V (1926–27), 226.

war claims against Greece was made out of a special loan floated for the purpose. This loan was given a special charge upon the revenues assigned for the foreign debt of Greece. It will be noted, though, that while their security was recognized, in both the Turkish and the Greek settlements, the bondholders took drastic cuts in their claims against the debtors, while the claims creditors appear to have been paid in full.

In the Venezuelan settlement there were claims which the intervening powers refused to submit to arbitration, for which immediate payment was demanded and received. There were also claims adjudicated by the mixed claims commissions of 1903. These were not all treated alike. The blockading powers secured a priority in payment of their awards over those of the neutral powers. However, both the blockading and the neutral powers were paid off, the former by 1907, the latter before 1912. Apparently no reduction in amounts of the awards was made. The foreign bonds were in a separate category and were converted, some at par and some at a discount of 25 per cent.

In the Dominican settlement (1904–07) the claims of foreigners were by agreement all scaled down to different amounts. The arbitral award of the Improvement Company was scaled down least of all (10 per cent), while the protocol claims of several nationalities were cut 50 per cent. Internal debts were cut even more and some as much as 90 per cent. It must be recognized, however, that many of the claims were grossly exaggerated and the cuts were in all probability not excessive.

The awards of the 1917 Dominican Claims Commission were met at par in bonds secured by a surcharge upon the customs.

The awards of the Nicaraguan Claims Commission of 1911 were met only in part in cash at that time. Nicaragua having defaulted on her debt in 1911, the greater part was left over until the settlement of 1917. Some of the claims were reëxamined by a public credit commission which cut those which appeared to be in the hands of speculators. The claims allowed were met eventually, partly in cash, partly in bonds secured on a surcharge upon customs duties. It will be noted, however, that in this case the Canal Fund of $3,000,000 was distributed by Nicaragua with the consent of the State Department in such a way as to omit completely any payments on the claims commission awards. Interest in arrears on bonds and various debts of the Government were paid off instead. Though not sharing in this fund, the claims creditors eventually received full compensation.

This mode of distribution was decided upon despite the proposal made by the American minister in Nicaragua to the State Department to pay off the awards first and distribute only the balance among the other creditors. It was decided, however, to subject all the awards to the scrutiny of a special commission which would reëxamine their validity and scale down awards in the hands of speculators.

In contrast to the treatment thus meted out to creditors, the holders of awards, the Emery claim which had been made the subject of a protocol between Nicaragua and the United States was paid in full, a large part of the claim being met in cash out of the Canal Fund, the balance in Treasury notes.

The awards of the Haitian Claims Commission were paid off partly in cash and partly in internal bonds. Meanwhile, the foreign bonds were called and paid off at par to take advantage of the depreciated rate of the franc exchange. The interest in arrears on the railroad bonds was paid off in cash.

In the postwar settlements, the claims commissions set up by the allied and associated powers were granted a special source of funds to draw upon for their awards. These funds consisted of the property of enemy nationals seized during the war in allied countries.

It would appear, then, that the awards of claims commissions have in almost all cases been met in full either in cash or in cash and secured bonds when insufficient cash was available. The fact that foreign loans, secured or unsecured, were subjected to reductions of interest, principal, or security as in Egypt, Turkey, Greece, Venezuela, and Haiti did not appear to affect the treatment of claims in those cases. Peculiar arrangements were made, however, in the cases of Santo Domingo and Nicaragua. In the former, protocol claims as well as foreign loans were severely reduced. In the Nicaraguan settlement interest in arrears on the foreign debt was met in cash, while the awards of the claims commission were subjected to renewed investigation and paid off partly in cash and partly in secured bonds.

SECURED AND UNSECURED BONDS

Holders of secured bonds have often successfully protested against attempts to treat them uniformly [61] in debt settlements with unsecured creditors. It is safe to maintain that the better treatment of secured loans

61. See II, 418–19. Holders of secured bonds protested against being subjected to the same stopping of interest payments as were the holders of ordinary bonds. English holders of secured bonds demanded preference for several years. *Corp. For. Bondh. Rep.*, No. 64 (1937), pp. 82 f. Protest against an offer by the Government of Uruguay of equal terms for secured and unsecured loans in the proposed settlement. "The offer would constitute a grave discrimination against the secured loans." *Idem*, No. 65 (1938), p. 43. It is clearly improper that the service of a later, unsecured loan should be made in full while an old loan with prior claims and government guarantees remains in total default.

has become a generally accepted principle.[62] The main justification for the differentiation appears to be that creditors regard the assignment of specific revenues or other security as giving a loan better prospects of repayment than it would have if it were unsecured, and that to gain this advantage they paid more for a secured bond than they would have given for a bond supported only by the debtor's simple promise to pay. Moreover, the credit standing of a debtor who was already issued unsecured bonds has in many instances deteriorated subsequently to the point where he would have been unable to raise another foreign loan at all without the grant of special security, with its implied promise of favored treatment for the bondholders. Numerous examples may be given of settlements where the secured creditors were accorded a preferential position.

The secured Portuguese tobacco loan of 1891 was not only serviced in full during a decade when two thirds of the interest due on the un-

62. At conferences held in 1937 and 1938 by bondholders' associations in Europe and the United States, it was agreed that, in general, secured loans should receive proportionately better treatment than unsecured loans issued by the same debtor, though it was recognized that, in the application of this principle, individual cases required to be considered on their merits. *Corp. For. Bondh. Rep.*, No. 64 (1937), pp. 9 f.; No. 65 (1938), p. 10. See, however, the Report of the Financial Committee of the League of Nations (1932) (quoted in Toynbee, *1932 Survey of International Affairs*, 80), which states that "while there is an obvious difference between loans which are secured on specific revenues and loans which have only a general charge, it is sometimes difficult to say, though in this respect individual cases differ widely, that any given specific charge is better or that any particular creditor can claim to be preferred to any other." Under the Brazilian readjustment plan of 1934, the secured external loans of the national Government were being serviced at a higher percentage than the unsecured loans. Similarly, El Salvador in its temporary readjustment plan granted more favorable treatment to the senior lien than to loans secured by junior liens on its customs revenues. Madden, Nadler, and Sauvain, *op. cit.*, p. 302. The financial commission charged with the settlement of the Greek indebtedness, 1898, classified the external loans of Greece into 3 groups according to the character of their original security. II, 329. (I. Monopoly loan of 1887 and funding loan of 1893, for which special safeguards had been provided to transfer pledged revenues to the bondholders; II. loans of 1881, 1884, 1890, which were secured by ordinary hypothecation of taxes; III. *rentes* of 1889, which were unsecured.) The holders of the bonds of the State of São Paulo Coffee Institute felt that they were harshly treated in the debt settlement decree of February, 1934, because they were placed a grade below the federal unsecured loans, in spite of the fact that they themselves had a special security in respect of an industry which provides the major part of the exchange resources of Brazil. *The Times* (London), February 23, 1934. But see Feilchenfeld, in Quindry, *op. cit.*, Vol. II, sec. 645 (b, 6), who denies that the creditor holding a revenue "pledge" (promise to pay out of certain revenues) has a right to demand any preferential treatment as against other creditors.

secured issues went unpaid but it also escaped the reduction in capital to which the latter were subjected under the settlement of 1902.[63]

In the Turkish settlement of 1881 a complex system of preferences was used, based chiefly upon two factors: the price received by Turkey for its bonds, which determined the basis of the conversion rate; the quality of the security for the loans, which determined the priorities in amortization.

In the Dominican settlement the claim of the French and Belgian bondholders was cut 50 per cent. Of the balance they received 20 per cent in cash and 80 per cent in bonds of the new loan. The British bondholders, protested unsuccessfully that they had been given poorer treatment than the Continental bondholders.[64]

In the Bulgarian settlement of 1926, the foreign loans were divided into three groups on the basis of the relative importance of the assigned security.

1. In the first group were the loans of 1902, 1904, and 1907 secured on the tobacco tax, which was under the control of representatives of the bondholders; these loans were to receive initially 49 per cent of the original interest.

2. In the second group were the less favorably secured loans of 1892 and 1896, the initial interest of which was set at 37 per cent of original rate.

3. The unsecured loan of 1909 was to receive 35 per cent of its original interest.

In the Turkish settlement of 1928, the loans prior to the decree of 1881 and secured by the revenues then assigned received preference in interest over the loans subsequent to the decree.

The Mexican debt settlement of 1942 awards better interest treatment to the secured than to the unsecured loans.

If the security attached to a loan consists in the guaranty by a third state or a group of states, no particular reason seems to exist for granting this type of loan preferential treatment in debt settlements, since the mere existence "of several promises which are all of the same nature does not make the debt a secured debt." [65] The practice of states, however, shows that guaranteed loans have frequently been accorded priority over other loans.[66] This was probably due mainly to political pressure exercised by the guaranteeing powers.

63. II, 377 f.; Feilchenfeld, *et al., op. cit.,* pp. 1120 ff.
64. See II, 254 ff.
65. Feilchenfeld, *et al., op. cit.,* p. 1129.
66. Under the terms of Egyptian decree of November 28, 1904, the service of the consolidated debts was effected in the following order: (1) guaranteed, (2) preference, (3) unified debt. *Corp. For. Bondh. Rep.,* No. 61 (1934), pp. 207–208. The Greek guaranteed loans were paid regularly in accordance with the arrange-

DOMESTIC OBLIGATIONS

The place held by domestic obligations of the debtor state in the order of preference as compared with external obligations depends upon their nature. Thus we have seen that internal needs and administrative expenses of the state and salaries in arrears as a rule have been recognized to have priority over the state's bonded indebtedness. Similarly internal loans made to pay off pressing charges are sometimes given priority over prior foreign loans, even where the charges are of a domestic nature.

In the Greek settlement the Government was forced to meet the pressing demands of the gold debt due to the Greek banks. This consisted almost entirely of loans from the banks of issue and advances made by them from their metallic reserve, the disappearance of which followed the establishment of a forced currency. The restoration of these banks to a normal situation being indispensable to a reëstablishment of financial order, they were repaid without reduction in bonds of a gold loan floated for this and other purposes.

In giving priority to the loans extended by the Greek banks to the Greek Government, the creditors were indirectly aiding in reëstablishing the finances of Greece to a desirable order so that the affairs of the Government could be properly conducted in the future.

In the case of the Portuguese default of 1892 the foreign bondholders protested that what they believed to be an unjustified preference was being accorded to the domestic bondholders. They contended that it was inequitable to reduce interest payments on the external gold debt by two thirds, while the interest on the internal paper debt was subjected to less than half that reduction.

Respect for contracts requires that these two classes of engagements should be treated on the same footing and that in the money in which they were respectively subscribed . . . It cannot be admitted that the external creditors may be subjected, even provisionally, to a reduction greater than that of 30 per cent fixed for internal stock.

In the Dominican case many claims against the Republic were represented by internal bonds and paper of the Ministry of Finance, held mainly by resident aliens. In the adjustment between the Government and its creditors completed prior to the 1907 treaty the internal

---

ments made between Greece and the guaranteeing powers. II, 328. See also the declaration of the Austrian Government of December 17, 1932, to the effect that "the priority of the Austrian Guaranteed Loan of 1923–43 as compared with all other Austrian Loans would on all occasions be faithfully observed . . . ." League Loans Committee, *First Annual Report*, pp. 12, 32. See also Phillimore, *Commentaries on International Law*, II, 14.

creditors took a reduction considerably greater than the 10 per cent of the arbitral award of the San Domingo Improvement Company, the 50 per cent of the foreign bondholders, or the 50 per cent of the protocol claims. Internal claims were reduced from 60 per cent to 90 per cent.

In the Nicaraguan settlement various loans had been made by the Nicaraguan National Bank to the Government secured by customs receipts. These loans went into default together with the foreign loans. The extensions granted by the bank to the Government were conditioned upon the promise of the Government to meet principal and interest due from the Canal Fund. The Nicaraguan Government in requesting the State Department's consent to allow a preferential claim in favor of the National Bank pointed out that if bonds were paid "the Government will be paying almost one-third of the capital of the bank with manifest injury to the agriculture and commerce of the country, those productive sources of prosperity." A payment was made to the National Bank out of the Canal Fund on account of loans and interest, thus placing the claim in a privileged category.

The internal bonds of Haiti were exempted from revision by the claims commission by special agreement of the United States and Haiti signed in 1922. It was declared that the internal funded debts represented in the three issues of 1912, 1913, and 1914 were liquidated debts and as such should be paid without reinvestigation. They were met, in fact, with a small reduction of 5 per cent to 25 per cent depending upon the issue.

It appears then that no categorical rules can be induced as to priorities between domestic and external obligations. Depending upon the situation, we have seen internal and domestic debts preferred over external debts or the reverse. In fact, however, the readjustment of a country's defaulted external debt and its internal obligations has rarely been effected by one comprehensive settlement in which the issue of priority between the two classes of indebtedness had to be squarely faced.

INDEX

bond, 25; legal character of, 24; obliging debtor to create loan, 24; prevailing over other loan documents, 25; registry of, with League of Nations, 25; signature of, by debtor, 24; similar to regulations of state agencies, 25 n. 24; statement of debtor's obligations, 24; use of, 24

General pledges. *See* Loans

Germany:
COMMITTEES TO PROTECT FOREIGN BONDHOLDERS, 213; an association, not a corporation, 213 n. 57
COOPERATION BETWEEN GOVERNMENT AND LENDING BANK. *See* Loans
THEORY AS TO IMMUNITY, 164
See also various headings

Gold clause. *See* Contracts

Governing law. *See* Law governing international loan relationships

Government control. *See* International government control

Governmental interference. *See* Contracts

Greece: causes of defaults, 148; rehabilitation after World War I, 148

Guaranteed loans:
DOMESTIC GUARANTIES BY CENTRAL GOVERNMENT, 101; a direct pecuniary obligation, 102, or promise to maintain debtor's solvency, 101, 102; discretion of authorities, 103
DUTY TOWARD CREDITOR, 105
GUARANTOR-CREDITOR RELATIONSHIP, 107; action brought by creditor, 109; claim governed by guarantor's municipal law, 109; claim of creditor based on bond, 108; clause for ordinary operation of guaranty, 109; creditor not forcing political pressure, 108; guarantor's intention disclosed on acts, 108; pecuniary obligation of guaranty, 108; political power not subject to private contract, 108
GUARANTOR-DEBTOR RELATIONSHIP, 106
Debtor's reimbursement of guarantor, 106; agreement for, 107 n. 23
Determined by international law, 106

Guarantor's forcing debtor to fulfill obligations, 106, 107; specific assignment of revenues, 107
Guarantor's right to interfere in debtor's fiscal affairs, 106
INTERNATIONAL GUARANTIES, 103; as promise to assert claims for bondholders, 105; basis for, 103; League's "special responsibility" for but not guaranty of loans issued under its auspices, 104; not to be implied from extrinsic circumstances, 104; precise terms necessary, 104; provided by international agreement, 104; term "guaranty" not always dispositive, 104
LEGAL SIGNIFICANCE OF, 105; obligation due immediately on any default regardless of cause, 105, 106
PROMISE OF THIRD PARTY, 101
RELATIONS AMONG GUARANTORS, 109
Joint and several obligations, 109; practical construction of obligation as proportionate, 109; regulation of, by treaty, 110
VALUE OF GUARANTIES, 111; confidence of subscribers, 111; payment or forcing debtor's payment, 111; stability of loans, 111

Guaranties, enforcement by trustee, 56; *see also* Guaranteed loans

Guarantors. *See* Guaranteed loans

HOLLAND, protective committee in, functions of, 214 n. 58

IMMUNITY:
BANKING HOUSE AS AGENT OR TRUSTEE OF DEBTOR, 166
DEPOSIT OF FUNDS AS SECURITY AS AFFECTING, Germany, 164
EUROPE MORE DISPOSED TO PERMIT SUIT, 162
EXPRESS SUBMISSION UNDER ANGLO-AMERICAN SYSTEM, 162
FOREIGN STATE NOT SUABLE IN MUNICIPAL COURTS, 166; instances of application of principle, 166, 167; principle rigidly applied to United States, 167

less clear or lacking in other instances, 290; Greece-Turkey treaty, 288, 289, implemented by local law, 289

Maintenance of political status quo, 287

Organization of, 291; control commission for Greece, 291, members of, 291, powers and duties, 291; control over Egypt, 292, changes designated by respective governments, 292, complete independence, 292, powers and duties, 293, similar to a proceeding in bankruptcy, 292; no uniform type, 291

Purpose of, 287

Reasons for, varied, 288; assuring prompt payment of war indemnity, 288; necessity for new loans, 288; necessity for reorganization of debtor's finances, 288

LEAGUE OF NATIONS TYPE, 296

Central features of League plan, 299

Control financial rather than political, 297

Control over Austria, established 1922, 297; arbitral functions assigned to Council of League, 298; initiative taken by state, 297; investigations, 297; plan embodied in diplomatic instruments, 297; two organizations of, powers and duties, 297, 298

Control over Greece and Hungary, established 1924, 298, 299

General character of, 296

Other controls on same pattern as Austrian plan, 298

Reorganization of economic life by new foreign loans, 296

NO SINGLE AND UNIFORM TYPE OF FINANCIAL CONTROL, 286

RESPECT FOR DEBTOR'S POLITICAL TRADITIONS, 286

TYPES OF, CLASSIFIED, 286, 287

See also Control

International guaranties. *See* Guaranteed loans

International law debts. *See* Priorities and preferences

International tribunals:

BOND CASES BEFORE, 266

COMMISSIONS' UNWILLINGNESS TO EXERCISE JURISDICTION, 266

GOVERNMENTS UNWILLING TO PRESENT CLAIMS DIPLOMATICALLY, 266

INTERNAL DEBT NOT BECOMING EXTERNAL BY ASSIGNMENT, 268

PROTOCOL FOR SUBMISSION OF CLAIM TO ARBITRATION, 268

PROTOCOL PROVISION FOR SETTLEMENT OF "ALL CLAIMS," 266

VENEZUELAN BOND CASES, 267 n. 211; bonds based on services for support to unsuccessful revolution, 268; bonds in payment of property transferred to government, 267; original bonds not produced, 267; various decisions of Venezuelan commission, 267

Intervention. *See* Diplomatic protection; Military action

Investment, prior capital after World War II, xxviii

Italy, protective committee in, 214

JOHNSON ACT. *See* Remedies

LATIN AMERICA: Loans to, in nineteenth century, xx, xxi; transfer problems of countries, 132, 133 n. 25; *see also various countries*

Law governing international loan relationships:

ARBITRATION CLAUSES, 36

COMPLEXITY OF SUBJECT, 64

CONTRACTS, 22 n. 14

GENERAL LEGAL PRINCIPLES, 65

INTERNATIONAL FINANCIAL LAW, 64, 65 n. 2

LOAN AGREEMENT BETWEEN GOVERNMENT AND BANK, 65; abrogation of gold clauses, 69, 71, and legislation exempting international payments, 72; agency agreements, 66; authority of debtor, 71; clause as to interpretation and construction, 65, 66 n. 5;